RYNT

WON TON LUST

Also by John Krich

Fiction

Chicago Is

A Totally Free Man:
The Unauthorized Autobiography of Fidel Castro

One Big Bed

Nonfiction

Bump City:
Winners and Losers in Oakland

Music in Every Room:
Around the World in a Bad Mood

El Beisbol:
Travels Through the Pan-American Pastime

Why Is This Country Dancing?
A One-Man Samba to the Beat of Brazil

WON TON LUST

Adventures in Search of the

World's Best Chinese Restaurant

John Krich

KODANSHA INTERNATIONAL

New York • Tokyo • London

Excerpts from this book have appeared in earlier form in *Condé Nast Traveler*, *Vogue*, *The New York Times Sophisticated Traveler*, *San Francisco Focus*, *San Francisco Examiner*, *Salon*, *Global Network Navigator*, *Saveur*, *Escape*, *Motorland*, and *East Bay Express*.

Kodansha America, Inc.
114 Fifth Avenue, New York, New York 10011, U.S.A.

Kodansha International Ltd.
17-14 Otowa 1-chome, Bunkyo-ku, Tokyo 112, Japan

Published in 1997 by Kodansha America, Inc.

Library of Congress Cataloging-in-Publication Data
Krich, John, 1951–
    Won ton lust : adventures in search of the world's best Chinese
restaurant / John Krich.
        p.   cm.
    1. Ethnic restaurants—Guidebooks.   2. Cookery, Chinese.
I. Title.
TX907.K75   1997
647.95'089951—dc21   97-25862
ISBN 1-56836-178-5   CIP

Book design by Steven Brower

Manufactured in the United States of America

97 98 99 00 QFF   10 9 8 7 6 5 4 3 2 1

With heaps of gratitude
and helpings of love—
to Mei Qian,
who cooks up all the
treasures of my life

MENU

Cold Dish: The Long Munch

China: The East Is Fed

Hong Kong and Taiwan: Two from Column A

Southeast Asia: Ginger Trail

South Pacific: The Endless Dumpling

North America: Like a Rolling Egg Roll

Europe: Let 'Em Eat Dog

Dessert: From Hunan to Who Knows

The rice can never be white enough,
the meat can never be chopped fine enough . . .
—Confucius

Class struggle begins at the end of one's chopsticks.
—Red Guard slogan

Acknowledgments

With the supreme gratitude of the well-fed, the author wishes to thank the many restaurateurs mentioned in these pages. Chef Chan Chen Hei, Moses Lim, Jimmy Man, Michael Tang, and Martin Yan each went several courses beyond the call of duty. No hosts offered us more eats or devotion than Bao Dao Ping and Elly Leung in Vancouver, Phunkhang Goranangpa in Beijing, Wu Gang in Paris, Tu Yingming in Los Angeles, Wu Xiaoying in Shanghai, Brian and Buni Lynch in Melbourne, Simon Wu in Sydney, Bruce Granquist in Bali, and Zhou Lin in New York.

Among the many unstinting guides and fellow eaters, we wish to acknowledge Wu Zu Kang, Li Ying, Li Lu, Mitchell Farkas, Mike Chinoy and Lynne Curry, Pamela Burdman, Prof. Wang Wenjiong, Prof. Li Hengji, Xie Jingli, Lynne O'Donnell, Marvin Farkas, Lu Hui, Amy Ho, Ma Shoupeng, Bob Halliday, Joanna and Leslie Wong, Chris and David Derauf, Ken Hom, Vincent Tai, Peter Kaufman, Martha Vallejo, Ron and Roz Levaco, Ira Rothstein, Jeff Greenwald, Han Yan, Hua Lei, Mark Epton, Mrs. Anne Lo, Catherine Yan, Wolfgang Krust and Agathe Romiere, Giovanni Lombardo, Toby Cole, Manina Jouffroy, Meixian and Bob Gunville, Christine and Julien Verniere, Diane Cassarino, Willie Chan and Gloria Li, Bayita and Brian O'Rourke, Mercedes Garoffolo, Maqué Calanche, and Carol Remes.

Highly professional aid and deluxe comfort was also provided by Japan Airlines and Morris Simoncelli, Stanley Yen and Taipei's Ritz Hotel, the Thai Tourism Board and Bangkok's Grand China Princess Hotel, and Dan and Cathleen Kaul of Livingstone's Murray Hotel. Ketan and Manish Kothari with Alphasmart Peripheral Devices provided computer consulting and all those meals were worked away at the sumptuous San Francisco Athletic Club. Final toasts are due to my wise and edibly erudite editor, Philip Turner, and my caring agent Judith Riven. Without all of these, the banquet would have been meager indeed.

WON TON LUST

Ground Rules:
A Journey of
Ten Thousand Meals

If diners from outer space were to land on our planet, odds are that their first earthly encounter would be with a Chinese restaurant. From Acapulco to Zanzibar, Pittsburgh to Strasbourg, only one cultural outpost has become so accepted a part of the urban landscape. During these last, multinational days of the twentieth century, *mu shu* and *won ton* form the most common, and least celebrated, of our ravenous species' unifying rites.

In an irony big enough to chew on, the country with too many mouths to feed has ended up cooking for the entire human commune. But what better way is there to enlarge a world growing ever smaller than to survey a field that's impossibly wide? The trip that takes us farthest begins with a curiosity about what's right down every block. To rephrase the oft-cited proverb, "A journey of ten thousand meals begins with a single bite."

Therein lies the premise of this expedition through a global institution's unexplored back kitchens. To make the quest more mythic, as well as specific, the Holy Grail being sought is the world's best Chinese restaurant. The goal that animates this voyage is nothing less than the imperial franchise closest to heaven, the banquet hall with the biggest bang, the top rung of a food chain as endless as a paper dragon.

As difficult as it may be to make such a delicious determination, the ground rules for this edible sweepstakes require little fine print. In the spirit of stir-fry, candidates from China's varied regional cuisines—deluxe and home-style fare, hotel roof gardens and dumpling houses, emperors' gazebos and mom-and-pop luncheonettes—have all been tossed into the mix. So have intrigue and indigestion,

1

booms and busts, even a wedding and a funeral—all experiences, sweet or sour.

Little attempt has been made at the anonymous tastings employed by ratings-minded food critics. In order to get the full treatment and learn the whole story, the traditional hospitality of Chinese chefs and proprietors has been duly accepted; hopefully, without the author losing "face" or credibility. Four-fork guidebooks and anxious tourist boards were consulted only as a matter of last resort. Instead, the way was pointed by word-of-mouth among the species' most picky eaters. Forget the usual disclaimer about close relations being ineligible. Befitting the time-honored Chinese approach, kin and clan have been called upon as much as possible. What good are seventh uncles and ninth cousins if not to widen the search and order more dishes?

For this first go 'round, the to-go itinerary follows the major centers of Chinese settlement, covering eighteen countries on four continents where prior wanderers have set up their woks. To get to the roots of the matter, the first and lengthiest stop must be China—and that pretender to its culinary throne, Taiwan—where the politics of food make a mere appetizer for the food of politics. The cooking, as well as the investigation, grows lighter in Southeast Asia, Australia, and the South Seas. A car trip across the United States powered solely by *chow mein* pit stops is followed by the ultimate impudence of tracking immigrant assaults on Europe's citadels of fine dining. While the tale is told chronologically, readers should feel free to hop around to wherever they may be seeking their next Chinese food fix.

Alas, they will find no review of the new glut of noodle joints in Budapest; the many *chifas* in Lima, Peru; the China Bar in Addis Ababa, or the wayward takeaway across from Leif Eriksson's likely landing spot in Newfoundland. There was no way to be exhaustive without busting all diets, budgets, and lifetimes—just as no single travelogue can encompass so widespread a culinary diaspora.

Of course, the world's *worst* Chinese restaurant might have been easier to find. But the results of such a contest would hardly be a service to readers, to a lofty cuisine, or to the author's intestinal tract. Recipes of signature dishes, adapted for Western cooks, have been contributed by select chefs. Though it is impossible to guarantee that all remain open or under the same management, a list of restaurants is provided for each geographic area, with the means to find the finest provided in Appendix 2. Where all manner of food reveals all manner of lives, what follows is not so much a guide as a succulent survey of the state of Chinese communities through their state-of-the-art caterers.

Among the thousands of jokes to match millions of restaurants, it's told that two Americans, arriving in Hong Kong for the first time, asked a traffic policeman to direct them toward "a really good Chinese restaurant." This Oriental bobby didn't hesitate before using a gloved hand to point them around the corner. Down a dark basement reeking of fish balls and disinfectant, our intrepid gourmets found a few dusty tables manned by an old gent in shorts and managed to order some greasy duck and a limited selection of greens. It was only after they had choked down the last of their repast that they noticed English script embossed on the red chopstick handles. The name of this noodle joint was there plainly and unarguably for all to see: A Really Good Chinese Restaurant.

This book hopes to do a better job of pointing.

Cold Dish
· · · · · ·
THE LONG MUNCH

Featured Restaurants:

Great China, Berkeley
Il Giardino del Giada, Venice, Italy
Peking, Jerez, Spain

A Romance with No MSG

We dream of another world, but we eat in this one.

At the Great China Restaurant, I feel like I'm dreaming. And it doesn't have anything to do with the walnut shrimp. A year's supply of TV dinners ago, I was just another emotionally starved single guy. A child of the sixties entering my forties, I had practically lost my appetite for a permanent dining partner. With nowhere to nest, my inadvertent profession had become accidental tourist—dispatched to write eloquently about traveling "around the world in a bad mood." Now my mood is improving with each spin of dishes on the lazy Susan, each glance toward a woman neither lazy nor a Susan. Setting out on the journey of a lifetime, she and I are actually thinking of journeying through life together. A half-dozen friends have gathered to celebrate what my fiancée's forebears would term *double happiness*. From the beginning, it's felt more like double gluttony.

Did our search for the world's best Chinese restaurant really begin outside a Berkeley, California, cinematheque? I'd been drawn there by a rare screening of *Zhong-guo*, Italian director Michelangelo Antonioni's documentary on China's Cultural Revolution. After four static hours of cycling peasants, a couple of film professors and I were among the few survivors in the lobby, trying to shake off too much cinema. When one of my crowd was approached by a distant cousin, her companions included an Asian woman who wore her tweed jacket with a dancer's bearing and whose shimmering dark locks fell nearly to her waist. I like to think that my instant interest was elicited by the woman's unusual poise, unguarded gaiety, and obvious sharpness. My urges probably had more to do with high cheekbones and long legs, as well as her enthusiastic reaction to an artless admission of my occupation.

"Really? I can't help admiring writers," confessed this fellow moviegoer, introduced as Mei. "You say it like the month of May but spell it the Chinese way. Not like Anna May Wong, that's too predictable."

Predictable Mei wasn't. By the time we completed a too-short stroll to the street, I learned that this arts enthusiast was an indus-

7

trial engineer who had been designing computer hardware for the past decade—a neat trick, since she didn't look older than twenty-five. "But I'm through with that corporate culture!" she announced. "And next week, I'm going to have a look at my Beijing home for the first time in nine years."

Just my timing! With atypical alacrity, and the doggedness born of much failure, I came up with the ploy of offering her numerous journalistic contacts in China if she'd take down my number. When the phone rang five days later, I'd already presumed that Mei was on her slow boat to the Middle Kingdom. Once more, I was taken aback by her vivacious wit and literary bent.

"You didn't lie to me about being a scribbler, did you? During the Cultural Revolution, we survived off the forbidden fruit of Turgenev, O'Henry, Victor Hugo." I wasn't sure that I could stand such comparisons, but her pronunciation was as charming as her sentiments. "Growing up, I could only remain human through reading."

Though Mei was hardly the girl next door, she and I found matches in many areas. We shared an appreciation for big-city pleasures—being children of biggies Shanghai and New York. As the offspring of persecuted intellectuals, we were likewise devoted to good fights and lost causes. In what Mei jokingly termed "a no-win situation," her folks were branded as "rightists" while mine had been blacklisted as leftists. Red diaper baby or almost Red Guard, each of us was the vulnerable only child of a turbulent marriage that ended in divorce.

From Glenn Gould to Lu Xun, the search for community, and the need for wanderlust, it seemed that we'd never run out of topics for conversation. And Mei lived right in my half-Asian borough of San Francisco! In a second, we found ourselves strolling through the rose garden in Golden Gate Park. Two hours later, I reached to stroke her hand under the table at a sushi dinner. Another hour beyond that, we exchanged our first deep stare while climbing the creaking Filbert Steps above San Francisco Bay. On that jasmine-cloaked night, I picked her a lily from someone else's garden. The next day came our first kiss. Or was there greater significance in our first shared Chinese meal, actually Singapore-style?

At this rate, I soon got Mei to postpone her trip. I knew this daughter of the Chinese translator of *Gone With The Wind* was the girl for me when I casually checked off thirty entries of interest at an upcoming film festival and Mei had rushed out to buy tickets for every single show. Here was a woman who sang both Peking opera and Puccini arias, played the accordion and the bond market, studied herbal medicine but was well-acquainted with Coco Chanel. And the best thing about these qualifications was that she made me want to throw away any and all requirements. By our fourth date, Mei was dragging me to the Department of Motor Vehicles to settle up several years' worth of unpaid parking tickets, followed by a trip to the shop for a new muffler. By coincidence, the mechanic turned out to be Chinese, affording me a first glimpse at Mei's formidable bargaining skills. In what Chairman Mao termed "the skipping of stages," we seemed to be setting a speed record for moving from dating to real life.

"Double skin!" she now cries with glee, referring not to our closeness but the perfect opening course for our send-off dinner. *La pi* in Chinese, this dish has nothing to do with any animal hide, but consists of sticky, hand-cut mung bean flour noodles topped with hot pork, then tossed together with cold julienned vegetables, crunchy jellyfish, and a stinging mustard sauce. "Some chefs call this a spring dance," Mei explains. "Just like us!"

But who taught me the steps? Could it be that I was primed to relish a Chinese woman thanks mainly to Chinese food? Like so many others, my first clues about the world's oldest civilization came in the form of a dusty dinette's carved screens, red-tasseled lamps, and pot-bellied Buddha toothpick holders—all the instant Sinosity imported from some dynastic supply house. No wonder Westerners rarely know what to make of the Middle Kingdom, when our advance intelligence comes in the form of *moo goo gai pan*—and Confucian thought is boiled down to preset menus in columns A or B!

As a freckled-faced kid growing up during the fifties, my palate's range extended from canned green beans to baked custard. After being fed hamburgers until age six, I graduated to sea shell pasta topped with ketchup and cottage cheese (Richard Nixon's favorite). Yet I had no trouble adjusting to my parents' weekly trek up Manhattan's Upper West Side to some archetypal Golden Dragon Café or to the curious, dark-haired attendants in bow ties and smudged ochre vests. I got right into the swing of this peculiarly Jewish-American ritual of ingesting illicit spare ribs, accompanied by bowls of pretzel-like prefab noodles. It was better than watching my sex therapist dad sneak out between patients to satisfy his oral fixation with a tongue sandwich. I had no idea that what I called yummy had long been categorized by *yin* and *yang*.

My first master in the mysteries of Chinese eating was Mike Chinoy, my precocious cousin, who started his long march to becoming CNN's man at Tiananmen Square by taking Mandarin lessons in junior high and decorating his room with a pinup of Red Army idol Zhu De. "Dig tunnels deep, store grain everywhere, and never seek hegemony!" Mike loved to declaim toward coeds on the Yale campus, a slogan destined to become my baffling toast at his wedding. While China remained closed to "capitalist roaders," my cousin's linguistic skills did him good solely in Chinese restaurants. The trouble was that no matter how fluent in Chinese he became, the waiters always replied in English. They simply wouldn't believe their own ears. And I couldn't believe what this nice Jewish boy was eating. In the basement walk-downs of New York and later in Hong Kong's mislabeled New American Restaurant, he introduced me to quivering blocks of bean curd, spicy chicken feet, and authentic hot-and-sour soup, laced with sinew-thick strands of duck's blood. We really crossed some sort of cultural divide when Mike suggested that we take a carton of boiled dumplings to a New York Mets game. By the third inning, our Chinese crackerjacks had stuck together in a glutinous mass. Perhaps the hot dog had its good points after all.

Food offered our politically conscious generation the kind of internationalism that couldn't be faked. But while novelty-seeking baby boomers moved on to pita pizza, Burmese-Cambodian, or Ethiopian finger foods, I never saw how any other ethnicity could offer a cuisine so varied in styles or social function—from the medicinal to the recreational. After moving west to join San Francisco's polymorphous eating orgy, I loved watching Chinatown lunch-counter wizards use their shovel fulcrums to flick toward the sizzling abyss just the right amounts of pre-chopped ginger and garlic, dried chilis, soy and vinegar, chicken broth and rice wine, five-spice powder, and cornstarch "binder." Was this short-order alchemy the glue holding together more than a billion people? Every recipe seemed to have been codified centuries ago, yet everything was so off-the-stained-cuff. Like Taoist philosophy, the stir-fryer's methods looked so practical, yet offered a glimpse of the infinite. For the Chinese, it was nothing new to declare, "You are what you eat."

How had Mei decided to eat at the Great China? I certainly wouldn't have chosen to stage our first and last supper in this narrow storefront set between a bifurcated movie palace and a grad student *taquería*, made Californian with ikat wall hangings and parquet floors, birdcage booths, and bamboo lampshades. Mei has much experience working her grapevine of a hundred close acquaintances for restaurant picks, then probing the place's owner about his specialties. The main way she is predictably Chinese is through her culinary tenacity. Tonight's protracted negotiations come to a successful close with long beans braised in garlic and stuff-'em-yourself crab and scallion buns.

"No flavor enhancer, please!" she requests. At this stage, there can't be any sugar-coating. Ours is a romance with no MSG.

Which doesn't mean Mei is immune to romantic enticements. In place of her long-planned return to China, I convinced her to accompany me on a retreat to Venice, Italy, not California. In order to get to this celebratory dinner, the two of us had made it through a Venetian winter holed up in a leaky, poor man's palazzo. I'm not sure that we discovered one another so much as the best brands of prosciutto, tiramisu, and sweet moscato wine. Our most delicious moment came when Mei and I got separated in Venice's maze on our shopping rounds and straggled home hours later to meet in a desperate embrace.

While I soon felt like a fish out of water, adjusting to the abnormal norms of yet another country was a cinch for Mei, who declared that "writers should be citizens of the world." Of course, it helped that every baker, bohemian, and bureaucrat went ape over a simple *buona sera* from the lips of *una bella Cinesa* (a beautiful Chinese lady). Perhaps Mei was so good at this because her ancestors had been officials in Suzhou, that canal-laden "Venice of the East." By Carnival, she even got me dancing in a papier-mâché mask of Vincent Van Gogh and toasting with Bellinis at Harry's Bar.

We soon found that nothing worked better against the damp of the lagoon than a bowl of sizzling rice soup. It may be trite to admit, but our travels in search of Oriental spice routes actually got started in the hometown of Marco Polo. In one setting, Mei could assuage her homesickness for China while I indulged mine for America. Without realizing it, we began a survey of every Chinese restaurant within some nautical miles.

They appeared to be springing up as quickly as canal moss, each duly marked with red lanterns the way striped poles mark barber shops. The upscale Il Giardino del Giada, or Jade Garden, enticed local Romeos with a brace of young girls in slit skirts. But I couldn't get used to hearing feline hostesses purr, "Ciao, ciao!" Or menus that exposed my prior conception of Chinese food as hopelessly Americanized. Home-style tofu became far more elegant as *Taufu Alla Casalingha*; the mixed greens got religion as *Misto di Verdura alla Buddista*; and I had more fun with *chow fun* called *Fettucine di Riso Misto*.

Besides, I was with the perfect person to turn dining into research. Aside from an uncanny ability to fight her way to the head of any line, Mei's socialist upbringing left her with a truly classless approach to people. Nobody was big enough to intimidate her, nobody small enough to be denied her respect. More than any translating skills, her common touch drew out Chinese whenever we ate out. So we quickly discovered that the staff of every pagan outpost as far as the gates of the Vatican hailed from Wenzhou. This port town in one of China's poorest regions is hardly a fabled name of the East— or culinary hot spot. Its citizenry have a reputation as born business-men, but not chefs. No wonder we found Italy's Chinese food so bland, the menus identical. China's loss was Europe's bad luck.

Wenzhou natives have even spread as far as Barcelona. But on an excursion to Spain in search of—what else?—sunshine and fla-menco, we soon tired of going *tapas*. In chilly Jerez, where life is just a bottle of sherry, we were attracted by a restaurant's fire-engine red facade bearing the name of Mei's hometown, Peking. Not only was the roly-poly owner a doctor of acupuncture, but this persecuted son of a former ambassador to Spain rehabilitated himself as a coach for the national ping pong team.

Señor Jang's only other customer was one of the many Japanese girls who flock here to steal Andalucia's highest secrets of dance technique. "Spiel-berg-a-noo!" Harumi purred, mistaking my bearded, bespectacled look for the Hollywood director. Several bodegas later and sometime past three in the morning, we had to settle for watching this Tokyo Carmen and a series of suitors strut to prerecorded castanets. Travel is the art of looking for what you can't find and finding what you aren't looking for. Searching for the obvious, we stumble on the unimaginable.

Perhaps that's how our dining habits finally crystallized into a concept. As soon we got back to San Francisco, I proposed—that Mei and I try to get paid for what we were doing already.

"You mean we don't always have to be starving writers?"

"I can find a publisher, then you can find us plenty of banquets."

"But how can you rank Chinese food by a foreigner's standards?" she objected.

"Don't get chauvinist on me. If my taste buds get educated, that's part of the story."

"And the adventure! Can we check out Thailand? Bali, Indonesia?

"We can go anywhere there are Chinese . . ."

"Counting all my cousins, that's everywhere."

"Just remember," I warned. "Travel is the ultimate test of a relationship."

"I'm game," Mei replied as always. She's one of those people who think they can do everything, from plastering to programming—and usually can. When it comes to hitting the road, Mei is a fine upholder of China's feminist slogan, "Women hold up half the sky." In our case, they would have to hold half the luggage.

"Shall we call this our long honeymoon?" I asked as we took a romantic sunset stroll down the Berkeley fishing pier that jutted out into the Bay, seeming to reach halfway to China.

Mei's answer to my proposition was the same French saying that she cites as we slither down the Great China's delectable noodles: "No passion is more sincere than the passion for food."

So where, I wonder, does that leave me? Who knows if our "long munch" in search of edible bliss will really become a long march to the altar? In turning down a host of well-meaning professional types, Mei has been waiting for someone to help liberate her artistic side.

In return, she offers China—which means a dozen rumors daily about government power struggles, a thousand tips for healthful living, a million proverbs culled from some unending Bartlett's. Back at the Great China, between courses of this personal milestone, she is Chinese enough to turn her gaze toward the fate of others.

With persistent interest and a humble way of listening with sympathetic nods, Mei soon breaks through the haze of anonymity that clings to the restaurant's oversolicitous owner. Though Yu Ching Hwa now calls himself Mike, the trials he describes to us would surely qualify this devout Christian to be named Job. With his family's land confiscated in 1949, Mike grew up in Korea and suffered the deprivations of war that led to a younger sister dying of starvation. Next came prejudice.

"I was only one of two Chinese accepted into a Seoul medical college," he explains in a soothing, radio deejay voice. Asked to accompany his sister to the United States, Mike later became one of the first licensed acupuncturists in California. Instantly smashing my stereotype of Chinese chef as desperate immigrant, he concedes, "I could have done a lot better by remaining a doctor in Korea. I lost more than a day when I crossed the International Date Line."

But Mike is a born foodie who always dreamed of opening a restaurant that would feature dishes from his native Shandong Province. He spent ten years in other people's kitchens before saving enough for his own place—then lost it all when a troublesome nephew caused Mike to have a heart attack right in the restaurant kitchen. While recovering, he found religion, along with this storefront in Berkeley. When partners pulled out of the deal, "I was saved only because fellow congregation members answered my fervent prayers."

Ten months into a one-man remodeling job, with all his cash gone and no insurance, the restaurant burned to the ground. "When I smelled the fire, I thought it came from the kitchen, but a lit candle had been left burning by a homeless man in the basement. I knew he was living there, but I didn't have the heart to throw him out," Mike tells us.

"But God wanted my wife and I to succeed," this true kitchen god concludes while fileting a steamed, whole Tilapia. "So tonight, I am serving you the fish that Christ used for his miracles."

Will Mei and I be able to learn from such lessons in adaptability? An awareness of the chef's travails only adds pungency to the delights that we now share.

"With a hamburger, every bite tastes the same," Mei observes. "American food is just like American people, sitting alone on the plate. Potatoes, steak, veggies. But Chinese people are always mixed together, bound in the same sauce. Bitter or sweet, there's no way out."

No wonder the quickest way to a Chinese woman's heart is through her stomach. Whatever the future may bring, this relationship isn't going to leave me feeling hungry in an hour.

But how much farther will Mei and I have to go to really feel satisfied? And how will we be able to separate real life from research, distinguish true love from our *won ton* lust? Our friends rise to clink together bottles of Tsingtao beer. Some wag toasts, "To Mei and John, may a thousand restaurants bloom!"

Recipe: Double Skin

From the Great China Restaurant

Cold ingredients, all julienned:
Pre-boiled calamari, 2 oz.
Pre-boiled sea cucumber, 2 oz.
Jellyfish, 2 oz.
Pre-boiled shrimp, 2 oz.
1 egg, scrambled
1 carrot, julienned
$^1/_2$ cucumber, julienned

Noodles:
Mung bean flour, 1 cup
Water, 1 cup

Hot topping:
Shredded pork tenderloin, 4 oz., marinated
   in soy sauce, rice wine, and 1 tsp. sugar
Diced white onion, 2 oz.
Wood ear mushrooms, 1 oz.
Diced garlic to taste

Dressing:
Soy sauce, 2 tbs.
White vinegar, 1 tbs.
Hot Chinese mustard, 1 tbs.

Mix mung bean flour and water to make a batter. Spread a very thin layer in a stainless steel bowl sitting in a wok full of boiling water. Spin the bowl to spread the batter and peel off as soon as it thickens. Cut finished, cooled noodles into long strips. Place in the middle of a serving platter with the cold ingredients, julienned and displayed separately. Stir-fry the pork, onions, and wood ears with garlic and spoon atop the noodles. To serve, pour the mustard-flavored dressing on the noodles and toss together all ingredients.

China
THE EAST IS FED

Featured Restaurants:

Sichuan, Beijing
Yue Bin, Beijing
Hong Yun Xuan, Beijing
San Xia, Beijing
Xinjiang, Beijing
Sui Yuan, Beijing
Kong Yi Ji, Beijing
Dai Village Big Shack, Beijing
Shu Rong Dofu, Beijing
White Peacock, Beijing
Fang Shan, Beijing
Li Family Restaurant, Beijing
Black Earth, Beijing
Geng Wu Big Cafeteria, Beijing
Sunflower Village, Beijing
Mao Family Restaurant, Beijing
Beijing Roast Duck, Beijing
Quanjude, Beijing
Jing An Temple, Shanghai
Shen Shen (Sunshine), Shanghai
The Box, Shanghai
Meilongzhen, Shanghai
Lao Fandian, Shanghai
Snack City, Chengdu
Chen Ma Po Dofu, Chengdu
Longchaoshou, Chengdu
Guangzhou Jiujia, Guangzhou
Bei Yuan, Guangzhou
Shahe, Guangzhou
Snake Restaurant, Guangzhou

Holes in the (Great) Wall

If the world of the Chinese is one big dumpling, then we're standing in its hot, juicy filling. On a searingly clear autumn morning, when Gobi winds scour the air of coal dust and construction grit, Tiananmen Square looks like the vast sinkhole of China's history. This silent stone epicenter of the stormy Middle Kingdom is terrifying in its flatness. Around the largest public space on earth, the feudal gates, dowdy lampposts, and Soviet-style officialdom coexist more uncomfortably than ever. Peasant pilgrims amble about in their best Sunday suits, come to tour the Great Banquet Hall of the People, peek into the emperors' no-longer forbidden kitchens, or inspect the moldering body of Chairman Mao Zedong—known to locals as "Hunan cured pork."

To comprehend just how much food means to the Chinese, I consider the 1989 pro-democracy hunger strikes staged on this sacrificial altar. While a few protesters now admit faking their abstinence and sneaking a sesame bun or two, the prospective Gandhis dropped like flies after mere hours. Was their downfall due to a lack of body fat? Or was their psychic dependence on the rice bowl just too great? Ancient brick shanties cling to the palace ramparts before us, testaments to this nation's unstoppable crescendo of want. Yet the most monumental view in sight may be each noontime's race of the million-fold masses, canteen tins in hand, sprinting toward lunch. A Chinese ceases to exist without a proper comeback to the customary greeting, "Have you eaten yet?"

Mei and I are about to do plenty of that. We've decided to begin our quest in the place where so much of China's cuisine once reached its apex. We must set our standards in the capital that for eight hundred years has attracted China's best and brightest scholars, generals, and chefs. Besides, this monster city of ten million is my fiancée's hometown. She approaches it more like a small village where a hundred leading elders can lead us to the eating houses that guidebooks miss. Though I can't help feeling a spine-tingling shudder, a sort of geopolitical orgasm when I stand in this place, Tiananmen is just part of Mei's old neighborhood.

"We used to ride the swings beside the Forbidden City," she

19

points out. "In winter, the moat around the palace was the best place for skating." Having grown up in a single room on the back side of the Great Hall of the People, this staging ground was her playground—with a million Red Guards as playmates, chanting nursery rhymes from the Little Red Book! More amazing than Mei turning up in my world is that she's turned out so emotionally sturdy—with a well-honed aptitude for maneuvering through crowds and responding to all forms of bullying. Inspired by the Brazilian tape playing on the Walkman strapped to the side of her jeans, she starts up a defiant samba on the Square's blood-stained stones.

Even as I join her in shaking my fanny pack, I can't believe that I am footloose once more in an anything-but-loose city that I vowed to never set foot in again. "Beijing Is Waiting For You!" read the ominous billboards on all sides, a greeting meant for Olympic committees that I cannot help taking personally. Six years back, I had approached this proletarian poster girl of a city like some starry-eyed suitor, my visions slapped down by a puritan schoolmarm in concrete. Now the city's remarkable entry road—one willow-draped meridian drawn across the yellow earth—has become an eight-lane expressway. Gone are the donkey carts and man-driven tricycles hauling unfathomably balanced loads of threshed grain and stacked charcoal coils. The rare deluxe taxis that once plodded along, content with their paltry quota of passengers, have become a fleet of scooped-out, suspensionless "bread box" minivans, loyal to the un-Maoist maxim that time is money.

"So how long will it take you to get from Peking to Beijing?" a confused British editor once asked his reporter in the realm of mistranslations. The question for me, as for all "foreign guests," is how long it takes to get from the Peking of our imaginings—somehow the outdated spelling has become the more exotic, conjuring up a Forbidden City of eunuchs and ideologues—to Beijing, the freewheeling city "for bidding." Though the veil of myths still hasn't lifted, I now have Mei to help me go native.

First, we conduct an experiment to find the eating place closest to ground zero. Crossing the Avenue of Eternal Peace where that emblematic lone citizen stepped before a column of government tanks, we start up a poplar-shaded avenue nuzzled against miles of imperial plaster. Forget about the Great Wall, most of which is a patched-up recreation. The most telltale sight in this city of boxes within boxes are the many walls that guard official secrets, the formidable front gates that encourage "backdoor" deals—all painted an indescribable tincture of vermilion, a regal Weatherbeater primed with dried blood. And we soon stumble upon our first hole-in-the-wall. As close as private enterprise can get to socialism's sanctified places, we spot a single-story brick hut with an unfortunate resemblance to the numerous public toilets that plague big-nosed tourists. Fittingly apt for our search, the crudely lettered signboard over the door proclaims in English, "The First Restaurant."

Of course, the owners really mean *best*. But this Maoist Freudian slip makes me wonder what the world's first restaurant might really have looked like. Somehow, I have the feeling it must have been called Wong's Place—Established 5,000 B.C. Since the Chinese claim the patent on practically every other boon to mankind, why not eating out? If they could invent paper and glass, surely they came up with tipping.

Even the discovery of fire, for the Chinese, was food related. Instead of wrathful gods sending down thunderbolts, legend has it that the value of flame-broiling was first understood when forest fires left animal carcasses extra tasty. Fond of such archetypal hors d'oeuvres as frog ovaries, Confucius peppered his Analects with hundreds of references to proper food handling as part of the path toward a just society. At a time when the West was still grappling with the concept of leavened bread, ancient Yellow River towns like Kaifeng boasted "72 first-class shops" each featuring as many as "234 famous dishes." Back in the Han Dynasty, around the time of Christ, restaurants were actually pleasure compounds where male patrons could linger for days, indulging all whims for women, wine, and song. Some of the complexes were so vast that miniature ponies bore delicacies from the kitchen. According to the early literature, the waiters were known as gong heads. Not only did they have to ring bells to announce esteemed patrons, but they were expected to accurately memorize every order—at a time when each diner could specify new combinations of ingredients. No wonder one classical account of the restaurant trade states, "If there is a green, inexperienced customer, they set down the chopsticks before him indifferently and he is the object of much laughter."

Funny, I've had the same experience in San Francisco. When asked for a heathen eating implement, one Chinese American waiter had actually deadpanned, "What's a fork?" Not only aren't there any forks in China, but there aren't always napkins. As a common Chinese saying goes, "If the table is dirty, just remember that you're not eating the table." Poking our noses into the First Restaurant's smoke-clogged atrium crowded with noisy noodle slatherers, I'm reminded of how much my initial disappointment with China had to do with the food—and an ambiance of slurping, belching, and heaving; tablecloths bombarded with gravy and folds of grime; floors that crunched under your feet from weeks of unswept chicken gristle.

If Chinese restaurants in China aren't anything like the false image I brought from the West—no plasticene booths or plastic packets of duck sauce—they also aren't much like the restaurants in China's past. With many great chefs having fled or been replaced by "work units," dinner at the commune cafe often meant gnarled chunks of meat suspended in pools of grease. Joining a 1988 tour of such cheery attractions as the world's largest open coal pit, I was almost relieved to consume banquets of fried baby sparrows and whole fish that hosts boasted were bred in the runoff water from a nuclear power plant! But the results of central planning were most obvious in the teams of listless waitresses refusing to "serve the people." There had to be something wrong with a system that could ruin something as good as Chinese cuisine.

Still, Mei has nominated a state-run establishment as our first candidate. Out of reverence for history and respect for her elders, she has arranged to treat her beloved stepfather to a welcoming lunch at the renowned Sichuan Restaurant. On our short cab ride past Zhongnanhai, the compound housing China's leaders, Mei explains, "We're going to the favorite spot of the top cadre—especially Deng Xiaoping, who came from Sichuan Province. During the Cultural Revolution, the place was shut down and used by Red Guards to interrogate their prisoners. About the time the restaurant reopened, I got a job in a medicine factory. I used my whole first month's salary to treat some friends to a meal here."

Given such a buildup, I'm expecting a top contender. I'm also a trifle nervous to meet the man she fondly calls *Lao Ba*, literally "Old Pa," but more correctly "Dear Dad." He'll come to refer to me as *Lao wai*. Old Foreigner—apparently that's the only name his new son-in-law needs. I suppose that's better than every second cabdriver's indiscreet inquiries about whether Mei can stand sleeping beside a hairy barbarian. This chess-playing pensioner proves most benign, still dapper at seventy in khaki outfits, with wavy tufts of gray hair, a small paunch, and a kind face accentuated by an overlarge upper lip. As an added attraction, he has brought along Li Na, a well-known writer, for what a winking Mei calls "a double date."

These two formerly persecuted "rightists" couldn't look more docile or out of place, awaiting us in a opulent private room off the restaurant's courtyard. With austere white gates, arcaded entry lined with photos of famed diners, and ornately painted overhangs, this palace turned top-of-the-line state canteen hardly looks like the haunt of revolutionaries. The Sichuan has the feeling of a house twice abandoned—first by imperial elites, then by Communist ones.

While we wait for our order, Li Na tells us of the dining habits in Yenan, the legendary stronghold of Mao and other Red Army leaders. "Everyone ate simply back then. During the anti-Japanese war, we had a dish that was named 'Bomb Tokyo.' It was a shrimp and tomato sauce poured over sizzling rice.' " She claims that the anti-Communist Kuo-mintang also had a version called "Bomb Moscow."

Our food is hardly that explosive. Sichuanese specialties like bean curd with minced meat, twice-cooked pork, a whole fish in chili sauce, are tough, bland, and quivering in congealed grease. In the school of cooking that one sign advertises as "hot and prickly," private establishments like the Dou Hua chain will provide us with more bang for our Chinese buck. But Mei's stepfather and his escort spend so much time harping that it seems they've come here in order to savor their disappointment. After a lifelong diet of lowered expectations, any other response might be too much of a shock. Or perhaps, turning up one's nose at the food is merely China's safest form of dissent.

"The Cultural Revolution destroyed our cuisine," observes Li Na, without evident bitterness, "as well as the ability of our people to think and to feel."

Though this fervent believer finds it easier to criticize our dishes than the ideals of Communism, she readily intertwines politics with food—and treats them as equally significant. "One can never be too serious about eating," Li Na explains. "We Chinese say that a meal must be tasted three times: once in anticipation, once on the tongue, and once with nostalgia."

From former times of scarcity, Lao Ba adds the homily, "Always sit where you can see the whole table." In the days ahead, Mei's stepfather will stuff himself as often as possible while sharing our realization that many of Beijing's time-honored eating houses have merely become old enough to have been run into the ground. With damning finality, Li Na concludes, "If Deng Xiaoping ate at the Sichuan Restaurant today, I'm sure that he would call for reforms."

One evening stroll through Beijing shows how much that culinary reform is already underway. Like China itself, the restaurant trade is on a long march back to respectability. In 1949, when the People's Republic of China was founded, there were upwards of twenty thousand restaurants in the Chinese capital. By 1975, at the end of the Cultural Revolution's ten years of self-denial, there were but seven hundred. Now the profusion of choices has already surpassed former levels. Along Wanfujing, the city's bustling Fifth Avenue, Mei and I notice such overeager entrepreneurial efforts as the Ban Po Hot Pot Primitive Beer Hut and the inscrutable Mister Beef Seafood Restaurant. Many of these newcomers are little more than spotless fluorescent-lit cabins fronted by teams of beckoning local beauties and lined with blown-up photos of ludicrously cheery alpine scenes.

It's hard to tell whether all this infusion of investment capital is enabling the Chinese to rediscover their heritage or abandon it. Where cheese was once anathema, Pizza Huts abound. A mock diner called the Broadway Cafe offers such unknown items as "Texas spaghetti." In the city's prime location is the world's busiest McDonald's, with some forty thousand customers a day. Though a Big Mac may be a "meal disguised as a sandwich," I'll be told that it hardly qualifies as a side-dish in the Chinese mind. After sampling this limited Western novelty, most Chinese don't merely ask, "Where's the beef?" but also, "Where should we go for dinner?"

Fortunately, I recall a place that Mei has never tried. One precious bit of prior reconnaissance leads me toward a back alley marked by stone lions and stacks of winter cabbage. With a single step, we've left behind the world's main streets for the world of the *hutong*, or traditional, enclosed courtyards. So many walled villages have turned urban that it is said, "There are more *hutong* in Beijing than there are hairs on an ox." Forget the China of flimsy fans and carved screens. This is the China of coal and slate. Places where everything is known and nothing thrown away.

After a wrong turn or two, we come to a door hung with colored plastic strips. I'm not surprised when Mei tells me that Yue Bin, the name of this neighborhood dive, means "Please the Guest." I've relocated the vaunted find of Beijing's CNN bureau, a hangout where Ted Turner once got a most unofficial welcome. The cracked walls are lime green and decorated solely with clocks and calendars; the enamel tables are covered with throws the thinness of cheesecloth.

The proprietor is seated before a register that consists of one trusty abacus and a plastic case that isn't for mints but tiny plates full of blanched peanuts, thin-sliced duck tongue, chopped cucumbers, and preserved "thousand-year-old" eggs. He is a jaunty old goat with a toothless smile, narrow eyes, and the flinty look of a Mongol horseman. Beneath a chef's cap as puffed as a soufflé, a bit of white stubble shows around the ears. He hardly looks like the local Toots Shor, but once Mei gets him talking, Mr. Guo reveals that he was among the first chefs in Beijing to open his own place.

With family ownership, the food is decidedly fresher. To fill an order, fish and chicken usually get thwacked to death on the sidewalk. Where menus consist of a handwritten guide on a stained piece of cardboard, fending off aggressive waitresses' "suggestions" can take agonizing negotiation. Whenever Mei gets locked into this ritualized form of self-defense, I realize that our meal will be made by the dishes she is trying *not* to order. But Mr. Guo quickly sends us the house specialty: soft strands of thin-cut pork and chicken folded into a thin omelette wrapping, then served in dense, wheaty pancakes along with a thick wheat-based sauce. Equally superb are deep-fried yet not too oily squares of fresh bean curd stuffed with Chinese ham. Yue Bin even does a decent rendition of *yu xiang ro si*, usually translated as "fish-flavored shredded pork," but actually chockful of wood ear mushrooms and covered in a tangy sauce that's mainly vinegar, soy, ginger, and sugar. Whenever I can on our journey, I'll order this hearty Sichuan favorite as a kind of test case. If a northern-style restaurant can't make this dish well, they can't do a decent job with anything else.

Mr. Guo actually learned his stuff in the kitchens of Zhongnanhai, the nearby encampment of China's top rulers. It's not clear whether he was a cook or some elite proletarian bottle washer. But he must have been around at mealtimes, considering his remark that "Chairman Mao was very frugal, with simple tastes. He was a kindly emperor."

Speaking of Mao's traitorous adjutant Lin Biao, Mr. Guo says, "He was a very picky eater. Lin Biao always looked like a dead man." As for Deng Xiaoping, "He was very clever and would never ask for more helpings while Mao was around. But later, he'd come around to the kitchen for his real dinner!"

Each time we return, the revisionist tales get more embellished. I don't mind, so long as they come with these heights of home cooking.

"Don't you feel comfortable?" asks Mei. I nod at the all-purpose word she uses to describe every state from contented to stuffed.

At Yue Bin, we get the real dish along with real eats—a sampling of Chinese food that, like China itself, is rougher, grittier, yet more rewarding than overseas imitations. In one location, I can shake hands with this town's Tartar inheritance, hear palace gossip, and eat my first poultry wrapped in pancakes. Nothing makes me feel more like I've made it from Peking to Beijing.

Some Like It Hot Pot

Who would have thought that our quest for the best Chinese food would be aided and abetted by a Tibetan?

"Tonight, my friends, I have organized a small welcoming banquet," we're told by Phunkhang Goranangpa, as this bear of a man paces in a cramped office daringly draped with rows of colorful prayer flags. The last thing I expected was such an invitation—or this Asian Paul Bunyan in a shiny, double-breasted suit, back from an Ivy League education, sharing space with a fledgling firm of twenty-something stockbrokers to promote "Tibetan self-development for mutual benefit." But Phunkhang—"Ping-kang" to his buddies—is no typical Peking Man. Himalayan in stature and Samoan in girth, he possesses the gentle smile and booming laugh, long nose and brown skin, pathos-filled round eyes, kinky hair, and pear-shaped earlobes of some bronze Buddha come to life. As the son of the controversial founder of Tibet's Communist Party, his presence in China's capital is as precarious as it is larger than life.

Overcoming the disapproval of Chinese authorities and Tibetan exiles alike, this lobbyist between countries had recently managed to stage the First Tibetan Plateau International Bicycle Rally. "Using the universal language of sport, we advanced brotherhood!" Phunkhang waxes, his huge, soft hands making circles in the air. "One night, our lead jeep had a small accident on a high pass. I sustained a few broken ribs, but we carried on. Athletes from twelve countries experienced true Tibetan hospitality. But no journalists were allowed to report the event!" Perhaps that's why he's so grateful for my contribution of an English "diploma" lauding the maniacal cyclists able to complete the three-week, thin-air course. "In return for your smooth words," the organizer tells me, "the least I can offer is Beijing's finest hot pot!"

We taxi to Baitasi, a lively warren of leafy back alleys centered around the ivory-white spire of an eleventh-century Nepalese-style temple. The tables set out on every inch of sidewalk are crowded enough to make this East Asia's Via Veneto. But these local literati and layabouts are leisurely poking chopsticks into portable cauldrons kept perpetually boiling with fiery chunks of wood charcoal. The distinctive, circular shape of the pot itself, with its fluted chimney in the center, was supposedly inspired by invading soldiers who turned their helmets upside down to make cooking vessels back in the thirteenth century when Kublai Khan took Beijing and established the Yuan Dynasty. Not merely the most gut-warming way to get through frigid North China winters, the Mongolian hot pot (literally "dipped lamb" in Mandarin) has been taken up enthusiastically as the cheapest form of all-you-can eat in a country that can never get enough.

Outside the brightly lit Hong Yun Xuan, meaning "Place of Great Fortune," the six p.m. seating has already spilled onto the street. But Phunkhang has reserved us an entire back room sealed off from the noisy rabble and decorated with flowered wallpaper.

The guests include a visiting scholar from Harvard and a considerable number of Phunkhang's sisters and nieces whose drooping jowls and quizzical stares make them pigtailed Mona Lisas. Also awaiting are platters of thin-sliced lamb, chunky squares of bean curd, and various leafy greens. Two long tables are already laden with half a dozen silver-colored steaming pots. While in Sichuan Province the broth itself is laced with chili, and in Canton medicinal herbs may be added, the true Mongolian hot pot should, according to an ancient food historian, "be cooked in water as clear as the relations between honorable men."

Before any of us can dig in, we rise to greet the restaurant's owner. This bald, stocky man in a dark, double-breasted suit has been asked to explicate the dish's derivation and preparation. Like most of the hot pot's high priests, he is a Muslim whose family once hailed from China's western deserts. (Often, their last names are Ma, shortened from Mohammed.) He had defected from the staff of Dong Lai Shun, a century-old institution in Beijing where "your President Nixon ate. But I always wanted to start my own restaurant and revive the old ways."

Not so long ago, sheep raised on the grasslands were marched through the northern gates of Beijing for slaughter. Now most hot pot places offer plates of frozen lamb shaved off by electric slicers. But Hong Yun Xuan serves only fresh meat, taken from ten different parts—the stomach, thighs, chest, tail, hooves, even, someone jokes, the armpit.

"See!" Phungkhang cries with pride, holding up an honorary first slice. "This little lamb's thigh is thin enough to read the *People's Daily* through it!"

Hong Yun Xuan's proud owner quickly adds, "A great hot pot is distinguished by its nine dipping sauces." I count sesame and chili oils; a kind of mustard; a red paste of salty, fermented tofu; rice wine; shrimp sauce; peanut and chive pastes; and a blend of twelve digestive herbs. We have to curb our appetites—and postpone toasts with Beijing beer—until the end of his seminar. Leave it to the Chinese to bring so much theory and protocol to the act of blanching meat! What follows is an Asian fondue party turned into an orgy of stirring. Lettuce leaves, nests of noodles, and almost everything else go into the broth. Phunkhang plies Mei and me with the most tender morsels, until we're filled with enough *yang* (Chinese for lamb) to balance our yin. "Dip the meat three times down and two times up!" our leader instructs, patting his Buddha-like belly. By then, my lamb looks so bedraggled that any of the sauces have to be an improvement. To prove the purity of the meat, he urges me to try some raw. The Mongolian No Pot. Fortunately, I can't keep up with Phunkhang, who loves to eat nearly as much as he loves to hold center stage.

"Old man river, that old man river . . . ," he croons in booming basso the kind of blues you can't catch down by the Yangtze. "My friend, how do you like my Paul Robeson?"

Next comes a half-tempo rendition of "Guantanamera," apparently popular among Chinese schoolchildren during a period of fraternal détente with Cuba.

Having downed enough rice liquor to match his body weight, Phunkhang tops his performance with titillating theories on Tantric sex.

"According to our knowledge, man must protect his vital life force! My friend, now that you plan to be married to a beautiful Chinese girl, I will offer some advice." He bats his watery eyes in utter seriousness. "If you can make love once a week for a year without ejaculating, at the end you will be able to fly!"

Do such dinnertime topics take the place of the politically illicit? In today's dog-eat-dog atmosphere, Phunkhang readily admits, "It's not easy to find a girlfriend once I tell them what I'm up to. My friend, shall we make our first million together on dehydrated yak milk? I'm the last nonprofit in China!" he bellows. "Talk about a black sheep!"

I will, so long as we don't have to eat one. But Phunkhang's jokes reveal the strain of being caught between his loyalties to an adopted culture and a native land that he hardly knows. Gripping me in a farewell hug, our host whispers, "Do you know what it's like to kiss a Tibetan?"

Over the next weeks, I come to see how his clowning hides the pain of nights spent sleeping on the office floor, always a marked man, the merry giant, the other. One time, he recalls the six years of his youth spent squatting in jail cells "until my behind became as raw as a baboon's." Corn cakes and gruel enforced a near-starvation that was particularly tortuous to this growing boy.

In private, Phunkhang reminisces about his naive, beloved mother, persecuted as much for offending a Chinese neighbor as for her political connections, who supposedly killed herself by slashing her wrists against a rusty radiator but was probably done in by rampaging Red Guards. He rarely mentions his illustrious yet distant father, also a victim of that dark period. That is why I am astounded when Phunkhang calls to announce, "My friend, I've achieved a rare opportunity for you to interview my father."

Rehabilitated by Deng Xiaoping and reformist premier Hu Yaobang, this transitional figure in Tibetan history retired among the highest ranks of his countrymen in China, a token Tibetan on the Minority Affairs Commission of the People's Congress. Mei and I call on Phungtsuo ("Ping-cuo") Wanjie in his small office on the second floor of a low-lying compound in the shadow of the Great Hall of the People. The father is the son's opposite: lean and guarded, austere and elegant, soft-spoken and deliberate. With straight, silver hair, elongated features, and just a slight tincture of high mountain blush to his complexion, he reminds me less of a Tibetan rebel than some Indian Brahmin.

"You can blame my life on Edgar Snow!" he starts our audience, referring to the American journalist whose early reports on the Red Army even inspired some within China. Born in eastern Tibet, now Sichuan Province, Phungtsuo was educated by American missionaries. Sent off on a scholarship, he became involved in the Communist underground, eventually escaping police dragnets to help form the Tibetan Democratic League and lead fighting units in horseback raids on the Kuomintang's rear flank. He was the first to translate "The International" into Tibetan.

After 1949, Phungtsuo participated in doomed negotiations to help the Dalai Lama and Chinese authorities reach some power-sharing arrangement. As part of the prelude to the military conquest of Tibet, Phungtsuo was recalled to Beijing by Chairman Mao. Accused of "nationalistic tendencies," he was sequestered in the capital until his sudden, if not unexpected, arrest. "All four top leaders of China had to sign the warrant," Phungtsuo claims. Ironically, he was held in a facility so top-rank that it wasn't even called a prison and "so exclusive that its whereabouts were completely unknown."

For eighteen years, he received no news of the outside world and endured absolute solitude. He was tortured regularly and forced to sleep on an iron board. Yet for many of these years, he remained fervently loyal to the Party and sought rigorously to understand the nature of his ostensible offense. When his health began to deteriorate, he could not bring himself to admit that his rations were being poisoned. Eventually, he learned to eat lightly and to keep up his spirits with Tibetan songs. "The darkest clouds," he repeats one lyric, "can't cover the sun."

To occupy his mind, he began to conceive a new theory of rules governing change in the universe. "I soaked my prison uniform to squeeze out some blue dye for ink, then scrawled my ideas on toilet paper," he relates to us. "I was so happy that I began to dance and sing!" But the guards confiscated his work and put him in such tight handcuffs that the scars took three years to heal. Released in 1980, Phungtsuo took time to regain his voice. When he began espousing ideas that he believed could shake the foundations of world philosophy, he was dismissed as mad. Finally allowed to address an academic meeting, he was given a standing ovation.

"In my latest book, I prove that there must be water on the moon," he explains, showing us two, massive tomes widely sold in China, complete with his prized diagrams—New Age Tibetan mandalas—for grappling with the eternal synthesis of opposites. Hoping to coax forth more of Phungtsuo's remarkable story, I suggest that we continue at his favorite restaurant. But the old leader rarely eats out. Home to office via limo is the customary route of this former guerrilla on horseback. Besides, he's still enough of a socialist to disapprove of the current-day tendency to dine lavishly. Hesitantly, he agrees to follow us to San Xia, a highly rated Sichuan place quite near to Tiananmen Square. The moment we get there, I know I've made a mistake. The place is lit too dimly to help reveal anything more of the man; the food is hardly worthy of our guest's stature.

Suddenly, more than a few minutes before closing time, San Xia's slovenly waitresses in hostess outfits and kitchen helpers in grease-smeared smocks fan out and begin dutifully, then mirthfully, ripping down every sheet of wallpaper. Though there is no explanation forthcoming, the restaurant is apparently due for remodeling. I've heard of many methods to keep customers from lingering at closing time, but this is ridiculous. All pretense of order is torn apart before our very eyes. Without explanation or apology, our dining experience has been turned into another of the new China's noisy construction sites.

Phungkhang's father looks horrified, and we help him beat a hasty retreat. What good is his martyr's vision against such insolence? Could this carnage be explained by his theories of change, Tantric or Hegelian? Is there anything about these sort of workers in *Das Kapital*?

"It's unfortunate, but the whole feeling is changing!" Phunkhang will lament when we tell of the abrupt end to our audience with his father. "Now everything in the culture reflects speed. We have franchised California Beef Noodles, with tables designed to seat only two. That's unheard of in China, where eating is always a social event."

To that end, the son now introduces us to a rare Chinese longhair, who boasts of having exported sandalwood soap to every American health food store. His Westernized occupation is now breeding dogs—for pets, not eating. But I face my greatest cross-cultural challenge when he drags us to a drafty Mongolian place and puts in a special order for camel's paw. "Finger lickin' good!" our guide declares at the delayed arrival of a bowl overloaded with what looks like chopped-up, quartzite crystals. Despite an hour's cooking, the delicacy has the texture and golden glow of hardened mucilage glue. How does one know when camel's paw is medium, well-done, or rare? Our host has to admit that the dish isn't supposed to be this chewy. Though there are no doggy bags in China, we leave with the sneaking suspicion that he's merely used us to bring something home to his hounds.

In Beijing's smoke-filled banquet rooms, you never know who you're going to break bread with—or what will go on top. For his pièce de résistance, Phunkhang arranges a special treat at the Xinjiang, one of Beijing's grittier and smokier Muslim-style grills. Because I've got a beard, the skull-capped waiters from distant Central Asian provinces move to embrace me as one of their long-lost brethren. Our cozy banquet room is hovered over by thick-lidded Scheherazades cloaked in wispy kerchiefs. Crammed with three tables turned into one, this is the sort of setting in China where little men come to make big decisions. We're joined by a group of VIPs engaged in some nefarious aspect of the giant Three Gorges dam, which is scheduled to inundate China's most fabled scenery, destroy ecosystems, and displace millions of undercompensated peasants.

"Gong An," Mei whispers, a guess that some of these fellows are part of China's untouchable Security Police. Who knows if they are looking for crime or looking the other way? The godfather of this gang has the seen-it-all lassitude of a former hit man. Just when I'm getting nervous, the entire, freshly torched carcass of a sheep is wheeled out for inspection. "Enough for a year in some village," Mei chastises. But the others just laugh. A glinting, half-moon blade has been jabbed straight into the brain. Before we dig in, every honored guest has to pose with the proof of our "whole lamb dinner."

Having been raised among meat-eating occupiers, Phunkhang leads the assault on the carcass. I can't imagine this jet-age nomad being satisfied with his people's native diet of barley and yak butter. I should have guessed from his girth: this lobbyist's most passionate commitment may be to China's edible—and drinkable—pleasures.

"It's true, food marks a major difference between the two cultures," he confesses, his plate heaped with bones. "As Buddhists, Tibetans only take the soul of the yak when absolutely necessary. You should see, the countryside is full of wild geese and fish! No one had to kill because nobody starved. But I can forgive another attitude toward nature. The Chinese, you know, always had more mouths to feed. And they are much too clever to pass up the chance to cook anything."

In his omnidirectional carnivorousness, Phunkhang is our best guide to a spartan capital's closet hedonism. Still, I'm not sure if he considers the Xinjiang a candidate for our search or if he's just seeking another excuse to forget his troubles. After fourteen down-the-hatch swigs of firewater, Phunkhang launches into an operatic rendition of "I Left My Heart in San Francisco."

He then confides, "Tibetans prefer to sing and make music. Compared to the Chinese, we are very gullible. We are children in their hands!"

Cocktails at the Penis Restaurant

"For every three people who walk toward you," says Mei, "one must be your teacher."

In her hometown, the ratio has to be higher. Even inside Ritan Park, flanked by the U.S. Embassy's line of desperate visa applicants and the cotton market's tag teams of Russian ladies haggling in hot pants, we find an outdoor academy of traditional arts. Beside lotus-clogged lakes and austere stone altars, pensioners coax a wail out of one-stringed violins or engage in the health-inducing spasms of *ch'i gong*, a morning exercise in which meditation meets hypochondria. While plenty of cities in the world provide me with an excuse to stay up late, only this one offers enough spectacle to make me get up early. Every dawn, I tag along while Mei seeks out Mr. Tsao, her very own round-bellied, chain-smoking master of martial arts. Soon enough, she is using a retractable plastic sword to mimic a lifetime's worth of lithe, concentrated plunges.

The instruction is not so otherworldly at Sturdy Pine Tree, the main vocational school devoted to the food industry. Competition is fierce for the chance at the three-year program, with one year of cleaver-on apprenticeship. Even sharp eyesight is required for entry. Due to the expansion of China's tourist-related trades, nearly all graduates can find work. Principal Hao Shou Ben ushers us through immaculate kitchens where late teens are acquiring the basic techniques. "That's stir-fry, boil, deep fry, sauté, simmer, dry fry, barbecue, grill, steam, bake, scald, iron skillet," he rattles off. "And cutting, of course. Cutting against the grain is what gives the meat texture and tenderness."

The bright classrooms are a far cry from the days when aspiring scullions proved their mettle by putting in three years' free labor hand-twisting noodle dough into microscopic "dragon's whiskers."

There's further professionalism at the school's attached Shu Rong Restaurant, a laboratory featuring Beijing's finest renditions of Sichuan tea-smoked duck and my test-case fish-flavored pork. Old gents in turbanlike headgear even practice the back-country custom of aiming hot water into tea-cup bull's eyes from brass pots held as high as possible above the table. The greater the height, the more respected the guests. Does the school give advanced degrees in pouring?

"Food is China's religion," declares the principal in yet another understatement. The son of the famed European founder of a restaurant in Tianjin, Mr. Hao adds, "While we still have to raise the social status of the chef, these boys will soon be making three times what I do." The need remains great because China's "quality of living is increasing and people have more leisure time." He reminds us, "When I was in the United States, I saw that even your suburbs have far more choice of eating places than does the center of Beijing. This is the legacy of underdevelopment. We need many, many more restaurants."

With the Gobi winds getting more fierce, the yellow clouds of heating coal more tubercular, Mei and I can't stick around to try all of them. When one restaurateur boasts to us that "Beijing's dining is now just like America's," he means that China's capital is finally reflecting the full variety of national styles. From Shanxi-style lamb at the folkloric Yellow Earth, we move on to home-cured Hunan hams at the cramped Sui Yuan and the chestnut-studded fried rice that makes an ordinary dish memorable at the Zhejiang-style Kong Yi Ji—favored by the conceptual artist Ai Wei Wei, son of China's greatest poet, and named after a character created by Lu Xun, China's wistful Chekhov. The Dai Village Big Shack is a Trader Vic's "with Chinese characteristics." In this thatched long house, tiny, sarong-wrapped women from Yunnan's minorities offer a floor show of trembling "peacock dances" while waitresses unceremoniously scrape sweet chicken dishes from tubes of bamboo.

One afternoon, Mei stops dead in her tracks at a sign in a storefront window festooned with red lettering. "I've never seen this in Beijing. Penises of All Animals!"

Too bad I've just eaten. Of course, the proprietor has moved here from Canton, where locals proudly uphold the edict to "eat anything that flies but an airplane, anything that swims but a submarine, everything on four legs but the table." The walls are lined with stacked rows of medicinal wines in see-through glass urns, spiked with monkey tails and whole iguanas, preserving a variety of glands and almost anything fetal. In its steadfast literalness, Chinese wisdom holds that any body parts consumed will benefit one's own corresponding organ. This young owner is dead serious about the increase in virility to be gained from a nibble or two of stewed male member, whether from donkey, deer, or cow. Helping out with the American trade deficit, he insists, "We import U.S. Grade A!"

I'm not sure what to do with "Fried manyplies," the delectable "Misce llaneous," crunchy "Bambwashoo," plus the unfortunate "Snobed Fish" and "Cold shredded." All of these are on the menu at the Fragrant Hills Hotel, the rundown showplace designed by overseas luminary I. M. Pei. Mei and I prefer the fragrance of hilltop snacks like sweet rice cakes crammed with whole dates, sold from the backs of donkeys. In an annual celebration of the fall's changing colors, half of China appears to have followed us out to these former imperial pleasure grounds. But the prettiest leaves have already been laminated under plastic to sell as souvenirs.

It's easy enough to walk in the footsteps of the emperor. The ambition of every Chinese is to eat like one. This includes the urbane professor who spent seven years translating the first volume of Proust's *Remembrance of Things Past* into Mandarin. For his own remembrance of things past, this world-weary rightist invites us to the White Peacock Restaurant and blows a month's wages on such splurges as springs rolls topped with deep-fried scorpions. Along with dessert, served by sullen schoolgirls disguised as imperial handmaidens, we're offered a chance to don silken robes and be photographed posing on a mock throne.

The Son of Heaven's first duty may have been to feed his people, but most people in China seem to know more about how the exalted man fed himself. "In America," one restaurateur tells us, "you know each dish by its calories and grams of fat. In China, we identify each dish by its imperial lineage." At a time when Europe's medieval kings were throwing quail bones over their shoulders, China's royal kitchen boasted 7,000 chefs. Out of some 4,000 palace functionaries in one period, 2,271 were involved in food handling—including 24 turtle specialists and 62 master vegetable picklers. Back in 1700 B.C.E., one Shang emperor made his chef a prime minister.

Forget scholarly examinations—China's main social distinction was always between those who ate to live and those who lived to eat. If Chinese businessmen pile on dishes to show respect, that's because the emperor once required 108 dishes per sitting. His wife had to make do with 96, the concubines a measly 60. (Like classical Chinese poetry, meals came in verses of 12.) The *grande bouffe* really got started when emissaries from neighboring vassals had to be impressed! As far back as the Sung Dynasty, astonished imperial guests reported that fifty pigs were beaten with sticks to "draw out energy" and tenderize the single dish that resulted. Milk from human wet nurses was also used to improve pork meat. The pièce de résistance might have been the palm of a fattened goose, cooked by forcing the live animal to stand on a scalding hot iron.

The higher the caste, the more one required "eight delicacies" like gorilla lip, leopard placenta, and camel's hump. Under the sway of Taoism, the Ming kings insisted upon "health foods" such as baby pigeon or orange peel and fish cooked in cinnamon. This dynasty also introduced female chefs into a profession that could prove dangerous. One traveling emperor was so wowed in Fujian by an arrangement of vegetables called "parrot's beak," he ordered the delicacy duplicated. When his Beijing staff served him an actual, inedible beak, all of the kitchen help were beheaded.

With plenty of clerical staff, the court kept strict records of every menu consumed. When ill, the royal family was monitored to see which foods proved beneficial. Qian Long, an early Qing emperor, used such meticulous bookkeeping to help create a unified Chinese cuisine. This galloping gourmet traveled farther south than any of the other Manchus, recording each dish tasted on food tours of the rich Yangtze delta. The resulting "Man-Han whole banquet" came to be known as the highest fruition of national cooking.

A daily breakfast of pork stewed overnight with cherries must have suited Qian Long. Of all the 208 emperors, who averaged a life span of forty-two years, he lived the longest—to eighty-eight. Last and most flamboyantly decadent, the nineteenth century Empress Dowager Ci Xi's dainty appetite required 128 dishes, filling some five tables. When the empress dowager created the first imperial railway, five cars were needed for food preparation. Fifty burners were fired for each meal, causing the death of a few chefs from carbon monoxide poisoning. When Ci Xi turned sixty, the imperial kitchens were redubbed the "long life" kitchens. All the silverware, napkins, and porcelain had to be remade to bear the lucky character. At each Chinese New Year, experienced eunuchs made certain that the superstitious empress always got served the single dumpling stuffed with a gold coin.

It's hard to believe that all this gorging ceased just a few hand-me-down recipes ago. In fact, items inspired by China's grand lady glutton are still on the menu at Beijing's Fang Shan Restaurant. No mere mock-up for the masses, the veritable mini-palace still hogs its exclusive position on the rocky island in the midst of the great lake in Beihai Park. To all sides, the waters are so thick with untended lotus leaves that a t'ai chi master could skip across them. Now these royal pleasure gardens have become a mobbed amusement park, with little room for contemplation along willow-lined banks dotted with cutesy refuse bins in the shape of open-mouthed pandas.

Approached through painted arcades, Fang Shan's decor is only slightly marred by plastic coverings on the antique divans. I doubt whether the emperors had to order from laminated menus with set banquets ranging from eight to sixteen dishes. Prices are still reasonable, considering that this is the one of the few places in Beijing that aspires to daintiness and nearly makes it. Balls of egg white float in sweet bean syrup. Layered petit fours made from pea flour quiver like Turkish delight, a see-through Chinese jello. I gobble the sesame buns stuffed with sliced lamb that resemble bite-sized Manchu burgers.

Free enterprise has spawned numerous pretenders to Fang Shan's throne. But if there's such a thing as exclusivity in the former Forbidden City, it belongs to the Li Family Restaurant. With a prix fixe that's close to the average worker's monthly wage, every foreigner in town seems to be dying to get into this place. The harder it is, the more they want to do it. Luminaries like David Rockefeller and

Bette Bao Lord are among those who wait months for one of two tables. But Mei calls right after a last-minute cancellation. Before we know it, we're searching out the unmarked entrance of a humble *hutong* abode that's at the cutting edge of Beijing's latest trend.

I don't mind another sunset stroll around Shi Cha Hai, the three narrow, manmade lakes that pour out of the back end of the Forbidden City. The change of seasons has stripped the banks of their droopy curtain of willows. Patient fishermen hunch before their supple bamboo poles, toking on their long pipes. To either side, the winding lanes and charcoal-tiled courtyards conjure the gritty essence of Tartar Peking. "In the old days, these lakes were clean and pure!" says a vigorous old man, approaching us to practice his English and apologize for his city. "Hundreds of food stands lined the pleasure grounds, offering fresh lotus seeds, the most marvelous candies!"

Such patent nostalgia for days "before the revolution" rarely surfaces. The cruel elites are dead as a door nail. But can mass rule, and mass production, ever produce similar masterworks of culture or cuisine? And what do the neighbors think of the steady stream of barbarians heading down a dead-silent row of gray-walled, one-story compounds? Little has been done to transform the Li family quarters. It's just the sort of quaint home most Chinese can't wait to get out of. The decor here is high prole: last year's calendar hung on a damp concrete wall, creaking red radiators, dingy floors ground into mud, a huge wall clock ticking loudly, cutout cardboard pandas in place of Mao portraits.

The only chairman here is Professor Li. Each night, this garrulous old gent with sprigs of white hair, distinguished in khaki lab coat, serves as a combination head waiter and master of ceremonies. This isn't exactly taxing, considering that he only has to deal with two tables, one filling the entire front room and a smaller adjunct shoved between a dresser and a cot. Yet for an economics graduate of Shanghai's Fu Ren University, this seems a strange form of retirement— reincarnation, really. We never glimpse more of his pediatrician wife than two thick calves showing from under the beaded curtains that barely separate our table from the Li family nuptial bed. The prof's eldest daughter studied internal medicine; his youngest, dentistry.

All help with the restaurant, except for the born chef among the bunch. "My middle daughter, Li Li," the professor brags, "won the citywide cooking competition by creating thirteen dishes in two hours." She's off in Australia establishing an overseas branch and residence.

None of these are the source of the Li family mystique. "My grandfather was a steward in the Forbidden City, something like a chief of security," Professor Li explains in advance of the first course. As a high-to-middle official, the grandfather lived in a large mansion quite near here—when power could be gauged by the exact distance one lived from the palace. His main duty was to keep an eye on the imperial kitchen's sauciers to make sure nothing lethal went down the royal gullet. As a result, he wound up with a number of original recipes, though Professor Li concedes, "Everything was lost or confiscated during the seventies." Cookbooks from the Qing Dynasty were the last thing one wanted to have found by the Red Guards. Being a descendant of a court official was enough to lose Professor Li his teaching post at the Beijing Economic Institute and have him sent to labor in the countryside. So the meal we're about to eat is based on an approximation of a memory of "imperial cuisine."

It's all whipped up by a Li daughter working outdoors in a chicken-wire hut the size of several telephone booths. Two black woks and a single chopping block—this is a far cry from the Forbidden City's facilities. So the meal comes out one dish at a time, making for a regal procession of food that leaves considerable free time for Professor Li's ramblings.

"You must never put a kitchen in the northwest corner," he explains. "To prevent fires, make sure the ceiling beams are crosshatched to form the character for a well."

The professor then dashes off to repeat the same homilies to the main table's party of Canadian students with Chinese girlfriends. "Foreign experts," the Chinese like to call all our fellow diners. But how can anyone be expert on so much time passed, so many secrets? Professor Li's life is revealed dish by dish. I don't know how he can keep the banter up every night with such zest. Maybe it's the turtle juice they chug, the t'ai chi in the parks, the respect accorded elders. Old people remain spry far longer than in the West. China is the perfect place to be very young or very old and one long frustration for everyone in between.

By the time our host is through talking, we've been through ten appetizers and eight main dishes. The best come first, in the form of such elitist treats as cross-sections of steamed, crunchy lotus root in a light mustard sauce. Other dishes are daringly plain: deep-fried scallops on a bed of bitter rape greens, pork fillets sauteed in a rice wine sauce that rival the best scaloppine marsala. While each dish seems a trifle unvarnished, the cumulative effect is quite stunning. Subtle sauces accent the freshness of ingredients hunted down each morning. All great cuisines are alike and the Lis have found the point where Chinese meets California-light Chez Panisse.

At the end of the meal, Professor Li drops into our laps the heavy albums of snapshots and business cards that catalogue the appearance of every ambassador and luminary. Do the "foreign ghosts" trek here for genuine Qing indulgence or an authentic dose of current-day deprivation? Billed as the ultimate in imperial cuisine, the Li Family Restaurant is the ultimate in slumming. Is it possible that all the dynasties—Sung and T'ang and Zhou—finish their chronology with a show for foreigners staged at two tables in a worker's hovel?

Seeking some ultimate wisdom, Mei and I are led to the connoisseur Wang Shixiang. This former curator at the Forbidden City recently donated his priceless collection of Ming Dynasty furniture to a national museum in Shanghai. During the Cultural Revolution, all the best pieces were confiscated by the Red Guards—perhaps Zhou Enlai himself wound up with a dinette set. Now this toothless aesthete lives in an unheated and toiletless room where every inch of dank, concrete space is crammed with mildewed texts and rusted coffee cans—a lifetime's scraps hoarded rather than displayed. Whither, I wonder, the unelaborated elegance that this man appreciates so well?

"Food in Beijing?" Eyes shut, his mind roams over a lost banquet—suggesting his last memorable meal may be too long ago to remember. "The great chefs are all dead or refuse to teach. The new generation has succumbed to mass tastes, speed, and commercialism. No, there is no place I can recommend. Nothing left."

Dominated by a spurious concept of luxury that's been reinvented in Hong Kong and Taiwan, there's no way that I can even imagine the opulence of China's old autocracy, really a foodocracy. As I lean closer to catch the final wisdom of this Eastern sage, Wang Shixiang suddenly brightens.

"I hear there are some good places in San Francisco. I recall a pretty nice restaurant on the outskirts of Washington, D.C. . . ."

But none can provide a mathematician's running commentary about black holes and filial piety—or the unique assurance that, like the despots of yore, no diner will leave poisoned.

Egg Dumplings with Crab Meat

From the Li Family Restaurant

Stuffing:
Crab meat, 4 oz.
Ground pork, 2 oz.
Shrimp meat, 3 oz.
Bamboo shoots, 2 oz.
Chinese rice wine, 1 tbs.
Chopped ginger, 1 tsp.
Salt to taste

Wrapper:
3 eggs
Corn meal, 2 oz.
Flour, 2 oz.
Peanut oil
Salt

Garnish:
Baby bok choy leaves

Chop finely and mix together all stuffing ingredients with a pinch of salt. Whip eggs in a bowl, then add a pinch of salt and corn meal.

Spread oil thinly on a large, flat Chinese dipper and place over high heat. Spoon egg mixture onto dipper and spread thin by rotating dipper. Place completed round wrappers on a dish and stuff with a small amount of filling. Wrap tightly and seal with the flour-and-water mix. Fry on medium heat until brown in a small amount of peanut oil. Serve on a plate surrounded by quickly stir-fried, shredded baby bok choy leaves.

Franchising Bitterness

What do you wear to a Cultural Revolution restaurant? Something homespun, to be sure. Not white tails, but model-worker blue muslin. A floppy Mao jacket, the better to dunk your cuffs in the soup. But the in-crowd at the Black Earth hardly looks like they've returned from forced labor. Beneath red banners exhorting them to root out "bourgeois elements," some eat gruel in Armani suits.

"People come here to network with old comrades from the country-side or simply to relive those difficult days," explains our escort Fan Gang, whose oxford shirt and blue blazer are decidedly preppy. With some chagrin, this rising star among China's pro-market economists points out a giant bulletin board that dominates the restaurant foyer. Every inch is covered with the business cards of Red Guards turned venture capitalists. In the early Seventies, approximately eighty thousand kids were sent from Beijing to slave and starve for the revolution in frigid Manchuria, near the Black Dragon River. The nostalgia and buying power of these "re-educated youth" now spur a revolution less cultural than culinary.

"The sky is big, the earth is big, but not bigger than the party!" Mei translates one exhortation among the many heroic posters punctuating the dowdy wallpaper of the Black Earth's second-floor dining room.

"Mother is dear, Father is dear, but not as dear as Chairman Mao!" echoes Fan Gang, before scanning the extensive menu. This boyishly handsome academic speaks with a humility that belies his title as one of "four young lions" in Beijing's new order. He's made time for us during an international conference out of respect for the fact that his father nearly married Mei's mother. But that was before slogans exhorted, "Our only love is the Communist Party!" When the Black Earth's capitalist manager pulls up a chair, I can't help asking, "Don't some of your diners get upset by all the marching orders?"

"But these posters are prized antiques!" Mr. Pan replies, with little repudiation in his tone. On his tour of the facilities, he appears genuinely proud of exclusive banquet chambers lined with strips of rough-hewn bark to simulate barracks huts.

"We've hosted reunions of up to fifty people from the same commune," the manager boasts. "Here, diners can feel completely relaxed to share the difficult memories and beloved, homespun tastes."

At the arrival of our first course, a thin soup with barley, even the placid Fan Gang begins to get teary. "How did we survive back then? Only young people could have found the hope and energy." Long before he became a Harvard grad student, he read economics texts in secret by a kerosene lamp. "The year's supply of grain ran out before the winter. We used to follow the local hunters, hoping they would drop some of their catch. We foraged for berries, husks, and wild ve etables. But mostly, we ate soy beans and cold water. We would hoard every precious bean in our coat pockets. Then we spent the whole night farting!"

Too young for work duty, Mei was among the many schoolchildren sent off with heavy packs for weeks of a meandering "Long March." She explains, "We walked thirty kilometers a day for twenty-one days, shouting quotations from Chairman Mao. Each night, we slept on the peasants' mud beds." It sounds like a swell field trip. "At night, we cooked cabbage and water in our own pans. During the day we had only a bun and pickled vegetables." Talk about a Reaganite school lunch program! "The first kid to finish got seconds, so everyone perfected a method of keeping their bowls spinning to cool their soup as they slurped. No matter how much we raced, everyone finished at the same time."

Still, the lessons learned during hard times have tempered this generation's ambitions. "Unlike the spoiled kids of today, the re-educated youth have the reputation of being China's most resourceful people," says Fan Gang. "Because we had the good life taken from us, we know that the good life has to be gained by our own work. It's not given by God." Or Mao. Or America.

Then why have they suddenly taken to frequenting trendy bistros with names like "Remember the Bitterness, Appreciate the Sweetness"? The fad in Cultural Revolution restaurants can be seen as the response to a regime that attacked the very concept of eating out.

"Most people were too poor to frequent restaurants," is Mei's analysis. "And those who could afford it would have gotten in trouble." Though he conquered starvation by creating the welfare state called the "iron rice bowl," Chairman Mao really meant it when he declared, "The Revolution Is Not a Dinner Party!" His Little Red Book was no Michelin Guide. After all, nothing is more inherently "bourgeois" than an institution where the privileged few enjoy a refined experience while hidden, low-wage hordes toil over the dirty dishes. And yet, no other collective enterprise provides more immediate gratification to the hungry masses.

If the comrades actually ate like we do at the Black Earth, I wouldn't have minded being sent to "learn from the workers and peasants." Especially to learn the recipes. The pork dumplings are thick and chewy, in the manner of *Dong Bei*, meaning the Manchurian Northeast. The bullet-shaped corn patties remind me of quick bread hush puppies and go perfectly with the soul food of stir-fried wild deer and mountain-gathered mushrooms. To top off the prison fare, candied chunks of deep-fried yams are bathed in cold water that hardens their chewy shell.

Our meal is just more proof that a century's ideological crusades have done little to shake the centuries-old Confucian consensus to "eat well, wear well, and live well." Fan Gang tells us about "sharp knife" restaurants, usually featuring Hong Kong chefs, where businesspeople are carved up by bills of three thousand dollars or more for a power meal of shark's fin and bird's nest. He repeats the latest rumor about self-made tycoons slapping down wads of bills and asking a chef to serve their guests whatever twenty thousand dollars buys. Only the worst boors bother to touch their rice and the many dishes stacked in pyramids of china are nibbled at with deliberate nonchalance. So flagrant is the excess of ordering that some municipalities in China have begun imposing fines of ten *yuan* per every hundred grams of food left unconsumed. Even for the average family, eating expenses occupy forty percent of the budget.

"The amount of money, time, and effort Chinese people spend on food is keeping us backward," we'll be told by Gao Xi Qing, another former Red Guard who has returned to build up his homeland. This Duke-trained lawyer now establishes fair rules for China's securities markets and spends his spare time hang gliding off the Ming tombs. Yet he still declares himself a Communist—and hits us up for unsordid Japanese sushi. "Unfortunately, the culture of eating goes hand in hand with the culture of corruption."

But the current fad in Cultural Revolution restaurants caters to jaded palates as well as jaded politics. In the name of hardships past, Beijing's success stories may be after the same thing Americans sought when they began switching from white bread to whole grain, Velveeta to Cajun. "We're tired of eating fancy foods to impress business clients," explains a customer at the curious Geng Wu Big Cafeteria. "We want flavor and nutrition, not some exotic ingredient that flies straight into the pan."

Wandering along a strip mall fronting one of Beijing's smelliest drainage canals, we have been lured into this place by the sculpted stone lions and a rare doorman, whose long pipe and wispy white beard make him a character out of sepia photos. Inside, the concrete shell is painted to look like it's made from courtyard bricks. The all-male staff are dressed in traditional, collarless black tunics. Somebody is trying hard to make China look like China.

The nostalgia evoked here is for the prerevolutionary cooking that goes by the name "Old Beijing." First come cold peanuts and soy beans blanched in the shell, then a couple of superb casseroles: black-skinned chicken with straw mushrooms, see-through bean thread noodles topped by light pork meatballs and wreaths of spinach. Mei raves over the Geng Wu's rendition of Five Flavor Meat, a Beijing favorite in which mounds of pork are cooked to a quivering, melting mass inside a cake of rice sprinkled with sugar. There are few pools of greasy kid stuff at the bottom of stir-frys. Cooking oil, scarce in prerevolutionary China, is no longer laid on like some long-denied treat. The luxury now is to leave it out.

Thank goodness, one tradition that can't be revived is the keeping of four or five wives. It's confusing enough having a fiancée with two fathers. Because he lives right across from the national headquarters of the dread Security Police, Mei and I can hardly linger over a home-cooked meal with her stepfather before some neighbor-hood shrew in red armband comes around to roust out the "foreign spy." Whenever I try to give Mei a public peck on the cheek, she whispers, "People are watching!" Now I get her point. Maybe I'm af-ter the state secret of preparing superb garlic eggplant on a single hot plate or preserving six courses of leftover stews without a refrigerator. Why do Chinese eat out so often when they've got home cooking like this?

There is a cook from Hunan and far less interference at the apart-ment of Mei's biological father. The only trouble is that he and Mei haven't seen one another in more than thirty years. The haughty el-der son of a landlord family, trained as a lawyer in Kuomintang days, Mei's father became a staunch Communist, but turned away from a constricted life with China's diplomatic corps to practice journalism for the state-run Xinhua News Agency. "I wrote what was required," is all he'll say in clipped En-glish of his years as a reporter, adding a sardonic laugh that softens a handsome face with cheekbones as pro-nounced as Mei's. When her parents divorced, Mei was just three and soon painfully banned from this household by a jealous step-mother. Now she's wary of a reunion motivated in part by the prospect of gaining a relative in the United States.

In the bargain, Mei gains a sister she never knew. Playful, with a warm smile, askew eyes, and hair in loose bangs, twenty-five-year-old Li Ying so looks up to her older sis that she offers to change her name to "the one who depends on Mei." She also wants an English name, of course, and I tease her by proposing "Kind Li" or "Sincere Li." A local representative of French aviation firms, her job consists mainly of a task she calls "pooshing the payment"—which means wining and dining Chinese creditors into honoring their bills. The job doesn't sound bad to me, but this neglected Cinderella dreams of a fairy-tale ending in America.

Near her home is the elementary school where Mei learned her Maoist ABCs. Its configuration of small, bricked-in classrooms has-n't changed much. With real schooling, she might have become a fine singer or dancer. Instead, she'd had to score high on a special exam for Cultural Revolution victims to be admitted to aeronautical college. Now her former school's principal is full of plans for a factory and hotel manned by student labor. Where Mei once sang paeans to workers, the only curriculum is capitalism for beginners.

"In first grade," she recalls, "there was a boy so poor and abused by his mother that I would sneak him a bun every morning." When not in communal playpens, Mei took the punishment that Mei's mother brought home from a re-education camp. "In China, human rights has to start with the family. Here, parents treat their children like pieces of property."

"If we have one, it'll be different," I try.

"And what if we don't have any?" Mei's upbringing in the whirl-wind has left some stubborn ghosts. Nobody has been left unmarked by the Cultural Revolution, especially the smallest foot soldiers.

"Toward the end, I was asked to go into the hills to fight against Mao," Mei now confesses. "We knew that terrrible time was over when the restaurants got crowded. The only way to get a seat was by planting one foot on the back of some poor diner's chair."

Yet Mei is as cheerful as ever, an indestructible rooster in the Chinese zodiac, entering the retrograde atmosphere of Sunflower Village. The seemingly innocent name refers to the once-bright "red sun" of Mao Zedong. This large compound along one of Beijing's outer ring roads is marked by hostesses in ankle-length red skirts and a gauntlet of red lanterns. Aside from wanting to sample the food, Mei has been asked here to appear in an American television docu-mentary called *The Wild East*. The director has chosen this lurid set-ting for a frank discussion of "sex and the Chinese woman." The panel gets off to a slow start when one innocent volunteer doesn't seem to get the director's off-camera prodding to describe how she "gets pleasure."

"My boyfriend and I find pleasure in taking walks through the park," this college co-ed tries bravely. "Afterwards, my boyfriend and I have pleasure in studying together. . . . I do not believe in sexy be-fore the marriage."

I'm relieved when Mei sticks to the question of China's one-child policy. To illustrate how the rich get around all regulations, she reaches for a proverb like some reach for cigarettes: "If you have money, you can make a ghost work for you."

Between takes, I become a ghostly presence in the halls of this gaudy proletarian playpen. Around an inner courtyard, each cinderblock cubicle is curtained with hanging sequins and painted up in a bright scene. Some folk-art murals feature merry-making farmers, others are perfect copies of Mao reviewing troops of ditch diggers. The first act of Beijing's burgeoning middle class seems to be to turn history into a consumer item. The first sign that people are getting rich is that they've begun appreciating the lost rustic days, the peasant look.

Nonetheless, the Russians could never turn their gulags into Siberian barbecues. Would Americans dare set up a chain called Joe McCarthy's Witch Hunt? Only in China—where food is the medium for all messages—are ideological shifts be so readily repackaged as cuisine. "The East Is Red" has turned into "The East Is Fed."

An advertisement for the Mao Family Restaurant, circulated in foreign hotels, promises hearty food prepared by Mao's "townspeople." When Mei and I get there, the hostess admits that only one chef actually hails from Shaoshan—the site of Mao's upper-peasant boyhood home in Hunan that is now infested with souvenir hawkers. The Mao Family Restaurant has been conceived in the same quick-cash spirit. Portraits of the leader drooling over adoring teen groupies have been hung by two Beijing middle-school teachers. All this married couple knows about the chairman's eating habits is the oft-repeated story of how Madame Mao tried to wean him off his favorite, fatty Hunan Stewed Pork.

"Chairman Mao's grandson came here to bow before his picture," the two claim, adding, "Fifty percent of our ingredients come direct from Hunan." This may include the dried black beans spread liberally over my plate of tart, blistered Anaheim peppers. The chicken in soup served out of a scooped-out tube of bamboo is certainly Hunanese enough. But the stewed pork is as dilute as the politics. On the way out, the schoolteachers give every guest a lapel pin of the chairman. The Mao button has made it to a merchandising giveaway.

"Chairman Mao would have liked to see China today because he was in favor of the improvement of the people," his non-family members argue. "We're sure that he would approve of our efforts because he believed in building up the country." And building up their bank account.

In an unguarded moment, the Great Helmsman himself is said to have boasted, "I believe the world will find that China has given it two great gifts—Chinese medicinal herbs and Chinese food." But while Mao championed a "great leap" from feudalism to socialism, he didn't realize that all societies have to pass through the theme restaurant.

"What we're doing here is honoring the time when we were fools," confides one diner who beckons us to his table. "But at least we believed in something!"

Five Ways to Duck

"To know how to survive in Beijing," says the news cameraman, "you better know how to duck."

If anyone can keep his head down, it's Mitch. This irrepres-sible veteran of state repression starts our final Beijing excursion by reminding me of the night I first tasted the danger lurking in this nervous capital. On the portentous first anniversary of the killings in Tiananmen Square, I had tagged along on a lark with the CNN crew only to find myself thrust into the middle of an illicit midnight protest at Beijing University. When student chanting and bottle-tossing attracted foreign reporters toward the high walls of the campus, we were scared off by the roar of several open-bed trucks filled with crack People's Liberation Army troops. Screaming insults about rumor mongers and running dogs, nervous recruits brandished rifles and shoved all of us toward the nearest patch of dark wall. For the first and hopefully last time, I felt cold steel at my neck and heard the click of magazine cartridges. How do you say *St. Valentine's Massacre* in Mandarin? The implacable Mitch kept rattling off a steady stream of Chinese, his all-purpose "May I lick your boots sir?" Then the Chinese officer in charge offered an imperceptible nod. As many journalists as could fit in one back seat scrambled and sprawled over one anothers' laps. Mitch burned rubber to haul us safely away from the scene of our meddling.

The mood tonight feels equally giddy, as he guns another Beijing Jeep to the beat of Bob Marley, cruising monotonous boulevards in a town that always feels under curfew.

"How many Chinese does it take to drive a car?" Mitch jokes.

"Three—one to steer, one to read the map, and one to keep an eye on the intellectuals. . . . But don't worry! I won't get you and your lovely bride in trouble tonight," promises this eternally boyish, half-Jewish, half-Korean "shooter" who hones his visual skills on the rising hemlines of the local ladies. "The only action these days is wrapping our hands around some fine Beijing duck."

"Anything you say, Mitch. You're the man who saved my life." And changed it. For only under the gun had I discovered the China that always attracted me—a country where every choice has immediate consequences and every fate hinges on an educated guess. Like the Chinese themselves, I had learned to approach the future with hope and the present with extreme caution. Like them, I could now settle for small victories.

Mei and I are encouraged when we pull up in front of the aptly named Beijing Kao Ya (Roast Duck) Restaurant. Imposing in Soviet-style granite, with canopied entries for Red Star limos and stacked tiers of dining halls, most of Beijing's Peking duck houses have become assembly lines for converting foreign currency. Unlike the block-long, state-run poultry processors such as Wall Street Duck and Sick Duck (named for its proximity to a hospital), this place, done up with plenty of rose-colored marble, resembles a Phoenix Hilton coffee shop. Far from the usual tourist haunts, though right in the center of the Sanlitun diplomatic enclave, Beijing Kao Ya caters mostly to Japanese businessmen.

"Your ambassador Walter Mondale came here straight from the airport," we're told immediately by the surprisingly young manager, Zhen Zhang Dong. "Afterward, the Security Police had a lot of questions." Mr. Zhen looks threatening only because he's the tallest Chinese I've seen outside of their Olympic basketball team. His dark suit and fiercely obsessional mood hanging on too narrow a frame. Yet he instantly asks, "Won't you have a look at our ovens?"

Here's a duck factory with no industrial secrets. We see for ourselves how an air pocket is blown into the cavity, separating skin from flesh, and how the birds are hung to dry and defat. According to Mr. Zhen, "These ducks are not dissimilar to the Long Island breed, which descended from Chinese stock." For browning, a honey-water glaze is applied and re-applied onto the hooked carcasses. The earthen ovens are kept fiery hot by the especially fruity wood of a kind of date tree. Wooden slabs blocking the oven door are removed to allow consistent air circulation. "The scent of the smoke, the balance of quick heat to slow moisture," claims Mr. Zhen proudly, "are most difficult to reproduce elsewhere."

The dish with which China's capital is so closely associated actually has its origins in neighboring Shandong Province. Having become popular as recently as the middle of the last century, Peking duck is still a passing fad by Chinese standards. At Qianmen Street's revered Quanjude Restaurant, an original hundred-year-old brick wall is lovingly preserved. There the finished birds, baked to a mahogany glow, are hung in a glass booth like a row of jets awaiting liftoff. A lucky Chinese character can be burned onto the hide for honored guests—though most are tourists on the two-day, three-bird stopovers known as "death by duck."

Leading us to a private room upstairs that has more of the traditional, carved rosewood feel, Mr. Zhen carries on with the morbid seriousness of a California wine connoisseur. "Though we're partially state-owned, I've instituted strict accountability among the chefs," he boasts. "Where the standards of the other duck houses are deteriorating, we maintain our own farm. And we take our time cooking every one to order."

I don't mind waiting forty-five minutes because the rite of the duck is supposed to occupy a whole evening. In the meantime, there are cold dishes of one's choice—jellyfish, cold meats, and cucumbers—followed by various forms of duck innards and gizzards. The shredded duck stir-frys added to please Westerners are far tastier here than any I've ever had. For Chinese, the real treats are the duck tongue, liver, and feet. A bowl of duck intestines in hot broth may also appear. The head has been split open to offer access to a soft morsel of duck brain, considered by many Chinese to be the best part of the whole affair.

Wheeled upstairs somehow in something resembling a surgical gurney, the duck itself is quickly carved in diagonal hunks. While most places include a tidbit of meat attached to the candied exterior, Mr. Zhen insists that the proper way to start is with two segregated plates of flesh and skin to be mixed according to each diner's taste.

"These are the traditional methods which we are reviving," the gigantesque Mr. Zhen insists, leading us through the proper stuffing of the pancakes. This involves no less than five variations on how to dress the duck. The Chinese would never leave something so crucial unelaborated. They again make the most of the least by using a simple change in garnish to create different courses. First, we have to eat the skin alone, sprinkled with sugar, a kind of appetite-whetting condiment. "To bring out the flavor of the date wood," our fearless leader claims. Next comes the traditional crunch of scallions, "to cut the duck fat." But that's just preparation for duck laden with a spoonful of chopped raw garlic. In North China, "the stinking rose" is always at the heart of the matter. What follows is a gradual cooling down, the equivalent of salad courses: duck wrapped in long strips of white radish, and finally, refreshing cucumber. Our table is running out of pancakes as well as the sweet flour paste slathered on the last four combinations.

"Don't add too much special sauce!" Mei cautions. After all, this isn't a Big Mac. And one doesn't want to overwhelm the most perfect of crepes with too much of the accompanying tart, gooey mud. Explains Mei, "We call this *tian mian jiang*." Despite the claims of misinformed food writers, it isn't plum sauce, duck sauce, or even *hoi sin*, which is a sweetened bean paste, but a wheat-based sauce that is created out of the same dough used for the translucent pancakes. The concept is to exhibit Chinese ingenuity right down to the duck soup that we now slurp.

"Maybe they should issue us regulars a discount card," Mitch suggests. "Punched for each duck." When a second bird arrives, we tear the thing limb from limb à la Henry the Eighth. Mr. Zhen hovers over us through every bite. If I hadn't already witnessed the Chinese devotion to eating, I wouldn't believe that one man could get so serious about poultry.

"My doctors have warned me that I work too hard," the manager admits between cigarette puffs. "Already, this responsibility has increased my blood pressure." Nor did I doubt it when he insists, "To maintain this heritage, I would gladly give my life."

Now that would be a true death by duck. In the meantime, Mr. Zhen volunteers to lead us on a day trip out to the farms where they force-feed the famed white-feathered breed. But Mitch warns, "You'll never want to eat Beijing duck again!"

I certainly don't want that to happen. What makes the concoction taste so good? Who first thought of wrapping candied duck skin inside a translucent pancake? For that matter, which anonymous geniuses first introduced mustard to sausage, chutney to chicken? Food and flavors like these lead back to the origins of taste, the origins of civilization. One needs such dishes as one needs water or air.

Not only is it comforting to discover that the finest Beijing duck actually comes from Beijing, but it's fitting that our search here should climax with the best rendition of what could be the best Chinese dish of all. Will we ever eat better? I see both Mitch and Mei nod when Mr. Zhen counsels, perhaps cribbing Confucius, "In food and in sex, you must go with what you like."

But what happens when the city you love to hate becomes the place you hate to admit that you love? We cannot choose our favorite places, no more than we can choose where to be born. Where I once felt lost in Beijing's empty boulevards and lunar landscapes, I feel increasingly at home in the congestion of a society passing through that awkward period between the infuriatingly feudal and the vapidly up-to-date. With the help of Mei and her friends, it seems that I've eaten my way to the very heart of this fortress city. Beijing's main obsession is more than the state. It's the state of the Chinese soul, expressed in the motto of one pensioner who tells Mei, "Where others get meat, I eat the soup!"

"Ganbei!" go the last urgings to down this town's stoic heroism to the last drop. After one more bracing hot pot laid on by our Tibetan toastmaster, there's but a half hour to run a steeplechase over the train station's squatting circles of displaced peasants and their permanent settlements of luggage. We'll never make it to our coveted "soft seat" sleepers. But Mei runs smack into her best girlfriend from grade school, now a stationmaster who hides a prematurely weary face under a ton of mascara and a state railway cap. This comrade in need guides our drunken caravan toward a blessedly unpopulated VIP hall, then unlocks an entry to the right platform.

Ruddy faces crowd our carriage window. Mei's newfound little sister's eyes are red with crying—the only red that counts in China anymore. I shed a tear myself as the train pulls past the gyroscopic silhouettes of Kublai Khan's observatory, underneath the last gray Mongol turret. At last we've found our own privileged "back door." Too bad it's the one that leads out of town.

The Real Eel

Shanghai has been called the Persian Gulf of Chinese cooking. That's because there's no shortage of oil in most of the dishes. After Beijing, the pleasantly moist weather and gangs of silk-suited hustlers make us feel like we've arrived in Miami. But Mei and I haven't just entered China's dynamic sun belt. More significantly for our purposes, sometime while we slept with one eye open for pickpockets, we crossed the great divide between wheat-based and rice-based cuisines.

Mei herself straddles a gap between Beijing and Shanghai that American guidebooks liken to Washington versus New York. But this game is a lot older than Yankees versus Senators. So it's woe to anyone who would lump together "the Chinese" when they themselves generalize Beijingers as dowdy, dreamy, and tradition-bound, Shanghainese as calculating, uncouth, and faddish. The twenty-something wheeler-dealers who treat us to a welcoming (and welcome) vegetarian lunch are already beyond making their first million; they probe us for the best overseas markets in which to invest. Is that why Mei doesn't like to admit that she was born here? This town's reputation, like its history, is brutal, short-lived, and best forgotten.

Shanghai is not a city, but an experiment in lack of leg room, head room, and eye room; a swampy river junction turned sadist's lab. It was here that I'd first disembarked in the Middle Kingdom back in 1988, only to be startled by flashbulbs going off at the arrival of another passenger on my flight, the French actress Catherine Deneuve. What a way to say hello to Cathay! Another shock was discovering that my hotel's Shanghainese staff all wore tags with names like "Josephine" and "Cleopatra." Escaping the quarantine of a forty-story tower on the outskirts of this former "Paris of the East,"

I'd taken a midnight stroll through the kind of blight associated with London after the Blitz. A few dazed vendors hawked bananas under bare bulbs amidst block upon block of Edwardian buildings reduced to rubble by reconstruction or slow ruin.

This time, our business hotel is smack in the formless center. Nominally two stars and perfectly nondescript, this is the class of hostel where you have to coax your key out of peevish girls assigned to each floor and where workmen hammer at all hours without asking permission. It's an impersonation of sophistication, as is much of the city. Stodgy, European architecture of the twenties dominates the avenues, while the side streets are more like holding cells, lined with laundry-laden slats of tiny apartments. Where East and West meet at their most charmless, Shanghai is the worst of both worlds.

Yet one feels braced and excited. The showiness and pedestrian crush are nonstop on Nanking Road, whose state-run department stores have become neon-trimmed warehouses of designer perfumes. Observes Mei, succinctly summarizing the results of China's great economic boom, "The streets are cleaner, but the people's thoughts are dirtier."

And forty years' isolation has turned high style into high camp. Pairs of Madonna impersonators in tight bodices are a common sight, reinforcing a certain mercenary impression. As we'll hear from numerous restaurateurs, "Every Shanghai chef comes with a bird cage and mistress." When he doesn't rise quickly through the kitchen ranks, it's the ladies who are known to fly the coop.

Since the time of Mei's grandfather, a well-to-do functionary of an American company, most of her family has dropped a few notches. Who hasn't in China? In between talk of raising funds to convert a state- run factory for parquet floors, several of seven siblings recall Mei's mom as the family live wire, vivacious and talented at music and dance—just like someone I know! Another self-possessed survivor, Mei's uncle Wu Yi Huang trained to be an opera singer and was branded a counter-revolutionary. In his sixties, he runs a chicken farm in rural Fujian and has just taken a wife thirty years his junior. When we take him to see China's longest-running Dixieland band, Mei's uncle finds it very old hat.

We get a more devoted escort in Mei's cousin Xiao ("Little") Ying—a rather overserious, overlarge woman with bobbed, brownish hair. In her thirties and as yet unmarried, Xiao Ying strikes me as one of those family members who unconsciously carry the burden of a previous generation's tragedies. All through our first Yangzhou-style meal together, she can't seem to take her eyes off her Americanized cousin.

She and her fervently Buddhist mother meet us for lunch at the Jing An Temple. Surrounded by construction cranes and thirty-story office towers, this centuries-old lair is crowded with incense bearers and smoky inner sanctums. Many have come to worship in the temple's fabled mess hall. One of the cooking nuns here is an aunt of Peter Fang, creator of San Francisco's most popular hole-in-the-wall, the House of Nanking. The monks wield a mean abacus to make sure each devotee gets no more than the dishes they pay for. Peeking into the kitchens, we see most of the shaven-headed scullions devoting their energies to kneading dough and peeling carrots. Theirs must be the order of the Clear Light Cleaver.

Perhaps we've been sent to the Nirvana Room, because the only other party in this dark-wood hall is headed by a fat abbot in orange robes. He gets about twenty dishes to our eight—a favorite Chinese sport is plate counting—but I'm not about to complain. "Se, xiang, and wei!" Mei declares at the sight of our food, teaching me about the time-honored Chinese criteria of color, aroma, and flavor. Since the monks have chosen our menu, there's little doubt that this meal is healthfully balanced in terms of yin and yang—passive and active, female and male, cooling and heating in more ways than temperature. But the more I taste, the more I realize that comparisons become impossible when the restaurants rise or fall mainly on what one selects. Variety, and especially a variety of the specialties that a chef or region does best, are the key to ordering. Every dinner worth noting should include at least four cold starters, eight main dishes that contain plenty of greens, and at least one whole fish, plus a finishing soup. There's far more to this art than Americans' democratic efforts to let each diner pick what they want.

At the Jing An Temple, for instance, diners would be sorely disappointed to stick to mere vegetables. Despite its long tradition, medicinal emphasis, and a variety of roots, fungi, and hollow stems that put the West to shame, vegetarianism in China is a backhanded compliment to meat eating. Exploiting the chameleon-like properties of protein-substituting bean curd, Buddhists have long simulated the look of pork, beef, and especially "temple goose" or "temple fish." I don't care what animal the chefs are mocking so long as they're as good as the Jing An's mock crab, made of scrambled eggs, ginger, and not a speck of fish.

Underappreciated in the West, Shanghai's cuisine, lumped together with that of the nearby canal towns of Yangzhou, Suzhou, and Hangzhou under the rubric *huai yang*, is one of China's great regional schools. Since this Yangtze River delta area has always been among the richest in ingredients, the cooking is lighter and blander, less darkened with soy sauce though often salty. Seafood is more varied, featuring crabs and eels, while fresh garlic stems and whole, green soy beans enliven the usual gray pork fare. At the state-run Lao Fandian—"Old Restaurant" is nothing derogatory in China—Mei delights in introducing me to my first plateful of bamboo shoots not from a can.

"If you eat canned," a Shanghainese chef will declare, "you're reminded that bamboo is a building material!" The fresh variety's subtle, woodsy flavor is complimented by flecks of a parsleylike herb and preserved salted vegetables. In Shanghai's packed bazaar, the other eateries specialize mainly in snacks like custardy tofu treats and *xiao long bao zi*, twist-top dumplings that contain a burst of hot broth.

To taste the authentic hairy crabs that are this city's full-time fall obsession, I have to get inside a Shanghai household. A family reunion is staged in our honor by Mei's mother's younger half-sister (the Chinese have a word for it). She lives in an upper-story slot of one of the characterless satellite towns that are going up as fast as concrete can be poured. Waiting for us are the oddest members of Mei's massive clan—twin brothers with identical high foreheads and Westernized button noses. Both should be models, though one works for the state railways and the other teaches a kind of English that I can barely follow. He guides me to an open-air market set in a muddy field between bleak citadels. The only sight in the area that is recognizably Chinese is the scrupulous way in which even these relocated housewives carry on the hunt for prime ingredients.

According to legend, China's prostitutes refused to eat crab, considering them their reincarnated spirits because the water bubbles in the crabs' mouths suggested prior kissing duties. Because the Chinese covet eggs, the fallen females among these crustaceans are best eaten when most often pregnant during the Chinese calendar's September. Searching for meat in the blue-tinged claws doesn't seem worth the effort. But I do feel one step closer to becoming a true Chinese when the twins guide me through my first round of mah-jongg. It's tough to slap the tiles properly when I don't even know what most of them say.

The next night, we're supposed to dine with a busy local architect. Who wouldn't be in demand where a new edifice rises every eight seconds? While this old friend's English fiancée is cooking up a curry, a call comes from a neighborhood restaurateur who very much wants to meet us. It turns out that the owner of the cutting-edge Sunshine, or Shen Shen, Restaurant is a Chinese turned homesick U.S. citizen.

"How are my Washington Redskins doing?" asks the affably ageless Tony Wang, a former student at the University of Maryland. "Is David Letterman still on? I miss him a lot!"

After twenty years, including some stints in the kitchens of Chinese-American restaurants, Tony Wang has come home to start his own place. "I don't care, Communist or capitalist, a man wants his own business. And in Shanghai, the businessman is king. I was educated as a Communist. From Mao Zedong, I learned to respect blacks as my Third World brothers. So it was a big surprise when I was jumped by a gang when I was riding my bicycle in the States. I tried to scare them away with my kung fu." Tony Wang cracks up. "It wasn't long before I learned to get along with all kinds of people. In the States, I learned how to self-promote, too. You hear the Muzak, see the recessed lighting, the counter seating? We're the pioneers in all China."

Come to think of it, the Sunshine does look suspiciously like a Denny's. Burgers and curried Singapore noodles are what attracts Shanghai's free-spending youth. But the dumplings are excellent, as well as the hacked slices of "drunken" or wine-soaked chicken. Already stuffed, we're spared a return to British cooking with an invitation from Tony's genial partner, Bright Yan. A waiting car and driver speed us toward his coffin-sized, bare-bones enterprise, which is aptly called, in English, "The Box." On the sidewalk beyond, pairs of Shanghai girls gotten up in hot pants and teased hair are in obvious search of male clientele. The Box does a big business in couples emerging from the behemoth J. J.'s discotheque across the street. Here, I get a luscious version of green peppers and pork shredded to near spaghetti.

Bright Yan says plenty of salt and a low flame is the secret to the cooking known in Shanghainese dialect as *muozi*—something like the revival of more earthy tastes that we've come to know as "Old Beijing." Charging diligently on to another home-style place called Lu Lu, still bustling at two A.M., Mei and I suddenly feel in the swing of China's only city of night.

"Maybe we can reschedule our flight," I can't help suggesting, overcome with the prospect of seeing China transformed into the land of the midnight snack.

"You know we've arranged for someone to meet us in Sichuan!" Mei explodes, cranky and tired. "Selfish American!"

I've forgotten. In China, you are what you arrange. Group loyalty provides one miracle cure for ambivalence. That explains Chinese politics, too. A billion people can't keep changing their plans, even when they know the plan is wrong. Besides, every one of my potential new relatives has assured me that Mei hasn't changed a bit throughout her decade in America—a compliment meant to imply that success hasn't spoiled her Chinese values. And being Chinese, I'm learning, involves a lot more than knowing how to press on a certain point on the wrist to instantly calm stomach cramps. In this worldview, the feelings of others are always in the foreground—often exposing my emphasis on "honesty" as sheer tactlessness.

On our final day in Shanghai, Little Ying takes us to the ancestral home where Mei's mother had been brought up with servants. "You know," Little Ying begins as she spills the predictable beans, "your third uncle got one of the maids pregnant!" The house is part of a block of attached brick mansions typical of the French concession.

"Once these were our three floors," Mei's cousin announces with abject resignation. "And now there are seven, eight, who knows how many families!"

No hippie commune in the Haight-Ashbury was ever so subdivided. Each pantry, each crawl space under the stairs, has been allotted or grabbed. There are people living in broom closets; one basic kitchen is shared by several floors of families, bathrooms by more. At Little Ying's own place, she and her mystical mom live in a single room that's ninety percent double bed. Crammed against each wall are items meant to simulate different living areas—TV and stereo on one side, papers and files on another, foodstuffs and tea bags on a third. Perhaps it's best not to have a personal life in Shanghai. There's no room for one.

After the tour, Xiao Ying leads us to an outlying branch of the ninety-year-old Meilongzhen Restaurant.

"Wu Mei, the famous actress, was the manager," Xiao Ying tells us to explain how this became a post-1949 showplace.

"But that was before Madame Mao got her revenge," Mei adds. "Jiang Qing didn't want anyone around to remember that she had once been a minor Shanghai actress."

With lunch hour just finished, we have our choice of tables in several small antechambers nestled into a Tudor-style building. Waiters fill a lazy Susan meant for eight with various samples of true Shanghai tastes. Xiao Ying can't see why I'm raving over the shredded bean curd with home-cured ham, chunkier tofu with scallops, and cold smoked fish that is better than any in a Jewish deli.

I keep waiting for the show stopper and grand finale. From previous scathing critiques launched by Mei's Shanghainese mother, I know that no dish is taken more seriously than Shanghai-style eel. I don't realize that it's sitting in a bowl right in front of me until Mei uses chopsticks to fish the buttery, boneless chunks from a thick sea of something that resembles Pennzoil. We degrease the pieces by holding them up to drip for as long as we can wait. The wait is worth it as soon as the tender eel slides down my gullet.

"Bad for you," proclaims Mei, "but awfully seductive." It's the perfect specialty for a slippery town.

Shanghai Stir-Fried Eel

From the Meilongzhen Restaurant

Ingredients:

Fresh deboned eel, 1 lb.
Green pepper, 2 oz.
Shaoxing wine, 3 tsp.
Soy sauce, 2 tsp.
Sugar, 1 tsp.
Chinese vinegar, 1 tsp.
Cornstarch, $1^{1}/_{2}$ tsp.
Chicken broth, $^{1}/_{4}$ cup
Minced garlic, 1 tsp.
Peanut oil, 6 tsp.

Slice the eel into one-inch-long chunks and the peppers into wedges of similar size. Heat 4 tsp. oil and stir-fry the eel until the skin is crisp, but the inside remains tender. Add the peppers and fry with the eel for one minute, then remove from the wok. Add 1 tsp. new oil to the wok and heat. Add the garlic and cook for thirty seconds. Next add the wine, sugar, and broth and bring to a boil. Add cornstarch mixed with water. When the sauce thickens, return the eel and peppers to the wok. Stir-fry briefly to heat through, then add vinegar and one more tsp. of hot oil for the glaze.

The Dish That Won a Hundred Million Hearts

"When you go to Beijing, you see how small a rank you hold. When you travel to Canton, you realize how little money you've got. But when you come to Chengdu, you find out how big is your appetite."

With this contemporary proverb, a sharp-talking deputy from the Sichuan People's Congress welcomes us to "The Storehouse of

Heaven." The capital of China's "bread basket" province for a thousand years, Chengdu is less recognizable to Western ears than its home-cooked, chili-laced specialties like twice-cooked pork, tea-smoked duck, *dan dan* noodles, and *ma po dofu*. It's said that travel, near or far, is always the shortcut to finding out who we are. But what sort of persons would fly to the western limits of Han China in a whining old Tupelov-154 just to sample a storied bowl of quivering bean curd, most likely too peppery for ingestion?

Apparently, we are Very Important People. Thanks to a well-placed friend in Beijing, we're met and led through the airport mobs to a black Nissan limo with siren and bubble-top light. Our lead blocker, Mr. Xie, is no sluggish party hack. His chubby cheeks, button nose, and deep-set eyes instantly suggest an impish koala. His full head of coarse hair stands at attention in uncombed swirls, leaving the impression that he's just got out of bed. Draped uneasily over a buttoned vest, Mr. Xie's standard-issue black, double-breasted jacket serves as a kind of shawl for his broad shoulders.

As our limo weaves around horse carts and tractors through a rain-speckled night, our front-seat barker fairly blows a steady stream of chatter in Sichuan's clipped and choppy dialect. This beer-bellied Buddhist's implacable self-confidence has not been the slightest bit sapped by twenty-eight years as a People's Liberation Army soldier stationed in Tibet border posts. By the time we're nearing the center of this heartland hub of six million, we've heard all about Mr. Xie's fluency in Russian and Tibetan, and extensive knowledge of Chinese medicine, including the various uses of pig bones.

"As a chef I've mastered at least sixty local dishes. I can teach you the best technique for deep meditation and people say I'm the best fortune-teller. Did you know that Chairman Mao himself used the I Ch'ing to find his safe hideout in Yenan?" As modern as he is traditional, Mr. Xie adds, "By the way, can I facilitate you in any form of economic investment?"

Mei and I can only glance at one another in amazement. What does this guy eat for breakfast? Who put the life force known as *ch'i* in his Cheerios? Or is this our first sampling of Sichuan's self-proclaimed "red pepper spirit"? Instead of depositing us in the usual musty banquet hall, Mr. Xie has our limo pull up alongside a mangy row of white-tiled, open-air stalls. At a four-table affair bathed in butcher-shop pink fluorescence, Mr. Xie barks instructions to several kids in white caps nearly as charcoal-smudged as their cheeks. The woks fire up and by the time you can say cornstarch, we have Sichuan's signature dishes laid before us: soft bean curd drowned in oil and a dollop of minced pork, hot-and-sour duck's blood soup, hand-twisted noodles flecked with pickled cabbage, and last but hardly least, my obligatory fish-flavored shredded pork. This first rendition in the land of its birth, tangy and decidedly fishless, sears my tongue toward Nirvana. Mr. Xie beams with pride. After five minutes in Chengdu, I'm already "finding out the size of my appetite."

Fancier isn't necessarily better in the city with China's liveliest street life. And this People's Deputy isn't in it for the luxury, either. Applying his formidable zealousness to the task of finding a bargain for two "humble writers," Mr. Xie escorts us to a backpackers' hotel where teenagers snooze with their heads on the reception counter. So much for free board in some cushy state *dacha*! This hotel lobby is unadorned but for the obligatory bank of clocks set to numerous time zones, all of them wrong. It's a bad sign when the mattress in our room has no sheets and we're relieved that none of the lights switch on. But Mr. Xie's face is too mischievous to ever lose face. "Come on! My friend is the manager at a much better place!"

We hightail it to a high-rise VIP suite hung with gold lamé curtains in what must be the Mildew Wing. The red carpet treatment would work better if the carpet weren't covered with black blotches. We wonder if the heaps of tea leaves have been left in the toilet for us to read our touring futures. Then we're refused the room for failing to show a marriage license, until Mei reaches for her U.S. passport—that worldwide license to get away with anything!

"When the sun comes out in Sichuan," Mr. Xie warns us, "all the dogs begin to bark." In the perpetually shrouded winter clamminess, Mei and I can hardly see the humongous statue of a saluting Chairman Mao, alabaster in his pea coat, rising above one end of the People's Road. Like all Chinese cities, Chengdu's population consists of millions more than you'd imagine and millions less than it seems when you're trying to get anywhere. The usual waves of weary bicyclists churn past this month's massive display of Party exhortation, "Fight Bravely Three Years to Make Chengdu Model Hygienic City!"

Fortunately, the ruled boulevards give way to an unhygienic chaos. Chengdu's wooden two-story houses look almost Elizabethan with their boxy overhangs and variations of exposed beam and thatching. Sichuan's famed bounty is showcased by a sidewalk abundance of straw baskets and bamboo bird cages, delicate stacks of budding eggplant, flowers and tobacco, fans and paper cuttings, and bonsai trees. Workers hand grind sesame oils in giant woks; old men puff on long-stemmed bamboo pipes. Kung fu epics are projected in converted, flap-covered teahouses—the only cinemas in the world where the seats are made of bamboo.

China finally looks the way foreigners have always imagined it. Along every river bank, temple courtyard, or bamboo grove, there's another teahouse. These are hardly sites for contemplation, but sprawling, noisy affairs where all age groups compete to stretch perpetually stained cups of soaked green tea leaves with composting piles of chewed pumpkin seeds laid beside cigarette butts. On every sidewalk, too, outdoor loungers stick skewers of frog thighs, pig livers, and baby sparrows into a sludgy, week-old broth that's divided into spicy and nonspicy sections like the symbol for yin and yang. I've been led to believe that the real popularity of the Sichuan hot pot is due to the opium that's added to addict customers. But Mr. Xie will assure us that any opium in the broth is just the non-narcotic flower known as the *keke*. Yet another of my Oriental fantasies shot to hell.

Mei and I prefer to stop within the calm portals of an immense, luridly painted-up model of a Qing Dynasty mansion that's topped with a huge neon sign saying, "Chengdu Snack City." Around a reflecting pool lined with covered pavilions, a dozen or so restaurants have been grouped together in government-sponsored competition. We get dizzy choosing among the trays of saucer-sized platters loaded with variants of noodle dough soaked in degrees of chili oil. Lounging on silk pillows under eaves covered with fiery dragons, we plow through as many as twenty-four dishes. Slippery folds of *wun tun* with little or no stuffing look like albino goldfish slithering in a truly red sea. No asterisks or printed peppers warn us of impending spiciness. There are no menus here and every snack is hot stuff.

Now my tongue has a true out-of-mouth experience. Or am I in heaven? Chengdu's much-extolled *ma la* numbness is provided by generous garnishes of ground *fagara*, a half-sweet and half-deadly peppercorn that was imported along the trade routes some five hundred years back. Judging by its ubiquitous presence atop every dish, it's difficult to imagine what the Sichuan diet might have included before that. According to Chinese medicine, the inner yang fires stoked by the pepper counteracts outer humidity and dampness. And the relative prosperity of the peasants has always made this a province with fewer distinctions between down-home and palace foods. Every dish tastes tugged from the earth.

"The four seas and the eight horizons all gathered into one cloud," wrote the seventh-century poet Du Fu, whose recreated cottage is Chengdu's leading tourist site. "You can't tell an ox coming from a horse going, or the muddy Ching from clear Wei."

Neither can Mei or I on our way to one of the shrines of Chinese cuisine. Suddenly, our taxi's engine starts racing inexplicably. The driver pulls over with a shrug. "Overheated," he tells Mei. Just coincidentally, there's a motorcycle rickshaw waiting on the spot. As soon as we've transferred into the carriage, the taxi pulls away, good as new. Two fares to get us three blocks.

Open to a busy, tree-lined boulevard, Chengdu's Chen Ma Po Dofu Restaurant is dimly lit at noon, with rotating ceiling fans, an old oak bar, a blackboard on which specialties have been scrawled in white chalk, and a monstrous charnel house of a kitchen. The level of noise and excessive rudeness of the waitresses augur well. This is the direct descendant of the roadhouse run by Mrs. Chen, a widow with facial scars from a childhood disease who became a legend through her *ma po dofu*, now appearing on menus throughout the planet but rarely translated in its full meaning of "pockmarked grandma's tofu." Transcending a life of toil following the accidental death of her husband in 1901, she created her signature dish by combining the products of a neighboring lamb butcher and bean-curd maker. Was it back at San Francisco's Hunan Restaurant that I first got hooked on this curious combination of crumbly custard topped with an Oriental ragu?

I can hardly wait to poke my sticks into the original. But impersonal state management and three moves from the original site have done little to maintain quality. The grand creation itself is served in a green plastic bowl that looks to have been recycled a million or two times. This *ma po dofu* is pretty much like other versions I'll have in Sichuan: a buttery slab of fresh curd plopped deep into red chili oil, topped with a dollop of pork meat, and garnished with numbing peppercorns. A meal in itself, as they say, without any of the West's frivolous scallions or peas.

I try to snap a quick photo back in the kitchen, but an aproned bouncer shoos me out, squawking as though I'm a corporate spy on a raid for Duncan Hines *ma po* mix. When Mei asks for some tea to rinse down the heat, the answer is *Mei you*. Pronounced like "mayo," that phrase was the trademark response to all queries during the Mao era, meaning, "We don't have any!" Mei is scandalized. Imagine a Chinese restaurant with no tea!

We get better service, and a heaped plate of smoked duck, from a former center of anti-Kuomintang activities that came to be called the Rat Hole Restaurant. And where will the ginger trail lead us next? Our stomachs, our eyes, our hearts demand an answer. Eating is more than necessity, it's the essential adventure, the quest that must be fulfilled most often and therefore offers the surest route to surprise.

Mei keeps asking for a restaurant called Rong Le Yuan and ends up getting pointed down darkened streets reduced to wreckers' rubble. With her accent, the locals think we're looking for a playground. So we settle for a private room in a new hot pot palace where a typically scrambled English brochure "invites gentle persons of all ranks to descend." It is here that I discover my new Sichuanese favorite, the killer *shui zhu ro pian*—hunks of steamed pork atop a crunchy variant of cabbage all drenched in chili oil.

Afterward, we poke our heads through hanging beads into a nightspot set glamorously beneath a circular highway rotary. The Casablanca Bar features a torch singer who mumbles her way through the Beatles' "Yesterday." The waitresses ruin the effect of their leopard-skin miniskirts by standing at attention like choir girls with gloved hands clasped together. The real entertainment comes from a back booth where a drunk "unit leader" is haranguing and slapping around a blubbering underling. The other patrons try not to look, but we can't help peeking at this spectacle of obeisance. The less dominant man presents first one side of his face to be chastised, then the other.

"Jesus said to turn the other cheek," Mei whispers. "But here, the god is money." When a Tibetan monk swathed in gold robes exits a nearby cabaret with a glazed grin, we're enticed to pay an exorbitant fee for glasses of lemon tea while the "live fashion show" is replaced by a Madonna video. Apparently, Chengdu hasn't quite got the hang of Western decadence.

For an Eastern touch, Mr. Xie transports us to the Da Fuo, or Big Buddha, carved out of the river cliff to a height of seventy-one meters. Sitting like some beatific lumberjack, hands firmly on its knees, this rather goofy, square-jawed Da Fuo appears to be waiting for the next helping of *dofu*. Recently, a peasant from Guangdong came up with the remarkable discovery that the entire bluff itself forms the supine body of an even more gigantic Buddha—with a pagoda erected right where a phallus should rise. Shouldn't a Buddha be contentedly flaccid? This prophet who laughs at the world can be taken home in the form of a battery-powered, rub- ber doughboy. "Ha-ha-ha! Ho-ho-ho!" goes this zen Santa each time it rocks from side to side in our satchels. The thing sounds just like Mr. Xie.

Of course, the main reason we've come to the grimy river junction of Leshan is for a luncheon laid on by local officials. Our table has been loaded down with such perks as stir-fried venison, deep-fried swallows, and boiled, whole turtle. Every second bite, we have to stand for toasts with fiery rice wines. I have no idea what our provincial hosts could possibly want from us in return, though one bigwig with oddly hazel eyes pulls Mei aside for information about getting a cousin into an American dental college. This food is given for the sake of showing what one can give. Enforced by Confucian ritual or Communist pecking order, that's the highest value in China.

"We have no mother and no father," declares Mr. Xie as he eats and drinks everyone else under the table. "The People's Congress is our family!"

Sounds like the Masons, but I doubt whether their meetings end in a private room made of sparkly foam walls, equipped with the latest karaoke system and projection TV. Mr. Xie is a born ham who joins Mei in a duet of rousing folk tunes from fifties' propaganda films about Chinese army conquests. Tibet's greatest hits. The accompanying "music videos" consist of ruddy-cheeked nomads strolling happily amidst herds of yak.

We don't get in touch with the true spirit of Sichuan until the wife of a local carpet exporter suggests that we have supper with her father-in-law. "He's something of a food expert," she tells Mei, in what turns out be quite an understatement. Whatever his profession, this occupant's service to the nation has gained him the biggest apartment I've entered in all of China, complete with parquet floors and a solarium. Though his business card is too small to hold all his titles, Mr. Liao Bokang could be anyone's archetypal bow-tie-wearing daddy. With his squared-off crew cut, bottle-thick glasses and salesman's smile, this Chairman of the Sichuan Political Association reminds me of a Chinese Ozzie (as in Harriet). Like many Sichuanese, the former underground fighter and government official is a tiny bundle of energy. Unassuming and highly practical, he embodies the best characteristics found in Sichuan's greatest political officer, China's number one "capitalist roader."

"In 1950, when Deng Xiaoping came to Chongqing and became the local secretary, he saw a bean flour noodle stand," Liao Bokang says of his mentor. "Since he had left the region when he was ten, he missed the food from his childhood so much that he went to try some. When the chief of the Security Police tried to stop him for security reasons, Deng said that the safest thing is to go where no one expects you to go, to eat what no one expects you to eat." The wit and wisdom of our supreme leader, according to Liao Bokang.

Once, Comrade Liao supervised the construction of the first bridge across the Yangtze River. Now he directs drivers, servants, and children with the unshakable confidence that is the product of China's unquestioned respect for age. The only challenge that leaves him stumped is where to find "the one restaurant to present you with the best of Sichuan." Like Mei and I, Comrade Liao is torn between authentic greasy spoons and elaborate, if less tasty, banquet houses. He settles somewhat grudgingly on Longchaoshou, generally acknowledged as Chengdu's premier dining establishment. We're whisked there in his black limo, then led through a ground-floor noodle house reeking of disinfectant. A table of honor is waiting for us in more exclusive surroundings, beside a traditional Chinese orchestra. As we're seated, Liao Bokang declares, "Food is the point where the material meets the spiritual."

Especially meals like this. Over the next two hours, we will sample eight cold dishes, five variants of dumplings in hot oil, chicken and pork over sizzling rice, chicken with peanuts and chilis, a whole fish, and of course, twice-cooked pork. In this version, the strips of meat are fatty and baconlike from the salty cure of a concentrated bean paste. Instead of cabbage, these are tossed in crunchy, hollow shoots of young garlic.

"There's the dish that won a hundred million hearts!" Liao Bokang swears with his broad grin, speaking for the entire populace of Sichuan. "And it must be made only with bean paste from Pi County!"

Mr. Liao tries to slow himself with the proverb, "When you eat, you shouldn't speak." But he clearly doesn't believe it. "Still, words cannot convey the best dishes, the true feelings in life," he waxes, turning coyly toward his demure and more wizened wife. "To say 'I love you' to someone, that's too easy."

Still waiting for those words after fifty years, the blushing Mrs. Liao tries to hush him up by joking, "Just tell them about the food!"

Pouring out his heart, the old man explains how everything essential to Chinese culture is connected to eating. After all, *"Min yi shi wei tian."* Liao Bokang is the first of a hundred sages worldwide who cite this scripture from Confucius. Translations range anywhere from "People consider food uppermost" to "Daily fare is as high as heaven for the common man."

"But don't ask Confucius for all the answers," Liao Bokang cautions. "He died two thousand years ago!" Better that I should ask him about the origin of *dian xin* (*dim sum* in Cantonese). "These snacks are called 'treasures to touch the heart' because they derive from buns which were easy for soldiers to carry when they left home.

During the wars of the Sung Dynasty, these foods were the only reminders of beloved places for men far from home."

His home province has taken their food highly spiced ever since traders brought the chili from India, because "we're in the center of China, and that means everything here has to be more intense." To him, pepper represents the "characteristic of our present time. To do things faster. It's like disco in music." But he corrects the general belief that *kung pao* chicken comes from the Chinese words "to explode." In fact, the dish was invented by one General Gung Bao, a renaissance man who was both gourmet and dam-builder, a master chef and the executioner of the Empress Ci Xi's favorite eunuch. As for the reason the meat is so lean in the centerpiece of tea-smoked duck, "That's because in Sichuan, to get our birds to market, we make them run a marathon."

With emphatic hand gestures, and a big smile that undercuts all seriousness, Mr. Liao illustrates how our tea cups are narrowed at the base to insure an even circulation of leaves. To him, "Chopsticks are a perfect example of physics, an application of the lever and the supporting point."

In China, the ultimate reference point is always food. Even Liao Bokang's description of the planet's cultural divide is based on eating. "In the world, one third of the people use chopsticks, one third use forks, and one third use their hands." So he's able to flatter me with the assessment that, "This makes you a one-hundred-percent man."

Liao Bokang is an inexhaustible fount of the Chinese beliefs that Mao's fevered crusades had sought to banish. "Just keep a big heart and your health in balance," he advises, dabbing his mouth with his napkin to suggest that the food orgy is nearly finished. "Try to look at everything that happens from the heights of history."

Which is how this one-time revolutionary can finish out his life surrounded by a table's worth of relatives who dote on his every pronouncement. But this contented cadre envies my work. Offering the best definition of travel, Liao Bokang confesses, "How I'd love to see what one hasn't seen, to hear what one hasn't heard, to taste what one hasn't tasted!"

Twice-Cooked Pork

From Longchaoshou Restaurant

Ingredients:

Pork leg meat with skin, 1 lb.
Garlic shoots, 10 pieces
Sweet flour paste, 2 tbs.
Pi County bean paste, 1 tbs.
Fermented black beans, 1 tbs.
Sweet red soy sauce, 2 tbs.
Pork lard or peanut oil

Boil the pork leg until the skin is tender. Let it cool and cut against the grain into thin slices—with fat, meat, and skin connected. Cut the garlic shoots into pieces of the same length as the pork. Heat pork lard or oil in a wok and stir-fry pork slices until the fat begins to be reduced. Add the sweet flour paste, bean paste, and black beans and stir. Add the soy sauce and garlic shoots, and stir-fry until the shoots are tender.

Revenge of the Snake People

The facade of the Guangzhou Jiujia looks like some antebellum plantation on steroids. This wedding cake of superfluous columns and balconies strung with Christmas lights seems about to topple onto the early evening rush of shoppers below. Above the stacked dining levels blinks a huge sign bordered with pink neon: "Eating in Guangzhou."

In English. Pronounced something like "Eat At Joe's." But something—like a qualifying adverb—has been lost in translation. Yes, we are all eating, as we must to maintain our existence. And Mei and I are happy to be doing so in Guangzhou, a.k.a. Canton, the Chinese city farthest away from the emperor and closest to Western imaginations. Perhaps each new viewer is supposed to fill in the sign's propagandistic blank, occasioned by a shortage of state approved words. Are we to infer that one can eat splendidly in Guangzhou? Eat prudently in Guangzhou? Eat anything that moves in Guangzhou?

The sign reminds Mei that ever since the Chinese have categorized such things, "it's best to be born in Suzhou because of the local beauties, best to be wed in Hangzhou because of the silk for dresses, best to die in Yenzhou where they have the hardest wood for coffins. And it's always been best to eat in Guangzhou—let's hope this restaurant proves why!"

Except for the hostesses in slit, velveteen dresses, I could swear that we're entering a hospital. But beyond the hygienic, marble-faced lobby and elevators, this is an updated version of ancient, all-purpose pleasure houses. Packs of kids play around the goldfish pond in the central courtyard. Three stories echo with the clatter of dishes, gossip, and drink. As in the many dim sum houses along the Pearl River, fine dining in Canton is never an intimate experience. One chooses ambiance by department store floors, men's formal to ladies' lingerie. In the sparsely populated first-floor unreserved section, we have the company of a half-dozen eager young bell captains, napkin folders, and plate changers. Compared to northern-style, the menu selection is vast.

We know we're on the right track when the shrimps we order are borne to us in a plastic sack to prove that they've just been plucked from the tank. But the high point is the Guangzhou Jiujia's signature Wenchang chicken, named for the nearby county that breeds the plumpest birds. Cold slices of deboned white meat have been arranged in a circle with equal-sized chunks of home-cured ham and chicken liver, then "married," as the cooking-show hosts might say, with a rice wine glaze. After weeks of oil-soaked, garlic-choked gristle, this feels like the gustatory equivalent of having one's windshield wiped.

Does the food taste this good merely because we haven't sampled this style in a while? How long, anyway, is the tongue's memory? Quite a bit shorter than the eye's or the heart's or the prick's. More than any other organ, our taste buds keep asking, "What have you done for me lately?"

In artistic terms, the cuisine in this far south city is to its northern cousins what Renoir is to Rothko. Here, the colors brighten, the taste buds glow, roseate. While bland Cantonese gets monotonous in the West, it's a welcome relief within China itself. Just as restaurants in the States scurry to repackage their reheated Cantonese fare as "Hunan-Sichuan," it's as fashionable on the mainland to advertise sophistication with the label "Hong Kong style," which originates in Guangzhou and its surrounding Guangdong Province. At the end of the eighties and the start of China's culinary upgrade, it was as difficult to get a good meal in the rest of the country as it was to get a bad one here. And we've begun with one of the best, where every blue plate is royal. "Until you've eaten at the Guangzhou," says the waiter, "you haven't been to Canton!"

But I feel like I already have. Here is the model for all overseas Chinese settlements, the original Chinatown. Though the streets are hardly lined with chop suey joints or phone booths topped with pagoda roofs, the old city center can't help giving me déjà vu. The faces that peer out from behind stoops and stalls are sage beyond their years, round as bowls, and faintly gold-colored, with broad noses and wispy eyebrows. These are exact genetic blueprints for the multitudes of San Francisco's Grant Avenue or New York's Mott Street. Their long-held *hai yas* of agreement and amazement are the familiar sounds that punctuate a diaspora's wheeling and dealing. The Cantonese cadences may be guttural, but how many cities can claim to have promulgated a language spoken in ninety countries? I'm actually more acquainted with some of the vocabulary than a northerner like Mei. Bok choy and dim sum aren't known in Mandarin, but they are standard American, Australian, or Malay. They're on the world menu.

This town meets all my criteria for being world-class: fast taxis, plenty of blue jeans outlets, and no closing hours on the nightly noshing. It is also a grubby place whose gray rows of sweatshops seem to be perspiring away before our very eyes. As in Hong Kong, khaki-clad police in British-style black cabs zoom along elevated highways that show nothing on all sides but windowless warehouses. Reared under two separate systems, these two cities are like twins separated at birth. Each is a no-frills, no-nonsense shrine to the family store. If the Chinese invented paper, the Cantonese invented the receipt.

Wandering down the back alleys called *gai*, there's a veritable tableau of every stereotype we consider Chinese: contented old neighbors seated at low tables for the strategic tile-slapping of afternoon mah-jongg; bald babies being washed in plastic tubs; doorways plastered with hygienic edicts plus paired decals of cherubic household protectors. Recovering from a delectable clay pot of duck and taro root at the elegant Bei Yuan, Mei and I take a bench in a pleasantly miniature people's park set before city hall. Here, an amateur Cantonese opera club begins to strut in patched pants. An ageless troupe declaims and bellows about the great deeds of warriors, concubines, and monkey gods. The head conductor in knitted vest and flat cap wants to practice his English while explaining every instrument and legend. But here, Beijing's blues have turned to crooning in Hawaiian shirts. Says the proud leader, "We do this not for money, only for happy!"

It's not for carved dragons, but for this everyday spectacle that people should come to Canton. Which means that there's nothing much to tour here, just lots to eat. The town's leitmotifs are the decapitated carcass, all glazed and shiny; the hanging rodent flank, tail included; the steam-pressed pig head complete with steamrolled eyeballs. Though a number of overseas Chinese insist that eating dog is entirely illegal, the barbecue shops of Canton are hung with stripped torsos too small to be pork and too large to be rabbit. "Woof! Woof!" is the explanation I both expect and dread. Apparently, poodles and schnauzers are out. According to ancient texts, young "yellow dogs"—but not golden retrievers—are considered the tastiest and most fortifying of breeds. Black ranks second; mixed, third; and white, last—cooks usually keep the tail to show the clientele. Considered a heat-inducing treat for cold seasons, Cantonese call man's best friend "fragrant meat" or "three six"—because the word for *nine* sounds the same as the word for dog.

Only the former British enclave of Shamian Island with its lush promenades and ramshackle mansions, lends a whiff of faded civility to Canton. Instead of coolie piers, tennis courts dot the waterfront. Past midnight, hordes of strolling teen dates pack the restaurant in our chosen Victory Hotel. I'm not sure which "victory" management means, considering we're on the shameful spot where the Brits grabbed their first chunk of Chinese soil.

Forget the Opium Wars, they must be talking about the pasta war.

In this, the cooks of Canton easily vanquish all infidels. Even the Italians can't top this obsession with one singular form of the staff of life. Always fresh, never limp or grease-soaked, noodles come at you in a breakfast nest of crunchy chow mein; rice flour versions are featured at a brunch of sausage and shrimp buns; heavier, eggier blends come in broth for lunch, mixed with shellfish at supper, and deep-fried in the wee hours. Life is an endless stream of steamed dough washed down with gallons of chrysanthemum tea. All our research quickly turns to noodling around.

Our quest for the ultimate leads us to the unlikely shrine of Shahe. This crowded suburban transfer point was once a separate market town at the foot of a small mountain. Over a hundred years back, the street stalls became known for the special taste achieved by mixing their rice flour with spring-fed wells from the top of the hill. Long before Olympia beer coined the phrase, Shahe's slogan could have been, "It's the water!"

According to the managers of the Shahe Restaurant, the perfect recipe came only when one couple ran out of flour and had to mix what remained at the bottom of their pot with some sugar. As usual, the origin is rooted in scarcity; hunger is the mother of Chinese invention. In the kitchens of the multilevel, state-run establishment, the long strips of rice noodles or *fun si*, are still hand cut by traditional methods. One batch at a time is prepared by spreading batter thinly across a wide wooden steamer, quickly peeling off the white crepes, and piling them in ready-to-slice rounds. Consolidated in 1953, and combined with the Shahe Hotel, the restaurant's abiding gimmick, shown in every window-display photo, is its five kinds of linguine-thick noodles. Colored spinach green, beet red, wheat golden, turnip white, or bamboo beige, they are duly labeled sweet, sour, bitter, spicy, or salty. I dare not admit before the proudly assembled brass who supervise our lunch that my heathen tongue can't always tell the difference.

"Our food culture is highly developed," says one of the head managers. Now where I have I heard this before? "In Shanghai, they put first what people wear. Here, we put first what people eat."

I can't register surprise because I'm too busy scarfing down the paired cold pigeon and chicken dipped in a green, garlicky sauce; the delectably sauteed pea-pod shoots; the "treasure tree" filled with gold coins, namely bok choy and black mushrooms arranged to look like a bush and its flowers. At weddings and other Cantonese excuses for elaborate feeds, Shahe's chefs can produce such luck-inducing menu items as "May you be together until your hair is white" and "Living in harmony for a hundred years."

In Canton, the Chinese obsession with fortune reaches full fruition and, of course, the most fortunate food item of all are the noodles themselves. Explains one manager, "No birthday celebration is proper without the unbroken strands that bring long life."

The problem with exporting Shahe's rainbow of noodle nests to the West isn't really the water, one manager explains, but the "chefs who might never return to China." But we've clearly come to the right place. On the way out, we're told, "If you haven't eaten at Shahe, you haven't been to Canton!"

It's only when reserving train tickets to leave that we see Canton's connection to the rest of the motherland's needy mass. The city's greatest spectacle is the main station's unstoppable, undocumented deluge of blue-clad peasants with bed rolls, stretching the borders of China's economy to bursting. Staring out across this portable village, this movable encampment of hungry stragglers, I feel some relief at surviving yet another bout with China—and getting out with my plumbing and relationship in tact. I've seen what I've never saw, tasted what I've never tasted—and with Mei by my side, I won't ever have to feel too removed from China's "red pepper" spirit. But it's going to be hard to top the mainland's soul food.

"Is it possible that the best Chinese restaurant really is in China?" I ask, feeling like a traitor to millions of overseas chefs.

"We'll just have to see," Mei answers, adding her battle cry, "Munch on!"

I may lose all appetite at the Qing Ping Market, a fitting final sight for food tourists. This covered gallery running crosswise through old Canton isn't for anyone who ever felt the urge to join the A.S.P.C.A. Among all the edible exotica, it takes a bit of effort to spot anything offensive to foreign sensibilities but that's just what foreigners come here to do. On a good day, there are caged monkeys, raccoons, civets, and, worst of all, fluffy kittens rubbing their noses against the wooden bars. Yes, Virginia, they really do eat anteaters by the truckload, wise old hoot owls, freshly stunned baby deer with open starlet eyes still seeking a gentler fate.

If "nature is one huge restaurant," as Woody Allen put it, then no place makes the point so vividly as the Snake Restaurant. Of course, it's located down a dark and serpentine street. But no identification is more obvious than this restaurant's ground-floor entry. To make our way upstairs to a table in the cushy mezzanine, or a private room where the snake comes with a high-tech singalong, we have to pass through a hosed-down, blood-splattered area. This tiled butcher shop is lined with snake cages. In the center are clinical dissection tables manned by more enthusiastic young handlers than might be found in an Indian bazaar. Rest assured, each is a certified trainer, deft slaughterer, chopper, or stripper. Only in China would this show be meant to stimulate, rather than put off, one's appetite.

"After you try it, you'll want more!" we are urged by an assistant manager with a four-foot-high beehive hairdo; a flashy, denture-regular set of choppers; and cheeks as rosy and polished as a Washington State apple. In ancient times, southerners were scorned for their love of frogs. Today, a younger generation carries on with another reptilian tradition. We follow her recommendations for pieces of barbecued snake, stir-fried snake with greens, and whole ginger in snake broth. The sauces are subtle, the soup lovely. Molts in your mouth! Some of the cuts are a bit bony, but they all taste like chicken. After this, I'm just not sure if chicken will taste like chicken.

A bonus for male clientele is available in the form of virility boosting snake spleen, excised with a knife from a caged garden snake brought to the table, then squeezed into a shot glass of mao tai liquor. Amazingly, the snake lives on unharmed, as do we. Fortunately, the manager isn't pushing the Stewed Three Different Snakes with Chicken Feet in medicinal herbs, the ever-popular Stewed Fur Seals, Snake with Cat Meat Soup, or the Stir-fried Ophicephalus Fish Ball and Stewed Frog.

"The entire snake is a treasure," purrs the politburo Nefertiti on her return. "It increases blood circulation, cures cough, builds the blood and organs, tones the skin and hair. Makes everyone feel energy, woman get beauty!" Apparently, we've come at the right time of year, too, since she hastens to rhapsodize, "When the autumn winds start, the snakes all grow meaty. That's the best time to eat!"

Now I now the origins of the term *snake oil*. Not only is snake meat very yang, or hot, in the Chinese system, but this woman claims it helped save the lives of some Cantonese injected with experimental serums by the occupying Japanese. She herself seems unusually pumped up. For a state-run place, morale in the Snake Restaurant sure is high. The whole staff is its best advertisement— including several other *Mädchen* in uniform with severe expressions and scary bouffants.

"Is it a cult?" I suddenly blurt out.

Not only do the waiters and waitresses act like indoctrinated converts, but they all seem unnaturally preserved, with taut skin, a stunning profusion of hair, and wildly bright eyes. I feel like we're dining in *The Village of the Damned*, that sci-fi flick where the children glow with an inner, alien light. I keep an eye on Mei to make sure she doesn't ingest too much cobra, lest she take on the same zombie stare. I fear that I'll catch her hissing each time we make love. Call this the Revenge of the Snake People.

"Can you guess how long I've worked here?" the head snake goddess asks ominously. "Twenty years!"

This grandmother doesn't look a single shed of skin over thirty-five. She nods fervently when I ask if she regularly tastes of the serpent. "One day, I'd like to open my own snake restaurant," she confirms. "With reforms, we have good pay and are able to travel abroad." But there's no place like home when it comes to snake.

"I'll bet you don't want to leave our country after a meal like this," observes our irradiated hostess. "Don't you think Chinese people really know how to eat?"

With a mouth full of snake, I grunt my approval.

Hong Kong and Taiwan
. . . .
TWO FROM COLUMN A

Featured Restaurants:

Maxim's, Hong Kong
Lei Yue Mun, Hong Kong
Hong Kong City Hall, Hong Kong
Lai Ching Heen, Kowloon
Yung Kee, Hong Kong
Tien Hsiang Lo, Taipei
Xin Yeh, Taipei
Peng Yuan, Taipei
Fu Yuan, Taipei
Yangtze River, Taipei
My House, Your House, Taipei
Ding Tai Feng, Taipei

The Golden Goose

The excuse is so very Hong Kong. An off-duty kung fu star, dashingly handsome in Vandyke beard, has offered to lead us to the shark's fin and abalone emporia that are his fast-lane haunts. After four or five tries to his cellular phone, including a brief chat from a Jaguar's bucket seat, he has to beg off. Shamefaced, our film hero confesses that his doctors won't allow him outdoors for another week. For the first time, I'm blown off on account of a face lift.

Reports of the death of Hong Kong are greatly exaggerated. Once the bargain basement of the world, Hong Kong might be called the ultimate designer-chic colony. The best Mei and I can do for under sixty U.S. dollars a night is lug our bags up one of the service elevators of a crowded office building in the midst of continually thronged Causeway Bay. Our headquarters is the Bao Bao Hotel, and though *bao bao* is what Chinese toddlers cry when they crave parental cuddles, there's nothing cozy about this windowless guest house carved from fourth-floor office space. Our room is the local equivalent of Japanese commuters' sleep-in drawers, a closet that barely has room for a bed and overhead TV—enough to put a crimp in any romantic commitment.

Yet within a single block, Mei and I can satisfy a thirst for the tropics by swigging three cups of fresh mango and melon juices, then purchase khaki slacks, Cadbury's chocolate, Ralph Lauren sunglasses, a new Casio watch, and a month's supply of film, soon to be filled with properly colorful views of neon signage above sidewalk bins of dried medicinal roots. No wonder this semi-extinct pseudo-nation stamps more visitors' passports than any of Asia's fabled realms. Even dour mainland rule isn't likely to destroy the appeal of an entirely nonthreatening Orient peopled with natives who tote cordless phones and public-school manners.

Few *gwei lo*—Cantonese for foreign devils—can compete with the uncritical consumerism found among this immigrant enclave's spoiled children. In fact, the toughest sector for the mainland to swallow will be a generation of Chinese who wear granny glasses, worship James Dean, and actually kiss in public while frequenting clubs with topical names like Post-97, the Yelts Inn, and the 6-4 Cafe (date of the Tiananmen killings). But are we really ready to ingest a Thanksgiving dinner at Dan Ryan's Chicago-style grill? At a distance, the timing of our arrival seems delectable. Up close, the canned candied yams and insipid gravy pored over thin slices of tepid, bird strike us as an unnecessary excursion into barbarism. A basket of nachos are enough to sate any homesickness.

"You know," I admit to Mei, "I don't want to waste a single mealtime in Hong Kong . . . "

"Now you're learning Chinese diligence," Mei approved. "Or Chinese guilt!"

At street level, the "fragrant harbor," as Hong Kong translates, is perfumed with heaps of chopped cilantro, the potent fumes of fish balls in broth served up by old gents in khaki shorts. After wandering the length of Hennessy Road past the weird mix of Seven-Elevens and herbalist shops, Mei and I settle for a second-story, full-floor representative of the chain called Maxim's—which has nothing to do with Paris, and everything to do with an owner named Meixin. Deciding that black bean chicken will be my baseline test for Cantonese cuisine as fish-flavored pork was for Sichuan, I'm happily surprised that Maxim's provides the best rendition of that standard I've yet had. Forget turkey with stuffing. I'll take these morsels attached to bonelets, flecked with salty bean halves in a light rinse of sugar, wine, and oil.

Any Chinese who does not run a restaurant someplace else will tell you that Hong Kong has the world's best Chinese food. When it comes to consistency of preparation and variety of seafood, that's surely the case. At creations like Lei Yue Mun fishing village (i.e., dining village), we can point at any seagoing beast, from soft-shell crab to large, meaty garoupa fish, kept shiny and slithery under bright lights until personally selected for steaming. One explanation for China's ongoing dispute with Vietnam and the Philippines over the waters surrounding the uninhabited Spratly Islands is that factory-processing ships come here to scoop up a large portion of Hong Kong's live seafood. In tropical waters everywhere, vast numbers of shark have been decimated for their vaunted fins alone. So edible cravings spill into geopolitics. Just as the United States went to war for oil, so would China for fish—steamed with a garnish of scallion and ginger.

Even the dead eat well in this town. During the holiday honoring ancestors known as Ching Ming, I once watched mourning relatives picnic atop the amphitheater rows of tombs chiseled into the hillsides. Roast chickens, cleaved half-pig, Fuji apples, and tangerines were then left before the stern portraits on every urn—enough snacks for eternity.

To that end, I can't wait to lead Mei on a ritual pilgrimage to Hong Kong City Hall. This dim sum house is surely no average government commissary. There's something especially tasty about the entire top floor of municipal offices being given over to the unabashed worship of any sort of gristle, web, or paste fit inside a pastry. We have to wait for the combination hostess/prison warden to bark out our number in Cantonese through a raspy mike mounted on her chest. By the time we've steeped ourselves in gallons of chrysanthemum tea and counted every tanker in the harbor, we've almost coincidentally had some of the finest shrimp *har gow* around. If the name *dim sum* really derived from soldiers who carried these pocket-sized treats, they must now fortify armies of accountants. Yet these "heart treasures" taken on the run and served unceremoniously from wheeled carts are the highest expression of a lifestyle that a film producer we meet says "is just like Hong Kong's movies, a mix of high and low culture, fast-paced and a bit unbalanced, but demanding total involvement."

For fun, we stroll over to the short-lived legislative council's weekly audience with Governor Chris Patten, Hong Kong's pathbreaking Last Emperor. The discussion sounds more like the Oxford Debating Society. But the latest accounting of harbor dredging and housing projects shows that these royals, in their desperation to hold on to the hearts and minds of the territory, have cooked up more social welfare than any Reds. Still, the colonizers never showed all that much concern about democratizing Hong Kong until they were about to lose it.

Unless it sets off another mass exodus of chefs, reunification can only improve Hong Kong's culinary provincialism. Despite the finest selection of Vietnamese food outside Paris, Indian food beyond London, Thai food east of L.A., this town can't do justice to China's regional variations. The best Mei and I do this time is the Peking, a northern-style walk-up amidst Wanchai's girlie bars. This is the favored hangout of Marvin, the father of our cameraman friend Mitch and a longtime "shooter" himself. With wry Brooklyn accent and a wink that attests to the pitfalls of this family profession, Marvin admits, "What my career needs is another war." Joining us, the proprietor of the Peking also speaks of an Asia in conflict.

"My father came from Wei Hai, on the Shandong coast. That was a recruiting zone for the British navy. The pay wasn't good, but after the Japanese invasion, my father got a bonus—the right to stay in Hong Kong!"

Apparently a frustrated mathematician, this chef spreads out napkin after napkin as he speaks, filling them with columns and graphs to illustrate each point. "From pig's feet with cabbage, I can turn a decent profit. But when you're starting out with abalone that costs three hundred dollars an ounce, how much more can you charge?" I'm not sure I follow his formula, but it's enough to keep the Peking relatively authentic. "In Hong Kong, raw ingredients have become status symbols. What can a good chef do with that?"

Invited to dine at the top of Hong Kong peak, I have hopes of finally getting to the heights of upscale Chinese eating. Our hosts—a hustling Pacific Rim developer and a renowned romance writer who uses white pancake makeup to exude her heroines' unattainable allure—lead us instead to the Peak Cafe, managed by the San Francisco chef Jeremiah Tower. Over quesadillas and salmon tandoori, the developer insists that I take a look at a newspaper column that expresses his vision. The headline reads, "H.K.—Model City for 21st Century!" I'm not sure I approve of such a sci-fi fantasy: a planet where there's no room for anything but the next banking conference or shopping spree.

Still, the more high-tech Hong Kong gets, the more cozy it remains—as cozy, say, as the back of a late model Rolls Royce Silver Shadow, steered by our Chinese Danielle Steele, its gray interior leather creaking with each bend of the switchbacks that bring us back down through the city's pricey Mid-Levels. Perhaps this is as real an experience as we can expect, the truest East of all.

Hong Kong's moment of dissolution may be its fullest flowering—

a chance to appreciate so unique a creation of cross-pollination. Would that each of us could transform our defects into assets as effi- ciently as this town's frog-into-prince act. Lousy weather? Say muggy, not moderate typhoon. Traffic jams? They're just proof of the highest percentage of millionaires per stretch of road. Have a swim? Mei and I have barely dipped our feet into the azure waters off Lan- tau Island when lifeguards hoist a flag festooned with the black sil- houette of a shark. Never mind if most of the sampans have been replaced with hydrofoils and the few floating restaurants serve up he- patitis. That's Pacific Rim progress! Yet I don't want to admit the possibility that the world's best Chinese restaurant may sit in stall 347-A of some sterile mall, between Giordano Jeans and Double Lucky Electronics.

On the very tip of the Kowloon peninsula, crowding out the colo- nial Peninsula Hotel, the Regent now commands one of the planet's most magnificent views. We've been lured to eating in chain-owned surroundings by a recent survey for the *International Herald-Tribune*. The only Chinese entry to break into the global top ten is the Re- gent's Lai Ching Heen. But Lai Ching Heen isn't even this hotel's number one restaurant, but rather a hushed basement bistro rimmed with wall-to-wall harbor vistas.

This is Cantonese world food, dished out with a bit too much pomp and not enough actual circumstance. The tablecloths and ser- vice are impeccable, but the baked barbecued pork in puff pastry isn't many rungs above the usual dim sum. More delicate are the dumplings in chicken broth stuffed with a favorite ingredient of Hong Kong chefs known as *conpoy*, dried and concentrated scallop. The steamed lobster, drizzled with a combination of crab cream and fresh mango sauce, could compete with anything French. And the deep-fried scallops on a bed of warm pears is an inventive signature dish that's already charmed a hundred critics.

Still, I can't quite see the point of a Hong Kong without damp- ness, tumult, and overcrowding. It is raining hard on our parade as we make our way to the correct double-decker to take us up into the northwest corner of Kowloon, a place where tourists normally fear to tread. Before heading off for even balmier climes, we're going to leave a sack or two of cold weather clothes with the aunt of Mei's half-sister. Her apartment is a half-mile climb up a public stairway, so we're properly drenched by the time we find the right gate to the right tower in a vast gray housing block.

This is the city rarely plastered on travel posters: ratty hallways, dim rusty corridors, rows of human beings living behind sets of double-locked, anticrime doors. Two bedroom boxes feed off a main chamber just big enough for a dining table, TV, and fax, with galley kitchen big enough to contain one female helpmate at a time. I feel guilty storing anything here. On either side of the ideological divide, the main competition is still to see how few square feet can accommodate the masses.

Yet after a homemade hot pot, the proud mother asks her elder son to speak English to me and the younger to give a concert on the violin. The parents cluck and contentedly close their eyes to take in the halting performance of their chubby man-child in British woolen jacket and short pants. There's a promise of gentility, if not affluence, in every squeak that we've got to sit through. "All happy families are alike," Mei cribs Tolstoy. "Especially when they're Chinese."

Bedraggled from wind and rain, we wash up next before the amazed receptionist at the newsroom of Hong Kong's leading English-language paper, the *South China Morning Post*. Mei has the bright idea that I should be able to sell these folks some dispatches about our search. Indeed, our premise gets a raised eyebrow from one laconic, red-haired British editor. But he turns the tables, preferring to write his own article about our book. Before I know it, he's led me down to the staff cafeteria and whipped out a tape recorder. Over a soggy plate of some of the worst stir-fry I'll get on our trip, I have to wax poetic over the meaning of our quest.

We're soon combing the Central district for locales where we can be photographed in action. Just below, on sloping Wellington Street, amidst a series of boiler-plate restaurants, we stagger into the venerable Yung Kee. By the time Mei has explained to me that *Kee* in Cantonese is the equivalent of the French *chez*, for "house of," we're sampling a dish of their trademark sliced roast goose—meat fragrant, skin candied, and sauce just sweet enough to bring out the gaminess. Next comes Hong Kong's most famous "thousand-year-old eggs," actually coated, heat-cured, and blackened with lime for days. At Yung Kee, I become permanently hooked on this acquired, gelatinous taste. The green yolks utterly transcend the gross, being slightly soft and perfectly pungent. The restaurant actually offers to refund your money if the yolks aren't runny. Of course, we also get numerous greens and shrimps in a perfectly moderated *kung pao* treatment. The cuisine here, we're told, mixes four cooking systems: those of Guangzhou, Chaozhou, Hainan, and Dong Jiang, or "East River." But this is the sort of establishment where what you see is what you get and every dish out of the kitchen looks just right.

Without fanfare, Yung Kee has quietly pleased four stories' full of the world's fussiest diners at every sitting for the past forty years. Packed elevators unload onto exclusive private rooms or noisy antechambers surveyed by carved phoenixes. Hordes of discreet captains in green vests manage the flow with walkie-talkies. The boisterous scene is surveyed by eighty-three-year-old Kam Shui Fai, instigator of this poultry-to-riches affair. Shrinking away in gray mandarin tunic, he's one Chinese man who nearly looks his age. Yet he still comes here daily to lunch proudly with his wife.

It's left to his diminutive son, Kinsen Kam, to explain that "Roast Goose" Fai, as his father came to be known, began this business as a takeout stall near the Macau ferry terminal. Word-of-mouth spread among the docks and in 1942, Fai used his life savings—four thousand Hong Kong dollars—to rent his first restaurant. The building was soon destroyed by Japanese bombings, but Yung Kee rose from the ashes. All three of its addresses have had the street number "32," which has the sound of the Cantonese word for *business*. By the fifties, the place was playing host to luminaries who came through the Crown Colony.

The next generation doesn't appear too troubled about the steep rise in rent—making Hong Kong real estate the most exorbitant on earth—or the mainland takeover. Though "lots of our old customers have moved to Canada," as one brother admits, the restaurant continues to feed three thousand patrons a day as well as prepare two thousand box lunches for carryout. This establishment is further proof that, for all its emphasis on social connections, Chinese food remains one of the world's more egalitarian pleasures. In France, you'd have to withstand far more snobbery to get the same level of poultry. Anyone can walk up to the take-out window here and walk away with one of the world's great delicacies.

As quickly as one reaches for superlatives, food criticism verges on the indefinable. How good is butter on warm bread just out of the oven? How good are soft *tournedos* topped with properly balanced Bearnaise? How good is it to be alive?

"Nobody can match our goose," we're assured by Kinsen Kam. "Now it's called 'the flying goose' because so many people carry it home to their relatives overseas."

His recipe begins back on the mainland. To be properly tasty, the goose must have black feathers and a short neck. They import three hundred a day from Qing Yuan town, across the border in Guangdong Province. In perfect middleman fashion, Young Kee has made its fortune by taking a raw material from China and improving it through clever repackaging.

"What the world doesn't get is that the business connections have already been made," we're assured.

Dust to dust, China to China. So why mess with the ingredients of this concoction ever at economic boil? Defiantly, and with enormous energy, this place remains an end game for middlemen, a long-shot gamble ever about to get cashed in. Like Hong Kong, Yung Kee's goose keeps laying dividends.

Deep-Fried Scallops and Pears

From Lai Ching Heen Restaurant

Ingredients:

1 fresh pear
8 fresh scallops
Peeled shrimps, 3 oz.
Yunnan ham or sliced ham, 1 oz.
Chinese parsley, 8 leaves
Cornstarch, 1 oz.
Lemon juice
Salt, $^1/_4$ tsp.

Clean and slit the shrimps, rinse under cold water, pat dry, season to taste, and chop finely. Slice the ham. Cut eight round pieces from the pear, slightly larger than the scallops, and dust with cornstarch. Place some minced shrimp and cornstarch on each pear round, then top with a scallop. Garnish each with a slice of ham and a parsley leaf. Roll the entire unit in cornstarch and deep fry until golden brown. Serve with lemon juice.

Cathay Gone Nouvelle

"A good restaurant? Pick any one!"

The Taipei street hawker, cart laden with a surprising snack of candied strawberries on skewers, reacts to our lunchtime inquiry with shocking fury. "Don't you know? The food has to be good. This is Taiwan!"

I hope he's right, since we've staked the next ten days' tab on just such a reputation. *Formosa*, or beautiful, is what Portuguese sailors once dubbed this teardrop isle dangling off China's Fujian coast. But Mei and I are willing to settle for "delicious." Now the prospect of finding the best restaurants has lured us both to the other side of China's cold (and hot dish) war—even though her nursery ditties were all about "liberating Taiwan," while my radical student chants had likewise branded this refuge a "U.S. puppet." Having learned the hard way that revolutions don't necessarily do much for haute cuisine, we must have a look at the counterrevolutionary enclave that fancies itself a safety vault for China's traditional glories.

But we don't make it to our first meal before being force-fed the sounds and sights of Taiwan's recent advance toward a most nontraditional pluralism. Lining every curb, planted in every available lawn, multi-colored party banners flap like the battle flags of ancient warrior clans. Campaign caravans add loudspeaker bombast to Taipei's controlled clamor. Mei and I have arrived a week before critical state and municipal elections that will test the strength of the pro-independence opposition to the ruling Kuomintang. Where a one-party state has given way to a rough-and-tumble openness, politics has become Taiwan's number one contact sport.

Descending into the underpasses that assure pedestrian survival, we're greeted with other sights that have been all but banished in the People's Republic. Doing quite well, if driven below ground, are rows of palm readers, mind readers, energy-charting acupuncturists, skull-scanning phrenologists. In dark tunnels, the proud practitioners of millennia-old prophecy and parapsychology discern fates for commuters on the fly. But can any of these seers tell us where to eat?

Perhaps it has something to do with Mei's mainland accent, but our attempt to locate a famed dumpling parlor only gains us more blasts of prideful defensiveness. At the back of a bakery where we finally help ourselves, cafeteria-style, to superb sesame-coated lamb buns and a cold, garlicky eggplant salad, my ever-alert aide notices that even the utensils are wrapped in poetic propaganda: "Chopsticks were invented eight thousand years ago when Confucian scholars were inspired by the birds feeding their young. Be thankful for such a long history! How lucky to be born Chinese on Taiwan!"

In this tiny seed of a nation, virtually unrecognized since 1979, we are bombarded with a nationalism as yet relatively latent on the mainland. When it comes to exchange rates, missile purchases, or human rights, Nationalists clinging to this rock (R.O.C. for Republic of China) have forged cohesion through unceasing competition with the nation they left behind. And it isn't easy always playing to an unseen audience of one billion. When I grumble about Taiwan's ostentatiously high cost of living, our first cabbie shoots back, "If you find our country expensive, then this shows our advanced stage of development. Soon, we hope to be even more expensive than Japan!"

Where "made in Taiwan" once meant the lowest quality, now it conjures high-tech exports and sophisticated movie hits like that recent portrait of a master chef, *Eat Drink Man Woman*. But it's a lot easier to create a new state than a cuisine. "Taiwanese" has emerged as a culinary category only as Taiwan has become a distinct enough entity to produce its own breed of energetic, restaurant-opening emigrés. Of all China's regional styles, what passes for local cooking here is the least immediately appealing to Western palates. Given that the island was one of China's poorer provinces not so long ago, the overfatty and oversweetened fare belongs very much to farmers and fishermen. It's no particular nose for the authentic that leads us to the ubiquitous street fare aptly named Stinky Tofu. These fried puffs aren't as rancid as they smell, just fermented to the level of gorgonzola and old tennis shoes. But I can't quite step up to the plate through the clouds of emissions.

When we beg a driver to take us to Taipei's most authentic night market, he steers us directly to its long-running tourist trap. "Snake Alley" is actually composed of several covered, sanitized galleries lined with overpriced cubbyholes that lure diners through every known gimmick—animal, vegetable, or mineral. "No videotaping please!" warn the signs, begging for a fat bribe. The real show—a late, late one in the insomniac tradition of tropical Asia—is in the many surrounding alleys crammed with stalls offering indigenous specialties like oysters embedded in omelettes that resemble a gooey concrete, and the favored form of thick wheat noodles topped with anise-scented chunks of boiled beef. I see why every Asian hand sent here to learn advanced Mandarin or intermediate kowtowing brought home rave reviews about Asia's finest sidewalk dining.

The most unusual offerings are saucerlike dishes of delicately arrayed vegetables—pyramids of baby eggplant and carefully crisscrossed stalks of Chinese broccoli—that aren't usually served at this un-Chinese cool temperature. Another tip-off comes when we notice that seaweed rolls are more ubiquitous than egg rolls. Fifty years of Japanese occupation has left Taiwan with a lot more than a craving for sushi. Decidedly Nipponized are an aesthetic weakness for white tile and sterile office facades, fast trains, swept streets, and back-alley bonsai. But each time I broach the subject of "external influence," some proud Taiwanese chef scoffs and shakes his head—before mentioning that both parents spoke Japanese!

Thank God, Stanley Yen has nothing to do with the currency of the same name. Recommended to this president of the local gourmet society, we discover that his day job is owner of Taiwan's Ritz Hotel. Like Taiwan itself, this hotel could hardly look less appealing on the outside: a smoked glass box in a northern district with all the charm of one vast auto-body shop. But inside, the hotel delivers a level of sophistication found only in Europe with a degree of hospitality entirely lost on the mainland.

Next lunch, we've got a reserved table at the hotel's Hangzhou-style Tien Hsiang Lo, an elegant, ground-floor boîte done up in flowery wallpaper. I don't recall ever eating this well in Hangzhou itself. What to call an imitation that's better than the original? We get refined versions of steamed West Lake fish smothered in a brown vinegar sauce and quiveringly stewed Dong Po pork. In his oft-cited classical poetry, the Sung Dynasty poet Su Dongpo not only offered a recipe for this dish but advised, "Without meat one grows thin, without bamboo, one becomes common. There is a cure for leanness but none for vulgarity."

Was he perhaps thinking of Taiwan? Before I can jab my chopsticks delectably forward, teams of tuxedoed waiters work before rolling trolleys to turn each dish into petite plates of individual servings.

"This is what we call Western-style Chinese," explains Fu Pei Mei, a matron in green business suit whom Mei has drummed up to be our lunch guest. I realize we're dining with the Chinese Betty Crocker only when she reaches into her purse and plucks out a half-dozen cookbooks. Who knows the number of Fu Pei Mei's published volumes, full of on-air recipes from her popular t.v. series?

"I've tried out forty-eight hundred dishes in thirty-three years on the show," she recites. "Because Taiwan has been kept from formal relations with many countries, I've also had to serve as a kind of ambassador through food."

In the late fifties, Fu Pei Mei was just another middle-class housewife who feared that she wouldn't have anything nice to serve the guests at her husband's frequent mah-jongg parties. "So I set out to learn everything," she confesses. "I put up twenty-five grams of gold per lesson to be taught by Taiwan's greatest chefs."

The investment in hocked jewelry paid off when neighbors asked her for secondhand tips. "Beijing-style is the most difficult—because the timing is so precise," is one tidbit she offers. Now Fu Pei Mei fears that her lifetime's work of preserving Chinese cooking will be lost in the rush toward a spurious sophistication.

"For the Chinese, eating means enjoying life, and that means the family and guests should share." Somehow, these doled-out dishes don't taste the same when everyone can't exchange germ pools. "Also, our ancestors weren't so stupid. They kept the food on one plate so that it would stay hot longer. Separated, everything grows cold—including the generosity of the host."

Somehow, the division of Chinese dishes doesn't seem quite as tragic as the division of China itself. But Fu Pei Mei's warnings are still ringing in our ear when we head crosstown for an early supper specially arranged by the Tourism Board. In a skyscraper basement converted into a fountain-dappled lair, one exacting chef-owner bears us the fruits of thirty years' time-and-motion studies. "Use of chopsticks is not hygienic," he declares, proudly offering us plastic knives and forks. His four-course set meal is served in compartmentalized trays. Salmon puffs go with bland slivers of shark fin. Is this all that's evolved from the historic exodus of all those renegade master chefs? It's proving more difficult than I expected to find a Confucian "middle way" between unrefined street snacks and this nouveau riche Cathay gone nouvelle. The schism in food reflects the gap between Taiwan's two versions of itself—as provincial backwater and high-tech showcase. When the owner boasts that his menus are entirely pre-fab, I know that I've tasted the first Chinese airline food.

West Lake Vinegar Fish

From Tien Hsiang Lo Restaurant

Ingredients:

1 whole fish, 3lb.–4lb.
Scallions, 1 $^1/_2$ oz.
Ginger, 1 oz.
White rice wine, 2 tbs.

Sauce:
Ground ginger, 1. tbs.
Zhejiang vinegar, 1 tbs.
White pepper, $^1/_4$ tsp.
Soy sauce, 3 tbs.

Sugar, 3 tbs.
White sesame oil, 1 tsp.
White vinegar, 3 tbs.
White rice wine, 3 tbs.
Cornstarch, 2 tsp.

Fillet any white-meat fish and cut into six pieces. In a large pot, boil enough water to cover the fish slices. Add the ginger, scallions, and wine, then the fish slices. Bring the water to a boil again, then reduce heat and simmer for five minutes. Remove onto a platter. Heat the peanut oil in a wok and add 1/4 cup water and all sauce ingredients except the white sesame oil, cornstarch, and shredded ginger. Mix the cornstarch with water and stir in the sesame oil and rice wine. Add to the wok when the sauce comes to a boil. After the sauce has thickened, pour it through a sieve and then over the fish fillets.

Home Cooking in Exile

There's just a slight hitch with the National Palace Museum, a small technicality. The nation that created Taiwan's number one tourist attraction is China. A three-tiered crypt built into the slope of Yangmingshan, the mountain north of Taipei, holds the former imperial art collection transported during the anti-Communist exodus. A sculpture in the entry depicts the main moving man, Generalissimo Chiang Kai-shek, pint-sized if imposing in military britches. But this artistic bank vault only serves to showcase the paranoia of Taiwan's past regime. Most of the good stuff, carted out of China miraculously unharmed, is still hoarded in underground bunkers. Still, cramped rooms showcase the greatest collection of Chinese antiquities anywhere. From jade rings to Tibetan textiles to equine watercolors, it's as awe-inspiring to us as it is to school kids on a field trip. They sit cross-legged, notebooks at the ready, respectful before such a vast array of loot.

"Did you know," Mei asks, "that even in our Communist textbooks Taiwan was called Treasure Island?"

Instead of feeling resentful, she is full of open-minded curiosity about this coveted trove of jade, tea, and ideologically unscathed lore. And we find our first buried treasure at the Institute of Chinese Culinary Culture. This dehumidified basement of yet another sleek office tower is lined with thirteen thousand volumes and innumerable recipes from all of China's provinces. Yet there's no place like this on the mainland. There is something quintessentially Taiwanese about the staff's excessive courtesy and the whole concept of this fully computerized, state-of-the-art facility dedicated to preserving a most ancient art.

Now I have renewed hope for our search. Not blessed with excess, this China in miniature cannot afford to take Chinese culture for granted. There is no place that can possibly savor the real China more than its rival.

"The tongue carries the deepest memories of heritage," waxes one of a squadron of patriotic hosts at the boisterously popular Xin Yeh Restaurant. We're brought plate after plate of Taiwanese-style pork knuckles with peanuts, baked eel, fried pork liver, delicately sour bamboo shoots in pickled herbs, even steamed chicken testicles. Call this haute peasant, but everything at Xin Yeh tastes a lot better than it sounds. I know we're on the right track now, even if we leave stuffed as much with local pride as delicacies.

I sense that we've found a gem as soon as we climb a mirrored staircase up toward the rosewood-trimmed confines of Peng Yuan, or Peng's Garden, billed as the capital's class purveyor of Hunan cuisine. Our host for supper is the self-confident Mr. Peng himself, nattily attired in blue blazer and sporting an impressive pompadour. He even wears rimless glasses that are almost pince-nez. But by this point in the journey, I've developed a sixth sense about "number one sons." Where filial piety is alive and well, one can almost feel it coming.

"My father personally introduced Hunan cuisine to the United States," Mr. Peng junior immediately volunteers. "A great man, he started cooking at thirteen and rose to become the private chef to Chiang Kai-shek."

By meal's end, we'll get a chance to shake hands with the tall, imposing patriarch introduced by his English handle, "Chuck" Peng. But he reveals no state secrets and neither does Junior. "In history, everyone knows that Chiang Kai-shek was a very simple person. He didn't mind to eat soup. But everything had to be the best for his guests. And my father was the best. When the U.S. Seventh Fleet was defending Taiwan, the admiral got a seven-day banquet. Then, in 1974, my father went to Manhattan. The same year that Nixon went to China."

The younger Peng says this as though the two were events of equal significance. "When his first New York restaurant failed, my father could not lose face by returning home. It was a waste—a great chef can't be appreciated where they only know egg rolls. But he stuck it out. Later, Peng's was a favorite of Henry Kissinger. He said that he never had food like that in China."

I can see why, if the New York version was anything like my minced pigeon soup served in half a winter melon, my taro-root pancakes stuffed with home-smoked ham. Every dish we sample is both delicate and hearty, as unique as it is wedded to the past. When Mei chews away in utter silence, nodding her head, that's the sign of our unanimity. America's Hunan restaurants are creperies to this *Tour d'Argent*. As Chuck Peng baldly puts it, "If we put all our dishes in the menu, it would read like a dictionary."

Now, the family has opened a place back in their native Changsha, essentially re-introducing deluxe Hunan food to Hunan. "Of course, those are our people, our blood, so we should be joined together. But it's not easy to teach them, especially when my father's motto is to do it good or not do it at all."

And how is it being the heir of so demanding a patriarchal head chef? "It's a free country, so they say," jokes Peng the younger with a resigned shrug. "But I'll tell you, I'd rather be his friend than his son."

There are no such conflicts at our tour's second garden. Gourmet society, Fu Pei Mei, and culinary librarians alike have pointed us toward Fu Yuan, Taipei's top-rated "Fragrant Garden." But none of the scuttlebutt has prepared us for the sight that greets us down a dark sidestreet off another endless skyscraper canyon. Wooden gates, bamboo bushes, and a stone garden in an octagonal courtyard lend privacy and exclusivity to three floors of a fantasy Ming Dynasty teahouse. There's not a bit of concrete, not a nail in the place. It's all wood beams and panels. Hallways are dotted with priceless armoires chosen for their simplicity of line. In the private rooms, massive, teak tables sit beneath equally circular, tentlike domes, supported by radiant spokes. The restaurant really is fragrant inside, having been constructed largely of sweet-smelling sandalwood.

Getting off the elevator at the second-floor vestibule, we're met by a stout grand dame in black velvet gown whose ample cleavage is merely a display pad for an enormous diamond necklace. A second gem, twice the size of a Dick Tracy decoder ring, twinkles on a chubby finger. From the pride Mary Yang takes in her guided tour, it quickly becomes obvious that this is her personal fantasia. It took three years to collect all the art for the building—a rarity, says Mary Yang, because "people in this country are still insecure about making long-term investments. They have the mentality of wanting to earn everything back in a short time." Now government ministers and corporate heads are the regular guests here. Mary Yang is Taipei's Pearl Mesta, the hostess with the mostest.

Even when we're seated with the peons in the relatively small basement space reserved for public dining—where the evening's set menu costs forty dollars per person and up—I feel that I've come as far as I can from the garish mom-and-pop joints of my youth. Just as the decor is unlike anything I've ever seen, the appetizers are like nothing I've ever tasted. There are seaweed-wrapped rolls of abalone, squid meats inside celery, leek flowers, vegetable-stuffed fresh bamboo. Since there are no menus here, I can't say what level of prix fixe we're getting. But the goose liver soaked in rice wine compares well with anything from Lyons. A dish literally named "coming back fully loaded" is a good-luck seafood medley of fleshy fish stuffed with sauteed shrimps and scallops. While the strands of bird's nest are no more exciting to me than baby food pastina, there's little doubt that the broth is exquisitely light. Mei's appreciative mooing assures me that this soup is at the top of its genre.

I find it all a bit Frenchified, but Mei argues that I've just never experienced the level of refinement that was once at the heart of Chinese culture. All my harping on the Japanese influence in Taiwan has raised her hackles. "After all, where do you think the Japanese got all this in the first place?" Mei's own answer is that "they took our highly refined court culture from the T'ang Dynasty."

Perhaps she's right to unglue all my misleading labels. Perhaps, back in the old days, things not only looked like this but tasted a lot like what we're getting. Besides, Mei has been assured through the rumor mill that "the chefs here make the best dumplings, too. They can be as Chinese as you like." With enough advance notice.

Taking time off from dashes to greet her regulars, Mary Yang joins us to let down her considerable black locks. She begins by admitting that she is the eldest, and therefore thriftiest, of six sisters. After her family came here from nearby Fujian Province, she worked seventeen years at various other restaurants before launching this place. She was even a waitress at a Sichuan-style hole-in-the-wall where "the original taste of the food was covered by hot sauce. But I always wanted to cook what I liked to eat."

As a rival restaurateur puts it, "Her secret is that she's had her own style and stuck to it. She lets the public come to her." Mary Yang amplifies, "I also took trips to Paris whenever I could to get new ideas." I'm not sure how this jibes with her pulled-up-by-her-own-bootstraps image. Fu Yuan, like much of Taiwan, seems to be a kind of shrine to upward mobility.

"Before, everyone was poor and there were few places to have fun," Mary Yang muses. "We had to have lots of grease and fat to make us feel full. Now, we've passed that stage and we can appreciate the art in eating. We're health-conscious and we are learning to use ingredients from all over the world, whether it's American beef or French *champignons*."

By dessert, the paragon of classical taste and dragon lady in black has melted into a single woman who can't suppress shy giggles and makes nervous jokes about not being able to meet the right man. "My only regret is that I haven't married. But men are afraid to approach me, because they think I've got someone powerful backing me up." Almost as quickly as she confides in Mei, she pulls out a road map and advises us on all the mountain sanctuaries we must visit. "Though we're living on a small island," she explains, "one can't help feeling very warmly toward it."

The high-class restaurateur even recommends a trip to the newly opened Taiwan Cultural Village, a popular shopping mall and amusement center built around such attractions as watching traditional cotton weavers on videotape. But all Taiwan is starting to feel like one huge theme park, a Confuciusland. Not so much Fantasy as Reality Island, this society seems dedicated to reminding the world that Chinese do not survive solely on shrewdness and rice, but also on generosity, refinement, and a dash of chutzpah. Taiwan's whole raison d'etre is being more Chinese than thou—especially when it comes to that most time-honored of Chinese measuring sticks, the sumptuousness of banquets.

"I want our next generation to inherit the very best of our culture," Mary Yang says with no undue pretension. "I want them to continue to have a Chinese soul."

For gourmets, Fu Yuan is the Taiwan's true Palace Museum. Have we hit pay dirt? Could this be our leading contender? If it isn't the best Chinese restaurant on earth, this Fragrant Garden is certainly the most beautiful.

Generalissimo Fish

In Taiwan, life is just something that happens between meals. With each of them, our mood seems to be improving. So what if there are too many phalanxes of motorcycles roaring off at each intersection, too many Kentucky Fried Chickens? If my eyes throb as much from the clashing welter of signs as from the chemical tinge in the air? By the time Mei and I stumble on Taipei's main baseball stadium—where a professional league builds on the fame of numerous Little League world champions—I'm enthralled to have discovered the only bleachers studded with carved dragons.

Forty-five floors above Taipei's brown, kidney-shaped sprawl, Mei and I are lunching with the Commissioner of Native Peoples. Trying to figure out why we've been summoned to these heights, I can hardly concentrate on the Yangtze River's superb Shanghainese dumplings. I'm not even sure what "natives" the government means. Certainly, the label does not refer to the indigenous Taiwanese, suppressed, even slaughtered in ways subtle and obvious ever since the mainland Kuomintang took over where the occupying Japanese left off. Only when the minister yields to an articulate adjutant do I realize that our hosts want to score points by comparing the Chinese occupation of Tibet with Taiwan's relatively benign treatment of their heavily showcased aboriginals—whose eighty tribes comprise three hundred thousand of the island's twenty-plus million populace.

"Taiwan tolerates everyone, according to the principles of Doctor Sun Yat-sen. Here, we've got eighty Buddhist centers, with many lamas," this exiled Tibetan boasts. Like so many others, he's here to prepare for a day of triumphant and vengeful return. But he holds himself in check when he notices that I'm having trouble listening while stuffing my face.

"Take your time," the spokesman says with a laugh. "This isn't Hong Kong, where all people live for is making money. In Taiwan, our tribal people keep the atmosphere easygoing."

Mei and I want to see for ourselves by visiting the high country that makes up most of the island beyond hectic Taipei. After all, man cannot live by Chinese food alone—not even a man spared from his aloneness by one Chinese woman. Could this be a maxim from a mutant fortune cookie? There are no fortune cookies in Taiwan, but there are plenty of mountains.

In the mezzanine of Taipei's modern train station, tekka maki and other seaweed rolls are available along with hanging strips of Cantonese barbecue and "California-style" pizza topped with curry, pineapple, tuna, bacon, and baby ears of corn. This isn't a food court but a food fight. Streamlined trains take us down the industrialized west coast through unaesthetic jumbles of poured concrete and advertising banners. Wandering through Changhua's motorcycle exhaust, Mei manages to discern the red gates of a Confucian temple. Across the street, we find what one Taipei food columnist calls "the finest pork chop noodles." In this unadorned stand, the chef boasts of knowing which time of year each part of the pig reaches its optimum moistness. This is the Taiwanese equivalent of finding that rare drive-in that still cuts its own french fries from fresh potatoes. The end result is still fries, or in this case, a homey bowl of noodles.

As soon as a rickety bus starts climbing toward the island's high-elevation interior, Taiwan reverts to its primal state as rugged Pacific Rim nub and tribal stomping grounds. I'm not certain if the rueful and wonderfully lived-in faces of our fellow passengers are the result of Polynesian genes or the harshness of peasant life. The cheekbones are more rounded, the eyes more winking and crow-footed than in any Han Chinese I've ever seen. There's something familiarly Indian in the stoicism, or downright fatalism, of the red-faced driver who replies to our inquiries about his frequent stops by proclaiming, "You'll get there when we get there." A fine philosophy for all forms of travel.

"There" is a clump of resort hotels perched around Sun Moon Lake, a shimmering field of tranquility in Taiwan's exact middle. Honeymooners favor get-acquainted sessions beside these amorous shores, but the name loses some of its romance when a chagrined grocer explains, "Once, we had a Sun Lake and a Moon Lake, until the Japanese dammed them up." Getting to our very own seventh-floor balcony just before sunset, Mei and I watch paddle boats and pagodas float in and out of a Zen-like mist.

In the village, we run a gauntlet of food stalls piled high with fetid dried cuttlefish and barbecued octopi shiny enough to have been irradiated. So Mei and I follow every other tour group in signing up for dinner in the Skyline Hotel. While waiting for our table, the manager of the lobby tea shop prepares us one sample after another. This porcelain-skinned lady's arched eyebrows and dignified bearing belie a natural hospitality. She is all too glad to suffer my endless questions about the difference between oolong and osthmanthus flower. Deftly, and with due seriousness, she manipulates a tiny pottery set, knowing when the brew is ready and the tea exhausted, how to maintain a constant temperature by sloshing water outside as well as inside the pot. Tea tasting, like wine tasting, is a lifetime's pursuit. These mountain areas of Taiwan produce some of the medicinal brews most beloved by all Chinese.

The hotel food is bracing, too. A stir-fry of local mushrooms, chicken with peanuts, and a bean curd soup are all washed down with hot rice wine. The house specialty is straight from the lake. "This was Chiang Kai-shek's favorite," explains our deferential waitress. "We call it President's Fish."

Even in the boondocks, it's hard to get far from the lingering presence of the Generalissimo. Back upstairs, Mei and I cozy up to a late-night TV broadcast of *The Barefoot Contessa* with Mandarin subtitles.

"How many hotel rooms have we stayed in by now?" Mei asks, snuggling up.

"Do you think we'll lose the thrill if we ever use the same mattress twice?" I second. What do we call this honeymoon that starts before the marriage? A prenuptial perambulation? A shotgun vacation?

A clammy December fog shrouds the lake by morning. A local cabbie is happy to shuttle us the fifteen miles to the much-advertised Taiwan Aboriginal Center. We're practically the only ones who buy a ticket to stroll the "villages" meant to evoke various tribes' traditional architecture. But the bark huts and log-hewn long houses come with lots of explanatory signs and refuse bins. So stark are these holding pens for humans that I'm almost relieved that we spot only one or two aboriginal janitors, toting authentic brooms. When a group of Taiwanese school kids pause to gawk at the only hairy barbarian in sight, I have to wonder just who's in the zoo.

The east coast of the island is billed as Taiwan's Big Sur, a string of towns protected from development by its plunging coastal range. Four hours by train from Taipei, we disembark at Hualien, a port town where I'm hoping to see more of the dominant Ami tribe. Mei wants to retrace the steps of her writing idol, the reclusive novelist Zhang Ailing, who wrote about her adventures among the Ami of Hualien and caused something of a scandal by reporting that she'd been bitten by fleas in her hotel. When the touchy Taiwanese reacted in angry denial, Zhang conceded that "the fleas must have been brought from the mainland." In the current standoff of missiles pointed across the Taiwan Straits, all sides could use such tact.

Hualien features rows of Bossini Benneton boutiques. But we sign on for the morning tour to Taroko Gorge, hyped to us as "better than the Grand Canyon." Surely, the quickest path to disappointment is to compare heaps of rocks, degrees of natural wonder. After a stop to promote purchases of the local jade, our forty-five-minute ride brings us to the scenic wonder's painted gateway. Away from the coast, Taroko's dense hills and striated cliffs keep narrowing, improving the view of turquoise waters below. More remarkable is the road that winds through numerous tunnels blasted from the steep walls. Not merely Taiwan's number one scenic attraction, Taroko is considered a monument to nationhood because four hundred and fifty workers died while completing this last link of the cross-island highway. Eleven million dollars was spent on the project at a time when, as our guide admits, "Taiwan was still an underdeveloped country."

At the top is the village of Tienhsiang, where everything remains nicely undeveloped. One tour member, rushing back with the rest for a free lunch, can't believe Mei and I are getting off when "there's nothing here." Nothing but miles of national park trails offering spectacular views and waterfalls; a Buddhist monastery across a mountain footbridge where we watch a pack of bald-headed nuns doing meditative labors; and a row of open-air restaurants heaped with steam tables of cabbage and black mushrooms. After an hour's hike through a mountain flank covered in straight-spine bamboo, Mei and I find the noodles especially bracing. No world's best restaurant is in sight in Taiwan's outer reaches, but we've never had better proof of Mei's proverb, "Hunger makes the best chef."

If I had come to Taiwan for the food, I would come back for its mountains. Tantalized by the possibility of stumbling on some hearty country inn, what we've found is an island unleashed from the burdens of an imposed cold-war identity. Mei and I even yield to our first and last "aboriginal culture" show advertised back in Hualien. Gift shops featuring the Asian equivalent of carved totems line the way to a large, concrete tent simulation where "warriors" with clip-on mikes and echo effects belt out chants to listless drumming. Even before the gods have been blessed, several busloads of Japanese men have been roused out of their seats and into the primal daisy chain by the lure of close contact with over-the-hill maidens in feathered headdresses. The Samurai clan seem to know the steps better than the indigenous Ami. Nothing translates quicker than the banal.

I'm about to scratch up another evening to ethnographic emptiness when our hotel's chatty driver takes our entire vanload on an unscheduled detour. I figure that he's just trying to stretch his ride for the sake of a bigger tip. Then he leads us all out onto a bluff and speaks with sincere devotion about the beauty of the few tankers moored in the dark of Hualien's tiny harbor. Before we know it, he insists on inviting all of us for a late-night supper at a popular seaside park. Lining scruffy dirt paths through a rutted field are the usual games of fortune, a potent cloud of stinky tofu, and steaming shrimp.

Our guide seems to know every vendor and just what to order. He secures a long picnic table at the back of an area set before a small, empty stage. But no matter how much beer arrives, how many heaps of noodles and crab legs, our driver shakes off all offers of money. Instead, he grabs one of my Taiwanese bills and holds it beside his face.

For the first time, I notice that he has very unusual features—deep-set, rounded eyes that appear greenish; nut-brown skin; and a bulbous nose to go with a clenched Ray Charles grin. It's his bald dome and squint that bear a striking resemblance to the equally hairless Chiang Kai-shek portrayed on the bill. Handing back the money, he asks rhetorically, "Why would I want you to give me more of my own picture?"

It's Mei who then realizes that he, too, must be an Ami. "Half Ami," he admits. "But I'm married to one!"

There are no formalities with him, no sense of obligation regarding any moment but this very one. It's amazing how quickly one can recognize it when one spots it. Exactly how many thousands of miles will people travel to be in the presence of one truly happy man?

"Let's drink to being on this earth together!" Our guide toasts us all with a clink of Taiwan beer. As he does, music pours out of the speakers onstage. The nightly karaoke singalong is about to get underway. Naturally, our Taiwanese Zorba is practically the first volunteer. He even grabs Mei by the hand and gets her to add her wavering soprano to make a perfect duet.

During this command performance, I notice that many in the crowd at these outdoor tables look quite a bit like our guide. There's a surplus of pug noses, broad foreheads, wide and easily elicited smiles. Our guide moves easily among them, greeting old friends. Just when I'm going to pester him about being taken to an honest-to-god Ami village, I realize that we're plunk in the midst of one. The spirit of the tribe is right here. And if travel is a kind of religion, this has to be one of the holier moments. On the brink of moving on, there's nothing like finding you've already arrived.

The Steamer Gap

For nearly forty years, martial law kept things quiet in Chiang Kai-shek's capital. Today, unfettered voting means that metal shutters have cracked down on every Taipei storefront. Maybe the Generalissimo's ghost is skipping about this instant ghost town.

The only signs of life within blocks of our hotel are at the neighborhood headquarters of the opposition Democratic Progressive Party. The devoted student activist supervising a squad of volunteer canvassers looks like the very Asian echo of myself when I worked for Clean Gene McCarthy's antiwar campaign.

"Today could be the most significant date in Taiwanese history," proclaims this starry-eyed kid sporting Beatle-like mop, black turtleneck, and granny glasses. If polls hold true, long-time opposition leader Chen Shui-bian is poised to become the first pro-independence mayor of Taipei. The successful completion of these regional elections will pave the way for the country's first open presidential contest, further deepening rifts with China. Asks this kid who would be more at home in Berkeley than Beijing, "Isn't it obvious that we're distinct from China, following our own path?"

Ironically, it's the hard-line anti-Communists of old who are still pushing for the ultimate vindication of reunification—and pleased to see increasing mutual ties between Taiwan and the increasingly capitalist mainland. More ironically, the rising clamor for a complete break with the past may be the very thing to bring down the full weight of that past. Any formal declaration of independence would likely provoke a Chinese invasion.

There will be no fireworks until the polls close tonight. In the meantime, the party activist knows his restaurants as well as his politics. He sends us along a desolate stretch of East Minchuan Road, and on second inspection Mei spots a rough-hewn wooden sign bearing the Chinese characters, "My House, Your House." We feel instantly welcomed in two wood-paneled rooms subdivided with fish tanks. This "house" offers a perfect winter melon soup and a terrific eggplant in brown sauce laced with basil.

"Mmm, just like Thai food!" Mei purrs. But the son of this house, back from studies in Australia, assures us that the use of basil is characteristically Hakkanese. This is our first of many encounters with the cooking of China's gypsies, the so-called "guest people" who wandered from the far North all the way to Taipei.

Our next fortuitous accident is to head toward Taipei's historic Wanhua district. With all attractions closed, we'll have something to see just by strolling through this "Chinatown" of an all-Chinese city. In a triangular patch of exoticism near the riverfront, most of the soot-blackened alleyways are literally given over to the dead. Dank warehouses display coffins and fanciful paper houses for eternity. The mortuary business carries on, politicking or no, and so does Lungshan Temple. This place is Taipei's Chartres, a cathedral to the kitchen gods that can only be classified as Frigidaire baroque. Here, we find a heartfelt fervency for ancient beliefs, unscathed by Communist China's antireligious campaigns. But even "religious" Chinese eschew posed spirituality or strict codes of behavior. Worshippers line up for half a block to throw wood blocks that provide a simple yes or no answer to all life's questions.

Lungshan also served as a sanctuary for Taiwan's democratic dissidents. Now, in this one locale, Mei and I get to view both of Taiwan's guiding passions. The main reason for the long queues is that the temple is doubling as an electoral station. The armed soldiers posted at several gates wave at us to come closer rather than shooing us away. They want the whole world to give Taiwan credit for its orderly balloting. Elections may cover a multitude of sins, but this one certainly makes a vivid contrast to China's succession game of seeing which octogenarian leader will reach for the respirator first. Even the Taiwanese kiddies get to help their moms pull the lever.

Soon, we are making the rounds of every shrine *cum* precinct. Inside a gray facade reminiscent of an American fire station, a group of elderly gentlemen use the temple for a social gathering. The conversation is aided by the crunching of soy-roasted melon seeds and the sipping of a knockout concentrate of oolong. Kung fu tea, they call it both here and on the mainland, because, as Mei explains, "the meaning of kung and fu is time and effort." A temple orderly accomplishes this ritual infusion through so much shuffling, so swift and sure a pouring and repouring out of tiny cups, that he could be mistaken for a card shark. After a moment's gawking, the men beckon us to join their circle on pint-sized stools. We even get initiated into that great vice of the East, chewing betel nut. The old pros laugh knowingly when small wads of the sour stuff give Mei and me brief, nauseating hot flashes.

One slick character sporting more gold jewelry than a Jersey mobster turns out to be the resident geomancer, an expert on propitious acts. But he doesn't have an opinion until he's referred to a large, glossy book of numerological charts. It's a kind of racing form for the universe, available at every local newsstand.

"So what's the luckiest day for us to get married?" I inquire. The fellow gets on the case right away, but he can't recall if his calendar holds true for events on the other side of the International Date Line. In a gesture that's ninety-nine and forty-four-hundredths pure Taiwan, he seeks an answer by whipping out a pocket-sized cellular phone in the midst of the temple and dialing up a pal in—guess where?—New Jersey. Naturally, he gets an answering machine. Our consultation ends in a deeper haze than when we began.

Like us, the tea circle hangs around to witness the opening of the neighborhood's ballot box, accomplished with the zeal of a New England town meeting. "And back when the Kuomintang ran China," an astonished Mei recalls, "they used to post signs in the restaurants that read 'No Talking Politics!' "

Now every tally is proudly read aloud. "The old days are gone," one of the tea sippers muses. "Now husband and wife don't even vote the same way." At this rate, it will take hours to get a count. But once we hop a cab toward the pro-independence candidate's headquarters, we're stalled by a huge celebration ahead. So we get out to walk, only to find ourselves smack in front of the noodle shop we'd been trying to locate back on our first day in Taipei.

Serendipity has led us to Ding Tai Feng, a neighborhood storefront that catapulted to culinary fame when a Japanese magazine rated it "the number one soft snack house in the world." There's no trouble distinguishing the place because the entire ground floor is occupied by an army of flour-dusted dumpling stuffers. By the time we've negotiated this strangest of restaurant entries, I feel like I'm batter-coated and ready for the deep-fry.

Upstairs, Ding Tai Feng is sterile enough to be labeled "Mc-

Dumpling's." On three floors are narrow, track-lit rooms that are all white Formica. As we peruse a long checklist of authentically juicy ravioli that come in a growing stack of bamboo steamers, I realize that this is also the Chinese equivalent of our trendy, fresh pasta stores. The quick turnover insures that every order is up-to-the-minute, every bite is properly moist.

"The secret is that every dough is different, more or less elastic, with varying flours and amounts of water or yeast," explains Ding Tai Feng's sociable owner. "My father started out making peanut oil. I'm not even sure of the name of the business, just that a *ding* is a kind of wine vessel. When he realized that homemade oils were growing obsolete, he hired a chef to make dumplings. Now we're known all over the world. The only trouble is that the Chinese eat quickly—a maximum of forty minutes—while these Japanese tourists like to drink and take their time."

He isn't boasting, just soberly offering himself up as another example of Taiwan's miraculous growth. "In middle school, I dreamed of having my own bicycle. By the time I was in the army, it was a motorcycle. Now, I can afford more than a few cars. And that's just in one lifetime!"

But the owner's pride is also linked to the old country. "My uncle was a graduate of one of the K.M.T.'s famous military schools. So we had to leave in 1949. All my family thought they'd be going home very shortly. Now we're criticized for buying a house back on the mainland. But aren't we still one people?"

The question needs no answer, not when we're scarfing down *bao zi* and *jiao zi* better than Beijing's. On our way to the rally for the pro-independence Min Jin Party, this owner offers the more entrenched point of view of a Kuomintang loyalist. In accepting the inherent power of mainland China, there may be a bit of the old fatalism—but there's also a grudging respect for adversaries still considered close relations.

"What's the point of pretending otherwise, especially when we can grow closer through investments? If we declare ourselves a sovereign country, we can never compete with their numbers. The mainland will wipe us out."

I don't see how that big, bad nation can pull off an invasion when it can't even run a restaurant that's as clean, quick, and superb as Ding Tai Feng. To my mind, a prosperous Taiwanese like this should be sitting pretty. In his eyes, I see only fear of the Chinese, fear of the native Taiwanese, fear of the future. As Mei says on our way out, "I'm sure that he already has his U.S. green card." On our table, we leave behind a tower of bamboo steamers starting to resemble a model rocket ship. Instead of worrying about a missile gap, this proprietor should take heart from his advantage in steamed buns.

Or from the joyous mobs in the street. So clogged is one of Taipei's major intersections that we can't possibly hear the returns being announced or glimpse the speaker's podium, set under an enormous billboard bearing the Progressive Democrats' logo—four open hands joined by an orange flame. The hundred thousand people who block our path are waiting for a victory speech by Chen Shuibian, the first pro-independence Taiwanese to win Taipei's mayoralty. Hundreds of kites fly overhead, paper dragons bob and snake above the crowd, and firecrackers explode in all directions. At once, Mei and I are given party pins to wear and handed banners to wave. I have never seen Chinese, individually or in a group, acting so giddy. The event is like a combination of a Democratic National Convention and Chinese New Year's parade—only noisier.

Yet there's no hint of anger or violence in this crowd, just a venting of steam on this pressure-cooker island. When Chen Shuibian begins to speak, his high-pitched voice and deliberate cadence remind me of a nerdy chemistry prof. I can't quite visualize him as a Malcolm X or a Martin Luther King. One of his first acts as mayor, however, will be to remove from city offices all official portraits of Chiang Kai-shek. This makes quite a contrast to the winning Kuomintang gubernatorial candidate whose entire program consists of the single sentence, uttered before TV cameras with stunning Confucian fealty, "I will follow the instructions of beloved President Lee."

The young people around us—modeling baseball caps, pens clipped to their shirt pockets—look more like well-groomed lab technicians than dangerous radicals. Still I feel uplifted just to be among them. "Since the eyes of the world are upon us, we've got to try twice as hard to be a good country," explains a pretty schoolteacher over the din. Few lands live under such intense scrutiny or insecurity—or produce people with such a charged sense of mission. Used to plunging into chanting crowds, Mei grips my arm with more than the urgency of keeping together. "For a Chinese, to have a little say . . ." she is shouting over the din ". . . to control the fate, just one time . . . an American can't know what that means. . . ."

No wonder Taiwan remains such a threat to China—as military foe, economic rival, and now, electoral example. Though she's hardly a flag-waver for U.S.–style democracy, Mei's eyes are filling with tears. "One day perhaps . . . in Tiananmen!" I can just hear. "One day, like this!"

Lifting higher the excited daughter who rests on her shoulders to get a clear view, the schoolteacher next to us shouts happily, "Now we take history in our own hands!"

Southeast Asia

· · · · · · ·

GINGER TRAIL

Featured Restaurants:

Grand China Princess, Thailand
Royal Kitchen, Bangkok, Thailand
Maple Garden, Penang, Malaysia
Overseas Restaurant, Ipoh
Hang Cheng, Ipoh
Madame Fatso's, Malacca
Lim Tian Puan, Malacca
Fatty Lee's, Malacca
Moi Kong, Singapore
Mui Chun, Singapore
Prima Tower Revolving Restaurant, Singapore
Hai Tian Lo, Singapore
Gandi, Singaraja, Indonesia

Thai Me Up

I n a perfect world, Thailand would be to China what Thai food is
to Chinese cuisine: scented with trade winds, flavored by spice
routes, playfully hot-tempered yet delicately restrained.

"Lemon grass and basil—I can hardly wait!" says Mei of this new-
kid-on-the-ethnic-eating-block. The evening traffic from Don
Muang Airport makes her wait an hour, two hours longer. Mop-
haired monks turned mirthful teamsters wave, wink and sometimes
run circles around their trucks piled with coconuts. Motorcycle *tuk-
tuks* put-put in place, adding to the unbreathable mire. A sunset
turning from orange to purple gives an otherworldly glow to enormous lurid billboards, which alternate between portraits of the
Thais' four-eyed king and the friendly staff at the latest, industrial-
sized massage parlor. As I've warned Mei, Bangkok is far from a
creamy chafing dish of coconut milk curry.

What will she think of her first look at a non-Chinese Asia? And
just how "non-Chinese" is it? Our vantage point could not be better.
A Hong Kong public relations firm with an absurdist bent has procured us a thirty-sixth floor suite atop the Hotel Grand China
Princess. This newly opened white hulk rises above the city soot and
fumes looking like a grounded ocean liner. From our roost, one continuous curve of smoked glass shows us the entire course of the
muddy Chao Praya River, clogged with speedboats and studded with
hotels. But the Thai capital is as planless and anarchic from above as
it is at ground level. The numerous temple spires look like the upraised tails of horseshoe crabs, stuck in an urban mud.

We spy none of the usual Mandarin gates marking ethnic bound-
aries. Braving hot twisters of fine-ground litter and motorcycle exhaust, we descend into a Chinatown that's among the world's oldest
and least easily delineated. So why not call this a Chinaclump, Chi-
nasphere, Chinarama? Quaint ghettoizing doesn't apply in Bangkok,
where the Chinese settlement actually predates the city. Estimated
at sixteen percent of the country, the Chinese have been intermin-
gling with Thais since the eleventh century. The national unifier
King Taksin, or Rama the Ninth, was widely known to be the son of
a Chinese. When he moved his capital to Thonburi, some three

thousand Chinese merchants followed and set up shop across the river in Sampeng. Eventually, he joined the Chinese in crossing over to create Bangkok. The king of *The King and I*—a minstrel show that insulted the Thais—was more likely to have looked like the Last Emperor than Yul Brynner. By the turn of this century, ninety percent of the Thai court had Chinese ancestry—leading to King Wachirawut's virulent campaign against the merchant class he termed "the Jews of the East." The very creation of the name Thailand grew out of national ambitions to regain institutions and territory long ceded to the Chinese.

Only here, in a land less tolerant than advertised, have the Chinese given up their vaunted family names. Yesterday's Sam Poon Kee is today's Suriwong Pramsapikipol. This doesn't help us any in spotting Chinese restaurants, especially when storefronts are plastered with the doubly inscrutable squiggle of Thai script. What lures people to the Chinese quarter aren't carrots, but karats. On prime corners for noodle joints, there are jewelers' counters, as overlit as pinball arcades, packed three-deep with a constant crush of women. The lines are for gold, or, to be exact, the white gold chains and trinkets so valued by Thais for investment and flaunting. The twenty or so Chinatown goldsmiths, one chef explains, "are trusted for providing percentages that are true."

Where Sampeng alley parallels the sooty riverfront, the specialties seem to be plastic buckets and piles of brocade, mangoes, and charcoal-charred satay sticks. The few pagoda turrets have been placed at the back of recessed courtyards. Chinese temples are announced mostly by splashes of color at the back of dank shops—red streamers, lucky numbers backed with gilt. Finding an explanation for every votive item would take a lifetime. We settle for a snapshot that proves we've been somewhere. Joss sticks and kitchen gods—don't leave home without them!

In the home country of bird's nest, the Chinese can at least indulge themselves in the soup made from their favorite ingredient. Collected by climbers who brave the heights of caves along Thailand's southern coast, these salubrious coils of dried spittle can be had at the bargain rate of a hundred *baht*, or four bucks per bowl. Numerous bare-bones cafes offer all-you-can-slurp of this prized swirl of tasteless, nearly translucent matting served in sugar water and topped on request with a poached egg. Other shops feature superb rice porridge laced with chunks of steelhead—so fresh the fish are hacked up before your eyes on a sidewalk block of teak. None of these are the kind of snack I favor when the temperature is over a hundred. But the Chinese prefer to keep what they ingest in the lukewarm range of the living.

In a filthy three-floor cavern that must be the world's most inappropriately titled Shangri-la Restaurant, young waitresses smirking like cigarette girls tote a minimal assortment of dim sum on metal trays strapped to their waists. Are these really pork buns or just cupcakes doused with cilantro? Like the rest of the Hong Kong tour groups that come through, we find ourselves retreating into the dust-free sanctuary of our hotel's restaurant. Besides, the suave Chinese-Thai manager invites us to sample what he calls "the best Peking duck in the world." The dim sum rank high, but we don't have the heart to tell him that the brittle skin served with thick, soft buns is a Cantonese cousin to the real thing.

An audience with the owner of the Grand China Princess provides us a glimpse into the Thai-Chinese elite. The grandfather came here from southern China about 120 years ago, the father is the austere lord of numerous real-estate holdings, while the son and heir looks just the way one would expect—prematurely chubby, hair parted and Brylcreemed straight back, wearing a navy blue blazer. He's just gotten home from four years at Tufts, near Boston.

"Trading is in our blood," says this scion, speaking what could be the creed of the bulk of fifty-five million overseas Chinese who have long lived in Southeast Asia, or Nanyang, as they call this limp claw jutting from the motherland's distended belly. By recent estimates, the trading has been good enough to earn them one-quarter more than the annual income of all China's billion-plus. Where ancestral ties govern business connections, the young man quickly points out that his heritage is Chaozhou, also spelled Teochiu. Supposedly, their syndicates have long controlled Thailand's opium traffic. More Chaozhou people can be found in Bangkok than in their original Chinese home of Shantou.

In an understatement, the young preppy tells me that the Thais and the Chinese have become "very well blended." His father adds, "Being Buddhists, the Thais are closer to our traditions." By now, it's hardly news when the old man informs me, "Restaurants aren't one of the traditional businesses here." The reason is that "most of the Chinese millionaires started with a small grocery or imports store. There was a big change in the sixties, when foreigners were allowed to own land. When Chinese prosper, the Thais prosper." The kid from Tufts puts the Chinese ethos succinctly: "I like to live in the States, but I prefer to make money here."

One brief exports boom ago, whatever was right about Asia was in Thailand—spirituality, charm, proud artistic traditions. When I drag Mei past the gauntlet of touts who line the way to the Temple of the Emerald Buddha, each one assures us, "Today palace close. National holy day!"

We've almost turned around and been coaxed into a cab, when we decide to seek confirmation ten steps beyond. There the world's most dazzling aggregate of spun glass mosaics is clearly open for business. Next stop, at the Temple of the Reclining Buddha, we don't even bother to stop when the Thais shout, "National holy day, sir! You go see parade in Chinatown?"

Later we do, but there's no parade. The land of smiles has become the land of guile. Our disillusionment deepens at Tum Nak Thai, which bills itself as "the world's biggest restaurant." In this suburban complex, the waitresses roller-skate between teak pavilions set on grounds no more mystical than a miniature golf course. Only tourists are eating here—a telling augury—and the greasy, half-baked Thai-Chinese dishes come with numerous unspecified charges on the bill.

After too many such experiences, I'm driven to look up an American ex-pat who works as a food critic writing under a Thai alias. Few have been able to tell that so erudite an aficionado of their cuisine is actually a *farang*, as foreigners are derided. Bob, a fair-haired sheep dog patting the sweat from his forehead with nearly every step, is the very opposite of the typical Asian hand. No bush jacket, no ambassadorial-level name dropping, no leering jokes about native beauties. He does double duty as the newspaper's classical music reviewer.

"I'm not even much of a traveler," he admits. "This was just the first place I got to and I have never been able to figure out how to leave." The humor downplays his passionate attachment to this town's every spice, fragrance, and sorry street spectacle—and his ability to huff and puff through its sooty, serpentine alleys. He takes us to several fine Sampeng noodle shops, then on for some rare Thai treats in teak-shuttered mansions just blocks from Thailand's various ministry offices. For a few hours, Bangkok reverts to the repository of Asia's courtliest culture.

All that's forgotten when Mei insists on a peek at Asian flesh on sale in the smoky lounges along Patpong Road. The famed girlie bars now co-exist with a souvenirs market that seems considerably more profitable. At Mei's insistence, we follow one haggard madam up-stairs and nurse beers in a booth while observing some of the Ori-ent's least appealing specimens of femininity. After so many turns around the block, they're assigned ping pong detail—which means squatting to pop sporting goods out of their lower orifice. Strings of razor blades, shown to cut paper, are shoved up labia dulled to all sensation. In my younger days, hormonal reflexes might have moved me to plunge into this orgy of wholesale disappointment. Now these gymnastics of the twat rate a perfect zero.

"When a society tolerates women's suffering so openly," Mei preaches, more bored than scandalized, "it's no wonder everyone loses their morals."

Or their marbles. At this point, I'd rather see the Thais legalize honesty. And the main bargains of the East that interest me are some very special bolts of Thai silk. Who would have thunk that just a condom's throw from the Silk Lips Massage Parlor, I'd be arranging for my wedding suit? My only choice now is whether to go with Good Humor white or a faded creme. In one particularly inviting shop, amidst snoozing kittens and fabrics of every known shade, a small village of women set about helping Mei pick out a pattern for her nuptial gown. That's tough enough under normal circumstances, but we haven't yet determined where and when to stage the big event, if we'll break a glass or swear allegiance to Chairman Mao.

"You Catholic?" barefoot lady tailors inquire, heads slightly bent in respect, searching for both the appropriate design and fantasy. "You Buddha? You city hall?"

Mei and I look at one another and shrug. Aside from trying to balance informality with sentimentality, we've got to arrange the participation of two sets of divorced parents residing on three continents.

"A marriage of inconvenience," Mei finally mutters, but these women didn't get her joke.

"Same same," says the Thais, who never stay perplexed for long. "You look in book, okay missy?"

I don't mind waiting out the afternoon for them to pick a pattern because these gentle seamstresses are the first Thais who make us feel welcome. Their boss is Chinese—a writer in his off-hours who serves as the president of Thailand's association of Chinese art and literature. His grandfather was a rice exporter who sent his descendants back to study Chinese culture in Canton. The head tailor assures us that there's even a Beijing opera troupe in Bangkok's Chinatown.

Along with proper measurements, we get a restaurant recommendation. Off Silom Road, that mire of construction, Hindu money changers, and rinky-dink pizza parlors, we hunt for the Royal Kitchen—part of a luxurious Hong Kong chain done up with huge murals of flying geese. The young Chinese manager says she feels "happy belonging to the Thai nation." Though the dishes come with more carved rosettes than food, she's also rightfully proud of the Cantonese fillet with black bean and a stand-out lemon chicken.

"We Chinese can't eat all Asian food," the young woman voices a common sentiment, "but all Asians can eat Chinese."

I'm not sure that proves Chinese superiority or insularity. Like the people who produce it, Thai cooking is explosive but limited in range. Reeling from too many chilis and too many half-truths, Mei and I are thankful to come away with one good meal and two wedding suits.

Laksa Luck

This is how it's supposed to work: balmy breezes, friendly porters, honest cabbies, a quick ride through a tropical isle half-tamed and half-exotic to a mildewed room where Somerset Maugham might have stayed. Beyond the pointlessly opulent Hotel Eastern and Oriental, a stroll along a moonlit, very Eastern and Oriental sea facing shuttered streets where the only menace comes in the form of a bidding war between horse-drawn buggies. Malaysia is Asia as country club, and Penang is its opening tee.

Hesitating before our very first sidewalk restaurant, Mei and I are beckoned to share a meal with the Pohs, an engineer couple up from Singapore with two kids and a Filipina maid to visit old Dad, who combines Malay vocabulary with Chinese obsessiveness to describe how much prawn paste makes a true shrimp *sambal*, how much tamarind in the red sauce makes a proper shrimp *assam*.

"Eat more," is the patriarch's familiar philosophy, "so you'll remember the dish!"

How can we ever forget Penang's crustaceans or this arrival? On this shrimpy island enclave, surprisingly unchanged and unbloated by beachcomber trade, even the outlying seaside promenades are highly civilized. Hawker stand after stand is cleaner and more fragrant than the next, offering us outdoor samples of such concoctions as *laksa*, a fish soup thick as molasses; *apom*, a crepe with a hint of shrimp puff; *kway teoh*, or bean flour threads in thick soy-based gravy; or the more recognizable cup o' noodles known here as *hokkien mee*. What's what with treats advertised as *wo mo cha cha* and *ba ba cha cha*? For four thousand Malaysian *ringgits*, approximately six hundred greenbacks, a party of eight can sup off a live *moo sei* fish, big as a tricycle and more lividly white in its tank than anything in sight, including me. Dining out beside the sea in short-sleeved batiks and getting serenaded by almond-eyed cowgirls in ten-gallon hats, I've never seen local Chinese looking so relaxed.

Malaysia is not exactly a melting pot; it's more like pot luck. Three major ethnicities simmer away, emitting their full fragrance while rarely coming to a boil. Garish temples built by Chinese family associations co-exist happily with domed Malay mosques and lemonade-pink Indian shrines. Under Penang's shaded boardwalks, all religions are outnumbered by magazine stands catering to Asia's most literate and sophisticated populace—one beneficial legacy of the British rule that forced all these peoples together. When the country became independent in 1957, the British forced the Malays into a pledge of equal rights for their large Chinese and Indian communities. After a failed insurrection led by the legendary Chinese guerrilla leader Thaiking, the thirty-plus percent Chinese have been virtually barred from attaining high political office. Even in banking and commerce, a Malay elite has increasingly muscled out Chinese investors.

On the food front, however, all indigenous outlets have long been outnumbered by the heavily patronized, one-dish franchises of "Hainan chicken-rice." Why bother with Colonel Sanders when you've got the original recipe of General Tso? These horizontally hacked strips of wonderfully moist bird sitting on bland scoops of broth-soaked grain strike me as a most tasty fare for sick men. As we learn, the dish was invented by the stewards imported by the British from China's tropical isle. But Penang boasts nearly as many Indian stands, where circles of *roti* dough are slapped on hot grills, adding a yeasty smell to the baking sidewalks. Here, Mei gets her first taste of curried lady fingers, yellow *biryani* rice eaten with fingers, temporarily betraying our mission to assess the spicy stew into which our favorite cuisine has been plopped. But why is it that the last thing one finds in urban Malaysia is a Malay? Maybe it has something to do with Malay food. For the first and last time, I coax Mei into a ghastly place where ceiling fans keep the flies off hunks of fish vertebrae that have been softened by weeks of sitting in a coconut sauce.

"No wonder the Malays are nervous about keeping us down," brags Mr. Sunny Lim, proprietor of the packed Maple Garden. "They've only got three ways to cook a bird while the Chinese have three hundred."

Who can doubt this suave owner once we've sampled his oysters and bean curd in a clay pot? Among the many dishes posted on wall menus, the waitress recommends fish maw as "good for complexion." The cooking here is more properly Cantonese, though Sunny's forebears hail from Shantou, the home city of the Chaozhou people, in these parts known as Teochews. If that's not confusing enough, Mr. Lim is soon whispering about keeping off-the-record certain topics relating to the fragile peace between ethnicities that is the dominant factor in Malaysia's politics. More telling than any rumor is the universal reversion to hushed, fearful tones. The whispers are a bow to the increasing repression of Prime Minister Mathahir, referred to eerily as "the universal warrior," whose every godlike pronouncement about the advance of Islam is the daily headline in Malaysian papers.

"The Malays are not diligent," Sunny Lim will concede, in an understatement of how the Chinese view their more languorous hosts. "Most Chinese here speak at least four languages. We send our kids to be educated in the States or England. But the trouble is that while we may have a few mistresses here and there, the Malays can have four wives each! So their population keeps outstripping ours!" It's ironic to hear a Chinese complaining about somebody else's ability to breed.

Soon, our own population crisis looms. Just when we've begun to bask in Penang's balm, we're brought back to reality by a tropical delay in Mei's monthly period.

"What will we do about all our research?" she begins our latest duet on the theme of impending familyhood, performed on a balcony overlooking jungle-choked curves of coastline.

"We can get it done in nine months, easy. Prenatal nutrition will never get this good."

For men of my Peter Pan generation, fatherhood is proof of having overcome one's dysfunction. But coming from a country where it's said that "having a child is as easy as laying an egg," Mei finds greater distinction in refraining from the burdens of reproduction. Can it really be that I'm the one arguing that we "accept fate" while my Chinese wife-to-be wants to master hers?

"We don't have to sacrifice everything just to be the same as other people," Mei argues. Another of her favorite sayings is that "Marriage is a package deal." And I have to admit that if Mei were just another aspiring housewife, I would never have been attracted to her in the first place.

"The world doesn't lack kids, just people who love them. Besides, a writer has to think first of the creations from his or her mind. It's so selfish to love only one's own blood. We can nurture other people's children . . . help orphans!"

"Either way, we'll face it together," I try to calm my own near-orphan.

Still, I'm extra careful to keep Mei from straining herself as we board a local bus for Ipoh. Three hours later, the monotony of undulating rain forest gives way to a bluish landscape dotted with a remarkable eruption of limestone nubs. The setting is strikingly like Gweilin, craggy inspiration of China's classical brush-and-ink reveries. But Mei and I aren't stopping here to plumb the mysteries of this valley's many natural caves.

Ipoh ("ee-po") is the capital of the state of Perak, which is Malay for silver. It was a tin mining boom at the turn of the century that drew many Cantonese immigrants into these foothills of the Malay Peninsula's central range. "City of Millionaires," they dubbed Ipoh back in those heady days. Now the place looks plain busted. The blocks near the bus station are half boarded-up and the billboards for shave creams and shrimp pastes haven't been changed in years. There's little evidence of Malaysia's high-tech boom, almost no flashing neon and not one chain hotel. Like vultures circling under a hot son, we head toward what remains of a modest guest house. The closer we get to the town center, the more shadows deepen and the populace appears to have run for cover. I feel like we're the only ones let loose on a film lot, suitably dusty for Westerns or Easterns.

"If you want to see old China, come to Malaysia!" Mei inadvertently coins some future tourist board campaign. Her discerning eye has recognized the peculiar cast to Ipoh's lulling time warp. Back in some archetypal South Chinese village, the posts supporting the covered boardwalks must have been painted up this gaudily, with red pictographs running down pulsing yellow. Once upon a time, the shop fronts in Canton must indeed have looked like these high-ceilinged slots of dank concrete, piled with sacks full of spice or stacks of gold leaf, inventoried by a scrawny patriarch at his abacus, identified with family name calligraphed in black on a wooden signboard. Though Ipoh's steamy boulevards are still broad enough for horse traffic, the main clatter now comes from the hammering of coffin makers. Instead of pigtailed rickshaw riders, the street traffic consists mainly of packs of schoolgirls: the Chinese in itchy gray knee pants and the Malays in one-piece jumpsuits with veils that leave a vapor trail of orange chiffon.

On every main corner, tiny wizards in khaki shorts lower wicker baskets of noodle coils into perpetually steaming cauldrons. "Restoran Wang" read the signs in Malay. "Kedai Kopi Swatow" for Swatow Coffee Shop. As though in a trance, Mei and I seek out shade and ceiling fans, then bend before bowls we must cool with our breath. The kway teoh for which Ipoh is justly renowned are slippery, see-through threads of noodle plunged in a brown sludge with a hint of fish sauce that has the viscosity of used motor oil. The Chinese specialty called "Ants Climbing a Tree" has shimmied up a coconut. While lusciously filling, I can't say that they are my favorite hot-weather snack. Still, Mei and I nurse our lunches as long as we can in order to get through a day that barely seems to wane.

Near sunset, we wander in the direction of glittering onion domes that look to be the most exotic sight in town. Up close, fronted by a green lawn and hydrangea bushes, it's the old British train station, an imperial homage to orientalism, a mosque to the prophet of iron. Wandering back along the Ipoh River, we spot a giant ceiba across the bank, reaching up at least two hundred feet and drooping with a solid fringe of crawler vines. So grand is this natural monument to the tropics' unchoked growth that I can't help declaring, "Look! The tree of life!"

Mei and I are only killing time—knowing that we can no longer postpone discovering whether or not we've created life of our own.

"Come on, let's do it," Mei urges, and I know she means making a stop at a storefront medical clinic. The reception station is open to the street, the waiting room a bare bench to the side of the green-tiled hallway. The place looks clean enough and before Mei heads inside, the U.S.-trained doctor assures us he's not only able to give a pregnancy test, but fluent enough in English to explain the results. But we'll have to wait twenty-four hours more.

We might as well see the town, hardly a rough task when the first woman we stop to ask about the tastiest night market packs us into her beat-up station wagon along with hubby and three small daughters, and insists on treating us to the internationalist dessert of *roti pisang*—Indian puff bread stuffed with bananas and butterscotch. In turn, Mei picks out a prize watermelon with knowing taps and has it sliced up for the kids.

All night long, I try to imagine what our child might look like. When it comes to people, the mixed strains are the most beautiful. The blending of Asian-Caucasian, or Euro-Afro seems to bring out the best of both. But I'm not sure the same can be said about places. At first glimpse anyway, the visitor wants to trace some genealogy of design. Where Ipoh ceases to show its pure Chinese lineage, it grows ragged with tin-roofed huts on stilts, Hindu temples pink-frosted as birthday cakes. In Malaysia, I'm never quite sure which country I'm in. Perhaps Malaysians feel the same way.

"Now we're going down Hume Street, only now it's renamed Sultan Iskander," begins the taxi driver we flag down to take us on a morning tour of the outlying caves. To add to the confusion, our driver, John Soong, presents us with a card that calls him the president of several international trade associations, with addresses in Hong Kong and Taipei.

"I just come back to Ipoh to rest up," says this free trader whose scrawny neck pops cartoonlike out of a flowery Hawaiian shirt three times his size. "You need a courier, I'm your man. From Hong Kong to China, it's just a matter of knowing the right customs man."

"And the right price?" Mei teases.

"The Chinese invented everything, including corruption. So call on our services when it comes to transport . . ."

We press him no further on the nature of his shipments. It's tough enough figuring out what's happening inside the curious caves. Not content with mere caverns of stalactite, the Chinese have added gatekeepers, ticket-takers, pink fluorescent bulbs, carved proverbs, figurines of Buddhas, and warrior gods in glass cases. Atop one called Perak Tong, steps carved into the limestone butte lead up and around to spectacular views. Behind another holy spot, there's a thousand baby tortoises struggling for life in a few inches of muddy, dirty water. At our insistence, John drives us ten minutes further into lush countryside, where one humongous arc of a cave opens onto undisturbed fish ponds and highland foothills. It feels as though we've stumbled upon the center of the earth.

For a tip, we treat our cabbie to a meal at the Overseas, no doubt Ipoh's fanciest Cantonese place. Four lasses in silk tunics attend every table. The shrimp with chilis are superb; the chicken in clay pots of the highest order. But no sweet and sour, like the way the Chinese have been treated.

"You know why the Chinese have problems here that they don't in Thailand?" John Soong asks. "In Malaysia and Indonesia, they're Muslims. They don't eat pork."

How does this country manage with one constitution when they need three separate cookbooks? But Chinese here also blame their failure to win full participation on the Chinese Communist leadership's refusal to stand up for their "overseas comrades."

"Mao and Zhou washed their hands of us, saying we were Malaysians," our driver complains. "Otherwise, 5-13-69 might never have happened."

"5-13-69?" The code sounds straight out of a spy movie.

"May 13, the Malays went on a rampage in Kuala Lumpur. Thousands of Chinese vanished. Young couples were pulled out of cars. Heads were chopped off. Since then, the Chinese just go about their business. You won't find anything about this in the schoolbooks . . ."

We'll hear no more of it, not even in Malaysia's most Chinese town of all. We know where our driver stands mainly by his order of spare ribs. Perhaps eating is the only way to know who's who and what's what. Could it be that one of the longest-running ethnic divisions boils down to an inability to share menus?

Is it possible that one of the more significant moments in my life should take place in so curious a hideaway, with its played-out tin mines and vast stores of bat guano? The moment soon passes—after some harrowing minutes of gutting it out on my hard bench. The pregnancy test comes up negative.

"It must be the heat, the stress of the travel," Mei assures me, beaming.

"Are you alright?" I ask.

"*Bao-bao!*" she commands, the Chinese kiddie word for a hug.

Not knowing whether to celebrate or commiserate, unable to distinguish between fate and just another highlight of our itinerary, the two of us continue along the dusty path to the next Chinese restaurant. For the first time on our trip, a dining recommendation comes with a doctor's prescription. The exterior of Hang Cheng is unpromising, but inside, a long hall is nearly packed. From the last table for two, we look straight into a smaller hall where a wedding banquet is in progress. A red paper sign over the dais bears so familiar a set of Chinese characters that even I've come to recognize them: "Double happiness."

We watch this nuptial rite like naughty voyeurs. Why do the couple and parents make the rounds, coaxing each table to stand in turn as they toast with Johnnie Walker Red? Why is the blushing bride so upstaged and ignored by her parents, even though she's all dolled up in Southern belle satin?

"The Chinese sure like to make spectacles of themselves!" admits Mei. But now, for the first time, we begin making serious plans for our own big show. Somehow, our near-miss at familyhood has brought us closer to making official our deepening sense of mutual obligation. At least Mei will be able to fit into her Thai wedding dress. "It's so much more romantic to get married alone, no? Let's go to San Francisco City Hall, then walk up Filbert Steps with a bottle of champagne . . ."

"But my father has got to be there. He suffered through all the lonely times with me. We can have a clambake at our summer house."

"Then your mom won't be able to come. And my mother will be in Europe."

"We can meet up for a ceremony in Venice. Is that romantic enough for you?"

"Can we finally take a gondola? Have arugula salad, prosciutto and melon . . ."

In the meantime, Hang Cheng provides the best black bean chicken with winter melon this side of Kowloon. A Chinese crowd is rarely wrong. And Ipoh is a truly Chinese town, where there's nothing much to do but honor ancestors through food, then digest in the quiet of lost fortunes.

After supper, Mei and I wander about holding hands, lured by the far-off sound of trumpets, clashing cymbals, and ceremonial gongs. We soon discover that the music is merely to lend a bit of pomp to a Chinese funeral. The plain coffin sits starkly in a storefront.

Along the street of undertakers, wrinkled ladies flapping paper fans perform a Cantonese wake on wicker chairs set out in the dusty street. Men with beards curled as question marks puff on long pipes that glint with silver. The great wheel of life and death turns, binding Mei and me to it. What does it matter if I feel ten thousand miles from home and just as far from being a father? In old Ipoh, the band plays so gaily.

Christmas at Fatty Lee's

If Malacca is not true East, where is? Commanding the strategic straits that bear its name, coveted by every Occidental power, cradling every Oriental people, this sultanate turned spice depot was for centuries the quintessential Conradian harbor. So why are we arriving overland via communal Mercedes-Benz limo with a spongy transmission and a grumpy Sikh driver wearing short-sleeved, hallucinogenic batik? How come the fabled waterfront is ringed with white hotel sentinels that resound with live Christmas carolers?

Apparently, I'm the last Lord Jim to learn that Malaya's fabled trading center has become Malaysia's leading historic zone—trading on its exoticism to the tune of a million tourists per year. The only way to find accommodation this weekend in the cradle of the Malay nation is to sign on for a "three-day holiday package," complete with Western buffet or Chinese-style Santa's repast. Guess which one Mei and I select?

Though the only trees to decorate are coconut palms, we're in the perfect town for a quaint Noel—where Ebeneezer Scrooge meets Robinson Crusoe and Hans Brinker. The red Dutch towers of Malacca's Stadthuys, or City Hall, and the adjoining Christ Church are the main landmarks visible from our room at the Emperor, among the tallest and most up-to-date buildings in town. Modern construction dwarfs the modest hill over which so many nations fought to place their fortifications. Down below, the tiled rooftops are arranged in curved aisles that open against a shimmering sea like a big Chinese fan.

As soon as we brave the equatorial heat to stroll toward the colonial center, old Malacca offers an Asia in concentrate. Along a two-block stretch of Jalan To'kong are three sunstruck religious franchises: the ochre-colored Hindu Vinyagar shrine, the cool green mosque of Kampong Keling, and the oldest Chinese temple in the country, Cheng Hoon Teng, or Green Clouds, with its black incense burners and gold altars. Thanks to Malaysia's rapid march toward modernity, each monument is duly marked by a tablet that's part of an American Express–sponsored walking tour.

The greatest Oriental mystery here is how the well-trod manages to remain so authentically undisturbed. Part of the explanation may be found in that dogged resistance to assimilation found among the Chinese—more accurately, the South Chinese variants of Hainanese, Fukkienese, and Teochews—who inhabit nearly all of the historic center and carry on with their trades and their vices no matter who's looking. Chinese calligraphy hangs over nearly every storefront. Back alleys echo with the slapping of mah-jongg tiles. Old men have their ears cleaned with ghoulishly long metal needles. What makes this culture as obvious as it is impenetrable? All open yet entirely closed?

These days, the Chinese community newspapers are full of a legal battle to stop the building of a housing development on the outlying Bukit China, or China Hill, resting place of a Ming Dynasty princess who married into the Malaccan court and now the largest (and most snake-infested) Chinese cemetery outside China itself. To try and get some background on local race relations, Mei and I seek out Malacca's nightly "Sound and Light Spectacular," billed as the only world-class historical recreation in East Asia. Along the way, we get lost along the spookily dark backside of Bukit St. Paul, the paltry mound over which so many invaders grappled. By eight o'clock, even the A. & W. Root Beer stand is closed up and we dash across unlit fields to find a place in the covered bleachers.

The structures beyond are just made for illumination: the moss-covered outer walls of St. Paul's church, the no-nails replica of a curvaceous sultan's palace, the cannons and single remaining stone gate of A Famosa, the Portuguese fortress, plus Memorial Hall, where Malaysia's independence from Britain was proclaimed in 1957. As colored spotlights alternate, waters murmur, maidens giggle, warriors grunt, and swords and armor jangle, the narrative is fittingly nationalist, conjuring an Islamic paradise lost and regained, a misty golden age of sultans that never was. We hear a stream of tributes to pre-Muslim despots who barely had time to establish the town before a pair of infamous brothers started its swift downfall by chopping one another up. Any tradition is better than none.

"All rulers are liars," whispers Mei, getting fidgety. If I were a Malaysian Chinese, the complete lack of acknowledgment given my people might make me more than a trifle nervous. Little credit is extended to the Indians either. As presented, the British Empire was single-handedly toppled by obstinate Malays. And the show's gory procession of conquerors—from the Chinese Admiral Cheng Ho just nine years after the village's founding in 1400, to the Portuguese, Dutch, and British—merely reinforce the impression that Malacca is the sum of what interlopers have made it.

It's the Chinese who rule nearby Gluttons' Row, a block of raucous outdoor dives facing the waterfront highway. We can't resist the one called Madame Fatso's. A business card is hardly required to identify the proprietress, on hand in all her domineering bulk. The massive tiger shrimps aren't exactly Beijing court fare, but why complain on such a balmy December twenty-third?

"Malacca, city of love!" chants our exuberant rickshaw driver between taped reggae and honks on his Clarabelle horn, as he cycles us home the long way. "I Malay, wife Chinese. You America. Come here! Love everybody!"

All that's left from all that bloodshed are lots of people whose features can't be found in any textbooks, as well as Southeast Asia's largest congregation of antique stores. To a forties rendition of "Rose of Malaya" played on a windup gramophone, an Indian dealer named Abdul—frighteningly reminiscent of Sydney Greenstreet in *Casablanca*—tries in vain to get us to purchase a canopied bed for two. Along this shuttered street is the Baba Nonya Heritage House, preserving the precious lifestyle of Chinese traders (Babas) who married Malay women (Nonyas). Barefoot girls lead a tour through airy atriums that re-create so-called Peranakan culture, which looks to me like Qing Dynasty gentility trying not to go moldy.

A nightclub or two claim to serve up some version of their gristly cuisine. Mei and I prefer to stick to such identifiable favorites as skewers of satay, grilled on the sidewalk and served by the dozen inside the old town's cavernous Satay House. On the less atmospheric main road out of town, between claptrap hotels and corporate towers, we also find Lim Tian Puan, a family-style, Teochew dinner house that's not only air-conditioned, but also packed with those appreciative of a multitude of fish soups done with such typical seasonings as lemon grass.

We stumble on the Malay part of town only when we go to purchase bus tickets. Stuck behind the noisy depot is the Kampong Mortem, a collection of tin-roofed, A-frame houses on stilts. At dusk, the call of the mosque's *muezzin* gives me chills. So do the veiled women who wave at us from their forlorn kitchens. The most memorable sight on Malacca's river tour—the river, after all, is nearly mud black—are the several immense lizards who lounge by the banks after feeding on the local detritus. Each critter is known by name to the ebullient boat guide, who begins his nonstop rap by identifying himself as "a Malaysian salad—part-Dutch, part-British, part-Portuguese, and part-Indian."

The last enclave we raid is the so-called Portuguese Village, actually a modest slum of flimsy, modern bungalows skirting an unswimmable stretch of southern shoreline. A community stage backed with stand-up Santas is being used for a game of ring-around-the-rosy by some children of the two to three thousand mixed-race peoples who prefer to be known as Portuguese. Through the imposing gates of Lisbon Square, there are open-air restaurants where a few old gents sip Portuguese wine with an air of majestic exhaustion. It was September 11, 1509, when the Portuguese flag was planted here, but those who still claim the nationality bear no connection beyond an irrational desire to horde *bacalhau*, the national codfish dish. If these guys are Portuguese, Omar Sharif is Swedish.

My few words of greeting cribbed in Brazil make me an instant celebrity in this circle starved for contact with their colonial motherland. "Please stay for our open house!" the old men all beg. We promise we will, especially after we run into an effusively friendly Italian kid—a Giovanni, no less, from our adopted second city of Venice. "Whomever is Lord of Malacca," went the fifteenth-century battle cry, "has his hands on the throat of Venice!" But the traveler, unlike the trader, is never quite sure what he or she takes away. When the locals head off for midnight mass, the dirt roads of the Portuguese Village become jammed with tourists come to eat fried fish and hear a country-western group do their Eurasian rendition of "My Achy Breaky Heart."

We return to the hotel to get our money's worth from our Christmas package. But the concept of a Sino-Noël sounds a lot better than it tastes—especially with an all-girl Filipina house band doing their best with a Bing Crosby medley. The diners beside us wouldn't recognize a homey Yuletide if they saw one. Mei is amazed to find they are on tour from mainland Canton. Our waitress forces us to don a strap-on party hat and blow paper whistles at the sight of our feast. Instead of a partridge in a pear tree, we get a "yam ring" with soy-drenched rubber chicken. Even Mei, who usually manages to make the best of anything, assesses, "This is the worst Chinese food I've ever had for Christmas."

Our present to ourselves is an unfinishable feast of noodles and various seafood in the unending tropical night—amidst the midnight mobs at an outdoor eatery called Fatty Lee's. There's no such big boy in sight. The cooking here is Chinese only in the sense that everything is flash-fried. But that's perfect for preserving the freshness of crab legs with ginger and bulging, double-breasted shrimps.

With most places shut down for the holiday, we venture guiltily into the air-conditioned comfort of Malacca's nifty new Mahkota Shopping Center, whose parking lots alone are as large as the old colonial center. Done up in designer pinks and creams, this latest outpost of empire houses the usual McDonald's and Benetton outlets. In the second-floor food court, we find a wide array of Malay satays, Nonya fish stews, Hainan chicken-rice, Hokkien noodles, and Hakkanese clay pot combos—a multicultural melange merchandised to perfection. As Mei and I stuff our faces, I can't help thinking that this mall will soon lie in ruins, too, leaving behind an eternal East that exists solely in Western imaginations.

Brave New Wok

In Singapore, eating may be the only public pleasure that isn't subject to fine or imprisonment. What else is left where all obvious sin has been banished, every vehicle is electronically monitored, and chewing gum is nearly a capital crime? With the antiseptic upgrading of Southeast Asia's one city-state run by Chinese, only Chinese food has been spared.

Or has it? Mei and I can't even locate what remains of Chinatown. Amidst the general white-out of new housing, a few blocks of shuttered Victoriana and a row or two of herb warehouses are all that

remains of unregulated local color. Even a "food alley" has been reduced to four restaurants identified by identical hanging shingles.
But as soon as we step inside the Moi Kong, we can't help running
into the town's number one bon vivant. Even in Singapore, a true
epicure is easy to spot.

"My qualifications as a food expert are quite obvious," jokes a rotund Chinese Orson Welles, quite youthful yet imposing in a black
vest. Aside from his boundless girth, our attention had been drawn
to the arrival of his party by a Laurel and Hardy scene. The group's
one willowy blonde, looking primly English to the core, tries to sit
down just as her nervous Chinese escort mistakenly pulls the chair
out from under her. With all due decorum, the girl flops straight on
her colonial bum. Though the others squelch their laughter, her
blush fades as slowly as an equatorial sunset.

"The Singaporean sense of humor is no longer up to par!" the fat
man apologizes in our direction. "Life has become too easy and we
complain about too many things. We have a saying that everyone in
Singapore is a one, two, three, four, and five. One wife, two cars,
three kids, four-room flat, five-figure income."

Judging from his business card, this Singaporean isn't doing too
badly. "Moses Lim Makan Around the World"—*makan* is Malay for
munching—is but one of the myriad enterprises listed, including
"Mac Bon Enterprise Pte.," "Him Peow Trading Co.," "Shin Shin
Beauty Therapy and Cosmetology," and the "Ganoderma-Dragon
Health Food Series."

"We have Singapore's favorite cooking show," says Moses, pushing his granny glasses up his pug nose with a pudgy finger. "Soon to
be syndicated throughout Asia!" The blonde young lady turns out to
be his new "on-air hostess."

Within moments, Moses is dictating a list of restaurant recommendations. Obviously, we haven't done wrong to start out at the
Moi Kong. Dominated by the Chaozhou and Hainanese origins of
most Southeast Asian Chinese, this city can't offer the variety found
in Taiwan. Yet it is still small enough so that each sample of a regional school is highly treasured—like this showplace of homestyle
Hakkanese with barely eight tables. One bite of the cuttlefish with
chives in brown sauce teaches me more than I need to know about

the distinctive flavors that mark the cuisine developed by China's so-called gypsies. The earnest brothers Wang continue the lesson with a chicken stewed in a blood-red wine made from the dregs of rice husks.

"This red wine is the essential ingredient of true Hakkanese cooking," says Tony Wang. "So we brew it ourselves in earthen jars out back. It takes about three weeks."

In a moment, they've brought us a pungently fermented bowlful, as good for cooking as bad Chianti. The Wangs learned all they know from their father, a chef for fifty years.

"I tried to leave the restaurant once and work in a shipyard," Tony Wang confesses. "But there was an explosion one day after a loading accident and the family was so worried, I had to come back." The dangers of the kitchen remain far less lethal.

In the meantime, Moses has hurried off, leaving us with numerous commandments for Chinese dining in Singapore. Without his guidance, Mei and I yield to the temptation of a nearby restaurant boasting "the world's most expensive fried rice." Served in a hole-in-the-wall as plastic as a Howard Johnson's, the twenty-dollar price tag for the Chinese staple is justified by the chunks of fresh crab lovingly culled from the shell by twin spinster sisters.

Like the fried rice, Singapore has become too expensive to attract the scroungier Western elements—once made welcome with signs reading, "Longhairs to the Back of the Line." Instead, Mei and I have been forced to the farthest edge of the island, in the barest wing of the town's lowliest YMCA. But travel's major consolation is the easy ability to find others having a worse time than you. Striding past dozens of Nigerian job-seekers who have formed a permanent encampment between the vending machines and the communal TV, we're approached by a couple of Los Angelenos outfitted in their best Banana Republic khakis.

"We only stopped here to make a connection for Delhi," is the hubby's new mantra. "The travel agent never told us we needed visas for India." Now they've got to wait through the New Year's holiday for the embassies to reopen. Travel nightmare number 379. A week in Singapore will devour all their funds, so I advise them to hop a train and hole up on some Malaysian beach. "How far is that?" the wife asks. These poor souls don't know which continent they are on.

I know just enough to lead Mei through Singapore's superb subway to Newton Circus, one of the more venerable and exorbitant of the town's famed outdoor food courts. Once upon a time, these aggregations of private family stalls displayed the same color and joy as those we'd seen in Penang. Now, they are just cafeterias under bare bulbs with concrete picnic areas. Signs reassure tourists by forbidding the crime of "excessive touting." So nobody pesters us with a prideful "come hither" and nobody bothers to compete over price, either. The tiger shrimps come huge and fresh, but the hawkers' centers have been merchandised into high-priced earthiness. "They've got one menu for locals and one for foreigners," a forlorn restaurateur will warn us. "You'll see an old man in shorts walk away from his humble stand and slip into his Mercedes 380 S.L."

"We Singaporeans find a methodology to out-organize everything!" we'll be told with a giggle by Joanna Wang. Short and stocky with thick glasses, she's hardly my image of a Chinese opera troupe's artistic director. Yet her company had once performed in San Francisco's Palace of Fine Arts thanks to Mei's tireless promotion. Just before we'd met, Mei had been asked by a friend to rescue the company's aborted American tour by arranging a stop in San Francisco. Mei ended up losing much of her life savings on the event, even cooking breakfast for all thirty-three performers. But she has no regrets, nor bounds to her zeal for helping strangers. After finding a third-floor classroom where housewives drill in the proper method of gliding about with bound footsteps, we're repaid with the offer of a midnight tour by Joanna.

"Did you know that my fellow countrymen are the ones who invented 'Tunch'?" she asks, both tickled and horrified by her hometown. "Combine high tea with lunch and you've got Tunch! Smashing! We've managed to squeeze another meal into the day!"

Aside from her high-falutin' elocution, she and her manager/husband, Leslie, are most Singaporean in conducting their marriage largely by car phones. After each rehearsal they form a convoy of dancers headed toward food. But first, we're given an exhaustive demonstration of the city's system of rotating-access traffic zones enforced by license-plate numbers and soon-to-come digitalized, dashboard-mounted chips. Here, the Confucian passion for systematizing meets corporate hierarchy; private anality becomes public policy. As for Singapore's grander contributions to world civilization, this feisty woman who has spent her life preserving classical Chinese traditions proudly shows us the last blaze of an annual competition in holiday lighting staged by the immense malls along Orchard Road. The mythical lion for which Singapore was named has been replaced by red-bulbed reindeer.

"Did you know we've just constructed a whole island full of theme parks?" Joanna asks. "And our garden city is surrounded with green belts! It's all so marvelously planned-out."

As a result, a waterfront once filled with barges and stevedores is now lined with banks and industrial parks. One can't even spy a seagull. Maybe it's too hot for them. Passing the Raffles, that one remaining bastion of the town's Kiplingesque past, there's no way to tell where the colonial roost leaves off and the shopping annex begins. Only the Indian neighborhoods emit signs of life in the form of peddlers' cries and record-store ragas. Banished are all normal, big city abnormalities. But we're still allowed to "pig out," as Joanna puts it, with a group of fledgling opera princesses at a listless hotel buffet. Later, the Wangs lead us to a special lunch prepared by one of the "four kings" of Cantonese cooking from a bygone era. Treated like royalty, we get our first abalone-choked bowl of Buddha Jumps over the Wall, a seafood medley designed to tempt even saints. But today's health-conscious crew wouldn't tolerate this king's mayonnaise-swathed lobster.

I am surprised, too, that Moses Lim has sent us to the basement of the popular Funan Shopping Center to find Mui Chun, a modest, modern makeover of a place that began serving Western-style grub back in 1935. "Outside of the Raffles, this was where British officers could come for pork chops with gravy and such," explains the suave second-generation owner, Michael Wong, who has no idea of the derivation of his restaurant's name. "I can only presume that my father called it after one of his mistresses!"

The menu is now billed as Anglo-Chinese, with the specialty a superb whole pomfret fish dredged in and caked with chili powder, then deep-fried to create the Asian equivalent of "blackened" Cajun spices. I'm not sure this quite qualifies as Straits cuisine. While we pick through the white flesh and wash down the heat with gallons of tea, our owner steers us through the dangerous straits of Singapore geopolitics.

"Being stuck between Indonesia and Malaysia, two large Muslim countries, even restaurant owners have to follow the political situation. In the fifties, when we still had good relations, we served plenty of Indonesians. Before the break with Malaysia in '63, we had to hire thirty percent Malay and have a paper Malay boss. It was a farce." Now I understand why the Chinese element in Singapore's mix of cuisines is at once overhyped and downplayed. It's as though the Chinese prefer to travel incognito through a rough patch of the world.

"Malaysia and Thailand are getting richer," Michael Wong continues. "Hong Kong has a great advantage over us because they can wake up in the morning, make a deal in China, and return to sleep in their own beds at night. For us to stay in the game, we've got to educate our children better than the rest. We've got to be like the Japanese: keep morals high, train our young to work hard and respect their parents." He expresses the essence of the Singaporean ethos: "There's a saying here that you can't fly with one wing. So our second wing has to be foreign investment. "

But in their obsession to satisfy international standards and placate foreign squeamishness, the Chinese rulers have made their food a little too clean to be properly Chinese.

"Since the government banned live slaughtering, you just can't get the same flavor of meat. The supply of good blood, good bones is gone," Michael Wong admits. Wong is especially bitter because he saw the shift in chicken processing as a golden business opportunity, opening five plants with the capacity of killing two thousand birds an hour. "But everyone saw what was happening," he complains. Wedded to its boosterist policies, the government allowed numerous competitors to open. So Wong and others went under—leaving the market open to "frozen imports."

Moses Lim soon confirms the slaughtering ban. "When we really crave some dogs or some bats," muses this galloping gourmand, "we have to cross the causeway to Johore Bahru in Malaysia."

We've finally caught up with the food expert for a monstrous feed at the Prima Tower Revolving Restaurant, part of a Southeast Asian chain. This showy parapet, with full bar and textured wallpaper, has been placed atop an unused warehouse and offers a vantage point for supervising a containerport's loading dock. But Chinese don't come to restaurants for the view—unless it's a view of what's on their table. Portions that are industrial-sized to match the setting are presented by a handsomely freckled chef-owner whose sleeves are unpretentiously rolled up. The Prima bills itself as a Peking-style eatery, though so near the equator and far from the emperor, some dishes have lost their sharp regional edge. Still, the Chinese go on gobbling their favorites, which are as unsuited to the local climate as these people are unrelated to the Malays they rule. The Peking duck is a reasonable facsimile but the show is stolen by a Chinese soufflé, its fluff stuffed with mock crab. The unforgettable dessert is a piping-hot flourless pound cake with the flavor of concentrated egg custard and the consistency of play dough.

"The three no-sticks," Moses calls it. Mei knows why: "Doesn't stick to the plate, to the chopsticks, or to your teeth."

Moses Lim's knowing nods are hardly a comfort. By the end of the trip, will I end up looking like him?

"There's not much else for us to do but stuff ourselves," he admits, "so long as L.K.Y. runs the show." As do most Singaporeans, he's referring familiarly and ambivalently to longtime president Lee Kuan Yew. Though the reins of power have passed down to Lee's son and a younger managerial elite, there's been little letup in press censorship or the mania for lifestyle fines.

"The government takes good care of us but they also guard our minds very well. They don't want their citizens to be troubled by too many dangerous thoughts."

Why should they? The average human would have few complaints with a realm where crime is all official, growth steady, employment secure, housing reasonable, environment green, trade winds kindly, trade deficit favorable, and shopping unlimited. The traffic keeps flowing and the food keeps coming. Except for its chickens, this brave new world isn't a bad place to eat. And much like the cringing old world, it appears to be largely a Chinese creation.

The Chef with the Four-Star Heart

Why is Singapore's premiere chef crying? We're sitting in the padded waiting lounge of Hai Tian Lo, or "Sea Heaven Chamber." With a view of turquoise waters halfway to Indonesia, this circular parapet on the thirty-seventh floor of the sleek Pan-Pacific Hotel is the pinnacle of the Straits' culinary world. But its relatively youthful boss speaks in soft tones devoid of self-promotional bluster. Looking to be in his early forties, Chan Chen Hei sports a carefully layered haircut, parted down the middle of an unusually square face, most handsome with large and deep-set eyes. His skilled hands—permanently bleached from too much soaking, supple but scarred from wok scaldings—are equally long and square, gesticulating hands that could conquer fire.

"The last time I was in China, I made a pilgrimage to the scenic West Lake," he begins his story. Chef Chan rode "hard seat" beside a sickly old man, dressed in blue homespun, headed to Shanghai to search for a grandson who was his last remaining relative. "The man was carrying his life's savings inside a kerchief. He showed me a few shreds of *fen* equivalent to less than one cent." Chef Chan was moved to slip him the equivalent of five dollars, more money than the man had ever seen and more than he could refuse. In gratitude, the old man kneeled down on the wooden planks. Describing how the old man wept before him, the chef breaks down.

"That is what it means to be Chinese," he tells us as soon as he recovers. "That is the true feeling that we cannot afford to lose." Chef Chan hasn't recounted the scene to boast of his largesse. He wants Mei and me to know that, despite these luxurious surroundings, he is a creature of China and his China is a place of unbounded need and mutual aid. "I was born in a small village outside Canton," he continues. "My father was a heavy drinker, his mind ruined by cheap alcohol. Whenever he drank, he would beat my mother." As a child, he ran away from the violence to a local Christian mission.

"A good woman there urged me to stay in primary school, even though I had to wash my one dirty uniform every night. Often, I sat in wet pants through my lessons." But his parents cursed the missionary and banished her from seeing their son. "I could only sneak

140

out to attend church when my father was feasting with what Cantonese call his dog and pig friends."

At thirteen, Chan managed to sneak across the border to Hong Kong, where the only choice for the poor was "doing car repair, signing onto a ship or going into the kitchen." So began his indentured training. Starting out making dough for morning dim sum, he had to commute across Hong Kong harbor at four each morning. "I worked sixteen hours a day and any time I made a mistake, or fell asleep on the job, the head cooks would throw boiling water at me." But he could eat for free and his starting salary was one hundred Hong Kong dollars, or twenty U.S. dollars a week—much of which he sent back to the family that had abused him.

"Chinese people think a man with a chef's hat is ignorant," he concedes. "But there are some thirty basic techniques to be learned." His high school and university was a Golden Wheel restaurant that stayed open for all but two hours each day, hardly enough time to turn off the cauldrons of broth. After dim sum came tea brunch, then businessmen's lunch, then more dim sum with afternoon tea, dinner followed by noodle and por-ridge snacks. This full-service canteen catered to the full Chinese eating cycle.

"I learned all I needed to know about life from peering out that kitchen door," Chef Chan observes. Gamblers and drug addicts abounded. The customers could be housewives, seamen, or in some cases, the staff of a local bordello. "The madam took care of disputes between her ladies by having the waiters push all the tables to the wall," he describes. "The girls would form a protective circle. The ones who were angry would get in the middle and slap one another until they became sisters again."

Gangsters from the neighborhood black hand society showed up, too, demanding their protection money. "Fourteen karat," recalls Chef Chan. "That was the name of their gang." When the manager got scared and refused to hand over red packets stuffed with bills on holidays, the local mob employed an unusual tactic. They didn't threaten or strong-arm. They simply sent their goons in to occupy every table, driving out all regular traffic and ordering only tea and noodles. The manager ran away and the restaurant shut down.

At this high-class joint, Chef Chan has no such worries. Multinational corporations take their cut. But he can't forget his roots, even if he spends his days and nights preparing fresh abalone, lobster-stuffed dumplings, or Chef Chan's Special Buddha Jumps Over the Wall. This seafood stew is so smooth and rich that nobody jumps at its devilish price of 200 U.S. dollars per bowl.

"You can only keep going if your full mind and heart are in what you're doing," he admits with an audible sigh. "Fortunately, our ancestors have passed down this food emphasis. Even in the Bronze Age, the Chinese already cared a lot about food. I think it goes back to the Chinese fear of death. People are always involved in maintaining their health, they want to enjoy life up to the last moment. So even in the most humble village, everyone is obsessed with what to eat."

Catering to the expense account crowd, Chef Chan can now use unusual ingredients to refine and embolden that Cantonese tradition. "In Singapore, the history of dishes isn't long," he says, explaining his search for new forms of Chinese balance by working with Western staples like beef and pumpkin. But he, too, feels hamstrung by the authorities' obsession with assembly-line methods. "People here don't eat wild things. Ninety-eight percent of the people can't remember how to kill their own chickens, to strip a quail, or skin a frog. All of this greatly affects the taste."

Chef Chan is less worried about the loss of living chickens than the loss of a living tradition of hospitality. "I rarely eat in other restaurants," he admits, "because they advertise the cheapest crabs but purposely overestimate the weight." Still, he takes time from planning his New Year's banquet to show us his few favorite spots around town. One is a street stall where patrons sit on half-sized stools to sample "mother's hen," a black-skinned chicken stewed in medicinal herbs. The bitter broth tastes like it can cure almost anything, even being human. The slumming master also leads us to a sultry Indonesian corner stand with ready-made curried fish and tamarind-laced stews plucked from a plastic display case. For Chef Chan, food is food, whether served at street-level or in his Pan-Pacific penthouse.

"People in Singapore are too easily impressed by show," he argues.

"If you know just two cooking styles, you are among the best. The government says that Chinese history isn't important and instead, everyone should study computers. Soon our culture will be gone." That's why he collects antique furniture with the same devotion showed to his cooking. "Perhaps you can't have the feeling unless you are born back there. My wife and son, they don't like China. To them, it's dirty and unpleasant. But I want them to see how people suffer so they can appreciate life. Here, you can't see a beggar. Our president hands out lucky packets to old-age pensioners at Chinese New Year. But if you always travel deluxe, you'll never see what's happening right next to you."

No wonder he suffers from vertigo at his restaurant's heights. Class consciousness is a fearsome thing to take into the kitchen. Meeting this cook with a four-star heart, I sense the pain of a Michelangelo forced to squander his generous talents on those who need them the least. Yet we keep riding the elevator at Chef Chan's insistence to sample dim sum delicately stuffed with chestnuts, and a trademark chicken that's moist inside and superbly crisp outside.

To see how this is achieved, we follow Chef Chan into the small yet gleaming laboratory over which he presides. A three-tiered system rules the division of labor. An outer phalanx does the heavy prep work, the cleaning and sorting of incoming foods. The important middlemen are the cutters, choppers, and slicers who group the proper combination of ingredients into rows of small stainless steel bowls. Then Chef Chan takes over—personally setting each dish into the pan. Holding a plucked, parboiled chicken by its neck, he patiently showers the skin with cup after cup of scalding oil. From long experience, he judges the magical moment when the chicken skin stands between candied and burnt.

The Chinese chef's job is truly Promethean. A millisecond too much flame can ruin a whole dish. This satisfying sleight-of-hand produces dishes that must be consumed just as quickly. So the Chinese master is a genius of timing and a paragon of endurance. To do this right, it takes a man who savors hardships. Each day, he goes back to where no man should stand. With every order, Chef Chan has to face the fire.

Chinese Parsley Orange Peel Duck

From Hai Tian Lo

Ingredients:

Half a fresh duck (about 1 $^{1}/_{2}$–2 lbs.)
Orange peel, 2 pieces
Ginger, 1 $^{1}/_{2}$ tbs.
Green onion, 3 tbs. chopped
Chinese parsley, 8 oz.
Chicken stock, 4 cups
Chinese Shaoxing rice wine, 5 tsp.
Salt, $^{1}/_{2}$ tsp.
Soy sauce, 1 tsp.

Clean duck thoroughly and marinate for several hours in soy sauce. Deep-fry the duck until golden brown, then pat to drain oil. Combine the chicken stock and rice wine in a pot large enough to hold the duck. Add the orange peel, ginger, onion, and parsley. Add the duck to the liquid and cook over low heat for 3 $^{1}/_{2}$ hours.

Superior Soup with Lobster Dumpling in a Baby Pumpkin

From Hai Tian Lo

Ingredients:

2 baby pumpkins (1 $^{1}/_{2}$–2 lb. each)
Fresh cooked lobster meat, $^{1}/_{2}$ lb.
Chinese celery, 2 tbs.
Chinese greens, chopped stalk, 2 tbs.
Green onion, $^{1}/_{2}$ tsp.
Chinese parsley, $^{1}/_{2}$ tsp.
2 large won ton wrappers

Chicken stock, 2 cups with 1 tsp. salt added
Sesame oil, $^1/_3$ tsp.
Cornstarch, $^1/_3$ tsp.
Salt, $^1/_2$ tsp.
Pepper to taste

Scoop out the center of each pumpkin and pour a cup of chicken stock into each. Boil in a half-full pan of water for 40 minutes. Dice the lobster meat and mix with all the vegetables and seasonings. Place mixture inside the won ton wrappers. Add one lobster won ton to the stock in each pumpkin. Steam another 15 minutes.

Supermarket of the Gods

The Garden of Eden is a hard act to follow. I have visions of ringing in New Year's Eve on Bali Hai to the tingling gongs of a gamelan orchestra. But these are swiftly drowned out by the crush of screeching scooters outside Denpasar Airport. What is this occasion to a people whose perpetual calendar charts 6,000 years, each made of 210 days divided into weeks of variable length, some running simultaneously? Along Sanur Beach's slapdash row of batik boutiques and mango shake shacks, circles of pony-tailed Balinese beach bums squat in grimy gutters dotted with banana-leaf offerings. They pass bottles of the local firewater, *arak*, and strum guitars while approximating the Eagles' "Welcome to the Hotel California."

On Bali, the laid-back locals make it easy to travel far and end up having gone nowhere at all. "You come honeymoon, boss? What's your program? Need transport? See cremation, okay?" But Mei and I have already got a vehicle to move us from tourist to traveler—and I don't mean one of Sanur's readily rented four-wheel Suzuki Jeeps. Per instruction, we wander over to Bob's Borneo, a frond-covered cafe boasting the best burgers east of Krakatoa. Out in back is the studio of an old friend from Mei's days at the University of Minnesota. A long stint in the tropics has only sharpened his jutting jaw and further melted away his lanky form. With close-cropped blond hair, this ex-pat artist strikes me as a Rasputin in scuffed jeans and rubber thongs.

"Welcome to the supermarket of the gods!" Bruce offers, his scarecrow blue eyes widening ghoulishly at the sight of Mei. On the run from the Midwest's lack of spontaneity and cheap studio space, this abstract adventurer has been forced to earn his livelihood by filling in the blanks on various touring maps. Instead of showing us his single brush stroke etchings, the painter volunteers to tour us around on the way to meeting a family who run one of Bali's rare Chinese restaurants. Suddenly, I don't mind that our New Year's party consists of some boxed Australian wine consumed in a mosquito-ridden atelier.

Denpasar, the island capital, means "big market." There's a city here somewhere, lost between embassy gates and rotaries that circle neo-Fascist monuments of mythic garuda birds looking as viciously patriotic as American bald eagles. In the dead center, where Bali momentarily flirts with the urban, there are two Chinese restaurants staring one another down across immense overhangs. But we have trouble recognizing them because they are stripped of neon ideograms. This is not for aesthetic reasons. Though we've heard that the edict is no longer enforced in Jakarta's Chinatown, here is firsthand confirmation that we're in the only country to ban the display of Chinese script. What could be the harm in exposing the Balinese to another ancient alphabet? Doesn't Indonesia's ultra-rich Chinese business elite ever stand up for its poor relations? We get pretty fair noodles in the Hong Kong Cafe, but no answers.

Clearly, the trouble with what Mei invariably calls "Bali-Indonesia"—to distinguish it from Bali, which is Mandarin for Paris, France—stems from the second part of the address. Back in 1965, the overthrow of the Nationalist Sukarno had been accompanied by the mass slaughter of six hundred thousand members of Indonesia's Communist Party, give or take a few hundred thousand. Since one of the main charges leveled against the nation's Left was that it sought to form an alliance with Mao, it made sense that a lot of Chinese (especially envied merchants) were caught in the general roundup. While it would seem that there would be greater tolerance for non-Islamic people on Bali, the one Hindu anomaly in the whole dour archipelago, history books claim that there were fifty thousand local victims of the great purge.

Still, Mei is especially eager to wake up in the back country of the realm Nehru tagged "morning of the world." Our expedition is delayed when Bruce uses our jeep on an unscheduled run for art supplies—and manages to run out of gas. In his enthusiasm, our guide has failed to mention that he hasn't driven a car in seven years. Until he gets the hang of it, our four-wheeler turns into a bucking bronc. "Watch out, this gets pretty organic!" he'll warn each time our backsides get jolted by semi-rotted road beds.

While Bruce has little patience for the usual tourist sites, he's willing to linger for hours sampling a smelly durian fruit and such mangy Balinese fare as *ayam tutu*, a chicken stew with a kick provided by some local grass pesto. At least, it's not Indonesia's staple of *nasi goreng*, the egg-topped, coconut-tinged fried rice that is one of the Orient's major disappointments. From our table at the humble truck stop called Gong of the Gods, we can at least trace the series of trembling volcanoes that are the taut mechanism winding Bali's precise whirligig of ritual and sacrifice.

If, as Eastern sages posit, it's all in the journey, then for Bruce, it's all in the detour. With no mention of our Chinese restaurant interview, he takes us to Sideman, a mountain village given almost entirely to ikat weavers, where we're the only ones around its bougainvillea-covered cottages overlooking amber fields of grain. Spotting a marker for a "Monument Nasional," our primitivist leads us down to the ruins of a Buddhist sanctuary beside a river bed complete with primeval waterfall—though, unlike the bare-breasted Balinese, modest Mei takes the plunge in panties and bra. On a jog west through a coffee-growing region dotted with dreamy whirls of clove bushes, the ridge-clinging town of Munduk echoes with the all-night chanting that precedes a cremation. Grimacing masked dancers flit about a ceremonial tower bearing excavated bones, until the bodies burn quicker than Kingsford briquets.

"The Balinese are too busy being religious," Mei can't help musing. "Why should they want the Chinese to come here and force them to work?"

Can these super-visions forming processionals really be the same creatures who by day till the fields and tend the shops? If so, where's the phone booth they change in? It's said that in the Balinese language, there's no word for *art*.

"But the local rituals have become 'culture,' " Bruce bemoans. "It's all gone from a verb to a noun."

That's certainly true in Ubud, offering one-stop shopping for anything Balinese. Where the population ratio works out to six videotaping tourists for every Balinese woman with fruit on her head, Mei and I break the record for nonstop ethnography by witnessing in one evening the ritual slaughter of baby piglets, a monkey dance accompanied by chilling jungle chants, the one-man ventriloquist virtuosity of a shadow puppet play, and the classic *legong* performed by eye-rolling prepubescents.

"For the first time in Bali," Mei admits, "I feel knocked out by something besides the heat!" Some say foreign exchange is the only thing that preserves these choreographic traditions. Some also say Indonesia is a model democracy.

Along Ubud's strip, we can indulge in a melting pot of peanut satays, tropical smoothies, goat cheese calzones—almost everything except Chinese food. But Bruce hasn't forgotten his promise. He fetches us for one last cruise up to Singaraja. The capital under the Dutch, this abandoned port has the most palpably Third World feel of all Balinese towns. The untended parks, windblown streets, and palace ruins have hardly been beautified by a recent government ordinance to paint all facades gray. In this eternal backwater, alleys divide the descendants of Moslem and Bugis traders. By a collapsing ocean embankment, bands of raggedy children sell peanuts and a Chinese temple faces the surf, its lucky red tiles impossible to disguise.

Thoroughly disguised in the corner of a small mall, whose lot is supervised by beggars, is a restaurant called the Gandi. Only in small print is the cuisine identified as "Indonesian, Seafood, and Chinese."

"We named the place after Gandhi because he represented tolerance," Bruce translates the Balinese of an elderly woman presiding over the register. Her name is actually Gunadi, which is a local adaptation of the Chinese *Huang*. But why should this family have to advance such a symbol in Bali?

"We have no problems with the Balinese. There's a deep connection between their beliefs and ours." Why not, when both are governed by a panoply of gods and luck-preserving rituals? "My great-grandfather came to Indonesia to work on the coffee plantations. When he didn't have a son, he went back to China and bought a son. My own grandfather came here as a slave. It was very common. He became the official son, but received no inheritance."

At each pit stop, another horror fills out the story of China's brutal past. "My own mother was also the daughter of a slave," this dignified proprietress admits. "She was a student at the local Chinese school when she fell in love with a teacher fifteen years her senior. They were married soon after. And when the rioters closed Chinese schools back in '65, my father was lucky to come away with his life."

Once the magic date has been mentioned, her volume lowers. Thirty years later, the Chinese only speak about that time in whispers. No one knows how many people were killed by the fundamentalist hit squads that ravaged the country, one village at a time. Yet there has been no acknowledgment of guilt and no guarantee that genocide can't happen once more—as Indonesian actions on East Timor seem to prove. So these Chinese cannot help but tie their future hopes to the growing strength of China.

"I was on a ship out of here, on my way back to Canton," admits a Chinese friend of the Gandi's owner. "But I was called back by word that my father had contracted cancer. Even though I can't write Chinese myself, I want my children to be educated in China."

To that end, he's procured as much Balinese beach property as he can buy up. But as the history of Southeast Asia proves, the Chinese have been able to procure everything except love.

"It's true, some of us have done very well in business." The Balinese-Chinese points at the black casing of my Nikon camera and, teaching me more than all our ramblings, observes ruefully, "If you pay enough, here is the place where black is called white."

South Pacific

THE ENDLESS DUMPLING

Featured Restaurants:

Shark Fin House, Melbourne, Australia
Taipan, Doncaster
Li Li's, West Melbourne
Flower Drum, Melbourne
Mask of China, Melbourne
Camy Dumpling House, Melbourne
The Bull, Melbourne
Kazakhstan Gourmet, Sydney
Golden Empire, Sydney
New Orient, Auckland
The Great Wok, Suva, Fiji
Maple Garden, Honolulu
Ja-Ja, Honolulu

The Lucky Country

Our journey is like an order placed with a thousand unknown kitchens. There's no more chance to turn back than there is to send back the food. Besides, all of this is becoming something of a dare. Anywhere the Chinese have gone, we can go, too. Where there's a wok, there's a way, even if that happens to be way "down under."

"Plannin' on sty-ing long, mate?" asks the plainclothes customs man who singles us out at the Melbourne aiport. "Got a marriage license, have you?"

Given Australia's longtime "White Only" policy, Mei is sure that her Asian features have set off alarms. After ten minutes of his impertinent grilling, she sets the man straight. "For your information, I have a masters in engineering and my fiancé is a travel writer."

"S'pose he's going to scribble a line about all of this," the officer jokes, quickly yielding. "Go on, then. No worries."

Why should there be worries in this bountiful continent divvied up by a mere nineteen million souls? "The Lucky Country," I'll soon hear Australia proclaimed. Somehow, I doubt the title is popular with aboriginals—or the luck-conscious Chinese. But nobody feels luckier than Brian, a commune-mate of mine during our wild sixties days. With prematurely white locks still in a ponytail, this lost beach boy is now the tenured director of an applied linguistics center at the University of Melbourne. Having rescued his actress wife from Hollywood casting calls and his mop-haired son from L.A.'s gang-ridden schools, he proudly presents Mei and me with our very own kangaroo lapel pins—and our own room in a suburban mini-mansion that comes with backyard barbie.

With its vast green spaces and evident civility, Melbourne is often ranked as the world's most livable city. Yet Mei and I emerge from Flinders Station—so near, yet courtside far from Flinders Park, where the Australian Open tennis tournament is starting—into a downtown at once stately Victorian and frontier shabby. Antique trams move through a sound-deadened grid where prim Anglican churches alternate with five-and-dimes. We stroll the boulevards of Australia's second city while shooing "outback" horseflies out of our faces. Passing imperceptibly under an airy blue four-story ceremonial gate, we turn down the straight-laced spine of the first continuous settlement of Chinese on this continent—a most livable Chinatown.

Little Bourke Street is more red brick than mandarin, dainty and quaint in its smattering of British-style pubs, scrubbed clean with barely a hint of burning soy, built on the petite and digestible scale of a barbecued pork bun. Appropriately, the miniature community's culinary distinction appears to lie mostly with its *yum cha*, quaintly Cantonese for "tea snacks," known to most of the rest of the world as *dim sum*. As we soon find out, "dim sims" are Aussie lingo for the doughy, greasy dumplings featured in horrendous takeaways. But everything is up to snuff and more at Chir Wei Tian—named for the Confucian quote "eating is uppermost," here curiously translated to English as the Shark Fin House.

This is where we meet Mei's cousin Lu Hui, her husband, and a Shanghai aunt whose acorn-round face makes her a twin of Mei's mother. In fact, the couple borrowed from Mei's mom to help pay for schooling that served as their entrée. Typical of a so-called "education rush" set off by the liberalization of quotas, the couple has used a post-Tiananmen amnesty to stay on while acquiring the technical skills to earn points that will eventually grant them permanent residence. Though university grads back in China, both work the night shift at a T-shirt factory while pursuing higher computing and accounting degrees. To meet us, they've traveled more than an hour from Dandenong, a working-class suburb less charming than its name. But family reunions, and food, take priority.

I've brought along my Aussie transplant friends, too, giving us more mouths to sample some of what the owner claims to be eighty varieties of appetizer. Standards like shrimp *har gow*, chicken feet in black bean sauce, and banana-wrapped sticky rice equal in delicacy anything found in Hong Kong. There are dazzling offerings like duck-and-black-mushroom rolls wrapped in Chinese cabbage, barbecue pork in flaky mini-loaves, eggplant and fish in clay pots, and pastry cups of shark fin. Here, the typically perfunctory waitresses don't just push carts while cawing out their wares. They also grill rice cakes, stir and garnish varied pots of rice porridge, cut greens with scissors, and pour on the oyster sauce like maple syrup.

Later, the food keeps coming on the cousins' "little weekend out-ing" along the Great Ocean Road—five hours each way of posing and picnicking through eucalyptus groves and coastal hairpin turns, hail storms, wind gusts, and double rainbows. Maybe this day's absurd diligence is pure Chinese bravado—or the cousins' effort to prove themselves worthy of Australia's open spaces and devil-may-care ethos. The whole country looks like California on steroids. California with no people.

This time, I've even got my own people here. There's a whole Aussie branch to my far-straying Russian-Jewish family tree, descended from our common great-grandmother named Taffapolski. Two of these properly Anglicized Tafts soon drive us out to their better end of town. In Doncaster, a suburb increasingly populated by skittish Hong Kong emigrés, their recommendation is the Taipan, which, despite its Japanese name, is a slick Cantonese seafood house laden with enough tanks to be an aquarium.

"They're brought live from all parts of the world," we're told by owner Charles Ng, an ebullient ex-microbiologist. He offers his theory on restaurant start-ups. "Nowadays, fish have more frequent flyer miles than humans."

I'm glad my cultured kin are there to order steamed versions of various Aussie invertebrates, including the single claw of a Tasmanian king crab. The world's an oyster for David and Angela, who after a long stint in London with the B.B.C., have returned to a house whose fruit-laden backyard is the size of a New York pocket park. All my extended clan live well within shouting range. As guests of honor at their post-Sabbath cookout, we get to hear them argue over a recent sex scandal involving various left-leaning government ministers. I can't keep track of the good guys and bad. In this egalitarian society formed by ex-prisoners, every politician seems to be named Bob.

"Every liberal deserves a mistress!" the patriarch argues. "At least that crowd's got some passion."

"Sexist swine!" snarls a daughter-in-law. "I suppose only fascists know how to keep their pants on. . . ."

Though they bear names like Marcus and Ronnie, there's something instantly recognizable about this family's wealth of opinions, the articulate sparring and neurotic nerve jangling. Mei can hardly get in a word—but this makes an enjoyable contrast to so many prior family reunions. For her stoic relations, it's enough to simply be breaking bread—or chomping rice—after so much time apart. Keeping their mouths full prevents the Chinese from stirring up old traumas or new indiscretions. Of course, the Taft/Taffapolskis also have a favorite neighborhood Chinese restaurant, but by the time we get there, we're already too stuffed with deli salads.

There's yet another family member awaiting us in Melbourne. Ever since we were wowed by the "imperial cuisine" in Beijing's Li Family Restaurant, we've been pointed toward their most illustrious daughter. From the elegant brochure for Li Li's restaurant, complete with endorsements from the brother of the Last Emperor, we hardly expect the place to be located on the downtown's semi-industrial fringes, near West Melbourne's train yards. Two stone lions guarding a carport are the way we know that we're nearing one of the more remarkable Chinese restaurants on the planet. The owner's new Honda nearly blocks the entry to the semi-attached home that's been transformed into a waiting room with bar and peach-toned inner sanctum.

Like her professor father back in her crumbling *hutong* home, Li Li produces set dinners for a limited number of reserved customers who pay around forty dollars per head. This isn't so much out of snobbery, as the diminutive chef explains, but because she's got to know how many people to shop for each morning. Will expatriation spoil the Li family's scrupulously homemade version of hand-me-down emperor's fare? A raffish waiter in black dinner jacket, matching kinked hair, and the inaudible accent of an Aussie mobster patiently describes each of the night's thirteen courses. Familiar to us from the Beijing branch, these dishes barely resemble anything that passes for Chinese food in Australia. The appetizers are unforgettable: fried rounds of lotus root with star anise, crunchy cabbage hearts turned special with a mustard sauce, pickled cucumbers with pork, strips of sesame-coated chicken. Later, comes the nearly Italian course of pork in wine sauce, plus a fair rendition of Peking duck. Like some Taoist experiment, the Li family banquet adds up to more than the sum of its parts. Each entrée sticks to the purposeful purity of bringing forward a single flavor: white pepper, Shaoxing wine, coriander. The flavors combine on our tongues, then in our guts.

Head chef Li Li is as timid as her mathematician dad was self-promoting. Accepting her culinary fame as fate, she admits to Mei with a sigh, "A fortune-teller told me I would get married late." Embarrassed, I try to hush up Mei when she starts playing matchmaker. But Li Li doesn't seem to mind at all.

"In the Qing Dynasty, Li Li would have cooked in the palace," whispers Mei as we linger to watch her close the restaurant. "Now she's an imperial chef for the world. Which is more of a prisoner?"

At least, she's traded the Forbidden City for the lucky country—where everyone is lucky to eat her food. "The Australian ambassador in Beijing wouldn't give up," Li Li tells us with a blush. "He made me feel that this country really needed me." A perfect fit with Melbourne's abundant peace and polite understatement, Li Li says of her adopted home, "It's so green and tranquil."

"Why don't we move here, too?" Mei asks, tempted by the local restaurants and welfare state. Though I doubt that our dubious expertise could earn us enough entry points, she's game for any and all citizenships. "It's still not too late. We can both marry Australians. No worries!"

Napa Cabbage Hearts in Mustard Sauce

From Li Li's

Ingredients:

Napa or Chinese cabbage, 2 heads
Powdered mustard, 1 oz.
Sugar, 1 tbsp.
Rice vinegar, $^1/_2$ oz.
Salt

Add enough boiled water to the powdered mustard to make a paste. Let cool and add the sugar, salt, and vinegar. Mix evenly. Peel the outside leaves of the cabbages, cut off the bottoms, slice and throughly wash the remaining 1 1/2 inch hearts. Put in a deep bowl, cover with boiling water, and let sit until the water cools. Pour off the water and repeat. Marinate the cooked hearts for one to two hours in the mustard-vinegar mixture.

Chinatown Without Chinese

What use are stone edifices if they cannot tell stories? Why can't I pick up a faded street hawker's echo in the breezy silence of dead-end alleys, the century of Asian life along lanes named Heffernan and Tattersalls? Prim missionary churches, family associations devoid of the usual flourishes, barely hint at triumphs and banishments, lives interrupted and lineage honored. What to make of an ethnic enclave more testament than neighborhood, a stage set bordered by stone lions but bereft of the usual cast of teeming thousands?

As in San Francisco, Melbourne's Chinatown had its origins in disappointed prospectors who stayed on to become merchants. While I've learned to identify my hometown as *jio jin shan*—the "old gold mountain" that Chinese tried to climb during gold rush days— Melbourne and the gem-laden foothills of its surrounding state of Victoria became known as *xin jin shan* (*hsi gum san* in Cantonese), or the "new gold mountain." Beginning just a bit later in 1851, this frontier had brought forth its own generation of forty-niners. Australia, too, provided a lure for quick riches, with veins to unearth and railroads to build. Some of the "Celestials," as Chinese were labeled, actually tried their luck here in order to flee the brutality and racism first encountered in California.

Still, only an estimated forty thousand Chinese worked the Australian gold fields at their peak. After the White Australia Act of 1901 prevented the first Chinese settlers from bringing over their wives, a bachelor society faced total ostracism from a God-fearing, Asia-dreading society—where tradesmen proudly stamped their products "made by European labor." Today, one or two thousand of the gold seekers' direct descendants remain in Melbourne, outnumbered by new ethnic Chinese arrivals from Vietnam.

It was in the mid-seventies, when Australia extended recognition to the People's Republic, that Melbourne's powers-that-be recognized the benefits of turning their very own bit of Asia into a tourist attraction. Little Bourke Street emerged from decades of seediness and exclusion. The tawdry row of laundries, flop houses, and chop suey joints was outfitted with globular lamps suggestive of paper lanterns. The neighborhood was revived largely as a venue for some forty restaurants. For tourists and local Chinese alike, this Chinatown isn't so much a place to linger as the place to eat.

On the Chinatown Heritage Walk, a neighborhood tour with won ton soup optional, my guide is Bettina, a serious German student of Chinese medicine. Instead of heritage, our curious group is offered a general primer course on Chinese daily life, a visit to the grocery store to explicate the mysteries of bok choy and bean curd.

"Can anyone tell me why these are called cellophane noodles?" asks our *fraulein*. I can't. A stop at the Bee Tin Hiong candy shop lets the daring few sample Chinese beef jerky, sesame rolls, and numerous pungent varieties of salted fruit. "Careful, please, these sweets are awfully sour!" She illustrates the basic precepts of Chinese medicine by having us watch an herbalist mix up his bag of leafy tricks. "See—that batch is for headache. Better than an Excedrin!" While many Americans could use such instruction, most would turn away in embarrassment from such condescension. Nearly a century and a half after their arrival, the Chinese in Australia are still treated as exotic.

Still, it's hard to say which promised land was the more cruel to its indispensable laborers and laundrymen, greengrocers and tailors. In this curious competition with America, the record shows that the easygoing Aussies were less murderous toward the yellow man, but equally less equipped with notions of a welcoming "melting pot." Is all to be forgotten and forgiven now that Australia is suddenly eager to join the Asian economic boom? Now that Melbourne is becoming a self-congratulatory ethnic welter, saved from Anglo stultification by its pockets of Greeks, Italians, Jews, and, finally, Asians?

"Fortunately, history here is very shallow," remarks one Chinese businessman. "Once the government signals a new approach, people change their attitudes." In his Kuomintang Building bookstore, the bellicose Martin Louey, longtime representative of Taiwan, argues, "Don't knock Australia! There's too much griping about the past! Who let forty thousand students escape from the Communist hell-hole? You've got to take things as a whole, the way Confucius would."

Instead of proverbs, we seek a prescription from a local pharmacy. Everyone tells us to look up Wellington Lee, Chinatown's unofficial mayor, usually found holding court at the back of his business on the bustling intersection of Little Bourke and Russell. Can this be the only drugstore in the world run by a proud holder of an Order of the British Empire? Taking to an extreme the Chinese tendency to tote up one's importance by titles on a card, Wellington Lee hands out mimeographed sheets. I cull from this community activist's crammed line of credits: "National Medal 1967 and Clasp 1977 . . . RSL State Council (proxy) . . . Chairman Hawthorn Mayoral Ball 1962 . . . Educational Vice-President Toastmasters International Club . . . District Governor Lions International 1967–68 . . . Elected Melbourne City Council 1977, 1980, 1985 . . . Moomba Board 1977–80 . . . Keep Melbourne Beautiful 1978–80 . . . Bicentennial Multicultural Task Force 1980 . . . Deputy Chairman Federated Ethnic Communities Council of Australia 1987–89 . . . New Board Freedom from Hunger 1989– . . . Member of Adult Parole Board 1994 . . ."

Despite these advertised honors, Wellington Lee hasn't grown bashful about his grievances. Dapper in bow-tie, striped oxford shirt, and blue blazer, this round-faced gent with distinguished white hair and a barrister's delivery is willing to hector almost anyone who drops in for a cough drop.

"You see, one of my grandfathers founded the first tin mine in this country," Lee explains. "But that didn't mean they would take me into the navy. When I served as an air force officer in Malaysia during the war, why, the Americans had to command my own men to give me a salute. Do you know that some Chinese were given tests in Spanish and Italian to disqualify them from entry? Now they've got these kids from China paying five thousand Aussie dollars to enroll in some sham English course. No wonder most of the families sent their sons home to Canton for schooling. They all wanted to be buried back in their native soil. I went around for twenty-four years in Darwin with a white wife, so I know what it's like. No country has offered us more shameful treatment. But we Chinese always put up with too much, like in Malaysia or Indonesia. It's our own fault because we only want to do business. The Chinese are afraid to reach for political power."

That's why this tireless officeholder says of himself, " 'Oh that Wellington, he's different.' I've been hearing that all my life!"

Yet such feistiness can only be a combination of Chinese staying power and Aussie irreverence. The only thing that disappoints me about Wellington Lee is his choice of restaurant. Perhaps his taste buds are no longer as nationalistic as his politics, because he leads us around the corner, down another dead-end alley, then up an elevator to the hushed and plush second-floor room of the Flower Drum. Posted clippings rank this as "best in Australia" and the Flower Drum's tuxedoed team of waiters are far more elegant in bearing and grooming than anyone who ever walks through their door. Their main dishes, while rich, are equally Westernized, like hunks of salmon and steak barely dressed in ginger and soy.

Mei blames it all on me. "With you, we always get the food that they think the foreigners want." If many of Chinatown's high-rent eateries are overdecorated and underspiced, the general level is still higher than back in the States. The Mask of China does justice to Chaozhou style and there are a surprising number of Malaysian-influenced eateries. Down the alleys, the newest generation of "fresh off the boats" have begun to offer more unadulterated home cooking, as we discover in the dumplings and cakes of the modest student hangout, Camy's Dumpling House.

In a half-empty mall off Flinders Street, a logo less Chinese than Chicagoesque announces "The Bull." Apparently, the reference is to an astrological sign, not Michael Jordan. But this modest establishment with scattered Formica tables serves some of the most authentic Shanghainese food around. Oddly enough, the Bull's owner, Wang Ren Kong, is a highly indulgent emigré who tells us, "I saved up to start this for my teenaged son. He showed some talent in the kitchen and wanted his own place to learn." He even hired an experienced chef to serve as his son's "master." Talk about spoiled!

Dwarfing his dad, Jackie looks burly enough to try out for some basketball team himself. Obviously, he already knows something about cooking. Mei is astonished at the tang of the homemade smoked fish, the salted duck, properly oil-soaked onion cakes, and flat strips of bean curd skins steamed amidst fresh green soy beans—a Shanghainese speciality that only natives would recognize. Despite dark decades when, as Wellington Lee describes, "white men could eat their fill of noodles and leave without paying," real Chinese food is obviously alive and well here. In Australia, as in no other country, it's made obvious that when hard times hit, the Chinese lean on their mean cuisine.

Only in 1985 were those times enshrined in a Chinese museum, constructed out of the former Cohen Brothers furniture factory. That's the reason Cohen Place is incongruously marked by imperial lions and a lacquered "Facing Heaven" archway sent from Nanjing. The gift shop is more extensive than the meager permanent exhibit of newspaper clippings, embroidered tunics, and leftover mining paraphernalia. In a basement exhibit entitled "Finding Gold," floorboards on mechanical rockers suggest the pitch and sway of a ship's hold bringing the miners to Australia. There's a tent for Chinese opera and, of course, a "Chong's Cook House" complete with cleaver and fresh wisps of scallion.

Upstairs, a slide show advertises the achievements of prominent Chinese businessmen. To an American eye, it seems vaguely pathetic that such points still have to be proved. But this sojourn in Australia is a chance to witness a nation in the first throes of a honeymoon with multiculturalism. And the moment has yet to be complicated by political correctness.

"For most folks, the Chinese are somehow slightly voodooish," admits a top aide to the museum's curator, thoroughly Caucasian herself.

"But shouldn't one of your directors be Chinese?"

"Oh my!" the Australian cries. "Wouldn't that be racist?"

My Dragon Is Bigger Than Your Dragon

The longest ceremonial dragon in the world isn't found in Hong Kong, Singapore, or even San Francisco. Coiled in the basement dark of Melbourne's Chinese Museum, ready to strike during Chinatown's street fair at Chinese New Year, is Dai Loong, some sixty mirror-laden meters in length. But top honors, we're told, belong to Bendigo, the main mining town of Victoria's get-rich rush, tagged by Chinese as the "big gold mountain" within Australia's "new gold mountain."

For Mei and me, getting there just means a pleasant two-hour train ride through a landscape remarkably like California's foot-hills—spotted with gnarled black oaks and scented with immense stands of peeling eucalyptus. For the Chinese prospectors driven out of Sze Yap—the four districts of Guangdong Province—by famine and filial duty, opium wars and Taiping rebellions, the journey meant months of travel by slow schooners during which thousands died of scurvy and worse. Thanks to a discriminatory head tax, the ships docked in Adelaide, forcing the "Celestials" to trek by foot up to five hundred miles across a hot and hostile outback.

Like the gold, their traces are everywhere. In the farming commu-nity of Ararat, a statue of a Chinese miner commemorates the fact that this is the only town in Australia founded when itinerant Chi-nese paused to stake a claim—that was just as quickly seized from them. In Ballarat, a living re-creation of gold rush days called Sover-eign Hill features an entire Chinese encampment (apparently staged without the benefit of Chinese actors). There's a large Chinese cemetery in Beechworth, stomping grounds of the notorious bandit Ned Kelly, who began his notorious career at age fourteen by "at-tacking a Chinaman with a stick."

Given the obvious parallels, I expect Bendigo to resemble Sierra Nevada mining towns turned into hokey Wild West pit stops, board-walks lined with pancake houses. From the train depot, flattened av-enues, rusted screen doors, stark white storefronts, and swarms of horseflies instead suggest the one-store outback outpost. Before we've carried our day packs two sunstruck blocks, we come upon the comforting familiarity of the Toi Shan Cafe. Named after the home district of the first prospectors—lured by a letter from Melbourne carpenter Louey Ah Mouey—this is Bendigo's oldest continuous ex-emplar of Chinese cuisine. The blue-eyed lass tending the counter is less interested in ethnography than in closing up the lunch service. We have to beg for the last scoops of pork chow mein and broccoli beef, which taste like they've been warming on the steam table for a century as well.

"And dont'cha want some dim sims?" she asks, forcing us to finish the half-cold lumps that pass for dumplings. "Short soup, long soup, dim sims"—that's about as far as Chinese menus go in the infamous takeaways that have long been Asia's most obvious contribution to Australia's frontier. Every Sunday, we're told, the local housewives would bring their pots and bowls to be filled by some "Chinaman." The ritual of the Chinese holiday supper is as much a part of outback life as digiridoos. What did I expect, stir-fried kangaroo?

Just when I think we're approaching the discernible edge of nowhere, Mei and I arrive at Charing Cross. Here, the town's limited pickup traffic chugs around a nonfunctioning fountain and the old tram tracks head off down the Pall Mall. The street names suggest that Bendigo's founding fathers were loyal sons of Britannia. While the town was officially christened Sandhurst, rough-and-tumble inhabitants preferred a name derived from a local sheepherder who was so good with his fists that people called him after British boxing champ William Bendigo Thompson. But the brawny chaos of the mining camps has given way to blocks of miniature cottages trimmed in cutesy "iron lace."

In every direction, there's as much Victorian opulence as some of the world's most abundant gold fields could buy. Bendigo once boasted the deepest mine in the world and one working mine continued to operate right in the center of town until 1922. Law courts, complete with striking clock tower à la Big Ben, sit beside a post office large enough for central London. Out in the middle of nowhere is what's claimed to be "the largest Gothic cathedral in the Southern Hemisphere."

A few blocks further down, we spot one modern intrusion. The Golden Dragon Museum is so pennant-strewn, concrete, and boxy that I mistake it for a gas station. Bulldozed away in 1964, Chinatown had formed along nearby Bridge Street's ramshackle row of company town cottages. The Bendigo Chinese Association was still active enough in 1991 to have raised the funds to create this impressive monument to their ancestry. There are two exhibit halls, a tea shop showing videos, and an auditorium meant for Chinese dancing and martial arts displays. If the place resembles a high-tech garage, that's because its main purpose is as a permanent parking space and spiritual abode for not one, but two, immense mythical creatures.

The attendant staff appears entirely Caucasian. Even the proud and well-informed wife of Russell Jack, the museum's guiding spirit, has near-Nordic features. Due to the dearth of Chinese women after 1901, Bendigo's Chinese community is unique in the world for its degree of interbreeding. Notoriously poor mixers elsewhere, Chinese like Lam See became Dr. James Lamsey—and the O'Hoys were hardly sons of the Blarney. At the same time, a surprising number of Europeans like Mrs. Jack have become thoroughly Chinese-identified.

The museum exhibition is a mishmash of acculturation: ancient Chinese instruments alternating with programs of debutante balls, recent college diplomas beside faded silk fans. These are presented merely to decorate the sweeping circle on whose spiraling levels is coiled Sun Loong, commissioned in 1969 to be made in Hong Kong and, at one hundred meters, supposedly the world's longest dragon. A second chamber holds the original Loong, brought to Bendigo from China in 1892 and now claimed as "the oldest Imperial dragon in the world." What's even more telling is that the dragon isn't made to dance for the upcoming Chinese New Year's. Though brochures boast of the town elders' authentic "awakening" ceremony, their mythic beast is bestirred solely as the top attraction for the town's long-running Easter parade, staged for charity by Christians and heathens.

I only hope they take their Chinese food more seriously than their Chinese lore. When Mrs. Jack recommends we go back to the Toi Shan for supper, I know that we're in trouble. If Mei and I are smart, we'll stay in the grandly restored Shamrock Hotel's homey pub, where waitresses who look fresh out of County Cork cheerily serve up shepherd's pie. If we were smart, we'd still be in Canton. As evening falls, crystalline to go with Bendigo's cut-glass uniformity, Mei and I make the rounds of three or four Chinese outlets in the town center, all ominously offering a house "smorgasbord."

Superior newspaper reviews in the window lure us into the House of Khong. As usual, there's not an Oriental face in sight. The frowsy hostess with accent straight out of London's East End assures us that the King Khong of the kitchen is indeed a Chinese, albeit from Malaysia—unforgettable Ipoh, no less. She should know, because she's his wife. Figuring she must know a thing or two about Chinese cuisine, Mei tries to bypass the menu with a simple vegetable stir-fry.

"Oh, dearie, I know what'cha mean!" the erstwhile Mrs. Khong caws. "But 'ere, we jes don't do it that way! I knows how you like it, but that ain't the Australian way!"

Neither of us can imagine the hows or whys of Chinese food without stir-frying, until the arrival of our "chicken in Thai sauce." A heap of soggy, stewed tidbits has been drowned in some maraschino cherry sweet ketchup poured from a jar. Of our many entrants for the title of "world's worst," this one may be without peer.

The next morning, Bendigo is boarded up shut for National Day, the Australian equivalent of the Fourth of July. Aptly staged on the shores of a lake left unswimmable by decades of mining effulgence, the town celebration is marked with brass bands, grilled hot dogs, scouts raising the flag, long-winded speeches. I've practically forgotten what country I'm in until a chorus of schoolgirls in Bo Peep bonnets breaks into "Waltzing Matilda." Does anyone but me notice that Bendigo holds its civic rites under a park pavilion with a pagoda-style roof?

While Bendigo's "talking tram," manned by a doddering conductor in bowler hat, takes tourists to the operational Deborah Gold Mine, Mei and I alight at the other end of the line. A short path leads to the Chinese Joss House, Aussie slang for a temple. This certified monument of the National Trust stands exactly as it looked in the 1860s: three brick halls painted red, utterly square and unadorned but perfectly Chinese in their symmetry. There is something very moving about the crudeness of this attempt to make a place in an inhospitable land for Guan Gong, a much-needed, protective warrior spirit. "Loyalty, utter devotion, benevolence, and courageousness" reads one of the altar inscriptions.

Allowed only to "puddle" through the white miners' leavings, isolated and ridiculed, under pressure to pay back their debts of passage, the Chinese had shown a persistence that the envious Aussies came to call "Chinaman's Luck." Thanks more to pluck, they dug 205,464 ounces of gold from the hills of Victoria—enabling their relatives to build a small railway back in Canton. A fifteen minutes' walk through Bendigo's last suburban subdivision is White Hills, former site of a Chinese camp where many of the miners lie in a small clump within a larger Christian cemetery. Who knows what these unlucky souls would make of their blue-eyed descendants? Fresh flowers, we've been told, are still sent to one grave by one grateful grandson who now lives in San Francisco. This is his homage to a man who kept sending money back to China despite being blinded by chili peppers thrown in his eyes. In silence, Mei and I try to pick up some echo of the seven thriving Chinese tent cities, one per district and dialect, that once drew the locals' ire over screeching opera and strange cooking smells. The Chinese writing has rubbed off most of the tombstones.

Back in Melbourne, Mei and I mark Chinese New year—appropriately, the Year of the Pig, with the widow of the first Chinese city councilman, her daughter, grandkids, and American "herbal gynecologist" son-in-law. But our feed is interrupted by an uproar out on the street. Having seen too many dragons reduced to museum pieces, I've almost forgotten that the real thing is meant to let loose its rage and shake its mane to the clamor of drums and cymbals. With the aid of a two-man team wearing white headbands, the restaurant gets blessed by this fire-breathing force of nature. Jumping onto tables to paw the plates, one hungry paper beast is enough to thrill the kiddies, rattle the silverware, frighten the ghost of bad times out of Australia.

Quotations from Chairman Maori

"Why would anyone possibly want to go to New Zealand?" asks nearly every Aussie when we tell them our travel plans. Their good-natured ribbing seems to imply, "What can you find there that you haven't already found here?"

I have to admit, it's tough to compete with Sydney—though we're staying miles from the opera house with another of Mei's cousins, the implacable Simon Wu. This sleepy but self-confident kid charms us with a combination of immigrant bluster and blasé Aussie chatter. After failing at his own restaurant, Simon has turned to sewing unofficial Sydney Olympics T-shirts by turning his garage into a one-man sweatshop. Though he's just married his childhood sweetheart back in Shanghai, his walls and carpets are sooted with years of bachelor living, Chinese cigarettes, and peanut oil residue. Like my Jewish forebears, there's nothing Simon won't try and nothing stopping him but the immensity of all he does not yet know. To impress us, he takes Mei and me for a lavish Thai supper, admitting only after he orders for everyone that he's never tried the stuff in his life.

Simon does know Sydney's Chinatown, an overcommercialized enclave that runs along Dixon Street toward a seaside park development. In one basement mall, all white plastic chairs surrounded by a dozen competing booths, Mei is intrigued by a sign that reads, "Kazakhstan Gourmet." This thoroughly un-Russian stand is run by a refugee *menage a trois* from Muslim China whose dominant wife/sister makes the best homemade dumplings and hot noodle dishes south of Taipei. Sometimes, paper plates are worth it. Guiltily, we sneak back to this place several times, even though we're giving up mealtime slots for other contenders.

Lured into the Golden Empire by front windows that display fish tanks big enough for most Sea World dolphin shows, we pass on the Tasmanian crab at a hundred U.S. dollars per claw. But we share some fine steamed Hong Kong-style renditions with a pair of droll local filmmakers. Since he's Aussie and she's Kiwi, the neighborly jousting takes up once more.

"You really shouldn't bother with those lonely set o' rocks out there," the Aussie cautions.

"But we've got a free stopover!"

"That's about what those Kiwis are worth!"

The documentarian's words will ring in my ears. While Sydney is like San Francisco with warm water to swim in, cross-oceanic Auckland pretty much suggests Oakland. The morning after our four-hour flight over, we find a harbor full of sail boats, a ring of green hills. But is there, to paraphrase Gertrude Stein's immortal words, a there here? Especially a Chinese one?

The downtown of the biggest city on New Zealand's North Island is a sterile collection of deadly straight boulevards sliding toward the sea. Old-fashioned movie palaces alternate with modest malls, and everywhere there are organic muesli cafes where, to the din of imported grunge music, listless hippies and scowling Maoris break brown bread in a palpable bath of boredom. I'm not surprised when I read in the papers of a high teenage suicide rate. Here's a country where things are so good, they can't help turning sour.

Without the native peoples—who've survived in large numbers despite Britain's onslaught a century back—there would hardly be any problems for people to sink their teeth into. No wonder New Zealand's modern-day distinction is as the place where daredevils from all over the world come to bungee jump toward the base of sheer canyons. As for a Chinatown to explore, we hear rumors of one suburb that nearly qualifies. There are not much more than twenty thousand Chinese in the country, some descendants of nineteenth-century gold miners who, following the regional pattern, weren't allowed to become New Zealand citizens until 1952. Downtown Auckland boasts four or five Cantonese-style dinner houses, though the aging, Hong Kong–style New Orient clearly caters to non-Oriental patrons. The owner says that he came here because of the New Zealand government's well-known, New Age tolerance.

"They're more welcoming to the Chinese than in Australia. The Kiwis make us feel wanted," he says. Few people are more politically attuned than the Chinese—able to take advantage of liberalism before their arrival, willing to turn conservative once they settle.

This place also knows how to take advantage of Mei's blind request for the house speciality. We get more mushy crab than we can possibly finish, coincidentally the menu's most expensive item. "Pushing the payment," it's called, both in Beijing and here. But for dessert, Mei can have volcanoes, hot lava, Maori chanting, sheep farms, skiing, certified knock-your-socks-off treks, seaside views, a hundred-mile jeep ride down a single strand of beach. All are available on the cheap along a well-trod backpackers' circuit. Bus tours featuring nonstop rock music leading to rugged mountain adventures can be ordered by number, and a youth hostel card seems the local equivalent of American Express gold. From our hostel, we have direct access to almost anywhere in the country—if the desk clerks ever figure out which order form to fill out. Life in New Zealand moves glacially.

In search of a glimmer of national identity, we opt for a trip to the Bay of Islands, scenic sight of New Zealand's first European incursions. Our ride up toward the northern tip of the country takes us through hours of a kind of twinkling, besotted green available in North America only when every sprinkler is turned on forever. By special request, we stop at the tallest kauri tree left in the country, amidst one of the few magnificent stands left unravaged by the colonizers. Roger, our driver, recites the life story of Mt. Everest conqueror Sir Edmund Hilary whose birthplace is along the route. But when the conversation turns to a book I'd once written about Fidel Castro, he admits, "Sorry, mate. Never heard of the fella."

If only Roger knew what mountains the guy climbed! Somehow, I expect a more universal awareness in this upstart land known for barring U.S. nuclear-powered submarines. Instead, everyone I've met so far—admittedly, most are in khaki shorts and under twenty-five—seem to mirror their country. At best, they could be called insular; at worst, they're about ten thousand miles out of it.

Dropped at sunset in coastal Paihia, we quickly discover the one and only Chinese mom-and-pop among a clump of sea breeze motels. I want to see Waitangi, where the infamous treaty between the British and the native Maoris was signed. A few days before our arrival, the government staged its annual commemoration of the event—a kind of bad sportsmanship akin to the mayor of New York celebrating the twenty-four dollar sale of Manhattan. This year, some Maori activists jeered the prime minister with more than tribal chants. If the show of fearsome facial tattoos wasn't enough, one pulled down his pants to show the leader his true opinion.

Set on an oak-covered isle, the early capital of Russell is a ramshackle row of nineteenth-century inns that look like the setting for the film *The Piano*. Mei tickles the ivories of an antique stand-up in the music parlor of the Arcadia Lodge where, oddly enough, nearly all the guests hail from Switzerland. Perhaps they hunger for the sea or are addicted to certain levels of pure oxygen. They should just get it over with and declare New Zealand an international ecological refuge—where the only wildlife will be hot dog skiiers and bungee jumpers, the *genus jockus*. But when it comes to Chinese food, the grass is always greener at the next table.

On Fire in Fiji

It's not a good sign when a country's biggest crowds are in the departures lobby. To get our first glimpse of Fiji's South Seas paradise, Mei and I have to fight our way past several dozen standing circles of mostly female Hindus. Flamboyant saris match the extravagant tears shed in farewells to husbands and sons about to board a midnight flight for Los Angeles. In a dimly lit snack bar where the cakes are as sticky-sweet as the air, Mei insists that we take a poll of one Indian brood.

"This country has a rattan ceiling," declares the quick-on-the-draw matriarch. While swatting the mosquitoes off her youngest child, she peers through a tarmac-level cutout at the refueling Fiji Air 747 like it's a freedom train. Looking straight out of the Punjab with arms full of silver bangles, she seems to know more about the economy of our hometown than we do. "Have you heard of a hiring freeze in Silicon Valley? Do you think NAFTA will affect the high-tech industries?"

This brain drain of middle-class Indians, the ancestors of cane-cutters imported by the British, started back in 1987 when strapping Lieutenant Siviteni Rabuka seized power in the name of native Fijians by invading the duly elected parliament in order to depose the country's first prime minister of Indian origin. About as separate from the world as any place could be, this new nation spread over 125,000 square miles of sea is tackling ethnic strife while attempting to enter the global economy. But I figure that's where the Chinese may have found an opening. In their timeless quest for appetizers, ships from old Cathay once combed the waters off Fiji for the best *beche-de-mer*, better known as sea cucumber. Given their roving gaze and proven seaworthiness, I'm sure four or five thousands miles of open ocean can hardly faze them now.

Meanwhile, Mei and I have to negotiate a dozen miles or so to the nearest bed. "Bula!" cry the Fijian matrons working the Polynesian brown airport lobby, in a greeting unrelated to the Yale fight song. These broad, tobacco-skinned ladies, look like misplaced schoolgirls in prim white blouses and black, ankle-length wraps. Closer to Australian aboriginals than Tahitians, everything about them is generously rounded, from noses to hips to the bushiest Afros this side of Capetown. With ultra-brite smiles and calm, gently accented English, they try to book us into Nadi, a town built solely on tax-free tourist shopping—or better yet, speed us on motorboats straight off to the best offshore resorts. With a planeload of neighboring Solomon Islanders having arrived so drunk that they literally crawl through customs, Mei and I appear to be their biggest score.

I hold out stubbornly for Lautoka, described by our guidebook as the busiest port town on the north side of Viti Levu, the country's main island. Eventually, a black van pulls up and offers us a ride there at less than a dollar each. Just beyond the airport gates, cane fields hiss in the darkness. The road skirts a rolling sea that keeps perfect time with radio reggae thumping loudly enough to vibrate the entire dash. All is too still and silent once we're dropped along a street of one-story shops fronting railroad tracks that lead to nearby sugar mills. Just around the corner, a small, blinking light indicates the Hotel Lautoka, rated as the city's best. There's no problem about vacancies. I have the feeling that we're the only ones occupying the shacklike boxes behind a second-floor dining verandah.

Tropical islands comes in two flavors—idyllic and not-so. On Sunday morning, we still seem to be the only souls stumbling about this unadorned town built blunt against a waveless sea. The architecture is so nondescript as to frustrate all labels: everything is smooth concrete flaking yellow. Down by the rocky shore are rusted piers and benches, one "resort" ringed with barbed wire. A bakery sells soft rolls sprinkled with sugar right across from the T-shaped overhangs we presume to be a bus terminal. Where most Fijians don't live in towns at all, Lautoka is atmospheric solely in its lethargy. The only signs of life are chords from a cheesy electric organ that cue the choir of an evangelical congregation. We poke our head inside a paneled storefront church to glimpse a preacher with microphone clipped to his long robes. Amidst empty rows of folding chairs, a half-dozen big mammas are standing and clapping, reveling in some serious South Seas gospel.

Every journey dictates its own story line. Only indigestion can interrupt this one for long. Among the dimmed businesses along the town's central block, we count three Chinese restaurants. Somewhere on the planet, we're bound to run into a town where the per capita exceeds one for every eater. In fact, these are the *only* restaurants around. Getting Fijian grub would mean attending some up-country ceremony where chiefs chant while preparing the national dish of *kava*—a lip-numbing, milky gray, pepper-root mash that doesn't sound like it can lure me away from twice-cooked anything. Fortunately, the practice of cannibalism in these parts (which has left gnawed and charred human bones dated as far back as 500 B.C.) has been reduced to the selling of tiny wooden "cannibal forks" to tourists.

"During the Cultural Revolution," Mei is reminded, "there were small villages where people ate the flesh of class enemies." There's no such danger in Lautoka's cavernous Hong Kong Restaurant, a linoleum palace that occupies the space of two deep storefronts with fifty or so red Formica tables. The minimal decorations include some strategic mirrors and the usual red calendars featuring cherubic, pig-tailed gods. Most familiar of all is the diffidence of the tall, teenage waitress just opening the place. She moves with that mix of resignation and untested superiority that can only be ascribed to those who have given up hope or never known it. For her, Fiji is no way up, just a way out. She tells us that she's from a village near Canton, as are most of the hundred or so Chinese who are still saving up to build the town's first temple. She brings us a passable chow mein and a fish fillet dotted with black beans that look like grounded flies. Fortunately, there's only time for a few bites before our noon checkout.

Back at the Lautoka Hotel, Mei goes up to pack while I'm paying up. Waiting for another imposing Fijian woman to complete the math, I notice a puff of white smoke coming from a vent on the far side of the hotel's inner courtyard. Within seconds, the puff becomes a continual silk-white gush. Without my having to alert her, the clerk glances back, registers shock, and reaches for the phone.

"Problem in the kitchen!" is all she'll say. That's enough for me to calculate that there's little between the flames and our room but a wall of perfect, clapboard kindling. I possess the slow reflexes of the chronically absentminded, a purposeful lag between me and reality's blunt edges. But it's amazing how quickly I get into motion when faced with a nearly risk-free opportunity to act heroic. In a New York minute—a Lautoka century?—I've dashed upstairs and am pounding Gestapo-like on our locked door. The brass number five starts to slant.

"Mei-Mei, open up quick!"

"Oh, it's you. I thought maybe it was a cannibal!" She's opened the door at last, but doesn't seem to get it.

"The hotel's on fire! No joke!" A moment earlier, I would have been embarrassed to shout so dramatically. Already, churning gray clouds are funneling up the backstairs and down our hallway. "Forget the packing. No, okay, grab the laptop!"

"Here—take it! I'll get the dental floss." By now, she believes me. But fatalism is the Chinese form of panic. With a few well-planned moves, she's pulled down a drying pair of undies, and handed me our half-zipped backpack. In the hallway, she pauses to stare at the hot cloud coming straight at us.

"Ay, ya!" That's Mandarin for "Jeez, Louise!"

We sprint past the desk clerk and out into the noontime sun. Our beat-up Nikes, dirty laundry, and stacks of collected restaurant menus fall from our arms in a heap—prompting a laugh from the crowd of Fijian kids who have begun to gather to watch the show from across the street. My medicine kit tumbles onto the sidewalk, splaying sheets of Pepto Bismol tablets into the gutter. Mei gives me a hug.

"My Lei Feng!" Mei is referring to China's most famous "model soldier" and rescuer of old ladies. "How did you move so fast in this heat?"

"You wouldn't make good barbecue."

By the time the Fijian fire truck pulls up, the whole back end of the ground-floor kitchen, town supplier of pineapple pizzas, is seriously aflame and nearly reduced to open beams. The firemen haven't bothered with a siren, and, as they leisurely pile out of their antique truck, the day is clearly too hot for much rapid movement under their asbestos suits. Mei and I stand back and enjoy the unfolding of a hilarious, slow-motion cartoon. The three-man crew are dressed like Third World Blue Meanies. Eventually, they drag the hoses back through the courtyard and aim their nozzle correctly. But nobody's in charge or imagines that the hotel has paying guests. We slip over the maze of flattened hose and tiptoe back upstairs to fetch our remaining Long March–brand slippers. Our room is filled with a level of smoke that might indeed have proved fatal.

"Lucky we got up early this morning . . ."

"Lucky we didn't linger over lunch . . ."

In how many strange towns, on how many hard beds, have I imagined such a revenge of the kitchen gods? But not in broad daylight, never on Sunday. On the long munch, this has been our closest brush with danger beyond ingesting excessive levels of MSG.

Catching Up with "Overcoming Difficulties" Wong

It isn't just Chinese food that's washed up on these far shores. "The Chinese question"—and a Chinese solution—are the talk of all Fiji. On our four-hour mini-van ride to the capital of Suva, we hear about little else than "the scheme," as it seems to be known. The details come to us via Tiffany, a secretarial student from Hong Kong who looks like she's found the ultimate party school. Short locks lightened in punkish streaks by months of sun worship, skin browned to a Pan-Pacific hue, this mousy girl is beachcombing with an ethnically indeterminate hunk named Mohammed. Along with her snorkel, Tiffany carries a sackful of family snapshots. But she clearly feels liberated from the crush back home. Now the presence of her fellow Chinese may be greatly increased due to a controversial government proposal to lure as many as thirty thousand Hong Kong people desperate to escape the Communist takeover.

"Isn't it bizarre? The generals need us to boost their economy! They'll charge every family fifty thousand U.S. just for a passport! And then they have to invest another hundred thousand! Can you believe anyone would be that eager to get into Fiji?"

I can't, though like the rest of the passengers, I'm made somewhat giddy by the absurd urgency with which our squinting, turbaned driver hurtles along the two-lane highway. At pit stops, the scents of curries and grilled flat breads, the shrill recordings of Hindu divas and droning flutes, only add to a general sense of displacement. The melange of music and heat, haggard men and swaying coconuts, make this island feel like a close cousin of Trinidad that somehow wandered away. Any remaining indigenous culture is somewhere up in the hills, accessible mostly by river traffic. Though Mei and I will later take a detour to stick our feet in the blue lagoons beside the fading "Man Friday Resort," the road we're stuck on is in between rain-forest ornithology and high-seas escape.

Yet it's only on this well-trod path that we'll find our favorite middlemen. "Good luck!" Tiffany wishes us. "There are at least fifteen Chinese restaurants in Suva!" With 140,000 residents, this natural port snuggled beside a large bay bills itself as the most sophisticated spot between Auckland and Honolulu. It's pleasant strolling about a city whose briefcase-clutching barristers and bureaucrats wear their brown oxford shoes beneath traditional, wraparound dresses. The place is graced with a core of colonial buildings with white wooden shutters and iron balconies, one leftover cricket green, and a single, basic-model Holiday Inn. For twenty dollars a day, we get a harbor-view efficiency suite, with kitchenette and balcony, the world's noisiest air-conditioner, and soggiest bed.

T-shirt shops are abundant, along with cheap five-and-dimes stocked mostly with Chinese-made dolls and sugar bowls. A few are owned by Hong Kongers who have arrived along with a recent wave of garment workers and vegetable growers, some using fake passports. Under the rusted tabernacle of the old central market, I see local herbs and weeds being hawked by a surprising number of young Cantonese girls. But there is certainly no "invasion" as yet. Due to growing crime and political instability, the Chinese population has actually declined since Fiji's 1970 independence.

The morning edition of the *Fiji Times* contains a page-two feature on a certain terrifying hotel fire in Lautoka. And the headlines confirm all Tiffany has told us. For months now, the government has been floating their "scheme" and pushing legislation aimed at luring Chinese money. But Fiji's stridently subversive press—an inheritance from the Indians as well as the Brits—is full of columns that question the plausibility of such large immigration fees. Commentators point out the opportunities for abuse in high places, especially with the father of Prime Minister Rabuka already implicated in shady dealings with Chinese businessmen. Others ponder the effect of such an influx on a society already so ethnically polarized. A leading local cleric warns that the Fijian body politic isn't "mature enough to deal with such change" and that the Chinese, "as people experienced in business," would "never lose out on the deal." To reassure a nervous public about new "yellow hordes," the government has even proposed housing the rich emigrés in a specially built encampment. Presumably, this would be the world's first high-end Chinatown, a technocratic ghetto.

In order to develop, the Fijians need to bring in other peoples—who'll undoubtedly give them a nice, modern country in which to feel like total strangers. It's amazing just how much of what passes for the latest incarnation of civilization has already washed up. The message in the bottle always reads, "Buy! Buy! Buy!" In Suva, Mei and I watch Demi Moore lay her sexual harassment on Michael Douglas in frigid Seattle, but the cinema's speakers are so raspy that we can't understand a word of *Disclosure*. As Mei says on our way out, "That's entertainment!" Sinister discos offer further distraction, but no video game arcades can yet compete with the purple cumulus clouds and unfiltered red sun dropping nightly into Suva's wide-open sea.

"Predictable," says Mei, repeating our favorite comment on anything this Cinemascopic. But each dusk, we follow a large segment of the population on their involuntary drift toward the waterfront balustrades. Arm in arm, Mei and I happily singe our retinas.

If there is any fear of some impending Chinese peril, that hasn't stopped Chinese restaurants from becoming the leading pleasure after dark. Six or seven lace-curtained outposts line several blocks of the main drag. Announced in black letters across its second-story balcony, the Sichuan Pavilion appears to be run, and run down, by the provincial government in China. We don't get to judge for ourselves because it is never open at the hours posted. Judging from the line outside its ground-floor take-out stand, the clear choice among the local Chinese and tourists—but no Fijians—is yet another Hong Kong Cafe.

Then a funny thing happens on our way to the wok. A classy sign in cursive script leaps out at us: "Leonardo's Italiano." Mei and I spend ten minutes on the unlit sidewalk trying to resist. How long has it been since we had a whiff of the roughest *ragu bolognese*, shaken up some grated parmigiano, or toasted with Chianti instead of chrysanthemum tea? How yawning the gap, at the moment anyhow, between plain old noodles and pasta primavera?

"We shouldn't, you know . . ." Duty calls us to more mediocre stir-fry, and our number of meals in one locale is limited. But the hallmark of post-feudal man, and woman, is requiring some variety in their feedings.

"I can't take this anymore!" Mei protests. "Do you really think we'll find the world's best in Suva! Or are you being cheap?"

"No way."

"Never save money out of the mouth of your wife," argues Mei, coining yet another of her instant proverbs. Casting better judgment to the trade winds, we take the plunge—and end up with plates of over-creamed spaghetti and wine-doused hunks of just-thawed tuna steaks that Mei insists on sending back over the protests of a Fijian Luigi. Italian food travels more poorly than Chinese. At least, with the latter, you can gauge authenticity by a visual check of the chefs.

Chastened, we're left with plenty of stomach room for the Hong Kong. The place is so crowded, we share a large table with a retired Singaporean couple who are enthusiastic regulars. But the general level of hygiene and the steely manner of the proprietress all reek of the motherland. When the owner's husband shows up, we meet a scrawny, chain-smoking, and possibly inebriated poet straight out of the classical tradition of Li Bai. He sits barefoot and cross-legged, scratching at his hairless chest, as though the busy eating house were his living room. Though he claims to "help out a bit," the man's main work is as a calligrapher. Mei translates one scroll about the poet's nostalgia for pretty Chinese maidens. Just the thing to console a spouse working fourteen hours a day. The man of the house points proudly to several watercolors of misty Huang Mountain that he's sketched from memory. In the Chinese vision of paradise, there are no palm trees.

So why have they all come to Fiji? For the millionth time, I hear about an uncle who came first, or a cousin before him, the original relative resembling original sin. Asking why the Chinese leave home is like asking why the sky is blue.

This time, the Fijian government will find few takers. Soon enough, they will be shamed into dropping the high admission fee of their Chinese "solution." We achieve our culinary solution with a five-minute taxi ride into Suva's paltry suburbs. A corner storefront, a distant branch of Auckland's Great Wok, has a contemporary, carpeted interior that is downright elegant by local standards. Co-owner and hostess Elizabeth Sorby looks more like a head librarian than a restaurateur. But one glance at the menu shows us that this place is for real, offering tea-smoked duck and more. That's because the Great Wok has entered into a rent-a-chef program with the government of Sichuan.

"Every other year, they rotate two chefs out from Chengdu," Ms. Sorby explains. "It's quite a challenge sometimes, getting them to adjust. But not these two! They like to practice their English by taking phone bookings. And they keep the waitresses on their toes by hurling cleavers at them!"

It may not be saying much, but thanks to this humble tandem, the Great Wok is the top Chinese restaurant for several thousand leagues in any direction. For us, these chefs provide a superbly fresh whole "squirrel fish," properly battered and carved, and honor a rare request for my favorite fish-flavored shredded pork, a taste of home as tart as these chefs' memories. Afterwards, the pair on lend-lease are eager to escape their deep-frying and oblige us with an interview outside the kitchen's screened backdoor. For them, Fiji is no day at the beach. It's a tour of steaming duty from noon to two A.M. Still, one says, "This assignment is a privilege earned by merit. Otherwise, we'd still be chopping carrots back home."

The tireless duo soon apologize for "lacking the true Sichuan peppercorns." They miss China almost as much. I press my poor translator, "Is that all they've got say?"

"They're not French chefs, they're Chinese," jokes Mei. "You should be happy just with their names!"

I am, since the handles given these stray children of the Cultural Revolution are dead giveaways of the epoch of their birth. In the midst of the Pacific Ocean, we are shooting the breeze with "Protect Mao Zedong" Zui and "Overcoming Difficulties" Wong. If only their ancestors could imagine such difficulties!

Surfing Doctors

Travel's great treasure is its anonymity. At seven A.M., Mei and I nonchalantly board a local Honolulu bus filled with Filipina nurses and overtanned Anglo insurance men. Only the two of us can know all that this brief, exact-change leg completes.

After six months on alien turf, we're welcomed back by some public transit loony mumbling about welfare cheats on Mars. The morning is about as chilled as Hawaii gets. Dropped at a downtown transfer point, I guard our still-rolling suitcases from Beijing's Friendship Store while Mei goes off to score a place to stay. She has no relatives here, but makes up for it with plenty of friends. Soon enough, we're having to coax a Vietnamese cabbie into conquering his fear of heights by taking us up to a subdivision built on a volcanic ridge.

Recovering from jet lag on a deck overlooking half the island, Mei and I reacquaint ourselves with a living standard to which we're not accustomed. Our hosts are not just roommates but siblings: both eligible M.D. bachelors with too little free time and plenty of disposable income. Highlights of the house tour are a refrigerated wine cooler, an industrial-quality cappucino maker (deployed with surgical precision), the top hundred world beat CDs from Swaziland, several prized Japanese woodcuts, and a collection of Oriental orchids.

As soon as we're properly caffeinated, we accompany the younger of these fair-haired midwestern transplants on the tiresome chore of trying to decide which duly-numbered site to purchase for his retiring parents. Every pace between wooden stakes driven into this windblown crest south of Waikiki adds up to another half-million down. No run-of-the-mill yuppies, the brothers have eschewed higher salaries to work in public hospitals, one in pediatrics, the other administering a walk-in clinic that deals largely with tuberculosis, drug addiction, and AIDS among Pacific islanders and fast-arriving Laotians. Despite having seen firsthand that Hawaii is no paradise, they've moved here from Minnesota because, like me, their lives have been unalterably tilted toward Asia—which means a taste for zen and anything that goes with rice.

We trust their warning to stay away from the high-priced Waikiki Chinese palaces, run for and sometimes by the Japanese. On a spectacular Sunday hike over the high end of an Oahu military base, accompanied by yet more doctors, our first samples of the local cuisine are seaweed rolls stuffed with sushi rice and chunks of canned Spam—a perfect marriage of these islands' dual heritage. For all its hype and golf course glitter, true Hawaiian style mingles Polynesian, Asian, and navy grunt. Can it be that the place in America with the fewest industrial workers has the most working-class feel? Most of the Chinese were brought here in the mid-1700s as near–slave laborers on sugar and pineapple plantations. Except for parts of Peru, their history is longer here than anywhere else in the Americas. Which leads me to think good Chinese food should be easy to find.

That certainly isn't the case in Honolulu's Chinatown, one of the grubbiest on the planet. How can the place look good with winos to one side and paradise to the other? Gnawed away by downtown development, lacking the continual transfusion of new arrivals, its Asian markets are struggling and most of the old-time chop suey houses have been boarded up. Like the culture, the cuisine has shrunken with isolation. When it comes to raw ingredients, the local vegetables aren't fresh enough and the fish is perhaps too much so. Mahi-mahi and opakapaka are just a bit too fleshy and boneless. Like Hawaii itself, they don't provide the Chinese quite enough to chew on.

Yet the purveyor of a popular Hong Kong seafood establishment in one of the few functioning Chinatown malls insists that he "loves the quietness of being out on the water." And he hasn't moved here for the weather. "I lived on the mainland, in Boston and Chicago. It was kind of scary the way people stared at me. I really saw fear in their eyes. But in Hawaii, even the natives have plenty of Chinese blood. Nobody would ever look down on you."

Hawaii may indeed be the leading-edge laboratory for a multiethnic America, but Mei and I are having trouble finding any genuine Chinese eats. The doctor brothers make a good diagnosis when they lead us to Maple Garden. This restaurant's exterior is pure suburban dinner house, but the interior is among the most delightful we'll see. The walls above every mahogany booth are covered with colorful murals of galloping horses drawn in spontaneous, calligraphic swaths.

"These horses give Chinese a feeling of racing toward success," says the Maple Garden's erudite, Taiwanese-born owner, Robert Hsu. He proudly tells us that they have been painted by Johnny Young, most collected of local Chinese-Americans artists. Mr. Hsu then leads us right to the table of this ebullient, gray-haired Hawaiian Picasso sporting a Picasso-like, striped fisherman's shirt.

"After five years of eating here, he gave me two small pictures," the owner explains. "I had to wait twenty years for these lucky murals!"

The artist corrects, "No, that was just when you could afford me!"

Well into his sixties, Johnny Young's round, browned face exudes a boyish self-satisfaction. He even whips out a magic marker and with a single masterly swirl conjures a whiskered catfish for us on a restaurant napkin. What really makes our young doctors' stethoscopes pound is that the artist is dining with a strikingly tall Japanese model at most half his age.

While we plow through the Maple Garden's hearty northern-style cuisine, the owner peppers us with theories: "Always keep your tables equidistant from the kitchen . . . A Chinese chef needs five years to learn about meat, five years about vegetables, five years about cold dishes . . . In Hawaii's restaurant trade, labor costs are thirty percent, insurance is thirty percent, food thirty, and rent ten. It's like having a temple with ten monks. If an eleventh arrives, you've got to shut down the temple!"

I'm not surprised to hear that Mr. Hsu started out as an engineer. How does this hard charger expect me to eat and take notes at the same time? "You know how old my daughter was when I sent her to school? One year and ten months! Start early. My goal is the Ivy League, nothing less! . . . So many official delegations eat here that the Taiwanese think I'm a Communist, the Communists think I'm a Nationalist! . . . I'd rather serve the Japanese because Chinese always criticize everything. One dish is too sweet, the next too salty! That's how they show off."

The surroundings are more humble at Ja-Ja—a name that means "good" and is fashioned with eight lucky strokes. I'm hardly expecting to find the best Chinese food in Hawaii in this narrow slot in the West Kapalama Shopping Center. But the owner is a zany Taiwanese painter who tries hard to turn his earthy northern dishes into works of art. He does quite well with rather limited ingredients, and for further after-dinner proof, presents us with a carrot carved into an anatomically accurate erection. This looks more edible than the real thing at Beijing's Penis Cafe.

We've come here to catch up with Mei's college girlfriend Zhao Li, who brings along her zealously libertarian husband, Ken, and their perfectly half-half daughter, Ken-li. Hiding out somewhere in Hawaii is Zhao Li's great-uncle Zhang Xue Liang, the legendary Nationalist marshal and war lord's son who, in a famed incident of the thirties, "kidnapped" Chiang Kai-shek in order to force him into negotiations with Mao. Too bad we can't lure the Marshall out for a meal! But Zhao Li has made some Chinese history of her own.

"I want the whole world to hear about what kind of country China is becoming!" she prefaces a saga that still rouses her to furious tears. A year earlier, she'd returned to the northern city of Tianjin to become the manager of a swank new nightclub—jointly owned by an American-Chinese friend and local investors, including the Security Police. Zhao Li figured that China had changed enough for her to run the business "in a high class, American way: no favors for anyone, no free drinks for policemen, no bribes to high officials." Rising tensions at the club soon proved her wrong. One evening after work, she noticed that the light bulb in her apartment's hallway had gone out. The next night, while she fumbled for her keys in the dark, three hooded men jumped her and began beating her with wood batons. They ran off when her loud screams alerted neighbors. Eventually, they found a cabbie to take her to the hospital—grudgingly. "He kept telling me not to bleed all over his back seat."

This was just the start of Zhao Li's woes. "At the Chinese hospital, the doctor on duty was in no hurry. He had to be convinced that I had plenty of money." Eventually, he began poking around in her skull, sewing her up with a dirty needle. "Each time that doctor said he was finished, I'd feel my head and find another cut, still bleeding." There were fifteen gashes in all. "I had to save my own life!" Before being granted a hospital bed in Tianjin, she was thrown out of the waiting room by a lady janitor. Once admitted, she had to beg for a scan to check for concussions. She was fed nothing until she figured out the system of bribing orderlies. Nurses taking tests and applying IVs purposely jabbed her arms over and over. "They weren't willing to find a vein until I paid them off, too!" Barely recovered and still bandaged, she was summarily thrown out one night. "Someone else must have paid more for my bed."

Zhao Li is so upset that she is one of the few Chinese on our journey who doesn't finish her meal. "The only efficiency I ever saw in China was the way the police got rid of me. None of them ever even apologized." When the local Chief of Security saw her off at the train station, he cautioned her about ever returning. "While he promised to keep me informed of the investigation," she recounts, "he could barely contain his glee." The club was taken over by the Security Bureau and since then, the American investor had not been sent a penny. "Please tell the world," Zhao Li fairly begs about her home country, "so that others won't suffer as I did!"

You have to overlook a lot to love China. But you have to overlook a lot to love just about anything.

After this tale, there's nothing left to do but thank our lucky stars 'n' stripes. We join our doctor hosts on their top-down sunset cruise to a rocky point beneath million-dollar homes where the world's most privileged surfers worship the blissfully down-market ocean. Patiently trolling offshore, these M.D.s in wet suits try to catch a therapeutic ride. It's just like *The Endless Summer*, that old movie about a worldwide search for the perfect crest of wave. But I'm hooked on riding the Pacific's historic tides, the curves and folds of an endless dumpling.

North America

LIKE A ROLLING
EGG ROLL

Featured Restaurants:

Peking Palace, Cloverdale
Royal Hunan Palace, Crescent City
Seven Stars, Portland
Honey Court, Seattle
Shanghai Garden, Seattle
Chongqing Seafood, Vancouver, Canada
Xi Lai Soon, Vancouver
Carrianna, Vancouver
Landmark, Vancouver
Victoria Restaurant, Vancouver
East Lake, Vancouver
Chinese Garden, Coeur d'Alene
The Golden Pheasant, Missoula
The Great Wall, Billings
Peking Way, Minneapolis
Beijing, Madison
Golden Bull, Chicago
Szechwan House, Chicago
Taipei Wall Sea Street, Queens, New York
New Flushing Seafood, Queens
Joe's Shanghai, Queens
Tse Yang, Manhattan
Pig Heaven, Manhattan
Shun Lee Palace, Manhattan
Sun Lok Kee, Manhattan

The Death of Chop Suey

Forget Mom and Apple Pie. Nothing is quite as American as chop suey. Derived from the Cantonese for "assorted stuff," this indeterminate hash was most likely concocted in Californian mining camps. One legend has it that some resourceful Chinese cooks made the first batch after a delivery of meat didn't arrive for an ambassadorial party. Life in the New World is always about cooking up an identity from available scraps.

"Steam vegetable very soft, add plenty brown gravy," one California restaurateur recites the time-honored recipe for mainstream digestibility, that warmed-over stereotype of a dish. "Too bad Chinese people never eat that."

Neither do I. But in order to remain faithful to our quest, I've convinced Mei to cross the forty-eight states' culinary expanse powered solely by unleaded gas and whatever passes for Chinese grub. No truck stops, no Denny's, no golden arches. We'll brake solely for the Yellow Emperor's frontier franchises. Instead of watery java, gallons of jasmine tea can keep me awake at the wheel. The two of us will measure the miles of the interstate by traveling from fortune cookie to fortune cookie. I'm willing to bet we won't ever go hungry.

Is there some portent in our setting out on April Fools' Day? My twelve-year-old Civic hatchback is freshly tuned-up and fully loaded with laptop computer, water crackers, and a duffel bag of cassette tapes including E-Z Italian lessons and Debra Winger reading *The Brothers Karamazov* (thankfully abridged). Heading north up the coast from San Francisco, we're ready for a first soyed fill-up in the one–A.T.M. town of Cloverdale, population: 4,500. Paying for gas, I have trouble popping the question. Will I ruffle local sensibilities by disdaining the native fare? Or is nothing more American than the constitutional right to cruise between ethnic flavors? I wait to get noticed by the bleached blonde cashier busy chatting with a former high school mate.

"And did you hear that Jennifer became a Witness? Roger, too!"

"To put up with him," the other responds ruefully, "she *had* to get religion."

"Ah, excuse me," I work up the nerve. "Is there a Chinese restaurant in these parts?"

187

"The Canton or Peking Palace?" I half expect her to add, "Name your poison." Can there be a Main Street U.S.A. with every city in China represented? The cashier's tone suggests that hundreds before me have made the same strange request. "Peking's on the right of the 101 loop, past the Hi-Fi Drive-in."

An interior dotted with dashboard Buddhas and Tsingtao beer posters doesn't quite go with the Peking's Norman Rockwell view of a major intersection crossed solely by single-file scouts looking ex-traterrestrial in their bike helmets. Piped-in Cantonese love songs don't sound quite right in the realm of 4-H. No wonder the Palace's Taiwanese proprietress is starved for company! Perhaps because her ancestors were Hakkanese, China's "guest people," there's not much that intimidates Lucy Huang, a bubbly woman wearing granny glasses, a black gym suit, and matching aerobic Reeboks. She shrugs her shoulders at clientele in snakeskin boots who only know how to order "a couple of number fours and a tea." For us, Lucy makes her husband cook up just-wrapped pot-stickers, nicely gingery—disprov-ing the contention that you can't make Chinese dumplings with American flour and pork. In these parts, call them Chinese Pups-in-a-Tent.

"In this town, all the business depend on Mexicans who work in the vineyards," Lucy Huang admits. "Pay by the bushel, work very fast."

About Americans, she wants to know, "When the kids put those rings in their tongues, how they eat?"

Her other main concern is that she has to drive her kids a hun-dred miles on weekends to the nearest Chinese school. "We let 'em take the bus back," she concedes, with a guilty giggle. "Up in Ukiah, we even got a Chinese temple. But that town was too quiet even for the monk! After a few months, he go back to Taiwan!"

Lucy Huang's self-deprecating humor isn't a form of bitterness; it's small town amazement at actually liking it here. She's no reject from some big-city Chinatown's Darwinian struggle. Some Chinese, too, prefer clean air and crime-free neighborliness. My fortune cookie reads, "Sell your ideas—they are totally acceptable." In the Confu-cian world view, I guess that's a compliment.

Heading north, Mei and I can't work up an appetite in time for the Yum Yum Tree in Willits. How can we possibly eat enough times in the day to cover all the places where Chinese have gone? The House of Lee is the first roadside attraction that bills itself as "Chinese and American." In a country straining to get more ethnic, can there still be such holdouts? After an exciting, eight-second journey through the world's only drive-thru redwood tree, we reach Eureka. Looming in the dusk is Chin's, a combination motel-restaurant with clock-mounted pagoda tower meant to stun motorists. The place is presided over by two whirling dervishes in black tights. One of these presumed Chin sisters greets her beefy local beau named Vince. But we pass up the chance to stay here after inspecting the re-education camp out back. The minuscule TVs in gun-metal frames are all stenciled "Chin's." The rooms haven't been remodeled since the Boxer Rebellion.

An hour further along, Crescent City is getting mighty multicultural. The manager of the Econo Lodge is an East Indian. "But I was born in Uganda!" she chortles, handing us discount coupons for the Royal Hunan Palace across the street. The waitress there hardly cares about the pedi-gree of the chef. Between evasive bubble-gum cracking, this "A.B.C." (American-born Chinese) finally confesses that her boss hails from Laos. Despite pancakes as square as frozen napkins, our *mu shu* pork is neither twice-defrosted nor half bad. More remarkably, we've come nearly five hundred miles without Mei having to strain her Mandarin over common Chinglish idioms like beef "chow yuke" and shrimp "sub gum."

The next day's drive takes us deeper into confusion. At Coos Bay on the Oregon coast, we're astonished to find that the yellow-colored fry shack that was Sun Wah Chop Suey has been outdone, shut down and altogether eclipsed by Kum Yon's "Golden Lotus— Hunan Cuisine." This massive coffee shop in copper tones, with discreetly Oriental bonsai landscaping, has a lot full of pickups and Ford wagons. On a Sunday afternoon, this Pan-Asian Denny's appears to be doing the lion's share of the town's after-church suppers. The blue-rinse set, dressed up in their finest flowered prints, are happily chowing down on sushi rolls. On a single rolling tray, I scan the dishes that we'll all be able to order at every lunch counter in twenty-first-century America: *kung pao* chicken with salad in sesame dressing, Korean barbecue with side of fries, teriyaki and tiramisu. I hear the all-Caucasian staff shouting toward the kitchen, "Tofu patty—light on the ginger!"

The only Asian in sight is a beatifically grinning Korean gent handing out mints from behind the register. "Toothpicks! You already got a pocketful of toothpicks!" one exasperated daughter is barking at her aged mom. Holding the door for Mei, I ask, "How would you categorize this place?"

Tripping through the bonsai, she answers, "It's not a Hunan. It's a Who Knows!"

We're back on more familiar ground at the China Doll in Davenport, a town barely big enough to support a single gun shop. The red leatherette booths are pure fifties; the lack of business, vintage nineties. A chef who could be the Chinese twin of Alfred E. Newman and a waitress who must be named Lily are diligently filling Dixie cups with a sweet-sour sauce that looks suspiciously like ketchup. Once we've allayed her fears that we aren't from the county health department, the waitress proudly boasts that she came here from Hong Kong thirty-five years back and has never bothered to stray anywhere else.

"Got work, have no time. Got time, have no money," she spouts, as though she's the first to arrive at the concept. Besides, "Uncle say to stay here, I stay here." Meanwhile, the owner is living it up with the proceeds down in San Francisco. But Lily has no desire to see the Golden Gate. "Too many Chinese," she says.

"Where is a good restaurant? *Dove un buon' ristorante?*" Mei keeps repeating to the tape until we've turned off Highway 1. In Portland, we can still find some Chinese-born Chinese. In fact, downtown is dotted with upscale Sichuan houses and there's even an elaborate *peilou*, or ceremonial gate, at the entrance to Chinatown—perhaps to shield the area from Burnside's winos and adult bookstores. I ask Mei to translate the lovely scrawls of gold calligraphy. "Por-ta-lun," she intones. And I was sure it would be something about the jade portal of fragrant clouds!

Portland's Chinatown tells a familiar story. An entirely white, over-forty Oregonian crowd is dining at the multi-lanterned Republic Chop Suey and Hong Far Lo—almost "one hung low." Across the way, the Seven Stars is hopping with packs of young Chinese and Vietnamese. This place has everything you'd want in a Hong Kong–style restaurant: overly bright lighting; sooty, paneled ceilings; a kitchen as big as a slaughterhouse; a corner shrine to ancestors like some baroque cobweb, with fake electric flame glowing; waiters who look like you've offended their ancestry when you don't order at once; a couple of tables where an exhausted staff is already slurping their post-shift soup. The table across from us is claimed by the designated father-in-law, withering away before everyone's eyes. He's so hunched over that I can't tell if he's scribbling some Taoist tome or using his abacus to fiddle the books. Remarkably, the owner is a sassy woman, curiously unaged by the travails of immigration, rearing four children, and coddling a husband-chef. Chinese life doesn't leave its marks on the face. If it did, you wouldn't be able to tell the smile from the scars.

"Reason we successful, we not like the old-fashioned kind," she observes. What's in fashion are the slimy green tanks blocking out every window, where the live crab are too crammed together to provide any proof of being animate. Claims the owner, "They not dead. Just sleeping."

That's enough to convince Mei to order one. The crab goes superbly with my pan-fried, cilantro-garnished noodles, unceremoniously cut into bites with what could be sheep shears. Tonight's fortune reads, "You are interested in public service." Does that mean someone may yet benefit from our curious research?

By the next afternoon, we're in an unpaved outskirt of gourmet Seattle. We crash with a Weyerhauser worker from Beijing who wants to lead us to "a Chinese buffet place with ice cream, not too bad." Trying not to offend, Mei suggests there may be too great a chasm between "not too bad" and "world's best." In America's capital of coffee, there are plenty of nouvelle places to try. But we head into the International District, which is more than a trendy avoidance of the word Chinatown. At a neighborhood museum, we learn of a community unique for its longtime hodgepodge of Chinese, Japanese, Koreans, Pacific-Islanders, and even African-Americans. Once, single Filipino men inhabited a racy Manilatown and there was something of a nighttime jazz scene.

Split by a freeway, chopped away by the lots that now surround the Kingdome stadium complex, what's left is plainly Chinese. The International District retains a homey feel thanks to minuscule storefronts like Star Tofu Manufacturers. Instead of sports bars, we find the Atlas and the Taitung, Chinese hash houses that have outlived the epoch when all foreign food, like all "furners," had to be Americanized. A refugee from Bronx oppression, one Chinese-American in a New York Yankees cap, answers our inquiries by admitting, "Hey, I only go out for paella!" His customers recommend a nearby newcomer called the Honey Court, where a rowdy young all-Chinese crowd enjoys vaguely Singaporean fare.

By the time we're seated, the Honey Court's glitzy proprietress fairly apologizes for having left a lucrative post as a hotel chain's public relations chief. "But what other business could I start where a Chinese bank would give me thirty days' credit?" We're more grateful for this hot tip on restaurant financing than the tangy clay pot of rock cod. My next fortune reads, "If your desires are not extravagant, they will be granted."

Still hoping that's true, we round a corner and, catercorner to the vast ballpark, find the Shanghai Garden. Too bad chef Hua Te Sun is away on business, because his food merits an in-depth interview. The house specialty, translated as "high nutrition hand-shaved barley green noodles" are the Chinese equivalent of Italian spinach pasta, but colored by the youth of the shoots and sliced off a thick block of dough. The concoction is wonderfully fresh and laced with yellow leeks, scrambled eggs, carrots, and pork. The menu claims this dish even lowers blood pressure.

These rib-sticking noodles can power me a thousand *li*—especially down the highways of Washington State, where every truck stop is blessed with a drive-thru cappucino stand. Instead of the pony express, there's now one drive-thru called Pony Espresso. Thanks to the gourmet revolution and new Asian immigration, the trail ahead is getting more cushy all the time. As for Mom and Pop, they're no longer with us. Chop suey has gone the way of the buffalo.

Van Kong

A t the border, the female Mountie unmounted in her toll
booth asks, "Purpose of journey?"
Why bother to tell her what she wouldn't believe? For
most Americans, Canada is just another place to set one's feet,
barely an excuse for cultural broadening. But I'm moving through a
nation whose territory is circumscribed solely by import-export
routes and the occasional annoyance of visa restrictions.

Snow-capped mountains loom but Mei and I ride through fallow
marsh fields until we bounce over the gentle humps of Vancouver
suburbs. I gun our li'l Honda to slip into downtown before rush hour
and within several hours of our appointed date with another of Mei's
long-unseen but well-trusted coconspirators. A flurry of last-minute
faxes has familiarized me with the tongue-twisting Bao Dao Ping. I
picture our latest local patron as another status-ridden fat cat with
bags under his eyes nearly as bulging as his bags of money. Instead, a
willowy youth in double-breasted suit charges out from his suite in a
shining office tower.

"Greetings, eh? Welcome to Van Kong!" I am no more prepared
for Mister Bao, Dao, or Ping than I am for this ultimate Pacific Rim
city. The man is a bundle of energy whose perpetually hoarse, high-
pitched voice belies a need to stay in command. With a single gray
streak in a carefully parted explosion of hair, eyes too closely set together, and a long, rounded nose straight off a Kabuki mask, he
could, and often is, taken for Japanese. But this former playmate of
Mei's reminds me of a Chinese Jerry Lewis, a brash brat full of me-
thodical mischief whose self-effacing giggle casts few doubts on the
outcome of many best-laid plans.

"Had my secretary work this up. Hope you approve!" While
I'm still seated in the driver's seat, he hands me a typed schedule
of our next five days in his fiefdom. Or do they call this a database?
In chronological order is every restaurant we'll be sampling, which
style of cuisine, name and number of managerial contact, along
with an attached promotional packet about our project and my entire career. So this is the way it's done out in the real world! After
eight months of traveling, we are finally getting organized. Our

organizer shouts, "Think you can follow me? I move pretty quick."

If I've barely time to see where I'm going to be eating through the week, I've even less chance of keeping up with this hyper driver. Because of our late arrival, we rush back to Dao Ping's two-story town house amidst a coiled development that feels like it's on the edge of the Yukon. Thirty miles is just a short jog in a city sprawled across three separate islands where one doesn't commute so much as migrate. After a change of clothes, we're off to pick up the rest of our culinary caravan. Han Yen, descendant of a high-ranking Kuomintang official killed when she was ten, is a recent emigré who runs a cooking show on the local Chinese-language radio station. Her dream is to open a restaurant that serves dishes out of the classic novel, *Dream of the Red Chamber*. Our next hanger-on is a hazel-eyed, slightly awestruck member of the local Chinese press, who holds himself with a stiffness that I take to be extreme shyness. But the most important member of our entourage is Elly Leung, introduced as programming director of the radio station and clearly our main door-opener. Awaiting us in our first banquet room, this handsome Chinese Yul Brynner projects a soft-spoken graciousness no doubt meant to minimize everyone's constant deference.

I'll soon learn the reason. But first, comes the food! A private table for twelve has been arranged at an elegant second-floor roost called the Chongqing Seafood. The regular fare may bear little resemblance to our VIP spread, but we're offered ample evidence that someone around here can cook. Right from the start, we're treated to the Vancouver trademark of smoked salmon served alongside heaps of stylishly arranged cold meats and rolls of "temple goose," really sweetened bean curd skin. Though the Chongqing Seafood is billed as Sichuan—father and son chefs actually hail from the home province of edible heat—they've toned down the peppers a bit too much. Orange rind dominates their beef; the peanuts are given prominence in their *kung pao* lobster served in a nest of crisp-fried noodles. The scallops arrive on a bed of spinach, and the world's thickest round of sea cucumber is slathered in a tangy *da qian* sauce.

"Mmmm! Munch on!" The last entrée has transported Mei halfway to heaven. "Wait 'til you learn to appreciate texture as much as taste! Then you'll be Chinese!"

It's the Northwest crab catch that Chinese chefs utilize to best advantage. How can I possibly feel crabby over our next five days' coddling when each meal comes with perfectly moist Dungeness claws done cold or hot, smothered in scallions and ginger and presented with the perfect, vinegary dipping sauce? For dessert, we're shown how the Chinese outdo even the best of Vienna's marzipan illusionists by turning candied bean paste into a perfectly believable harvest of faux plums, tangerines, and blushing peaches complete with fake baby pits inside. Adults all, we're caught playing with our food.

The group is tickled when I tell them that this meal shows a higher level of care and presentation than any we've had back in California. The explanation is obvious. For more than a decade, Canada's more liberal immigration policies and British Columbia's geographic proximity have made this the haven of choice for both Taiwanese and Hong Kongers seeking a hedge against overcrowding and political instability. These days, Vancouver is one-quarter Asian, with a Chinese population of two hundred thousand and counting—and a culture that's even begun to produce its first Chinese-Canadian rap singers. While the natives complain about being driven out by rising prices, they can't question the rising level of local dining spots. The greater the numbers and the more recent the arrival, the better the chance of finding great Chinese food.

Dao Ping declares victory and hurries us toward the next battlefront. A relentless booster of his adopted home, our host cruises past downtown's original Chinatown, one of North America's largest but already somewhat obsolete with its cavalcade of fruit stands and failing mom-and-pops. We dutifully bound out of the car at midnight to inspect the venerable Sam Kee Building, a most evocative symbol of Chinese overpopulation, tabbed by Guinness as the world's narrowest edifice.

"Canada is my first love," Dao Ping gushes. "But photography comes a close second." In the motherland, his grandfather had been a cinema tycoon with controlling interest in ninety percent of China's movie theaters. His father, a Shanghai *xiao kai*, or playboy, known to have partied around with the future Mrs. Mao, was sent off to college in America carrying "a book stuffed with dollar bills." But Dao Ping's dad quickly grew homesick for his favorite haunts. Returning to a life of privilege, he ended up in a People's Republic labor camp. So his own son was forced to retrace the journey west with hardly the equivalent of a movie stub in his pocket.

It was no "smooth road," as the name *Dao Ping* translates. Enrolled in a junior college, he found laws against foreign workers strictly enforced. Desperate, he made a plea to friends who had already "come out." Mei's mother and American stepfather had come through with a life-saving thousand dollars. He saved precious pocket money by walking seven hours a day to and from school (no log cabins in these Lincolnesque sagas). Thoroughly broke and lost, he wandered into a Chinese grocery but couldn't communicate in Cantonese. Another shopper translated, later lent him his first bicycle, and became his first friend in Canada. Always hustling, Dao Ping. He scraped together his savings and let a large apartment. Providing cooking and cleaning, he rented out rooms to Hong Kong students at a profit.

After months of scrimping, he purchased his first camera. Now he traded tuition charges for work on the college catalogue and started working at every Chinese wedding and function he could find. A place of honor in his home is reserved for the daughter of Winston Churchill, who befriended Dao Ping after he'd been sent to photograph a reception in her honor. "But there was one Englishman I'll never forget," he tells us. "He turned his head aside rather than be photographed by a Chinese."

Eventually, he opened his own video production service, then moved into the higher ranks of entrepreneurship by becoming an investment consultant on mega-bucks People's Republic construction projects. But money isn't "uppermost to heaven" for Dao Ping. "Any Chinese who came to me," he tells us about his work on Vancouver's Expo, "I got him a booth for free." Today, he still rents out a room of his condo to newly arrived Chinese students. "The pressure is so great to succeed, there's no turning back," he tells us. "Chinese people feel that coming to Canada should be a snap compared with the Cultural Revolution. I had a friend who was down to selling his clothes when he gave up and returned to Shanghai empty-handed. His parents denounced him as a coward. His wife divorced him."

On the drive home, he admits that he feels partially responsible for the condition of the reporter we met earlier. "Maybe you noticed the way he carried himself, the scars around his neck? He's a college guy who was forced to take work in an illegal Chinese mushroom farm, just for room and board. I warned him to ask about health insurance. Months later, I knew there was trouble when I was awakened by a caller asking for 'Mr. Ping.' The Vancouver police had found my name among the poor fellow's papers. Instead of installing a proper valve on a hot water pipe, the farmer used a stone. While treating the mushrooms, my friend was sprayed with boiling steam over ninety percent of his body. I was the first one to the hospital, the only one who visited him until he was well."

Dao Ping is one of those for whom the links of memory and community cannot be broken. That doesn't stop him from kicking off his wing tips and unveiling his thousand-dollar home karaoke machine. Dao Ping struts about in pinstripes and stocking feet, practically wearing a hole in his living room carpet. He concentrates his frustrated artistic ambitions into one hoarse wail.

Lacking Dao Ping's guidance in the morning, I take a wrong freeway turn and drive twenty miles back toward the U.S. border. The place at which we finally arrive looks more like Taiwan. As in San Francisco, the secondary and newer Chinese encampment goes by the name Richmond. But this is no quaint Victorian neighborhood overrun by Chinese hordes. Risen from the flat farmlands that surround Vancouver's International Airport, a new neighborhood has emerged entirely out of Asian traffic not just figuratively but literally "just off the jet." The multicultural city has already yielded a multicultural suburb, proving once and for all that modernity can have a Chinese face.

At first, I'm a bit taken aback that our typed itinerary has taken us to a drafty room with Formica tables no more inviting than a Dunkin Donuts. But its front window displays fresh onion cakes being grilled. Xi Lai Shun, while named in honor of the famed Muslim restaurant in Beijing, bills itself as a Taiwanese snack shop. They do all sorts of northern treats about as well as anywhere we've been. Moist twists of steamed buns, homemade dumplings stuffed with fluffed-up eggs and chives, Chinese knishes stuffed with fatty sausage, and a cold eggplant salad laced with seaweed are packaged between perfectly crisped peanuts that I can't stop popping down. The owner is a Taiwanese lady, chic in a suit of gray tweed, with a cellular phone that's never out of her hand.

A more humble chef confesses that he could do better in terms of salary back home: "For my son's sake, I came to Canada. I like the education but also the parks, the room, the fresh air."

In Canada, we have stumbled upon an entirely new breed of diaspora. Call these eco-immigrants. Over and over, these people tell me that they aren't in it for the money. One look and it's obvious that the real boom is on the other side of the Pacific Rim. Chinese are coming to Canada for many of the same reasons that motivated the first European settlers: a way out of the Old World's social pressure cooker, wide open spaces and wider exposure for their minds, rugged individualism and communion with nature.

In the fresh breezes of British Columbia, I finally learn to warm up with a hot pot. At the Landmark, a Vancouver branch of a popular Hong Kong chain, we're led through the ritual by a confident family scion with a doctorate in dipology. This chubby first son has a smooth and easy rap about the different kind of broths: Cantonese-style is clear consommé, the brownish mush is spicy Sichuanese. The Landmark also offers a medicinal brew made from Chinese herbs and especially beneficial fruits like dates and "dragon's eye" loquats. At the same time, the owner is an astute and honest observer of the political scene. "It's strange, because there's little overt racism here. Whites just move to the smaller towns. They don't admit feeling threatened. At the same time, Asians who want full participation are dealing with a society where minorities have rarely acted together. There's been no civil rights movement here. There's no experience of accepting minorities as a permanent fact of life."

He manages to make the point while shoveling heaps of green mussels, giant clams, oysters, halibut, crab roe, lobster, chicken, won ton, bean sprouts, chives, thinly sliced sirloin, and beef tongue toward their boiling bath. For the first time, I can't get enough of whatever I scoop from the cauldron. So many ingredients, so little appetite. I can't argue when the owner states that, "We can do better here with our raw materials than back in Hong Kong."

Unfortunately, Vancouver also outdoes Hong Kong in terms of

government regulation and higher taxes—yet provides but two sitting's worth of diners each night to Hong Kong's six. "You have to be careful in Canada," the Landmark's boss says, repeating every Chinese investor's motto, "because for every dollar you earn, you can only put fifty cents in your pocket. But for every dollar you lose, you lose the whole dollar."

As the economic tables have turned in recent years, up to twenty percent of Chinese immigrants have returned home and, in the Chinese parlance, "traded a lonely heaven for a happy hell." Others have become "astronauts"—in permanent orbit between jobs in Asia and families in Canada. But no one seems more at home in his new world than Elly Leung. Through whispers among our entourage, Mei and I learn that Leung was an actor whose screen name was Yue Wha. Only Mei's considerable prodding gets him to bring us his scrapbook full of stills and clippings. With full head of pigtails, sometimes a false beard, our tight-lipped toastmaster appeared as the valiant hero in a hundred Hong Kong historical flicks. A star in the stable of the legendary producer Run Run Shaw, Yue Wha gained fame as a fighting monk and Mandarin noble in such epics as *The Monkey King Goes West*. Dashing on horseback and slashing with kung fu, he specialized in portraying Lancelots in silk, including his most memorable role, the drunken knight.

I can hardly imagine the gentle, impish man before me in broad-chested military bearing. What's harder to fathom is why he would give up Hong Kong's fast lane to dawdle over luncheons with the likes of us—or to dash off to late-night talk shows on the rates of child immunization among the Chinese.

"Our life is more peaceful and much healthier," he answers, coaxed between meals to face me across a conference table in Dao Ping's office. Gazing out at the perfect mountain scenery across the harbor, he tells me, "You appreciate your own Chinese roots better when you're no longer in the majority."

Yue Wha's roots can be traced as far back as a grandfather from Zhongshan, near Shanghai. His father was an inspector for the British and left for Hong Kong in the early fifties. "That wasn't easy, being the only one left behind," he admits. "You were a kind of hostage, always under suspicion, always reporting to the police."

Raised by a grandmother, he managed to study voice and flute at the Shanghai Music Academy. After reaching Hong Kong in 1962, he auditioned on a whim for a drama company. Now his performing skills are utilized at all sorts of fund-raisers for charitable causes, like a recent "Walk with the Dragon" for the United Way. It's Dao Ping who interjects that Elly's work with the community has won him a prestigious Citation for Citizenship Award. But fame is not the issue. "I just hope to do my best for the new arrivals here, to raise my daughter well, to pass on a little of what it means to be Chinese. I feel that I'm part of the last generation able to do it."

Though Elly Leung is still a relatively young man, he may be right. His authority doesn't stem from stardom, but out of respect for Chinese services rendered. Later, Mei will hear him referred to as Yue Da Xie—"Warrior Yue." Like Dao Ping, he is more than a community pillar or perennial elder son. There is no proper word in English for this sort of person, because back across the border, so few of them exist.

A Banquet a Day Keeps the Doctor Away

Once in a lifetime, everyone deserves an idea like this. Or could it be that this trip is a reward for prior lifetimes well-spent? In Vancouver, my entire worldly duty consists of consuming the courses laid before me. We wake up and check the schedule, we cruise and we eat, then we join our kung fu star to eat again. Not even the emperors ever kept up this pace, or had to praise cooks while in the midst of head-throbbing MSG attacks. A tough job, but Mei and I have to do it. Another day, another banquet.

"Eating is our prime entertainment, "says Janet Chiu, manager of the Carrianna, a mammoth marble mausoleum complete with turbaned doorman, Ming vases, and glassed-off function rooms. But if this is a movie, I have no opportunity to walk out. Our entourage plows through some resplendently arranged platters of blandly Chaozhou-style specialties, starting with cold jellyfish—"Rubber bands," says Janet—followed by chicken marinated in pomegranate, fluffy pieces of fresh cod on beds of smoky Chinese ham, rolls made of cucumber and dried scallop essence, Chinese broccoli arranged in the shape of a spread fan, a white duck-egg pocket with chicken and mushrooms, and probably the best rendition in town of cooled-down Vancouver Island crab. Dare I fail to mention cameo appearances by the blanched beef with bean sprouts in satay sauce, the sizzling freshwater goby fish? Stick-to-the-ribs desserts like "red bean banana ball" and deep-fried taro root make for a bang-up ending. But too much of a good thing began yesterday.

Another evening of after-dinner chit-chat is passing in conversation that I can't understand. If only I could attach a book holder to my forehead—I'd have gotten through *War and Peace* by this point! To entertain myself, and add up my observations on Chinese rituals, I take the risk of generalizing. To the approving smiles of another owner who thinks I'm making copious notes about each and every dish, I enumerate my hosts' banqueting behavior:

1. Exchange business cards. Who's the fastest draw in the West?
2. Host makes apology for humble food. The more apologies, the more food. Impolite to groan.
3. All talk at once about what they're going to eat.
4. Inquire about family members.
5. Volunteer to help one another with import-export.
6. Preliminary toasts.
7. Pose for pre-appetizer snapshots. Food better dressed than people.
8. Eat.
9. Critique what they're eating.
10. Matrimonial matchmaking.
11. Offer plenty of free, unsolicited advice on intimate matters.
12. Spread malicious rumors, especially if political.
13. Delight in catching errors of logic, making puns. Easy when nearly every word in Chinese is a pun.
14. Secondary and tertiary toasts.
15. Secondary and tertiary poses. Photographer always jokes, "Food stand still better than people."
16. Look at snapshots of previous similar occasions.
17. Sit back and picture themselves doing business.

18. Sit back and picture themselves posing.
19. Picture themselves looking at pictures.
20. Picture themselves celebrating matches made.
21. Picture themselves eating again.
22. Final toasts.
23. Tug-of-war over the bill. The treat is to treat. Winner pays all, loser loses face.
24. Final poses with chefs in stovepipe hats.
25. Final exchange of business cards, for latecomers.
26. Profuse gratitude to all. Subtext: "What do I owe now and to whom?"
27. General, unsupervised digestion.

At the next day's forced feeding, my attention is stirred by the mention of one genus of flesh that I've never previously associated with the Chinese. The full brass of the Victoria, a popular meeting grounds whose dappling waterfalls are set in a downtown skyscraper basement, have gathered to initiate us into the multiple uses of the ostrich.

"Ostrich meat is low cholesterol," declares one of the erudite owners, a lean and balding man whose high-collared tunic makes him look like a chief adviser to the Last Emperor. He explains that Canadian farmers are breeding ostriches and exporting them to some fifty countries, so the Chinese community wants to do their patriotic duty. "Every part can be used for something. The feathers can clean computers, for instance. Bear paw and all are not for the environmentally conscious. Despite the present regime, Chinese have always practiced living in harmony with their surroundings. Otherwise, how could there be so many of us?"

I'm not sure that makes the ostrich dumpling the ultimate environmental statement. It's pretty damn tasty, but then, so is anything the Victoria's chefs manage to encapsulate in quivering dough. Afterwards, we're brought a single ostrich egg, big as a game-day football, which is duly passed among the twelve of us like the intoxicating "orb" in Woody Allen's Sleeper. Next, I'm brought another assortment of crunchy mystery meat drenched with sweet-sour sauce.

"Can you guess, please?" This blind big-nose's bluff is cause for a lot of hilarity.

"Pig's feet? Duck elbows?" I'm hoping that I'm not getting warm.

"Chicken knee caps! . . . That's why there are a lot of handicapped chickens walking around!"

The talk turns more scholarly when management brings out their best bottle of the sweet rice wine from Shaoxing, China's *sake*. This special vintage is known as "daughter's red wine" because "each family used to bury the best wine to save for their daughter's wedding. In olden times, an unmarried daughter didn't just mean shame. It meant the sorrow of never tasting that wine! In that case, daughter and bottle lay buried together!"

Everyone nods in sad sympathy at the legend, utterly incongruous amidst redwoods and Indian totems. As the owner puts it, "Canada is only half as old as my family tree!" To my usual question about the origins of China's food culture, this scholarly fellow offers the unusual answer, "When each man has so many wives, a competition develops to create the best dish. Just imagine, five thousand years of pleasing the husband!" So why wouldn't that lead to gourmet Mormon restaurants? The logic gets further skewed—or delectably tongue-in-cheek—when the Chinese love of shark's fin is explicated with a rhetorical, "Did you ever hear of a shark who had cancer?"

I can't say that I have. But I've never met a duck with diabetes, either.

Later, I'll read that scientific studies have proved the benefits of shark bones in shrinking tumors. I'd like to know why Elly Leung and Dao Ping don't seem to have gained any weight through this week. At our last stop on the eating marathon, an East Lake Restaurant that's nowhere near a lake, we learn from yet another chef, "The most prized is the dorsal fin. Bought dry, it must be softened in water for twelve hours, then cleaned, braised, and added to the best broth—a three-day process." Dare I tell him that I prefer his more plebian quickie of salt-baked squab? "And we sell twelve to fourteen fins a week." No wonder the shark stock in tropical waters is decreasing. How many other endangered creatures are gobbled to death by this billion-plus set of Chinese jaws?

Anorexics excluded, we are all mere open mouths, constant machines of ingestion. At each stop, I swear that I'm just going to nibble. One bite tells the whole story, old boy. But each time, I go the whole hog. Is this a tribute to my infinite capacity or the infinite temptations from Chinese cooks? Forget global itineraries. After eight months of this, I still can't go more than a few hours without another feeding.

Back at Dao Ping's condo, I'm quite ready to yield to the grandeur of peristalsis. Blessedly, tomorrow is the day of rest for my stomach. But that doesn't mean we can't trek off for Sunday brunch, Chinese-style, at a popular Shanghainese place that's an indoor whirl of squalling babies, bamboo steamers, and kitchen steam. The family who run this place share a genetic propensity for spilling soup onto the heads of their customers—be it bowls of scalding soy milk or hand-stretched noodles in detergent-scented broth. At this point, I'm willing to holler uncle—or Dao Ping.

For our trip's finale, we are driven to the base of Stag Mountain for a funicular ride up to the best viewing area in the region. None of our party is prepared for the inch or two of icy spring snow at the top. Besides, this is a hike à la Chinois, which means stopping for snapshots every six feet. They made it through the Long March only because the Instamatic hadn't yet been invented. Stopping in a raucous après-ski bar where lumberjack types swill Molson "green death" ale, I see how ill at ease my hosts are in a non-Chinese setting.

"What's a hot toddy?" ask Han Yen, the expert on *Dream of the Red Chamber*. Even Dao Ping has yet to learn about the three-martini lunch. Called to our reserved table in a swank mountaintop lair, my Chinese entourage expect me to be as adept at ordering Western food for them as they've been at planning my banquets. I'm no more at home than my Chinese hosts in this candlelit, pseudo-French chalet, except in the sense of knowing that salmon likes dill and both like Chardonnay. So I thank one and all with a toast to Vancouver, center of authentic Chinese cuisine in North America. Clinking my glass, I proclaim, "The only way to go on a diet is to get out of town!"

Stir-Fried Ostrich Steak

From Victoria Restaurant

Ingredients:

Ostrich tenderloin, 10 oz.
Soy sauce, 3 oz.
Peanut oil
Cornstarch
8 asparagus tips, blanched

Slice the ostrich into thin strips. Marinate for 30 minutes in soy sauce along with a pinch of cornstarch and a few drops of oil. Fry in pan over medium heat, without oil, for about two minutes per side—or until brown. Serve garnished with blanched asparagus.

Looey and Clark

So far, so fattening. But three thousand miles of franchised wasteland await. Picking up the old Lewis and Clark trail that is now Inter-state 90, we hang an eastward left that may last for weeks. Our four-cylinder covered wagon faces a test of survival in the form of a pass through the Cascade range. The hulking spires highlighted by a white gouache of spring snow remind Mei why the Chinese call America *mei guo*—"the beautiful country."

For some hours at the wheel, I ponder what makes this Peking cowpoke so at home in the Wild West. "Nature is the number one cure for depression," she states confidently. "Once we settle, let's rent a cabin in Yosemite. You have to reserve a year and a day ahead!" I suppose that backpacking with granola bar in hand is preferable to the old days of forced marches. She's actually better suited to this journey, since her favorite foods, bar none, are corn on the cob, salad greens, and watermelon. As the road stretches on, she keeps proving that she's "okey-dokey" for exploring almost any "neck of the wood." It's a long way—for Mei and my Honda—to Ellensburg, the only reasonably sized settlement for a hundred miles on the dry, stark side of the mountains. I only wish that my road map indicated the number of woks per hundred square miles.

"Ten bucks says we find what we're looking for!" I wager as we turn down a one-way main street through dusty feed shops and somber bank branches that still come with old-fashioned analog clocks.

"No dice, unless you give odds," Mei answers, knowing the wandering Chinese all too well. A moment later, we've pulled up at the mock-deco doors of the China Inn, its corner location marked by a neon pagoda that looks more like a squashed accordion. We're the only customers in the front room, though I glimpse a galley of red booths kept authentically opium-den airless. Our waitress, however, shows not the slightest hint of that Chinese caution bordering on suspicion.

Before we've made it through the menu, this Filipina manages to fill us in on her romantic life since puberty. All has ended well with a green card and marriage to some salesman who sits at the bar, providing child care for their beige kid. In such marriages, why is the bride always dress size zero and the groom tall enough for the NBA? "The last trip home, Manila looked so dirty!" is the waitress's backhanded pledge of allegiance. As soon as Mei heads for the bathroom, the Filipina starts musing aloud about why a traveler like me hadn't ended up with one of her countrywomen. "Of course," she adds with mischievous giggle, "your wife is just perfect!"

The China Inn's menu is a lesson in applied probabilities. The deep-fried variables—sweet-and-sour, breaded shrimps, and what Mei calls "egg foo you"—are shuffled to make the maximum number of combinations. The next table gets some fried won ton skins as big as frisbees accompanied by a dipping sauce that's the color of carcinogenic maraschino cherries. Mei employs the last-resort option of stomping into the kitchen to demand rice fried with "just egg, salt, and scallions." In Ellensburg, the emperors would weep.

We're actually hard-up enough to be looking forward to the choices in Spokane, but I have my heart set on spending the night in Coeur d'Alene. I'm not the first motorist to fall for this town's Francophied handle. Does it mean "heart of Alene" or perhaps "ailing heart"? It's nearly dark when we roll into this bit of poetry just across the Idaho border, only to discover that a resort hogs all access to the lake of the same lovely name. Along the strip, Mei eagerly rates identical motel chambers for their firmness of mattress, heat of shower, and freshness of artificial scent. We make our selection based on the eagerness of one desk clerk to switch on their hot tub. But Mei and I shiver in a shallow, heart-shaped spa set in a wood-paneled garage. Dripping our way across the chilly motel courtyard, we escape a tub that never gets more than lukewarm.

Downtown Coeur d'Alene has more cappucino parlors than the Via Veneto. We spot a sushi bar and two Chinese restaurants, selecting the one that exhibits live customers—though following the crowd may be the greater risk in these parts. Inside the Chinese Garden, we find nothing floral, just the usual row of booths and take-out counter. At the one table with a view, there's a retired couple—he in lumberjack's shirt; she in quilted, lavender vest—who immediately inform Mei in their best Mandarin that they started the first Chinese place back in Spokane, then moved on to Boise. With their son having established the Garden, these proud parents could be counted as the Chinese Ciprianis of Idaho. Still, the sanguine grandpa confides that he once worked at the National Museum in Taipei—as close to the heart of Chinese civilization as Coeur d'Alene is at the periphery. Now he cares for his camper instead of T'ang Dynasty vases. He'd rather talk about the three kids that he's managed to put through college.

Since their kin once hailed from Beijing, the couple treat Mei like a long lost daughter. My bilingual mate quickly throws off the coyness of her English-speaking persona. Throughout our entire dinner, across adjoining tables, the couple and Mei carry on a tiny segment of that one vast, portable conversation.

"Was the wife of Taiwan's mayor really crippled by Kuomintang thugs? . . . Can Jiang Zemin consolidate his power? . . . Did Mao's doctor die as a punishment for writing his book? . . . Does ginseng cure the common cold?" We may be in Coeur d'Alene, but Chinese topics transcends state lines and new citizenships. The points of reference are as fixed and readily used for navigation as the North Star. Whether the break is a moment or decades, Chinese people are forever taking up wherever their Chineseness left off.

In the meantime, I coax an order of fish-flavored shredded pork from the couple's son, a genteel type who doesn't seem to have his heart in the business. He personally whips up my test dish, which is pretty darn good, if lacking in wood ears and a trifle tangy. Or does the mountain air make me gobble the heap down as though it were a T-bone? While Mei chats on, I mosey past the rest rooms to conduct some interviews through the galley kitchen's pass-through. Once I've spied his all-American cooks, the chagrined son explains, "They only do the combinations." One stir-fryer keeps his long locks out of the grease with a red bandanna. He has no inkling of a five-thousand-year tradition, only his eight bucks an hour.

Somewhere between the next rosy dawn and my first chance to flip on the *Today Show*, we're awakened by repeated, agonized shrieking. Just what I hope never to hear through such membrane-thin walls. The first wail makes me reach involuntarily to call the front desk. With the second and third cry, I hunker down under the covers. By the seventh or eighth, I'm not sure if the man in the next cubicle is grunting in agony or howling with delight. Perhaps chamber number six is equipped with more than our quarter-per-minute vibrating bed. As we're packing the car, a genial gent carrying a guitar case emerges from the same room to give us the world's biggest "Howdy."

The morning's drive is just another stretch of asphalt in the West, where I-90 plunges across the top of Idaho's forested jigsaw. We're at the crest of some monumental ridge—the sort of that makes you feel that the planet still has room for a surplus of human trials and errors. Would that the hordes of Shanghai, sharing their subdivided mansions, could all be plopped down here! Still, I can't explain the zeal with which Mei poses before scenic lookouts and plunges into the depths of all-purpose truck stops to emerge with silver earrings, beef jerky, and postcards of Sitting Bull.

"How many do you want? A hundred million, two hundred million?" Deng Xiaoping is supposed to have inquired when Ronald Reagan began giving him a hard time about Communist restrictions on free travel. Knowing the density of the East lends greater force to the openness of the American West. I'm not interested in Lewis and Clark or the others who first trudged this way, as valiant before dangers as they were blind of consequences. What astounds me is how *hoisin*, ginger, and sesame oil could have crossed such fearful terrain. Without the snooping eyes and echoing taunts of close neighbors, how did the first Chinese pioneers even know who they were? Right on cue, a discreet signboard announces that we've made it over the hump of the Continental Divide. East of here, all the soy sauce runs into the Mississippi.

Big Stir-Fry Country

At the top of the pass, we're welcomed to "Montana—Big Sky Country!" Downhill, where each hill takes hours to cross, we come to the signs that really grab me, the ones announcing gas, food, and lodging. On official highway placards, I spy "The Pagoda" listed right below Hardee's Big Boy.

We're entering Missoula, an oasis of college-town civility nuzzled against bare hills. At the junction where four stampede-broad avenues form the city center, we find a potential candidate called the Golden Pheasant. We're not certain because, as in repressive Indonesia, there's not a bit of Chinese script to identify the place. The front-room-plus-bar is an artsy expansion with high ceilings, recessed lights, and an unfinished wood floor. The mandarin-red booths have been shoved into the back like some dirty secret. The only waiter is an affable student big enough to be a football lineman, yet with curly, dark hair and recessed eyes. Adding to our confusion, Jeremy Wiles says that the chef is his "mother's husband," who may or may not be the grandson of Golden Pheasant founder, Ruby Wong.

To get the genealogy straight, Jeremy brings out tributes from the hometown papers to Ruby, who put in twelve hours a day until she was in her eighties. Though her family came from China to Seattle, Ruby was sent off to Helena to fulfill an arranged marriage. Her husband died after seven years, leaving Ruby with three small sons and a four-month-old daughter. Somehow, she found time to learn the restaurant trade as a cashier and waitress. Then she struck out for Missoula, choosing to start up on the site once claimed by the town's first gas pump. In 1941, on the night she opened the first Chinese restaurant, four hundred people lined up outside. Pork chow mein cost fifty cents. That was four months before Pearl Harbor slowed business and ignited anti-Asian hostility. Eventually, her second partner Ming launched a rival restaurant and the Golden Pheasant was handed down to Ruby's son Jack, then to Jack's daughter. The current chef is her husband. But something is still wrong with this picture. Bill Wiles emerges from the kitchen, a strapping, sandy-haired Caucasian with a courtly manner. Aside from his genetics, he looks far too happy to be a Chinese cook.

"I spent two years in Chinese studies at the university. That's about enough time to learn to play mah-jongg efficiently," he concedes. "After I met my wife and her parents taught me their recipes, I looked on this as a way to get through school. I just never found anything else I enjoyed as much as running a restaurant."

Both all-American father and son seem amazingly at home as the Wongs' inheritors, though Bill admits, "Every day, I still expect Ruby to come around." He honors her by "trying to push the envelope" of Chinese cuisine—hardly a Confucian concept. His pot stickers and his pan-fried noodles with pork, taste like the kind I do in my kitchen. They're nicely light and fresh, but they bear the curse of rote approximation. What's missing is the indefinable grit of suffering, the slightly burnt glaze of low-wage freneticism. Or maybe it's the MSG. I leave wondering what old Ruby would think of her trendy joint now. Every life sets in motion unrecognizable results. In their abiding practicality, immigrants just do it quicker.

"Faster, slow poke!" Mei commands for the next few hundred miles. No matter how heavily I push our pedal, some Montana granny in a pickup passes me by. We're hurrying to meet up with a writer friend who recently moved from San Francisco to Bozeman. These days, the North woods are thick with hyper-realist scribblers, but our comrade is a Billings native who actually knows how to handle the hunting rifles he plucks from his bedroom closet. He's proud that the backyard of his A-frame stretches "for a hundred miles to Yellowstone." His Brazilian wife isn't faring so well with the adjustment. "It's the people," she whines in a slow, Rio singsong. "There aren't any!"

Just to show that some things never change, we see snapshots of this girl from Ipanema dancing in drifts of snow wearing nothing but fur boots and her dental-floss bikini. Surely, Chinese people should have no trouble adjusting to a place where most menus include the infamous "prairie oysters," or cattle gonads on toast. They'll just need a four-wheeler to find twice-cooked pork. My friends lead us down a snow-dusted driveway off the main strip to sample the newly opened Great China Wall.

"I've lived in New York, New Orleans, Dallas. I just prefer the peaceful life," says the proprietor, a classically wan ex-cook. But this articulate man, looking far younger than his forty years, is fleeing more than I can know. "Back in Guangdong Province," he recounts, "soldiers came to our high school to tell us we had to leave for a military training camp. There was no choice. All they told us was, 'If you understand, you will go—and if you go, sooner or later, you will understand.' "

He understood well enough to wait two weeks on the coast for his chance to swim hours across open sea to Hong Kong. But he now argues, "In America, Chinese people are supposed to be united. Thirty years back, the family associations gave shelter, lent money. Now the rich ones don't help the poor ones."

As for Americans, "they don't like Asians because we're used to working harder." He's still shocked to see "some ignorant people who disrespect and say bad things about the Native Americans. You have to fight to oppose such ideas!" His steely will seems to inspire a fortune cookie that reads, "You will be rich not only in wealth but in other areas."

A night fog clings to the road all the way to Livingstone. "Stay close behind the trucks!" Mei keeps instructing. Her theory is that it's worth reckless speeding to be guided by the lead traffic's bank of red lights.

"Just let me handle things, please!"

"That's what I'm afraid of." From her autoless upbringing, Mei has a natural distrust for anyone at the wheel, along with an unchecked tendency to backseat-drive my life. But our moments of mutual annoyance come from the pistonlike friction of naturally close parts. The harrowing ride is worth it when we get to rub together in a down-covered, four-poster bed at the Murray, an old railroad hotel recently refurbished by some more of Mei's step-relatives. As an only child, I've stopped feeling inferior. I just feel outnumbered.

One of four Montanans live—the word is used advisedly—in

Billings. Coming into a town as stripped of notable features as the surrounding high plains, Mei and I are thrilled to spot a full-fledged, wide-screen highway billboard touting "the best Chinese restaurant in Montana." There's a self-damning boast, if ever I heard one. The ad even features a considerably larger-than-life dessert item—the fortune cookie that ate Chicago. Hardly original, this one is named the Great Wall. Why not, for a change, the Dynasty Diner? Perhaps the Chinese prefer not to tamper with a winning formula.

The Great Wall turns out to be one of those glowing red, monstrously large affairs dominating an ugly strip mall, right beside a donut shop recently transformed into "Khataly's Egg Rolls—Laotian Cuisine." Wisely windowless, the Wall's loaded interior is packed with elderly couples. This looks to be one of those places that charges more for chicken by calling it *fowl*. The staff is both ultra-blond and ultra-chipper, but no one is friendlier than the mistress of the house. Poised and well-appointed in a dark-blue business suit, gold-framed designer glasses, and lapel pin of Native-American silver, I don't have to be told that she's Taiwanese—compared to Hong Kongers, the upper caste of the restaurant trade.

"My husband was a jet fighter pilot in the Taiwanese air force and he could have worked for the commercial airlines," owner Li Li tells us, confirming my hunch. "I used to be a piano teacher. But we thought, at forty, that if we get out now, we have a chance to start another career. When my husband was stationed in Washington, we'd always eat in Chinese restaurants. And we'd finish the meal by asking ourselves, 'Now if we had this restaurant, how would we run it?' " The chance came when an old friend in South Dakota said he needed partners to set up an outpost in the unconquered territory to the west.

"Where you need large investment in the big city, it was easier to make a start here," Li Li explains. "Besides, the schools are better for our children. And people in a small town are better neighbors. All the pianists and the pilots started coming around." An odd clientele at best. In the beginning, she admits, "my husband and I felt like we needed six arms and four legs." But the couple appears to have been guided by one of Mei's favorite proverbs: "Nobody ever dies from a little hard work."

Says Li Li, "After six years, our partner sold out because we could handle it by ourselves." Given the attention to every detail, I'd say so. "Before this, everyone in Billings was used to Wong's, an old-style place. At the beginning, our customers would tell us, 'This isn't Chinese food' because it didn't taste like Wong's. Do people go into McDonald's and ask for their money back when their hamburger isn't just like the one at Burger King? We have our pride, too."

As a result, her food may indeed be Montana's best. We get an above-average Cantonese beef with broccoli and a fancified shrimp served in a deep-fried potato basket. Li Li swears that she uses "hardly any MSG," a sort of semi-disclaimer. Her shrimp are absolutely "top-grade frozen" from the Louisiana coast. From the live fish tanks of Vancouver, we've come even farther than my odometer can measure.

"Everyone has been so kind," we're told, "because they consider us brave to have to come to this strange place!"

Can the same be said of us? The Great Wall's owner phones ahead to reserve us a table at her ex-partner's place in Rapid City. But we're two hundred miles late and another bleating sun is setting already. I guess the wagon trains didn't brake for every egg drop soup. Nor was Mao's Long March punctuated by signs, "Next rest stop—twenty-nine *li*."

In the far eastern corner of Montana, the earth seems to have been given a crew cut. There's no place to hide near Little Big Horn and no Chinese takeouts. Maybe that's why Custer succumbed so quickly. The battlefield closes at four, massacred by funding cutbacks. We barely have time to take a snapshot of thousands of graves and stare with four brawny cowboys at a plaster-of-Paris model on which colored lights trace the general's skirmish with oblivion. Mei remains uninvolved with the drama of European settlement.

"They look like Tibetans," she says of the ruddy-cheeked, black-banged Blackfoot kids at the Big Horn gas station *cum* jewelry depot. Spurred on, we check out a neighboring Indian town, only to find all the descendants of Buffalo soldiers lining the sidewalk outside every bar. Nonetheless, Mei tells me, "It wasn't until I saw the Indian Museum in Denver that I really felt the roots of this place. Before then, I always felt unsettled in America."

I feel especially unsettled as we skirt a thoroughly lunar corner of Wyoming, only to discover that Buffalo, one of many little towns with larger-than-life names, is too small for any Chinese restaurants. For the first time, our search is frustrated. At last, we've identified the outer limits of Chinese forbearance—as well as our own.

Washing My Brain

I never thought I'd be so thankful to get to the Midwest. Unwilling to cross the Black Hills in total darkness, we settle for a night in Spearfish, the first town across the South Dakota border. At a hippie cafe where comatose junior-college kids chomp on tabbouleh, waitresses in ankle-length Bengali prints point us toward the customary Chinese outpost. How did we miss it? The Golden Dragon is painted hazard yellow. But the lights inside go off just as we pull up. Undaunted as ever, Mei dashes out and around to the kitchen entrance to try and catch the help. I dash after her, fearful that she'll be met with a shotgun.

Instead, the lady inside is all too happy to have a chat while she empties the till of today's meager take. We simply must see the wallful of photos of her son, late of Harvard, recently transferred to Stanford. This budding success has posed and interned with not one, but both of the state's sitting U.S. senators. I may be glimpsing the future first Chinese president himself. Unlike the culinary world, it's Japanese-Americans who have proved themselves more palatable as politicos. Meanwhile, the proprietress's ten-year-old niece is aching to get home. A restaurant isn't a place for homework, and besides, business is bad. Poor kid, she pines to go back to New York, where classmates don't call out taunts "about the way I talk and the shape of my eyes."

Continuing in this patriotic vein, we spend the next morning following back roads through scrubby pine forests out to Mount Rushmore. "It's worth the detour," I insist, "in case the monument has its own Chinese takeout." This is also part of my sly, unspoken attempt to make my future bride feel a trifle more American. Too bad the chiseled faces are more puny than I'd ever imagined. Our constitutional emperors all have double chins made of sliding rubble. "These stone figures aren't much beside the Big Buddha," Mei says of Washington, Lincoln, Jefferson, and Teddy Roosevelt. "Compared with current politicians, I guess they look about as good as Jesus Christ!"

I've always harbored warm feelings for any state that could produce a senator as sincere as George McGovern. This time, I'm willing to nominate South Dakota for most bereft in the lower forty-eight. Following the interstate's plowed line through plains covered with dirty snow, all there is to look at are billboards touting Wall Drug, a small-town pharmacy whose promotional bluster extends for hundreds of miles. Free sarsaparilla for the kiddies! Wall Drug! Indian beads made in Taiwan? Wall Drug! America's "Great Wall" of promotions leads to the town of Wall, just a few gas stations and storage silos. Don't miss it, next exit! Wall Drug! The meaning of life? Turn back, you missed it! Wall Drug!

On a bluff to the far side of the Missouri River, signs seen in nine states announce a combination salad bar/gift emporium. There is no salad bar inside, but two of the four diners have tubular breathing aids up their noses. Mei and I practically sprint toward the Pizza Hut. A matronly attendant tries to tempt us by inquiring with heartfelt excitement, "Have you heard about our brand-new extra crispy?" Something's wrong when you're driven to McDonald's for your green vegetables. A trainee in paper hat says she thinks there's a Chinese place in Mitchell, ballyhooed home of the Corn Palace. Predictably, it's neither made of corn nor a palace.

Hooray for plain-speaking Minnesota! The convenience store in tidy Worthington is manned by a couple of Nordics whose flat accents and no-frills helpfulness scream out Middle America. There's not a soul downtown and the screen doors on every shop look rusted and torn. If only there were a Norman Rockwell for the nineties who could paint the telling details of decay as well as he once captured the small town's smug confidence! Today, the barber shop quartet has been replaced by a grunge band of skinheads. Even the Chinese takeaway has moved off Main Street to make way for J. R.'s Lao Diner.

There are two teenage kids manning this narrow, immaculate galley while watching Thai videos on a giant monitor. One rushes back to the kitchen to whip up our curried chicken over rice vermicelli and a spicy Lao-style eggplant. While-u-wait, there's free clove-spiced tea from a giant canister. As for "J. R.," he's not a character from *Dallas* but a typical, football-jersey-wearing Minnesotan who happens to have been born in Vientiane. Sis, boom, bah, go Luang Prabang! His chili-laced cuisine hasn't exactly caught on with the Lake Woebegoners. After so much purposely bland Chinese food, these vicious victuals pack all Asia's heat and fervency into paper cartons. As we drive off, Mei stuffs me with musky jasmine rice, one spoonful at a time. A hundred miles down the line, I'm still licking my lips for the lingering flavor of coconut and coriander. There never was a truck stop like this.

At the end of our longest driving day, we enter the flow of free-ways that dive and duck through Minneapolis. A city at last, but more important, we've come to Mei's college stomping grounds and the place where Mei's mother married a widowed microbiologist. Even on this freezing midnight, Mei senior—whose corresponding name in English is Macy, just like the store—crosses their suburban lawn to greet us. I still can't get used to this former belle of Shanghai modeling a sweatshirt that reads, "University of Minnesota Mom." Her peach-round face and droopy eyes now remind me of numerous relatives met on the road. Watching her with her American Bob, a couple in their late sixties with time to roughhouse and giggle each day, I see a harbinger of my future life with Mei. Just the way I do, this Anglo-Saxon down to his eyelashes revels in each opportunity for connection with China. The couple's trips to the red motherland are the annual highlight of his Christmas newsletter. And there is definitely something familiar about the determined way that Mei's mom offers her mate a sane and tranquil existence rich with the ben-efits of Chinese wisdom, Chinese health tips, and, of course, Chinese cooking.

For our own welcome dinner, she makes a barbecued chicken. "Too salty again, Ma!" Mei teases. "Just like that precious chicken we were able to get on the night before you were sent away to re-education camp. What a shame—you put on so much salt than we couldn't eat it!" Considering that she'd been raised with cooks and servants, it is remarkable that Macy can produce Shanghai-style dishes on a portable range while camping in Yellowstone, Glacier, and Big Bend. By her own admission, she was a spoiled brat who "wasted my youth with parties and dancing." But decades of deprivation have honed her survival skills. "I always thank the Communists for reforming her," jokes husband Bob. "They're the ones who tamed the woman warrior and gave me a good wife."

Around the dinner table in Minnesota, there's finally a chance to hear tales of Mei senior's privileged Shanghai childhood, which came to a crashing end when her own mother died of appendicitis that could not be treated in time because of the Japanese occupation of the city. "All I remember is hearing my mother moaning," she admits, "and thinking she had a stomachache."

Though her father had worked for an American firm, Mei's mother was typical of a generation of intellectuals who threw themselves zealously into building the new China. At an elite school for training revolutionary leaders, one of her classmates was China's current leader, Jiang Zemin. Like Jiang, who shows off for Western reporters by crooning "When We Were Young" from the Hollywood version of the life of Johann Strauss, Macy remains enthralled with American films and culture. Once, this top cadre's job was to do simultaneous Chinese translation for *Gone with the Wind*. Often, she served as an interpreter for visiting directors. "That's how I learned the British were civilized," Macy says. "They were the only ones who stopped talking in order for me to have a bite of the banquet!"

Such tasks, of course, did not put her in good stead once the Cultural Revolution struck. No brownie points were accorded for volunteering to labor among the peasants when Mei was only a month old. Left in the care of a stingy relative, Mei had been provided with a wet nurse who couldn't produce milk. No wonder she can now hold up her end of gobbling down the whole planet! "Oh, my!" says Macy. "This little girl was so thin when I got her back!" Still, mother and daughter share a laugh as though they're telling another cute baby story.

Despite her stentorian English and relative erudition, Mei's mother gets most poetic when recalling the fresh fish from Tai Lake and the soups from her native Suzhou that were "so rich they made your lips stick together." After supper, she sits down at the piano and warbles out a fine rendition of "As Time Goes By"—showing a talent, and vivacity, passed down to her daughter. I also see where Mei gets her determined self-sufficiency, drummed into her by such methods as each day's six-thirty A.M. run around the Great Hall of the People.

"The government sent me to a re-education camp to plant rice and assured me that I would never return," Macy tells us with a flicker of pride. But return she had, at least as far as the suburbs of Minneapolis. In a corner alcove, she spends much of her time watching Oprah while writing letters full of generous aid and blunt advice to families the world over. It takes some getting used to Mei senior's no-nonsense manner—and a mother-in-law whose phone small talk is sometimes as clinical as a doctor's questionnaire. "Just don't ask for too much sympathy," she warns. "I've run out of tears for this lifetime."

A drizzly Easter Sunday hardly looks like the day for egg rolling or an egg roll. If anything can resurrect this city's iron gray sprawl, it will be a Chinese restaurant. This time, we aren't just scanning two sides of a street, but two sides of the highway for signs borne on ninety-foot stanchions. We have to backtrack to spot the Yangtze River, which Mei recalls as among the most authentic in town. She coaxes a surly waiter to get us a special order of my favorite fish-flavored shredded pork, then complains about its red sauce and thick-cut chunks of meat. "This is foreign-style fish-flavored shredded pork," the red-jacketed fellow insists. When pushed, this Cantonese admits that he has no idea what the real thing tastes like. As we stomp out, Mei hears him cursing us for "too small an order and too much talk."

Through a freezing rain, Mei's mom leads us downtown to meet some friends she's made at Peking Way. This lunch place along a mezzanine of the Minneapolis Law Center offers do-it-yourself Mongolian barbecue. As usual, the couple that runs the place are a lot more interesting than the premade dishes in their steam table. Of course, they don't come from Peking at all, but from Xiamen, the lively southern port whose colonial enclave of Gulangyu is called "the piano island" for producing so many classical musicians. Mei and I had once wandered Gulangyu's tree-cloaked paths in search of Chinese Cliburns, then slurped snails and squirrel-fish with Shu Ting, a food enthusiast and leading "misty poet" of China who claimed she would write even better if she had my "sad eyes."

Trained as a ballet dancer, the Peking Way's fledgling chef escaped the mainland with a scholarship to Brigham Young, studied Martha Graham techniques, and landed a job with a company in Phoenix. "But I was used to China, where the state still supports the artist," he admits. The long hours, low pay, and insecurity of a dancer's life in America made him consider alternatives—especially with his wife and son coming to join him. He hired himself out to gas stations and car washes before enlisting as chief bottle-washer at another Peking restaurant in Arizona.

"The cooks there were the most bad-tempered men I'd ever seen," he said. "But they also taught all the techniques I needed in a very short time." This sounds like the corporal education by which China forged its opera stars. "For instance," he explains, going into an empty kitchen to demonstrate, "Northern-style food is cooked in small woks with handles, while I was more familiar with Guangzhou-style, where they use the larger, pot-bellied wok and stir more slowly."

While others speak of the change from Arizona to Minnesota in terms of the climate, he speaks only of the "local preference for brown sauces over clear ones. Every region of Chinese-American is different." But not as much as each restaurateur—united solely as men with a plan. Perhaps only such determined people would dare enter a field where so many are sure to fail. "A good operation here can clear ten thousand dollars a month," he insists, though he hasn't reached that point. "That's why I chose to help my restaurant with the word *way*. That is very positive and also sounds just like the Chinese word for flavor." Sheepishly, he adds, "I've thought more about the name for my restaurant than I thought about the name for my son."

Between trips with our in-laws to their local gym—a veritable indoor city, complete with walking tracks and fake shrubbery—Mei leads me on excursions back through her earliest days "just off the jet." I don't know if it's part of her bravado, but Mei professes to have had little fear regarding her new country. In the precious Chinese passport that allowed her to immigrate, the photo shows a smiling, unpainted innocent, with hair in dowdy, curled coif, who looks closer to twelve than twenty-six. She certainly doesn't look like someone who was ready for modern art or corporate culture, but then neither does she look like she had already labored in a Chinese medicine fac-tory and gained a B.A. from Beijing's Aeronautical College. "I never told you and I can't tell you now!" she reveals. "We had to swear that we wouldn't give away the secrets of China's rocket program!"

So Mei really means it when she says some new challenge "isn't rocket science." Within a year in America, she was on track for her graduate degree and found a place among a wild crowd of artists like our friend Bali Bruce. But the first stop in her acculturation was a Chinese restaurant run by Cambodians where she'd put in some months as a waitress.

"Even you!" Yes, even my Mei had undergone that trial by wok fire. "Someday, they'll put up a plaque."

She finds the wretched place unimproved, still miles of checker-board linoleum floors behind a brick facade that reminds me of a Polish veterans' hall. Heading through the back entrance to a kitchen smeared with grease, Mei inquires about owners long fled.

"There was one dirty old man who always asked me out!" she ad-mits. "He also stole my twelve-dollar tip from the son of Prince Sihanouk! I remember now—Sihanouk couldn't come because a gunman was found waiting nearby." Is this restaurant under new management or under United Nations protection? I can't believe that the prepossessing Mei ever worked here. Nor can I fathom how she shared a room with two other Chinese girls at the back of an off-campus, evangelical mission. All the born-again proselytizing soon drove her away.

"Coming from China, I had my brain washed already," Mei tells me, as we speed past her first American sanctuary. "I didn't need to have it washed twice."

Egg Foo Youngstown

It's still snowing on the late April morning when we leave Min-neapolis. I suppose they feature hot chocolate at their Fourth of July picnics. We think we've escaped when a fresh storm turns a Wisconsin highway into a field of foam fill. So confused are the mo-torists stranded with us at a Friendship Inn chain that I overhear one phoning relatives to say, "We're stuck in a town called Friendship!"

By late afternoon, we're passing Madison. I can't resist a detour to inspect a campus that was once my "safety"—the one college you could always get into even if every other admissions department believed those nasty things that your principal wrote about you. Besides, the percentage of Chinese has to be higher in almost any college town. Sure enough, we hardly have to make a pass along the parking garages that border the campus before noticing a Beijing Restaurant in one half-occupied, concrete walk-through.

Briskly run, with decor that features marble tables, mock red columns, and a calligraphed Li Bai poem, the place exudes an updated style that emphasizes China as a place of culture rather than coolies. The food is also more scrupulously prepared, because the chef is a recent arrival from *dong-bei*, the cold Manchurian Northeast. Unless he's wild for pasteurized mild cheddar, I can't see how Wisconsin is much of an improvement. In Chinese food, who cooks is not as important as who orders. Mei recognizes that the dish translated as "pork with vegetables" is actually our old engagement party centerpiece, *la pi*—the "double skin" cold bean-thread noodles, tossed in hot mustard and a variety of crunchy veggies. The fortune cookies come with Hershey's kisses. With prophetic hindsight, mine reads, "Your business will assume vast proportions."

That evening, we're enveloped by vast Chicago—known for its ethnics, but not its Chinese. The original few to make it here were railroaders whose wives stayed in China. Though the Second City was always second to New York in terms of Asians east of the Mississippi, there were only about seven thousand Chinese in Chicago at the start of the 1970s. There are now around twenty-five thousand, along with ten times that many Koreans. The original Chinese enclave at Van Buren near Clark was pressured out of the Loop by rising real-estate values. So the Leong Business Association began buying up property near 22nd and Wentworth. Today, Chicago's Chinatown is quarantined in that no-man's-land south of downtown but not yet "South Side"—a checkerboard of littered lots, flophouses, and abandoned print factories. Despite some dragonesque flourishes, Chicago's Chinatown is a lot like Chicago: jauntily ugly, defiantly industrial, and windscrubbed.

Mei and I resort to flagging down Chinese men-in-the-street for food recommendations. The random polling is inconclusive, though Mei zealously pesters a group of old men milling outside a church, waiting to ascend into an endless stream of funereal Caddies. None of these mourners seems to mind mixing their bereavement with a discussion of life's most pressing need. We are finally swayed by two enthusiastic brothers up from Indianapolis, one a math professor, the other a pathologist, and both named Ng. "That stands for nice guy," is their motto. They and their young wives are so nice that they even drop into their recommended Golden Bull a half hour after our side-walk encounter to see how we've enjoyed the hot-and-sour fish slices and the spare ribs. The Hong Kong couple who run the Golden Bull haven't had a vacation in five years. Tuesday is their only day off. Chicago really is the city of big shoulders, even small Chinese ones.

Our fortune reads, "The old believe everything, the middle-aged suspect everything, the young know everything." In the days when I knew everything, my roommate and radical main man was the rebel-lious scion of an illustrious Chicago political dynasty. Close to this Chinatown, at the last convention of the Students for a Democratic Society, Mark was the first to show me how to properly wave Mao's "Little Red Book" at sectarian foes. That doesn't mean he knows much about Chinese food—his taste runs more toward Chicago's sausage staple of "red hots." When our Berkeley commune wanted to eat out in San Francisco's Chinatown, he sloganized, "Don't go chowin' down in no oppressed community!" Since we were only af-ter a couple of egg rolls, the rhetoric seemed a bit of an overreaction. Still, I'm looking forward to visiting the first of my circle to marry so that I can show him the woman with whom I'm finally going to make it to the matrimonial promised land. When I phoned ahead, my friend sounded even more like a low-down Chicago bluesman than usual.

"Two Jews blues," Mark reminded me of a favorite band from the old days. "She's hitting the wind without warning." Just a week back, he'd been given the news that his wife of nearly twenty years wanted to part company. This puts something of a damper on our weekend. But Mei plunges headfirst into the situation, soon discovering that my old pal and she share a love for the revolutionary Russian novel, *What Is to Be Done?* I suppose the question might as well apply to modern divorce. Instead of offering understanding, she prefers to bestow plenty of practical tips. I never thought I'd see my coffee-chugging, street-tough friend straining in his Converse high-tops to follow morning stretching postures that Chinese call "one-finger zen"—Mei's prescription for heartbreak and most other ills.

My friend also finds solace in coaching the soccer team of his speedy ten-year-old son Abraham, a precocious geography buff who can never quite fathom all the places on the map that his father's old friend has actually been! Together, we go cruising to find the oddly titled Paris City Inn, a Chinese favorite from the brief stint when Mark and I shared a grimy North Side apartment and a single bed that we used in alternating shifts. Our old hangout has been crowded out by dozens of Thai places favored by Chicago's hip set. So we put in an appearance at a big family reunion in a swank apartment over-looking the so-called Gold Coast. My friend's wise-ass uncle, a magistrate once so feared by Puerto Rican gangs that they called him "the hanging judge," has enough wits at eighty to offer to marry Mei and me on the spot. "On one condition—the judge gets a night with the bride!"

Of course, all these well-heeled, canasta-playing Jews go out for Chinese noshing every Sunday night. On their recommendation, we try one of the high-priced establishments along Michigan Avenue's un-exotic Miracle Mile. At the below-ground Szechwan House, owner George Kuan puts out a spread that's most impressive to young Abraham, who plays food critic for a night. There's nothing the slightest bit Sichuanese here. The owner himself is a circum-spect, blazer-wearing former representative of the Taiwanese foreign ministry. Like Mei, he studied engineering and did computer design before starting his first restaurant on the North Side. He is another of those men whose placid exterior belies a life of considerable risk. It is one of the great strengths and also great banes of the Chinese that they are so good at making themselves respectable, which so of-ten means invisible. The "middle way" doesn't make it in America—nor on this menu, which falls in that gray area between homemade and deluxe. The highlights are the appetizers, including a cold chicken smoked on the premises. To the boy, the owner explains why Chinese disdain the white meat on chicken with the saying, "If you eat it, it has no taste; if you throw it away, it's a waste." But does it rhyme in Chinese?

If Mei and I are going to make it on time to New York—and our planned Italian wedding—we've got to spend the next night in Youngs-town. God knows why I expect to find a decent Chinese meal in a rust-belt city known largely for the De Bartolos, Eddie and Eddie Jr., shopping mall developers and football-team owners. But even here, as Mei and I navigate a dark freeway and squint toward the proper exit for downtown, there's a tingle of anticipation at entering a speck previously unseen, a name on the map risen out of the inanimate. A traveler knows the excitement of a seduction nearly every mile. In lifting so many veils, he or she undresses the world. But do we really want to see Youngstown naked? Or partake of its very late dinner? By night, Youngstown appears to be a patchwork of bars, chicken shacks, and insurance towers. We share the mean streets solely with bubble-topped cruisers. The center has not held and what's loosed upon the world is not "mere anarchy" but sheer policing.

A two-laner leads us deeper and deeper into the black ghetto. When I steel my courage and pull up beside a barbecue shack in the midst of nowhere, I'm dismayed to peer through the front windows and see nothing but two arms swinging a pink Wiffle bat from behind a counter. I take this as some disembodied warning to all potential holdup men. A mile or two further on, we pull into the packed lot of a popular pizza joint. At Mei's urging, I roll down the windows and call out to an African-American girl leaning against a car filled with friends. Will she think that I'm one confused honky?

"Chinese? Well, there's the China Coast, that ain't bad but it's kinda far for you." She and her pals are actually willing to escort us there through the spooky Allegheny night. Instead, we get directions back to the strip that services traffic on its way to New York. One Chinese place is actually a motel's dining lounge, so we cruise on until spotting another mall occupant called the Golden Hunan. "Sorry, it's takeout only after ten," we're informed in familiarly Americanized tones. Not so much a dumb blonde as a second banana—as in "yellow outside, white inside"—this sweet kid soon admits that she and her sisters are trying to get out from under the burden of two restaurants bequeathed by their dad. They can't compete with all the franchised outlets and clearly, their hearts aren't in cooking, or being, Chinese.

"I wish my dad hadn't passed away, so he could tell you his story. I think he was some kind of a cook back in Taiwan. I know he had a brother someplace in China, because they were reunited after fifty-three years. It was all written up in the papers, that's how I remember. Jeez, it's terrible, I can't tell you the brother's name! We've had a lot of trouble since then, because all they wanted was for us to send money."

When Mei has difficulty understanding the girl's Ohioan pronunciation of her family name, the girl confesses that she can't write it. But wait—there it is on her key chain! The Chinese character for *Tseng*. She continues, "My dad called himself Ben. Through a friend's recommendation, he was sponsored to this country by Ira Gershwin. For several years, he was Ira Gershwin's personal chef."

This is worth our detour—though I'm somewhat dubious about the path that might have taken her dad from the glitter of Hollywood to grimy Youngstown. "Oh, he had some partner who convinced him to start a restaurant somewhere around here. Pittsburgh, I think! I wish he could tell you!"

Dad's gone and our food has arrived, so we're left with hints of a delectable history. We transport our containers back to a local motel where the coffee machine is broken, the cable TV keeps fuzzing out, and archetypal weirdos in jacked-up trucks drag race in the parking lot. Holed up in number seven, drapes tightly drawn, we venture no further into Youngstown. We don't even dare open our door to throw away the copious remains of our final foray into portable Sinology. Bulked-out with cubes of canned water chestnuts, the food isn't just bland, but bordering on rancid—not Hunan but Who Cares.

Our final fortune reads, "It is better to have a hen tomorrow than an egg today." How about an egg foo Youngstown? The threatening toughs and highway traffic aren't the worst of this night. For the first time, and hopefully the last, I'm awakened in our unsanitized bed by the potent fumes of congealed cornstarch, uneaten *kung pao* exhaust.

Joy of Flushing

The first New York restaurant we choose to sample is closed on account of murder. Only in the Big Apple! Mei and I have rattled out to the end of the Queens subway line in search of Min Feng, a rare Fujian-style eatery praised in the *Times* for its fishy authenticity. But genuine Chinese food comes with genuine Chinese trouble. Most newly arrived Fujianese are indebted to syndicates of snake-head smugglers. There is something decidedly fishy about the eviction notice posted on the door. The locked entrance, leading down into the basement of a slapdash mall, has the hurriedly vacated look of a crime scene. The Mandarin-speaking girl in a donut shop confirms our hunch. So does the next restaurateur on the block.

"Yes, there was a killing," he confirms in a whisper to Mei. "But how do this *weiguoren* know so much about our neighborhood?"

There's nothing like being called a foreigner in the place of your birth. Doesn't it count that I began emerging into this world when my mother's water broke on the Number One Broadway Local? Even then, I couldn't wait to try my first takeout. Back when a token still cost a quarter, there wasn't the panoply of multiethnic snacks for a big-eared, freckled-faced American kid. On the daily ride to and from my Riverdale prep school, me and my buddies would turn the subway into private dining cars by noshing Italian heroes and Hostess pies. When the whole city went dark with an electrical blackout, I'd already spent my "emergency" money on a jumbo ham and swiss. What use now my expertise in egg creams and salted pretzel sticks, two for a nickel from the candy-store jar?

This homecoming, I head straight for the safe haven of the Public Library's reading room. For kicks, I want to see what's spewed from the computerized database when I type "Restaurants, Chinese." Out of several hundred references per year in the New York press, few have to do with eating. Most would be cross-referenced under "crime." One irate apartment dweller sued for damages because of his abode's proximity to the constant fumes from a restaurant's kitchen ducts. The courts have yet to determine just how much soy soot constitutes a litigable nuisance—probably because judges are being kept busy with the remarkable number of homicides in Chinese restau-

226

rants. A few are the result of straightforward cash register robberies; some involve gangs seeking retribution for unpaid protection money. Most stem from owners seeking the most effective means to do away with the competition once and for all.

Growing up, I was robbed so many times at knifepoint that I thought every kid in America carried two wallets. I barely made it out of kindergarten when a fledgling schizo tried to toss me off the thirty-story tower of Riverside Church. Not long after, a gang of Puerto Rican playmates extorted money for candy by threatening to dognap my Scottish Terrier. How had I survived to become another adult seeker after stolen innocence? Why bother showing Mei the old neighborhood? The block of Riverside Drive that felt interminably windy on my way home from school is now conquered in a single adult stride. I can almost peer into that tenth-floor apartment where I spent my first seventeen years—the very window from which my pet chameleon leaped to an untimely death.

For Chinese who have survived famines and purges, New York doesn't seem such a dangerous place. A few years back, a promising painter name Lin-Lin had flaunted his survival skills by putting his studio in Harlem and making his living as a sidewalk artist on sordid Forty-second Street. He was killed for talking back to some heckling gang members. Hardy bohemians all, the mainlanders I meet through Mei like to swagger through the subways and streets at all hours. Real men don't eat quiche and real Beijingers don't take cabs.

In a gauge of the swiftness with which the Asian influx has hit, I can easily recall a Manhattan bereft of the black-garbed Oriental kids who crowd every art school and publishing office. I can testify to a town that functioned perfectly well without a single Korean grocer's multinational buffets. I can swear under oath that Stone Age apartment dwellers actually came home to cook rather than call out for Chinese banquets in a box. Down in the East Village, you couldn't find a single Tibetan joint, where we discover the yak butter being churned by Puerto Ricans. The Indians had yet to create their blocks of curry houses supplied from one vast underground cauldron. By the late sixties, Hell's Kitchen may have already been crammed with *Comidas Criollas*—the odd bisection of Cuban and Chinese cuisines that took hold here after a giant exodus from Havana—but

227

my taste didn't run to plantain omelets back then. Thirty years later, Mei and I still dare not foray into the perfunctory Chinese side of Chinese-Cuban menus. Nor coax a word from the decrepit waiters, in English or Spanish.

Where my parents once led me by the hand to my primal mom-and-pop restaurant, the sidewalks of old New York are increasingly encroached by the glassed-in terraces of an Empire Szechuan or Hunan Balcony. All put out an underspiced product, suspiciously over-fortified with canned baby ears of corn and the like. As one owner bemoans, "Chinese food here was all Cantonese until the seventies. Then the yuppies discovered that Chinese food could be spicy. There may not be any Hunanese in New York, but every place has to call itself Hunan or Szechuan." To survey each one of them on even a single avenue of Manhattan would send me straight to a Park Avenue shrink.

So we concentrate on another local subgenre. Call it "power Chinese." Scattered through Midtown's mid-Fifties, from Fifth Avenue toward the United Nations, are a number of discreet outposts of the Orient reserved for the captains of the Empire State. "Yes, we train all our waiters to keep their ears closed if possible and their mouths shut," says the comanager of Tse Yang, a darkened lair full of smoky mirrors, tropical fish, and elaborate wall carvings shipped from Taiwan. Instead of willowy cooks in torn undershirts, there are bell captains; instead of steamers, perfectly refrigerated wine coolers. The raucous chatter and crying babies of Chinese families has been replaced by the hush of insider information. Declares the manager, "Henry Kissinger ate here." And probably practiced his chopstick skills before a first encounter with Mao!

"A restaurant like ours is always the victim of a double standard," says Larry Woo, the assured young heir of Tse Yang's late owner. "We're called high-priced if we charge twenty dollars for a dish that takes six hours to prepare, but nobody says anything when some Italian joint charges the same amount for a simple pasta. When a French restaurant adapts Asian influences, they are praised as innovative. But if we offer French wines and service, food writers complain that we're not authentic."

I must confess that I've already done as much. What I like about

Tse Yang is that it sticks to recognizable standards, enriched with the finest ingredients.

"We're part of the world's largest group of deluxe Chinese restaurants," Woo reveals. Blushing, he goes on to admit that he's cemented the company's near-feudal alliance by marrying the daughter of the owner of the chain's Paris flagship. "Of course, I thought it was a terrible idea at first, but things just sort of worked out."

This young man in blue blazer seems the perfect American-born Chinese success story. "In fact, I'm a licensed attorney," he admits, not exactly a shocker. Like so many others we've met, Larry has opted out of the rat race for the homey life of family inheritance. "My father came from Shanghai, moving first to the Philippines. At the triumph of the revolution, the Communists were throwing out all the top chefs. My father even had to burn his wedding pictures because he was dressed in Western clothes."

In the plush surroundings of Tse Yang, it's not easy to keep hold of Chinese history. It's only in restaurants like this that one begins to imagine a China that isn't defined by suffering. But it's still tough to savor a Chinese restaurant where I can't loosen my tie.

That certainly isn't the problem at Lucky Cheng's. When we accidentally stroll past the First Avenue tenement housing this cutting-edge publicity stunt, Mei and I can't resist having a peek at what might be the world's strangest Chinese restaurant. Circulating on tiptoes and pouting in the back kitchen are Lucky's trademark transvestite waiters/waitresses. But what's the use of being hip enough to employ Asian boys in blonde wigs when the hip clientele does their best to act unfazed? Long tables are packed with young white lawyers in love, unwinding after a long day uptown by chowing down on enormous portions of Pan-Asian *shitake*-and-*salsiccia* pastas as polymorphously perverse as the staff. Culinary bisexuality leads to the bland, though it's tough to rate a menu this pointedly androgynous. The Chinese have sure come a long way in New York, or perhaps I just haven't come far enough.

If the sons of the Yellow Emperor could find their way to Queens, I should too. Growing up as an Upper West Side brat, my universe was bounded by the Hudson and Central Park. I know the layout of Lop Buri, the back roads of Tuscany, and the rail lines of the New

Territories better than my native city's other benighted boroughs. Having left before an influx of Dominicans, Koreans, and Hindustanis, I wrongly hold to the stereotype of Queens as the site of unending, Archie Bunker, lower-middle-class backlash. The last time I'd been out this way was for that ill-fated Mets game when I first substituted hot dogs with cold dumplings.

At Flushing Boulevard's last stop, I step out to find street stalls manned by Arabs, rows of signs in Hangul, and just enough ethnic color to relieve the brick primness and past-its-prime East Coast grime. California, that's the promised land! New York is merely the practiced land. If so many immigrants are content to stop here, that has to be because they are the people most primed to take the first best offer. And "Floo-shing," as it's lately been sinologized, started attracting Chinese settlers about ten years back. Like San Francisco's Richmond District or Los Angeles's Monterey Park, this second-tier Chinatown supposedly offers better Chinese food because it caters to more established diners. In addition, the recently populated enclave draws its residents more heavily from Taiwan and mainland China—thereby breaking the cultural, and culinary, stranglehold of the Cantonese.

"When I came to New York," one of Flushing's Shanghainese restaurateurs admits, "I felt like an outcast among my own race. I didn't even know how to speak their language. And sometimes, the Chinese can be so clannish." Within a few blocks along Roosevelt Avenue, Mei and I sample a genuine purveyor of Sichuan spice called the Golden Monkey, then complete our lunch at the Taipei Wall Sea Street Restaurant, as tiny as its name is big. The small sushi bar in back is a mark of true Taiwanese authenticity. Another positive sign is the scullion at a back table shucking a bucket's worth of garlic bulbs. Manager Kai Ting, a former hotelier, has big plans to transform the home-style dishes of the owner's wife into a thriving concern. "Top secret" and piping hot from the kitchen come distinctive casseroles that make liberal use of cilantro and basil, beef slow-cooked with anise, a sticky rice smeared with a tangy sauce that employs, of all heathen things, pureed tomatoes.

Spurred on by our best eats since Vancouver, we hang around to have dinner at the New Flushing Seafood Restaurant. The unappetizing name is a poor substitute for the untranslatable *Lou Wai Lou*, a phrase from the poet Su Dongpo suggesting his native Hangzhou's pleasures in "chamber beyond chamber." On a previous trip to China, I'd eaten in this legendary West Lake restaurant turned into another stained-rug, state-run tourist trap. There are few local customers joining us in the New York version. The over-refined decor and matching prices are probably scaring off the skittish masses.

"Chinese always get frightened when they see flowers on the table," the manager admits. "Besides, we haven't been open long enough for any mouth-to-mouth."

I know he's not talking about first-aid techniques—except as they apply to resuscitating his nightly take. The house specialty here is West Lake Vinegar Fish, nearly as tart as in Taiwan, accompanied by "sister-in-law's" fish soup, jumbo shrimp, and unusual *shu mai* dumplings packed with sweet rice. The "vegetarian birds with a vegetarian heart" are big, soggy, bow ties of tender, brown bean-curd skin stuffed with sprouts and heavily gravied. They are much too healthy for me to keep popping them in like junk food. This Lou Wai Lou ships its eels live from Shanghai weekly—the neighborhood's least nefarious form of smuggling.

By the end of the first course, I feel there's some experienced hand behind all of this. Sure enough, the affable Tommy Chan emerges from the register shadows. Trained as a journalist, Chan found a more lucrative calling as the proprietor of Midtown's most prestigious Sichuan House. As he tells it, "John Gotti was a regular. I don't know if he was the Godfather, but he always said 'please' and 'thank you.'"

Chan sold the business to go into real estate just at the moment when Manhattan prices took a collective swan dive. So this place represents his modest attempt at a comeback, as well as a September song to his native Shanghai.

"When I went back home, all the kids called me a foreigner. Even when I spoke to them in Shanghai dialect, they yelled, 'Look, the foreigner speaks perfect Chinese!'"

Chan is full of a professional host's practiced quips, such as the claim that "Americans like to age their steak a long time, but we Chinese like to chop it a long time!" He tries to stay away from chefs who gamble, employing the maxim, "If a cook loses money, the dishes lose flavor." But just to insure good luck, he's changed the traditional name of clay-baked Beggar's Chicken to "Rich and Famous Chicken." His menu is a form of wish fulfillment.

My only wish is to endure the subway ride again the next day to try a more crowded place around the corner. If I could put a finger on what makes me so strangely pleased to be thus wasting my life, I'd know for sure just how to keep from wasting it! With every good meal Mei and I have, it seems that we're willing to go even farther for the next. Perhaps the only true pleasures are repeated pleasures. If that isn't a Chinese proverb, then it should be.

Joe's Shanghai, while begun in Hong Kong, more than justifies our return trip to the same Queens block as the New Flushing Seafood. Wearing a mint-green polo shirt like the rest of his staff, the owner isn't a Joe at all, but a kindly, burly fellow who calls himself Peter. Yet everything about this cozy, wood-paneled place exudes this young man's calm faith in Chinese traditions. "Maybe I'm part of the older generation," he admits, "but I want all my employees to feel part of a family."

To that end, I count twelve college-aged waiters hovering around the same number of tables. There's a staff of fifteen more in the small kitchen. Though he lives with his mother and wife back in Manhattan's Chinatown, where he will soon open another branch, Peter confesses, "I see my cashier more than my mother, I talk to my partners more than my wife."

Peter tells us that the lucky character emblazoned on the uniform stands for "deer." He serves us a tender braised pork shoulder big enough to be from an elephant, Carnegie Deli portions of chow mein, shaved blocks of rice cake tossed with leeks, deep-fried fish sticks uniquely combined with soft wedges of eggplant, and some of our journey's most tender *xiao long bao zi*—the twist-top, soup-filled Shanghainese pork dumplings to which Joe's Shanghai has added a stuffed dollop of salty crab eggs. There is no pretense here, just bold flavors served up straight from the Chinese heart. Around a single corner, Mei and I have come upon two of the best Shanghainese restaurants in the country.

Unlike his competitor, Peter is a fervent believer in anything that will bless his efforts. "There should always be eight or nine fish," he informs us with gravity about the good luck aquarium in his entry. "But our business has been so good, that when one of the fish died, we were afraid to replace it."

On a ledge above the door to the kitchen, he's also placed one of the gaudiest shrines I've ever seen. Food offerings and a simu-lated electric flame are set before the scowling countenance of Guan Gong, the righteous judge deity. "People in the restaurant business pray to him for protection because he is the one to know right from wrong." Does that mean this god knows how to order? Or does Peter need all the help he can get to subdue the evils of the big city?

"Back in China, we had the wrong idea about New York. We were all pretty disappointed. This is a rough town, dangerous and dirty." But it's worth the risk when you can find bliss in Flushing.

Shrimp and Clams in Beer Broth

From Joe's Shanghai Restaurant

Ingredients:

Shrimp, 1 lb.
Fresh clams, $^1/_2$ lb.
Celery, 1 stalk chopped
Cilantro, 4 sprigs
Fresh tomato, 3 slices
Fresh garlic, 2 cloves
Sugar, 2 tsp.
Salt, dash
Chinese vinegar, $^1/_2$ tsp.
Rice wine, 1 tsp.
Beer, $^1/_2$ bottle
Sesame oil, $^1/_2$ tsp.
Peanut oil
Chicken stock, 1 cup

Heat the wok, add a small amount of oil, and stir-fry the shrimp until they turn red. Boil enough water to cover the clams and cook them briefly until they open. Heat and oil the wok again. Add garlic, tomato, and celery and stir-fry one minute, then add beer, chicken stock, sugar, salt, wine, and oil. Pour entire mixture into a bowl atop the shrimp and clams. Serve immediately, garnished with sesame oil and cilantro.

Beijing to Bagels

Pig Heaven is not the place to go on Yom Kippur. Yet that's where Mei and I will eventually find ourselves—the only ones about to order swine on the very day Jews are supposed to atone for a year's sweet-and-sour sin. This Upper East Side fixture features the forbidden flesh doused in hot bean paste, glazed with barbecue, dotted with sesame, bedded on spinach and oranges. It's brought to us by an octogenarian waiter who ought to be in a Beijing retirement home but tells us with a most Hebraic shrug, "So what else have I got to do?" Somehow, I'm not surprised to learn that Pig Heaven's cook gained his first restaurant experience in Haifa, Israel.

"Every year, we do great take-out during the High Holy Days," the merry Taiwanese owner whispers, to keep some higher authority from hearing. "Don't tell anybody, please, but the Jewish people are our best customers!"

So what else is new? "The Jewish calendar goes back six thousand years and the Chinese goes back five thousand," goes one of many jokes. "So what did Jews eat for the first thousand years?"

Come to think of it, a weakness for won ton may be the main trait that I share with my coreligionists. If I can get to the bottom of this most curious crosscultural craving, perhaps I'll even know a bit more about what's bonded me and Mei in yet another Jew-Boo (as in Buddhist) linkage. Already, one such pair has joined forces to market a teriyaki sauce called "Soy Vay!" The mutual admiration stretches back into China, where a small community of Jews—reform or orthodox?—was once centered in the ancient river town of Kaifeng. One big-time Hollywood agent actually hired a Chinese train to stage his half-Chinese daughter's *bat mitzvah* there. But how do all red Chinese know that Freud and Einstein were "orange Jews"?—as Mei likes to tease while ordering breakfast.

The theories are nearly as plentiful as the gags. Some posit that both peoples are ruled by strong moms and extreme politics, noshing and guilt, respect for the written word and for medical school diplomas. Yet as much as marginalization has forced them to play retail ends against the wholesale middle, both Chinese and Jews share a tendency toward a mystical utopianism. Living too much in the material world, they put their faith elsewhere. Where Judaism parts company with Confucianism is in uplifting the right of complaint. To my eyes, the group-oriented Chinese are masters at suffering in silence—a bit too adept at patiently tolerating the intolerable. In Mei's eyes, there is nothing more inconsiderate than my relations' constant kvetching. Whatever the cause, Chinese figure things are bound to get better while Jews figure things can't get any worse.

Yet their joint battle cry could be *Ess, ess, mein kindt!*—"Eat, eat my child!" All of the above guarantees that the two groups should meet at the Chinese restaurant—like the apocryphal Chinatown joint where a Jewish man entered to find all the Chinese waiters speaking fluent Yiddish. When he went to compliment the proprietor on his staff's amazing bilingualism, the worried owner winced. "Not so loud! They think it's *English!*"

But if every Chinese restaurant is crowded with Jews, as comic Jackie Mason has asked, how come you never see Chinese in a Jewish deli? Mei goes straight for the rugelach cookies—"Just like sesame paste buns"—in Zabar's, that museum of modern food art where the lox slicers would greet my dad with a guttural, "Doctah Krich! Have we got some sturgeon for you!" I take her on my annual pilgrimage for real corned beef—like fine Beaujolais, it just doesn't travel well—to the Carnegie Deli, whose half-pound, high-cholesterol sandwiches have, as the black humor goes, "killed more Jews than Hitler." Coincidentally, I share a mile-high mound of chopped liver with a Bejing friend of Mei's who claims to have had a Jewish grandmother. Mei completes another circle by ordering borscht, a childhood favorite due to Beijing's Soviet influence. The Carnegie's caustic waiters, so proud to assure customers that "you'll never finish that, *bubi*," share an eerie affinity with their Chinese brethren.

At the Shun Lee Palace, a classy mainstay of New York's gourmet Chinese elite, Mei and I are put in the experienced hands of just such a waiter/kibitzer.

"I ran away from the Communists in '49," Tommy Chu begins, setting up his kicker. "Nothing personal, you know."

Spreading napkins on our laps, he continues, "Now I hear you can get back the house that they took, except that they charge you for forty years of painting." The deadpan delivery of this son of Beijing is accentuated by sad Buster Keaton face, bowl haircut, and gapped front teeth. Aware that few customers expect him to speak such good Brooklynese, Tommy adds, "I don't wanna go near another Peking duck myself, not after serving seventy a night. Just gimme a bagel in the morning and a can of Bud at night!"

When I compliment Tommy on his use of the vernacular, he assures me, "An empty stomach is the best teacher. Believe me, if you'd landed in China with six bucks in your pocket, you'd learn to talk Chinese real fast."

I'm not sure this explains the basso articulations of the esteemed Michael Tang, Shun Lee's suave founder. After all, *shun* means smooth. With every hair in place, and every nail manicured, this assured figure reminds me of a glibly ingratiating uncle of mine who once headed up the New Jersey Bar Association. Tang runs his ship with the seriousness of a great war lord. It's hard to believe that this son of a Chiang Kai-shek adjutant was a busboy when he first came to the States.

"Even while I was studying at Oklahoma State, I would work in New York restaurants during the summer," he explains. "By the time I graduated, the owner of a place called the Dynasty trusted me to take charge." What Michael Tang soon created was "New York's first four-star Chinese." Thanks partly to the endorsement and friendship of *Times* critic Craig Claiborne, the iconoclastic Texan who first championed ethnic foods, Tang came to hobnob with French chefs and improve the stature of each new venture.

Though the Shun Lee Palace menu is full of well-worn items, the owner returns with each of our courses to ask rhetorically, "Who else would dare to serve an oxtail?" More superb are his meaty *kung pao* frogs' legs and a *dong po* pork, the Hangzhou specialty that's a side of uncured bacon baked to the consistency and sweetness of a Black

Forest cake. Shun Lee's chicken in black bean sauce is the best this side of the Mississippi. Whether crunchily Chinese or wisely Westernized, every order comes out up to snuff. With one chef each from Beijing, Shanghai, and Canton, Mr. Tang is able to keep up with all regions. "The mainland chefs are fine," he observes, "after they quit splashing oil on every dish." Shun Lee recently won some publicity by offering a tie-in dinner to re-create up to thirty dishes from the hit film about a Chinese chef, *Eat Drink Man Woman*. Tang has to do it all with eighteen helpers in his kitchen when, in Asia, they'd use a hundred.

"Overtime! That's the American way!" seconds Tommy Chu. With its constant flow of plates from the kitchen, its voluminous menu of consistent quality, Shun Lee Palace reminds me of—what else?—an imperial Jewish deli.

"It's the take-out business that's brought down Chinese food," Michael Tang moans. "The vegetables get all soggy in that cardboard box. And now everyone wants Japanese. Sukiyaki and raw fish? Do you call that a cuisine? Chinese food, on the other hand, has no limits. Where Americans prefer to change their furniture every year, Chinese people don't care what they have to spend to celebrate with friends."

Michael Tang wants us to know that he's just dropped a cool million to do his first redesign in thirty-five years. A famed decorator has brightened up the place in tones of royal blue and burgundy, plus a rich carpeting inlaid discreetly with dragons. Which doesn't mean he's dumped his old, gold-trimmed Oscar de la Renta plates.

"But all the monkeys are still from China!" whispers Tommy Chu as soon as his boss wanders off. He points toward a giant of a busboy. "Look at computer Yang over there. He started out sleeping on the subway. Now he installs software on his days off. Was a swimming champ at Ohio State. Even my daughter is at Columbia Law. I know I've made it because she won't have to be a waitress!"

I'm not sure how Mei and I make it to the end of Shun Lee's feast. While we're groaning with the last of nine courses, Tommy inquires, "How 'bout some tiramisu with soy sauce? An MSG sundae? The boss is gonna kill me, but why don't you skip it? Chinese make lousy desserts anyway."

Still, his shtick isn't finished. A couple of tanned Texan tourists at the next table hesitate at the prospect of gripping their duck-stuffed pancakes like hand-held burritos. When these gentiles ask for a knife and fork, Tommy Chu complies with a plastic smile. With perfect George Burns timing, he barely gets out of the diners' hearing range before muttering, "Barbarians!"

Crabmeat with Snow Pea Leaves

From Shun Lee Palace Restaurant

Ingredients:

Fresh crab meat, without shell or cartilage, $^1/_2$ lb.
Loosely packed snow pea leaves (*dou miao*), 8 cups

To cook and flavor the snow pea leaves:
Chicken stock, 1 cup
Minced ginger, 2 tsp.
Minced shallot, 1 tbs.
Shaoxing rice wine or dry sherry, 1 tbs.
Peanut oil, 2 tbs.
Salt, $^1/_2$ tsp.

Sauce for crab meat:
Minced ginger, 2 tsp.
Minced shallots, 1 tbs.
Shaoxing wine or dry sherry, $1^1/_2$ tbs.
Sesame oil, 1 tsp.
Cornstarch, 2 tbs. mixed with water
Salt, $^1/_4$ tsp.
Fine ground white pepper, dash

Heat the wok until smoking hot. Add the chicken stock and when boiling, add the snow pea leaves. Cook for one minute, or until the liquid just boils and the vegetable is barely wilted. Drain immediately and thoroughly in a colander. After cleaning the wok, reheat until smoking hot, adding oil, ginger, shallots, the blanched snow pea leaves, Shaoxing wine, and salt. Stir once or twice and cook for about one minute. The snow pea leaves should be bright green in color. Drain in a colander, pressing the leaves to extract all the juice. Set the leaves on a serving platter and keep warm while preparing the crabmeat.

Heat the wok, adding oil, and when the oil is smoking hot, add the ginger, shallots, and crabmeat. Stir the mixture once or twice, then add chicken stock, wine, salt, pepper, and sesame oil. As soon as the mixture starts to boil, add the cornstarch mixture and stir the sauce until it thickens. Add more cornstarch if necessary. Pour the crabmeat sauce over the greens and serve immediately.

Mott Street Meditations

"Walking down Canal Street, not on every door," goes the sailors' saw that kept us grade-school kids snickering. "Walking down Canal Street, trying to find a whore!"

At the time I sang that ditty, I had no idea that Canal Street was the northern boundary of the largest Chinese community in America. As a kid, I rarely had cause to go near the place. As a grownup, however, that's straight where I head. Now I'm walking down that ribald avenue with my wife-to-be, not just knocking but sticking my head into every door, hoping to be enticed by far different forms of flesh. In most of these houses, however, the distinctive perfume is made of cold duck fat and disinfectant, dish detergent and the faintly soapy steam rising from stale mounds of bok choy.

Back in the sixties, I'd been lured to Bo-Bo's, a single front room of a tenement that served the softest Cantonese version of steak fillets, surrounded by fresh chunks of pineapple. Twenty years later, I'm not willing to see if the place can withstand new owners or the withering standards of my new-found knowledge. Since one has to eat three meals a day no matter what, perhaps it is better not to know too much. How do we choose our pleasure when nearly every walk-up window is plastered with some glowing clipping come-on? New York is the one town with enough press to cover every hole-in-the-wall in glory. In Chinatown, everybody is a star, sometimes three-star or four.

Or are they? Approaching the end of the twentieth century, the average wage for waiters in New York's Chinatown still hovers somewhere around fifteen dollars a day for a thoroughly nineteenth-century work week of approximately sixty hours—bow ties and stained vests not included. Only a hefty influx of tips brings these peons' paychecks up to the legal minimum. But no labor statistics can possibly add up all these masses huddled over woks, the lives sizzled away. Chinese dumplings of the world, unite! You have nothing to lose but your wrappers!

Yet unions have made little headway among this boss-fearing group. Just a year or two back, the annual meeting of a Chinese business association at one of the largest Chinatown restaurants had turned into an oversubscribed mob scene—there to show support for management's attempt to turn back yet another organizing drive. Even when one state investigation turns up $1.5 million in a single restaurant's unpaid wages, sentiment here runs in favor of keeping the tables filled by holding labor costs low. No wonder I'm having pangs of liberal guilt as we wander the hodgepodge of grocers, wok shops, and Kuomintang clubhouses along Mulberry, Orchard, and Mott. How these pockets of soy-drenched poverty sound like scented country lanes!

For Mei, there's only amazement at street vendors grilling home-style rice flour pancakes or hawking fresh bunches of the longan fruit that Chinese call "silver thread." She can't resist initiating me to the benefits of this spiny white lychee that is supposed to cure fatigue and restore women after pregnancy. With her finely honed instincts, she coaxes me into one grimly fronted, aluminum-lined soup kitchen, uncharitably lodged on a block facing a ramp of the Williamsburg Bridge. This quite decent Shanghainese place is a "joint venture" of the America-Shanghai business council. But doesn't "venture" imply going somewhere one hasn't been before? The first business is always a restaurant because it gives the board of directors someplace to meet.

No businessmen want to go on record about the protection rackets and property-grabbing schemes of such black hand societies as the Fukkienese Flying Dragons.

"This is American-style, we've got to speak up!" one restaurateur will declare bravely. "We're safe so long as the black societies know you are in with the whites." No racism intended. But the conspiracy of silence speaks louder than a few oblique references to "trouble." Only when speaking of Brooklyn's smaller Chinatown does one proprietor tell us, "It's not so easy for the gangsters to get there. . . . Of course, on Chinese New Year, everyone comes around for a packet of lucky money." Nobody says how much buys enough luck.

"Criminals are in every country," I'm told by a friendly family patriarch from Hong Kong. "If you already got capital, Hong Kong's a good place. But New York, that's a good place to get capital!" Taking a distinctly American tack, this Chinatown chef adds, "Maybe China remains poor and backward because we waste too much effort on cooking and shopping. When do we have time for anything else?"

In Chinatowns like this, one forgets that Chinese can do anything else. Certainly, none of the Chinese whom I meet through Mei would live anywhere near here. The one exception is avant-garde composer Tan Dun, whose full-floor loft faces the Henry Street Settlement, once the renowned uplifter of Lower East Side Jews. Where Eastern European "green horns" faced their first tests in the New World, Mei passes hers by talking about her friend's work with John Cage, adding, "I'm not as green as my cabbage looks!"

I'm not sure what color you'd assign to Tan Dun. Who else could combine Bach and the Chinese *pipa*, gurgling water and Red Guard hymnals, Shakespeare drawled over shamanistic chants?

"I'm a product of Si Mao, a typical Hunan village near where Mao grew up. And Hunan is closer to the Yellow River culture of China," he explains while he cooks. Dressed entirely in black, with nearly shaved head revealing a wide brow and cheekbones surrounding intense, darting eyes, Tan has lived long enough in Manhattan to cultivate the image of artist as cat burglar. But he hasn't entirely forgotten his roots, explaining, "Hunan's music is more atonal, speechlike, and ghostly. It's very mysterious, both peaceful and violent. That's why I prefer a lack of balance, a lot of surprises."

This effervescent son of Hunan surprises us with some superb salt-baked shrimps. "Fan-tah-steek!" he comments on his own cooking. After supper, he leads us to the far end of the single oblong space barely cluttered by his piano, plus plenty of gongs and bells of his own invention, and, turning up the stereo, conducts the latest squeaks and blasts of a suite of sounds made entirely from blowing, rustling, or rubbing paper. "The *New York Times Magazine* is best instrument!" That's his accompaniment to a ballet based on the erotic imagery of China's ribald classic, the *Jing Ping Mei*. Commissioned to write an opera about Marco Polo, Tan bubbles over with themes for such scenes as "Marco Polo making love to the Yangtze River." On the entire planet, how many people could be so rooted in the traditional while racing so far into the future?

I'm amazed to hear that even this guest conductor of orchestras the world over started out playing Chinese violin on the street. Shown the ropes by a Chinese painter more experienced in Manhattan's jungle, Tan Dun was told "I could keep the paper money while he kept the worthless coins. You know who came out ahead!" All is forgiven because, "Every artist who makes it here has that special edge," he cries with eyes a-twinkle. "The competition, the cross-pollination. Fan-tah-steek!"

Maybe there is something fantastical about a street like Mott, where steam rises out of every dank basement dive and our lucky number turns out to be thirteen. A local tip to the restaurant at this address—its name is the forgettable Sun Lok Kee—leads us to the quintessential Chinatown joint. Mirrored walls expand a small space occupied with bare bones Formica. The scrupulously fresh dishes run from hot squids and steamed steelhead fish heads to the more standard lo mein variations. The head waiter/owner walked eleven days to escape China, then spent an equal number of years washing dishes in Jersey. Success has done nothing to burnish his beaten-down air. He's a perfect match for the group of aging hep cats at the next table who speak loudly enough to advertise the fact that they can actually order in Cantonese. Their familiarly abrasive tone and New Yorkers' ease with living in public make it easy for me to eavesdrop. As I suspect, these three are jazz sidemen taking a break from world-hopping gigs, using a Chinese lunch to compare notes on touchy tenors and officious orchestrators.

Something about slurping soup alongside these guys triggers a memory of a winter day in high school when a buddy and I had managed to escape parental watch for an afternoon. For some reason, we chose a Chinese restaurant to grouse and moan over girls we'd lost or could never get. In that moment of burgeoning sophistication, I'd first come to see the Chinese restaurant as a perfect locale for exploring life's sour-sweet edge, a temple of the beat where dislocation comes with the fortune cookies and disappointment is always on the menu. Just the spot to blend in with the world's tawdriness.

On a drizzly Sunday morning, I can't rouse Mei to take the long ride down to Canal with me. At this point, she'd rather deal with cheese danish than another Chinese breakfast. But I have a rendezvous at a popular dim sum parlor with Eileen Yin-Fei Lo, billed as New York's leading teacher of Cantonese cooking. I'd read that this hard-driving ex-housewife, nicknamed "Shrimpy" by her Americanized kids, rules her family and students with commands to work harder and study longer, enforced with her unbroachable explanation, "Because I'm Chinese."

Trying to find Eileen Lo and her husband amidst the standing-room three floors of the Golden Unicorn is like scanning the mug shots of the entire Red Army. After three passes up and down smelly stairs, I'm about to go home. At a corner table, I finally find one "happy couple"—as Mei likes to refer to every Caucasian-Asian mix. They soon order more rounds of paper-thin chive dumplings and excellent *har gow*. The petite Ms. Lo and her longtime Italian-American mate introduce me to yet another manager boosting his pet project, a nearby lunch counter that serves up fifty or so variants of *tam sui*, hot and cold soups made from sugar syrup boiled up with medicinal fruits and herbs. He brings a sample of the sweet potato variety, much more delectable and fortifying than oatmeal. At times, the tongue knows so well what's good for the stomach. At other times, how the tongue chooses to forget!

Through his lifelong association with Yin-Fei, husband Fred has become a professional gourmand. Will this be me in twenty years, become more Chinese than Mei? In a Hong Kong hotel restaurant, he tells me, another food writer was foolish enough to remark that fine French wine was a waste with so "poverty-stricken a cuisine as the Chinese." So the couple immediately called the hotel manager to testify that his Chinese restaurant outspent the French in ingredients by four to one. "Every holiday in New Jersey, I'd put together a ten-course supper for neighbors," Eileen explains about her own culinary indulgence. "My reputation grew with each Chinese Christmas!"

Most of her students are Chinese-Americans trying to regain their lost culture by following such admonitions as, "Treat the lowliest vegetables with love." Says the teacher, "I learned everything from the aunt whom I watched as a child in Guangdong. We Cantonese are born to cook."

But am I born to go on eating? I wander back to the subway through crowds that choke the sidewalk as effectively as those on Shanghai's Nanjing Lu. Without Mei at my side, I feel as muffled as the scant patches of New York sky. After a year's wanderings, I can nearly manage to order a meal that's balanced in yin and yang. I've become aware of how to avoid committing the more common forms of crosscultural offense. But have I learned anything about how it really feels to be inside the skin of a Chinese? Except to note certain mass tendencies, how dare I speak for those at the center of such a sturdy web of traditions and obligations?

I catch myself in a sigh, inhaling the sour plums, the rain-dampened produce, the Manhattan trash. I revert to the pose of a hands-in-my-pockets white man, a fugitive from sterility and false manners, discreetly agape at the infinitude of Chinese gestures and the urgency of Chinese life. But Chinatown's people are still somewhere "out there" and I am still over here, mum as a ghost amidst their noisy haggling.

Europe
. . . .
LET 'EM EAT DOG!

Featured Restaurants:

Palace, Frankfurt, Germany
Il Tempio del Paradiso, Venice, Italy
Hong Kong Palace, Sidari, Greece
Jenny Lo's Teahouse, London
Kenneth Lo's Memories of China, London
Imperial City, London
Poon's in the City, London
China City, London
Kai, London
The Oriental, London
Lai Sin's, Dreibergen, The Netherlands
Chou Chen, Paris
Dragon d'Or des Arts et Metiers, Paris
Chez Vong, Paris
Au Mandarin, Paris
Tse Yang, Paris
Chinagora, Paris
Zlaty Drak, Prague
The Great Wall, Prague
Cinske Zatisi, Prague

For Better or Fatter

In the midst of complicated lives, everyone wants a simple wedding. From Apex fares to Italian red tape, Mei and I are finding out how tough that can be. Back in San Francisco, we had to round up four witnesses to personally swear that she and I aren't potential bigamists. Next, we have to travel via Frankfurt to the U.S. Embassy in Milan to complete more paperwork. But nothing is more daunting than trying to accommodate two sets of divorced parents on three continents.

My bride-to-be stays in New York while I catch up with my father, a retired sexologist who is very much my active writing collaborator. He lives "in sin" with his seventy-plus girlfriend in a converted Massachusetts textile mill. "In winter, a Buddhist," he describes his quiet life. "In summer, a nudist!" His luscious potato pancakes and homemade scalloppini soon remind me of where I got most of my interest in cooking. Between feeds, my most maternal dad and I compare notes on books read lately, jazz epiphanies heard lately. While I fill him in on real-life realms that he would never dare cross, he reads to me from the more prodigious achievement of five years spent on a hundred-page poem in rhyme about the Holocaust.

"Life is short but art is long, Jackson!" he cautions, along with the obligatory, "Neither a borrower nor a lender be . . ." For now, though, he takes possession of my trusty Honda. This first-born son of immigrant car dealers, once handed the keys to every Hupmobile on the lot, looks nervous and frail trying out my Nipponese clutch.

Most of our visit is taken up by a blitz of phone calls as Mei and I try to purchase air tickets for Europe while choosing final dates for both our nuptial ceremony in Venice and a subsequent celebration at Martha's Vineyard.

"Stop, you're driving me normal!" my father jokes. When everything is set at last, this man who gave up his own literary life to support a family by counseling married couples, reaches for the phone to offer Mei both a personal blessing and professional reassurance.

"If you can put up with so many complications and so much indecision," he diagnoses, "I think you and my son will get through anything!"

I'm not sure that includes *Fruhlingsrolle mit Fleisch unde Gemuse gefultre Teigrollen fritiert*. That's the first appetizer listed by the Chinese restaurant nearest the Frankfurt train station. Maybe we're crazy to make our snack on this brief German stopover anything better than a wurst. Perhaps it's the jet lag, but I'm quickly losing my appetite. In fact, this menu is giving me the flop sweats. There's no way I'm going to order, or devour *Kong Pao Huhnertfleisch mit Bambussprossen Marchein unter Wasserkastanien, Scharf*.

Tossed-together Chinese dishes don't translate too well into uncompromising *Deutsch*. Nor do the Chinese feel that welcome in Germany. We run the gauntlet of Frankfurt's sex-shop district, peopled by the brawling, tattooed dregs of the Master Race, to hear the owner of the Palace Restaurant offer tales of junkies leaving needles, locals screaming insults, and police making regular raids to check for illegals. Of course, Frankfurt is in many ways the world's most "green" town, with more bike paths than truck stops; a surprising number of Turks, Vietnamese, even Haitians; and a range of Asian restaurants sophisticated enough to include one trendy Ginger Brasserie. Yet this Chinese chef quickly reveals, "I dream of America, where everyone is a stranger."

He also trots back to his kitchen for a recent newspaper clipping. We can't read the German, but see a photo of formally dressed Chinese restaurant owners at a Berlin press conference. They have gathered to deny persistent rumors about Chinese chefs stealing dogs and serving them up to unknowing customers. The racist slur that has followed Chinese people, and Chinese food all around the world, is still alive in the land of mordant Nazism.

"Every day, I fear that my house will be burned down. Why should people spread such lies?" pleads the cook, before undermining his case. "Don't they know that real dog meat is very expensive?"

It can't be as inflated as a marriage license in Venice. Thanks to an influx of Japanese couples seeking a romantic backdrop for their nuptials, the Venetians have added the heftiest surcharge in Italy for wedding ceremonies. When we're made to present our documents in yet another musty palazzo, the one office-sitter in sight informs us that we need a series of official stamps for each sheet, purchased at untold *lire* a pop. Perhaps Mei is too forcefully reminded of battles with the Chinese bureaucracy. She is ready to pull the plug on our water-logged fantasy.

"Have we lost our marbles?" she quaintly asks, as we sprint past marble facades to catch another water bus. "Why are we going through all this to get a piece of paper that we won't even be able to read? Even your mother says that marriage is a form of property!"

Actually, when my mother first dragged my father here to escape the regime of King Richard Nixon, she took up the habit of shouting to the brides passing in their virginal white *gondole*: "Don't do it! Don't become a lifelong slave!" Though her old neighborhood is full of social clubs for old Comunisti, nobody listens to her in a city where the word for "slave" evolved into the harmlessly loving *ciao*. It's strange that we're all here to stage a marriage where my parents had once moved in hopes of saving theirs. But Venice's serenades had failed to do their magic. Instead, my theatrical agent mom traded Broadway flops for the stage set designs of Palladio; my therapist dad gave up his fifty-minute hours for happy hours with the gondoliers. Though I can't quite respect my elders in the full Confucianist manner, I pay homage by trying to see this town through their loving eyes. Venice remains the one tourist trap that takes me in—I still experience a vicarious thrill from Mei's gaping over Byzantine arches and watery reflections.

"The golden clasp on the girdle of the earth!" declares my mother, citing Ruskin. I'm used to more rabble-rousing quotations from my righteously angry Chairman Mom. Like: "The end of the world—it can't come soon enough for me!" She's been thumping for lost causes ever since Depression days when she was given the hook for preaching revolution at a New Jersey burlesque house. Yet the myriad injustices of mankind only seem to fuel this red-haired zealot's will to go on battling. Now that Mei's mother and stepfather have arrived for the wedding, each day of delay brings amiable political sparring. Old Bob has never met anyone like this out in Minnesota! Once a faithful cadre herself, Macy can only respond to calls for socialism by recalling, "All that word means to me is five years of planting rice shoots in mud up to my hips." At the mention of politics, she prefers to head out along the canals and lose herself in age-old mirages. "It's so easy to save the world," Mei's mom whispers, "when you're sitting on a beautiful terrace in Venice!"

At this point, we decide to chuck all legalisms and stage the "surrealist ceremony" that Mei has envisioned all along. Ever since our first stay in Venice, she has wanted our high priestess to be Manina, a worldly wise painter of "automatic" dreamscapes; uncrowned Empress of Venice; Viennese-Jewish survivor of the Nazis, Hollywood, and just about every modern artistic movement. No wonder this modern artisan has found a refuge amidst the unchanging back alleys of a city Manina calls, "So darling! Venice is formed like the inside of the human brain!"

At first it seemed a most unlikely friendship—but Manina is touched by Mei's curiosity and open heart while Mei has found a model of female independence and unshakable civility. Whether discussing days with Thomas Mann or throwing the I Ch'ing over a white wine *schpritz*, Mei and Manina spend hours together in the artist's water-stained salon. Mei even volunteers to help with an upcoming show by hosing down every phantasmagoric canvas in the bathtub. For our wedding, Manina, or "little hand," presents Mei with one of her handmade sculptures of a graceful, feminine paw inlaid with jewels, mosaics, and holy kabbala emblems.

Hobbling a trifle, but radiant with aging Garbo eyes and long gray locks, she leads our two mothers and assorted hangers-on into the Campo Santa Maria Formosa, an ample, L-shaped piazza always chockful of fruit vendors, coffee sippers, and howling tykes on bikes. On this spot, the axis of Venice turns. It feels like the center of some eternally enlightened city without name. Enacted before the locked portals of a rotting cathedral, our unrehearsed, impromptu ceremony consists of Manina placing Mei's palms against mine. Symbolically, neither man nor woman presses down on the other, equal partners.

"A marriage shouldn't be celebrated just once, but every day, every year!" declares Manina, hardly knowing how right she'll be in this case. My mother represents my absent father by reading one of his poems about "sinking in Venice." Afterwards, we pile into two *gondole* for a quiet glide past the world's most beautiful backdoors, service entrances, and laundry lines on a still, glinting June afternoon. Though I've been coming here since I was nine, both Mei and I are initiates when it comes to this touristic ritual. But they don't make *gondolieri* like they used to. Ours may be named Mario but he's a portly widower who can barely croak a tune and shows inordinate interest in being set up with Mei's half-sister back in "Pecchino." To top it all off, my truculent mom, anxious to get our money's worth while equally concerned about setting out the food for our reception, keeps warning Mario not to stretch his fare like a New York cabbie. Before long, I feel like sending out an SOS: "*Uomo in mare!* Best man overboard!"

On every bridge under which we glide, crowds gather to gasp and cheer. Venice echoes with the cries of "*Che bella sposa!*" What a beautiful bride! And if only they knew how she could cook! Play the accordion! Do rocket science! Softened with rouge applied by a gay Italian department-store artist, veiled in netting ringed with satin rosettes formed by her mom's own deft hand, at once eager to be seen and discreet in her feelings, Mei exemplifies the two adjectives that most often accompany the word *bride*. She's both bashful and radiant. The dress design chosen so haphazardly in a Bangkok shop now perfectly fits the occasion. The Thai silk shimmers like Venice's waters; the sleek form and slitted fins make Mei into a risen mermaid, a Botticelli apparition.

As I help her out of the gondola, she whispers, "It's not too bad having a Chinese wife, is it?" I stare into bright eyes, inspect a ready smile with a single gap caused by a childhood accident. Such are the imperfections necessary for perfection. As is her childlike habit, Mei stretches a single, elongated finger toward Venice. I want to be at her side as she points toward all the world's wonders. Back on dry land, we finish our rounds with a trip for champagne-and-peach-juice toasts at Harry's Bar. But the admiring crowds in the Piazza San Marco barely part for us. "*Auguri! Auguri!*" the Italians shout. Best wishes! For one moment, I know exactly what it must be like to be the Pope. The greatest adulation comes from achieving the ordinary, not the extraordinary. If you ever want to earn the cheers of the crowd, do what's utterly expected!

For our grand finale, Mei and I pose for a photo before the Bridge of Sighs, under palace gargoyles of Adam and Eve. Alas, there will be no video record of the event. Our volunteer cameraman is none other than the Venetian kid we met with his Singaporean girlfriend on Christmas Eve in Malacca. Though we failed to find him again that night at the Portuguese Village, he had run smack into us one morning among the San Marco crowds. With his angular form, pointy noise, charming grin, and scabrous squint, Giovanni is a figure straight out of *commedia dell'arte*. A true son of the lagoon despite dark hair that won him the nickname "El Greco," he claims grandiosely to "live in Italian-occupied Venice." Fitting world travels between fitful law studies with a come-what-may attitude born of a coma-inducing encounter with an out-of-control police car on Cyprus, Giovanni has arrived in Venice an hour *after* our ceremony.

"At least, the trains weren't on strike!" he declares when we run into him along an embankment, searching in vain for our wedding party. "Just kidding, just kidding . . ."

He makes up for his transgression by lugging off the boats not four bottles but four cases of Prosecco and Bardolino from the vineyards of a friend's family. The wine goes well with our reception's mini-pizzas and rolls of raw carpaccio.

"A humble gift from the underdeveloped land of Cicero to my dear friends!" Giovanni toasts. "No matter how poor, the Chinese and the Italians always know how to eat!" For the moment, Mei and I don't mind that there's no Chinese food in sight. We've already had our wedding banquet a hundred times over.

Your Pasta or Mine?

Along the mildewed shortcut to the one fruit stand in Venice that carries fresh ginger, Mei and I stoop under a medieval pass-through into the Corte dei Milioni. Home to a modest carpeting store, this laundry-strewn atrium appears misnamed. However, these millions aren't *lire* in kickback scandals but the amounts of Chinese riches described by Marco Polo. *Il milione*, the merchant would be called in Venetian puppet shows. Past the far end of what was once his family's courtyard, beside an especially brackish canal, there's a palazzo as unadorned as it is unknown to tourists. Perennially obscured by renovation scaffolding, a plaque attests to this having once been the abode of said Signor Polo.

Is it possible that he was the first man to set out for Cathay with visions of silken treasure only to return with a sackful of noodles? Did such hometown fare as soured sardines and squid-ink risotto send him on his way to the realm of pre-parmigiano pasta? Returning with odd spices and stories of cannibalism, Marco Polo probably had nothing whatever to do with the greatest controversy of cross-culinary pollination. Some revisionist scholars now suggest that this primal travel writer never even made it to China. After all, his detailed travelogue makes not one mention of chopsticks or tea! His description of the markets in thirteenth-century Hangzhou record the local craving for shellfish and duck, as well as vegetarian "temple" food, restaurants with menus and memorizing waiters, steamed-bun vendors, and yes, noodles, which he termed *lasagne*. Historians believe the Chinese had been consuming boiled wheat starches since a thousand years before Christ—and twenty-five hundred years before Italian shopkeepers learned to mix dough with bare feet and hired night watchmen to guard their precious comestible.

The case would appear to be open and shut. Yet back in San Francisco, a local judge who enjoys throwing his court open to historical controversies actually staged a hearing in which Chinese and Italian community leaders each staked their claim. The Italians cited the 1279 inventory of a Genoese soldier that included the word *macaroni*—probably from the Greek *makar*, meaning "blessed." The Italian director Antonioni, in the fateful film about China that led to Mei and I meeting, even speaks of "getting depressed to find *our* spaghetti everywhere."

Just a few bridges over from the house of the man who bridged cultures, they're dishing it out the Chinese way—though the menu diplomatically refers to dim sum as *Ravioli Cantonesi*. Practically at the starting point of Polo's journey to Peking, the circle has been completed by a restaurant called Il Tempio del Paradiso—a Latinate tribute to Beijing's Temple of Heaven. Down a cul-de-sac near the Rialto Bridge, as perpetually shrouded from sun as only poor locations in Venice can be, this *ristorante Cinese* is identified by obligatory red lanterns and decorated with sumptuous carvings and scrolls. Only the ceiling's unfinished wood beams remain from some former Venetian *osteria*.

The Chinese couple who run the place are equally formal. A bearish husband models a starched white shirt; the wife's cautious face is as unmoving as a Venetian carnival mask. Yet once Mei explains our mission, both turn warm and generous, offering a lunch on their covered verandah. Before potted flowers sits an oddball clientele: one Japanese businessman dining alone, a group of Russian tourists ordering in voices that boom back to Moscow, a rich Filipino in golf cap scowling beside a wife and daughter loaded down with Armani and Missoni.

In an effort to pull out the stops, the owner has dressed up our plates with parrots made of carrot with toothpicks for legs. The pleasant shrimp come in a deep-fried nest made of potato. Temple of Heaven's *shu mai* (meatballs in pastry) are certainly the best in Venice. What I really crave is some hearty peasant stuff like spicy eggplant or chewy duck—which is just what they're getting at the next table. Mei and I spy cold meats sliced thin, a bubbling clay pot of leeks with fresh bean curd, and thin, curry-scented rice noodles.

The three Chinese men doctoring each plate with heaps of chili paste look as comfortable here as in their own living rooms. They are in their twenties, bone thin, with slick hair and teeth that have gone their own way. All are overdressed in the way of new immigrants: striped Lacoste shirts with plaid pants, flashy gold watches, belt buckles stamped with Playboy bunny insignias. They could be sailors spruced up for shore leave, but the Chinese navy doesn't call in Venice yet.

Striking up a conversation, Mei discovers that these are off-duty chefs from Milan, a town they term *ma-ma hu-hu*, that perfect Chinese equivalent of the Italian *cosi cosi*, the English *so-so*. Referring to risotto, the pride of the Milanese, one garrulous cook observes, "The Italians say that we overcook our rice but we say that their rice is only half done."

As for how they made it here, one answers with a wink, "We dropped from the sky!" Secrets of the Orient? All you have to do is ask. "Sure, Wenzhou people makes those fake bags the Africans sell on the streets of Brescia, Firenze, on the Rialto Bridge when the police aren't there! We know how to do things cheaply. Even the *People's Daily* has called us the Jews of China," one of them reminds. Are they now the true Merchants of Venice? Their biggest complaint is an inability to find some women. "There are enough Chinese girls over here, but all of them want to marry the boss," the lead chef observes with both logic and swagger. "But if I become the boss, who will do all the work?"

The three kids are soon joined by "Mario"—the local version of something like Ma Lin—who isn't a gangster but the godfather of Venice's very first Chinese restaurant—where my parents had taken me when I was still smooth-chinned and freckled. After more than two decades in the restaurant trade, this chain-smoking wisp has taken early retirement.

"Every day, he goes to the casino," the others tease, with more than a tinge of envy. Chinese cooks don't come to Venice to see the Tintorettos. These pay up and head off toward the Piazza San Marco to find their favorite *Agenzia Ippica*—the Italian equivalent of off-track betting. This isn't the first time that I've witnessed a predilection toward gambling in an occupation where off-duty games of chance don't merely provide relief and excitement but practically serve as hiring halls.

"Paradiso" proprietor Cheung Hung Chen doesn't have that problem, though he offers the explanation that "everybody takes risks in life, no matter what way." Raised in the Fujian countryside, he went on to teach in a mainland elementary school. "I have a sister with a Ph.D. from Columbia," he wants us to know at once.

"In Wenzhou, we say people have shallow roots. Everyone is always looking for a way to come out." Given the number of its citizens spread across Europe, there can hardly be enough left there to raise a quorum. In terms of politics, these exiled owners are more identical than their menus. But the Chinese "middle way" means appreciating the good points of one's adversaries. "Actually, Mao was extraordinarily capable. Here was one man who could control a billion people—and hold them back from doing anything useful!"

But Mr. Cheung hastens to add, "Now the standard of living in Wenzhou is higher than in Venice. Ninety percent of the people have newly constructed houses."

Then why had he left and why would he stick it out here? It's clear that this fellow isn't in Venice to admire the view from the Rialto. "My father-in-law established himself in Holland," is all the explanation Mr. Cheung gives. There is always a previous relative, a first link in the pipeline. Instead of a reason, there is an uncle.

"I figured that if I couldn't make a business here," Mr. Cheung says of the tourist trade, "then I couldn't succeed anywhere." And he adds quickly, "The Italians are much closer in personality to the Chinese. They are family-oriented and the two things they love most are to dress up and to eat."

Apparently, there are other links to China besides the love of boiled noodles. "The legal system here is also very underdeveloped. You have to know the right people. In a contest over corruption with China, I don't think the Italian government would place second."

So Italy has proved no *paradiso*. "The neighbors shun us—except when they complain to the city to make us repair our home. When all the houses here need repairing! Besides, we can't legally own anything but a restaurant and to get a passport is harder than climbing to the sky. Our dark hair, our eyes can't be changed."

Despite its connection to the trade routes of the East, Venice remains a closed place. After eight hundred years, noodles still travel more easily than understanding.

"Have you seen it?" asks Mr. Cheung, aware of his unique location. "Marco Polo's house is less than a hundred meters away!"

Misfortune Cookies

The vagaries of travel! Can they rival the ups and downs of just-married life?

One moment, Mei and I are being feted at the Gritti Hotel and the next we're crashed-out with a mangy student crowd in airplane seats on the ferry to Corfu. For the hell of it, I attend the nightly raffle held in the ship's casino. When I run out on deck holding the winning ticket, Mei thinks I'm pulling her leg. A moment later, we're collecting shopping bags full of duty-free ouzo and cartons of cigarettes. Just what we need at the start of a beachcombing trip! What's that about Greeks bearing gifts?

Mei and I are heading down to the closest Mediterranean island to see if we can find any Chinese restaurants. Along the back alleys of Corfu's port where we wheel our suitcases, there's something indefinably Oriental. Past midnight, an old couple sells seared skins of lamb from a car lit by a single bulb. With hotel clerks, all transactions honest or angry are done quick and gruff, take it or leave it. Yet by day, Corfu town must rank as one of the quaintest meeting points between East and West, among the top ten spots to while away a weekend, a decade, a lifetime.

To go where none have gone before you—that' s a simple matter. To travel where so many others have already been, there lies a subtler and more necessary art. Along the German-occupied coast, former fishing ports have been overwhelmed by slap-dash strips of discos and money changers. But any uphill turn with our rented Fiat takes Mei and me to an unspoiled village where she can partake of her love for Greek salad under trellises hung with grape vines and bougainvillea so purple they strain the eye. I find her a perfect balcony overlooking the blue-into-green coves at the mythic landing site of Odysseus. Following a hot tip from an Athenian lawyer toward an "almost virgin" beach, we track down far-off Santa Barbara, where host Spiros—named after the patron saint who protected Corfu from the Turks—grills swordfish at a seaside tavern incongruously named Mandela. "If Nelson himself ever came here," he admits, "I couldn't tell you what he ever did!"

Between Sidari's beachfront bars offering Schwarzenegger videos and "Greek Dancing Nightly," we discover the Hong Kong Palace. Owner Spiros—who needs name tags on this island?—is a former waiter who decided to open his own place, only to be told by Chinese friends that he'd hung Chinese lettering on the restaurant sign upside down! There's definitely something topsy-turvy about the brawny, hairy Greek waiters tiptoeing around with dainty pots of tea. A couple of cooks in the back are actually from Hong Kong. Wearing aprons that cover their shorts and make them look naked underneath but for their rubber thongs, these carefree kids on an endless world junket admit that they gamble away much of their summer wages. They show me that I've still got to work on my Cantonese accent, because when I confidently ask them to whip up some *chow fun*—fried rice noodles—we get *chow fan*, the infamous fried rice itself. The Malay-style satay beef is surprisingly good. But does it really go with the evening scent of fresh oregano?

The ritzier Peking House is built smack on the water overlooking Ipsos Bay. We arrive in time to watch the dinner preparations of a young head cook nicknamed "Lemon." Like the usual two Chinese per each restaurant, he's on loan for the summer from "one of seventy-five Chinese places" in Athens. He tells us, "The English people don't like salt, but the Greeks like it a lot. So you have to adjust. This is European-style Chinese, it's not the real thing." This convinces us to keep cruising and spend our last night sipping Greek coffee high in the mountains. Our appetites are also somewhat slackened by the sweat dripping off this macho man's bare chest straight into the dumpling stuffing. What shall I call him, Chairman Zorba? And what am I supposed to call this detour among so many trips? Travel writers don't have honeymoons. For a few days, they just quit rating every stop.

Returning to Mei's mother and stepfather in Venice, we find that my father has sent us the final, printed invitations for our upcoming Martha's Vineyard party. The Venetian paper we've chosen looks lovely—appropriately etched with bunches of grapes. But in his lifelong habit of lovingly revising my copy, my father has added a *u* after the *q* in Mei's middle name. The *pinyin* transposition looks more readable in English but makes no sense in Chinese. I'm infuriated with my interfering old man. But Mei's mother calms me with her Chinese perspective: "Spoiled boy! I hardly even knew my own pa! What if you didn't have a father to put on your parties?"

On July 17, exactly halfway between our Venice ceremony and our planned American celebration, Mei and I spend the day doing some fix-it jobs around the apartment. One blood-red splat of paint gets on my white sneakers.

"Every event in the universe is interrelated," Manina, our interdenominational oracle observes over supper. Later that night, already tossing in the airless bog of a scalding sirocco, I get the phone call that I've been dreading my whole life. In a waking dream, I give out a low moan. My reporter cousin Mike, who years earlier had offered the urgent bulletin of his own father's death in a car accident, now tells me that my dad collapsed without warning. He had spent a typical summer day in the country, joking around with his best pal of fifty years, then retiring after lunch to the cabin where he worked on adapting Chinese love poems to be read in our honor. In the late afternoon, carrying a customary cocktail, he'd gone out to trim a smilax bush and keeled over. Damaged by a prior attack, numbed by one too many cocktails, clogged by kielbasa, choked by Cuban cigars, flummoxed by regrets, his heart had no more ticks. Though I will soon hear plenty of U.S. Grade A baloney about a "happy death," at least my father stopped in the midst of preparing wedding songs.

In our last phone conversation, he had been discouraged by the latest rejection of his epic, rhyming poem. But he was cheered by the news of a waiver on the time needed to get a marriage license in Massachusetts. Mei and I finally would make our legal vows in his presence. "More than a clam bake," as he said, "we'll have the whole *mishpucha*"—Yiddish for family. When I ended our call with an afterthought about whether he'd been paying my car insurance bills, my father's last words to me were, "That's my religion."

Never again would I be offered such unconditional faith. Having met Mei, I have at least made a transfer of loyalties to make the loss less severe. When she and I finally register for our marriage license in the New England country town, we realize that her given names plus my family name now give her the same initials as my dad. Was it conceivable that I'd spent the last year apart from him in order to sample Chinese restaurants? Could I now go on sampling all the pleasures he could no longer savor? Will I remember this as the summer I got married or the summer my father died?

Unfortunately, life isn't a menu, offering every preference on demand. My dad cannot share in our happy ending, while Mei is once more denied a crack at having a real father. Instead, she has to board another plane and see me through another crisis in a relationship that sometimes feels like one continuous arrival in unknown territory. Hurriedly scrawling the first words I have ever written that my father will not edit, I declare that I have lost my "full-time tutor and co-collaborator on books not yet written or impossible to write. . . . Ph.D. schmoozer, Dostoyevskyan kibitzer, existential vaudevillian . . . Depression child seldom depressed, sensitive lad in Buster Brown suit beneath Bogart bravado, driven to be a 'somebody' but turned out better than that . . . As they say, whoever 'they' are, he died as he lived—with a drink in his hand and a poem in his heart."

I read a eulogy over my father's grave, having just found the poem he had written for our wedding:

259

Fortune Cookies

Eating out in ideographic dives
We taste the flavor of other lives,
Tempting us toward exogamy
And the end of junk-food monogamy.
Two, they say, can live as cheap as one
On love-nest soup and won ton,
The sayings of Talmud and the late Chairman Mao.
So, go East, young man! Vow,
With the paper parasols that shade
Scoop of vanilla, chocolate, to evade
Those universal abasements
Printed in Mott Street's basements.
Think, when you break them open, unfold,
These fortunes are at random told,
For others intended those just desserts.
For John and Mei, they're just desserts.

Lo and Behold

"Why is the English woman always on top? Because the Englishman, he always fuck up!"
An amateur comic from south of Barbados is testing his saucy material at Speakers' Corner in Hyde Park. This shrine to free speech is the first London sight that Mei wants to see.

"Even in China," she says, "we heard about a place where you could scold the government, even scold your mother!" If bobbies now circulate to make sure that nobody defames the queen, this is still a far cry from Beijing's infamous "English Speaking Corner." Before the Chinese security police put an end to the place, I had joined China's conversationally deprived amidst the shrubbery of Purple Bamboo Park to answer such subversive questions as, "What is the price of porcelain in America? Is it true that a gay can marry a gay?"

The British soap boxers hardly do better. One old-timer baits the crowd with a cardboard chart of insults for Irish and Jews; a pair of angry Platonists in army fatigues rehash the Rodney King incident; a hard-line anarchist literally foams from the corners of his mouth. No wonder the crowds gather around the one honest-to-goodness laughingstock. "Yah, how did the Englishman make his symbol the lion, when there were no lions here? As far as I can see, the symbol of Britain should be a hamster! Like his hero Tarzan, he goes to the jungle in Africa and finds—a white woman, Jane! Then he looks for a best friend. Does he choose an African man? No, he hangs out with a monkey, Cheetah! And that's how we got AIDS. . . ."

What the Englishman did to the Chinese is a sorrier tale. From the dismemberment of Canton to the burning of Beijing's Summer Palace, the introduction of opium to the wartime abandonment of Shanghai and the more recent sellout of Hong Kong, no intruding imperialists have so earned the epithet of "foreign devils." No second country has taken more Chinese out of their silks and put them in Buster Brown suits—as swabbies, coolies, and cooks. Yet the loyal Chinese subjects who washed up on Britannia's home shores were greeted with race riots and the creation of that enduring villain, Fu Manchu.

The only good result of the last two centuries' Sino-Anglo tangle may be that London serves up the best Chinese food in Europe— some claim, the world. But first, Mei and I must explore the trend toward noodle bars. We've rented an exorbitant cubicle just across the street from Princess Di's favorite Italian cafe, in a Chelsea condo complex crammed to the gills with job-hunting Japanese schoolgirls. The British Museum is likewise occupied, but here at least Mei can get wondrously lost amidst the Egyptian loot. On a nearby side street, we join a continual line outside Wagamamma, one of London's many high-tech, minimalist purveyors of the basic Japanese ramen. There are a thousand such joints in Japan, but here shorn waitresses take orders from computerized pads holstered to their hips. Touted as a healthy part of a "process-oriented lifestyle," the menu even claims that the loud slurping of noodles heard all over the Orient offers the system an unwitting oxygen boost.

Mei and I can hardly resist a woodsy, Chinese imitator called the Great Culture Revolution. Having escaped from the real Cultural Revolution, a chef from Beijing plucks orders of dumplings from the deep freeze. Though the prices fit the needs of the budget-conscious, there's hardly anything revolutionary about repackaging the food of China's past as the nutritional wonder of the future. "In earlier centuries," wrote Kenneth Lo, Britain's leading popularizer of China cuisine, "if an innkeeper could produce a large bowl of steaming noodles after a day's journey through biting wind and sand, he could bring untold joy. The eating house provides a beacon to guide the weary and alienated traveler . . . to find refuge and identity."

We are looking for refuge in busy Belgravia after discovering that his restaurant, Kenneth Lo's Memories of China, has been bought out by Italian managers. But right around the corner, we stumble onto his daughter's newest entry in the noodle wars. Jenny Lo's Teahouse caters to a lunch crowd with hearty bowls of thick egg *mein* topped with "mountain vegetables." The menu features "therapeutic teas blended by our herbalist, Dr. Xu," plus soya milk and the popular side dish of seaweed. Jenny herself is a quick-talking, sharp-shooting, chain-smoking Brit.

"They call us B.B.C.s—not British Broadcasting Company, but British Born Chinese." In aerobic sneakers and sweatshirt, she does not look quite right behind a wok. "The noodle shops are a response to England's post-eighties recession," Jenny explains, using a word banned from discourse in the States but about as common here as patter about the weather. "Besides, everyone fancies a change from kidney pie! In this area, at least, we ethnics have the advantage." Her accent is harsh, her humor Monty Python–sharp. What remains Chinese is Jenny Lo's evident willingness to warm the bellies of two weary travelers.

In another of those connections that make China appear to be a country of one thousand instead of one billion, Mei's closest friend in America is a first cousin of Kenneth Lo—both descended from a leading statesman-scholar of the Qing Dynasty's final days. While in Venice, we spoke with Kenneth's wife, who promised an interview as soon as her husband returned from the hospital. But our arrival had been unavoidably delayed. A week after my father's funeral, I was shocked to see Kenneth Lo's obituary in the *New York Times*. Felled by cancer at eighty-one, he was survived by innumerable eating companions. Was it really a surprise that the most famed Chinese

Englishman, and most English of Chinamen, should be a food writer?

Born Luo Xiaojian in Fuzhou, Kenneth Lo was given his future pen name by a British doctor who prescribed medicine for the boy and his two brothers during a flu epidemic. As the son of a high-ranking, high-living Chinese consul to Britain, Lo developed a zest for the finer things. A member of China's Davis Cup team, young Ken's first passion was tennis. After partying his way through Beijing University and Cambridge, Kenneth worked during World War Two with Liverpool's Chinese and Indian dock laborers, often soothing tensions by inviting the two groups to dine together. As the British public became more curious about Chinese cooking, it was natural that the restaurateurs and publishers with whom he socialized should turn to Lo. With a degrees in physics and English, Lo was overqualified for the job. Yet British erudition combined with Chinese pride made him a perfect culinary promoter.

"The area of Chinese food, like China herself, is too big a territory to wander in and out at will," Lo observed in his autobiography, *The Feast of My Life*, "and once I was in, whether serious or not, it was not easy to extricate myself." I know the feeling. In time, Lo admitted, "I did develop something of a mission. All along I had felt that Chinese food and cooking had something to offer the western way of life. For all the labyrinth of Chinese culture, Chinese food could most easily convey the power and subtlety of Chinese civilization without it being necessary . . . to master . . . complexities . . . beyond the wielding of chopsticks. It could take decades to appreciate Chinese literature, philosophy, painting, music or dance, but it took no special skill to appreciate good Chinese food."

In this spirit, he produced some thirty books that sold over a million copies. He organized a gourmet club that sampled the best Chinese food in London and finally yielded to the temptation of opening his own, highly rated establishment. It's at the second Memories of China, set in the ghostly mall of a Chelsea Harbour development, that we're met by Mrs. Lo.

"This was a risky move and our trade never quite recovered from the Gulf War scare," she admits, displaying photographs of her husband with the likes of Paul McCartney. Accompanied by a blue-eyed, fair-skinned grandchild, the former Anne Brown appears shaken, her bangs wilted and her eyes darkly circled from sleepless nights. Long the sturdy British lass to her bon vivant mate, she has been dealing with her loss by maintaining a heavy work schedule and stiff upper lip.

"My husband always knew good food. But at the start, he didn't know a thing about cooking. His first experiment was to boil a chicken in an urn without taking out the innards," Mrs. Lo confides, while supervising the presentation of dim sum, peppery medallions of beef, and squid with pea pods—food as decent and straightforward as Lo himself. "While Kenneth may have played tennis with the snobs, he aimed his cookery books so every British housewife could read them. Even the London cabbies would tell us they'd use his recipe for long-cooked pork."

Thanks to her husband, Anne Brown can probably tip us off to more of the history of Chinese cooking in Britain than nearly any Chinese. "In the beginning, the Chinese would open restaurants and move on before the V.A.T. man—the tax bill—came calling. There was one Mr. Wong who started and closed eleven restaurants before he fled to Taiwan. It seems that Chinese food has come in waves. First came the Old Friends down by the docks—and now we've got the Zen group of restaurants. It's all gotten so sophisticated."

That's in no small part due to Lo's groundbreaking efforts. "Kenneth always said that he was all Chinese," Mrs. Lo tells us, "no matter how long he was in England." His widow recounts a life that was "really very lucky, with an ambassador father, luxurious mansions, skating on the lakes of Beijing, then punting in Cambridge and eating, eating everywhere."

The meal is so touching, and the moment so awkward, that I can hardly recall eating a thing. Two grieving non-Chinese are brought together and consoled by our mutual connection to Chinese food. Yet we can only skirt around the main subject. As much as we fail to acknowledge the power of death, we can never fully articulate the attraction that Chinese culture holds over us. For as many hours as she can keep us, Mrs. Lo finds a meaning to her life by presenting the food—as I do in consuming it.

She has already known a lifetime of this distinctly Chinese pursuit. "Ken's relatives back home had a dreadful time of it. But if we sent them money, they used it at once to go out to eat." I know Mrs. Lo is thinking of her gourmet husband when she adds, "In China, they even worry about feeding the dead."

'Anging Out Yer Red Lantern

I t's not easy to find the best restaurant in London's Chinatown. But it doesn't take long to find the best pub. After running the pressed-duck gauntlet of Soho's Gerrard Street, Mei takes it upon herself to take a survey of patrons at the cozy King's Head. In this dark, corner venue for downing a lager or three, the habitués are straight out of a Somerset Maugham tale from the East. A rotund, boozed-up Malayan Mama harangues a couple of bemused barristers with her pidgin cries of, "What you do, Charley?" Near the door, a teahouse circle of Cantonese ladies are nursing their pints of stout.

"We're a mixed crowd here," says the barkeep, in an understatement that may apply to the entire country. "But we all rattle along."

Under rows of tankards turned on their end, singing along to Broadway show tunes as he drains the tap, this merry, one-earringed leprechaun lives up to the sign over the bar: "Michael—Charming, Confident, and In Control." While chatting with us like we already live at the pub, he receives various videotapes that pals keep slyly sliding across the bar. Soft-core porn? Michael insists that these are travelogues about Hong Kong. But why plan a holiday there when half the place is already in the King's Head?

Most of London's 150,000 Chinese arrived from the rural areas known as the New Territories before the sixties when laws restricted the flow from former colonies. After Tiananmen Square, the Conservative government allowed another 50,000 "top Hong Kong people" to qualify for residence. But despite the calls of Chris Patten, Hong Kong's last British governor, the home government has done all it can to assure that any post-1997 influx won't upset the nation's "racial balance."

"When I'm off, I go for Fook Lam Moon," recommends Michael, a well-balanced bloke.

"Don't listen! New Diamond bettah!" insists a Vietnamese-Chinese card dealer from a nearby basement gambling club. "You follow Numbah One, right?"

"Number One!" the bartender teases. "Is that how your mum named you?"

Neither of their suggestions make our top ten. Unsatisfied, we follow the lines into Wang Kei, the most infamous of Chinatown's chow mein factories. Here is the archetypal Chinese experience that Caucasians from here to nowhere have come to savor—perhaps as just punishment for their race's pillaging of the East. There's a long wait, three floors of noise, hard seats, and bare linoleum tables shared by groups of strangers with barely enough elbow room. The legendary waiters are so brusque and haughty that customers actually come here to get insulted.

"Every floor full, so must be the best," declares our surly server as he slaps down some decent Cantonese duck over rice and curry-tinged Singapore-style noodles, all at the bargain rates that are Wang Kei's ultimate draw. Trying to provoke the waiter, Mei teases, "How can you make it so cheap?"

"Because *you* so cheap!" he snaps back on cue. Asked for the secret to Wang Kei's success, the waiter deadpans, "Some information you got to pay for."

Instead of paying for ours, we require further guidance from some local Chinese. Crisscrossing Gerrard Street for the tenth time, I muse in Mei's direction, "If only you had a relative here! It's hard to believe that you don't."

"Wait a sec! Actually, I do," she now remembers. "A distant cousin from Shanghai that I haven't seen for fifteen years. His grandmother is the sister of my stepfather's mother."

While I'm trying to untangle the genealogy, Mei steps into yet another Chinese grocery to continue her impromptu survey. She strikes up a conversation with a thick-set bull of a man who loudly barks out dining recommendations. As I join them, this pinstriped gent presents his business card. Not only is he the vice president of the London office of the Bank of China, but this Mr. Li turns out to be the very same cousin Mei just mentioned! Think of the odds! As soon as we get back to California, I'm going to make her play the lottery.

This busy VP and VIP begs off on unspoken familial obligations by whipping out a mimeographed chart from his attaché case to prove that every lunch is booked solid for weeks. But the banker promises to ring up management at the few Chinese places where he can take visiting deal-makers without "losing face." Is that why Mei's cousin barely cracks a smile at our amazing encounter? Speaking of his own march toward affluence, Mr. Li trots out a new Chinese aphorism: "It's a lot easier to sell half a chicken (*ji*) than half an airplane (*feiji*)."

Awaiting his introductions, we make our way to the Imperial City, a surprisingly ritzy restaurant, considering that it's in a basement snug against the back end of the Royal Stock Exchange. The exposed heating ducts have been improved with painted dragons, and the Chinese- American food writer Ken Hom—fitting heir of Ken Lo—has created the menu. Owned by a consortium that specializes in Thai restaurants, the Imperial City is run by a suave Hong Kong–raised Englishman named Richard Miller. He suggests that we try an assortment of half-portions that are light, fruity, and certainly among the most original in London. The stir-frys here sit pertly on the plate, braided with red and yellow peppers. A Sichuan pork uses fresh chili paste, à la Singapore, not the more authentic flavor of charred chili pods. The food here is less Chinese than pure Ken Hom. As soon as the British boss hurries off, an agitated Chinese head waiter slinks up to Mei and whispers, "A thousand apologies. We haven't shown you true hospitality!"

Since that's usually measured out in shrimp, scallops, and lobsters, I'm quite relieved. But the clash of cultures is illuminating. I can see why the experimental Imperial City isn't on the list of recommendations from our traditionalist, mainland banker. The financial-set hangout preferred by Mei's cousin is Poon's in the City, as distinguished from various other Poon's that crop up on every major double-decker route. Arriving just after lunch, we're greeted by the proper, if slightly bedraggled, Mrs. Poon, who fights through the effects of a morning's root canal to tell us that Poon's brought the first "homemade wind-dried meats and sausage" to London. After eighteen years of success near Covent Garden, they had been forced out by high rents and a young crowd whose idea of dining "consists of little more than jacket potatoes."

The original Mr. Poon (pronounced "pung") is an abstracted fellow, chugging on a curved meerschaum pipe as he shuffles about in sandals, soiled white T-shirt, and pants that are about to slip down his backside. The descendant of numerous chefs in Hong Kong, he helped launch the restaurants of four Poon brothers and sisters. On the side, he's quite a patron of the arts. The walls of his restaurant are a gallery for Chinese artists in London. Fledgling opera singers and numerous Tiananmen exiles have filled his staff. Is that why Mr. Poon exudes the air of a painter just out of his garret?

"Yes, I love art and Chinese food, which is an art in itself. Why, we can make a great meal out of anything, even pig trotters. Just like a painter with his colors, the chicken stock is the soul of the cooking. Mine is concentrated like a jelly. The first scoop is always reserved for shark's fin soup."

A tall and elegant waiter, whispering in upper-crust tones, turns out to be the next generation of Poon, identified by his father's disbelieving remarks about having "raised an English boarding-school boy." Yet the son loyally bears forth his father's scrupulously adapted Cantonese cooking, which includes a memorable pocket fish—steamed Dover sole stuffed with its own flesh. "You've got to adjust to British ingredients," says the chef. "When they brought a Chinese over to demonstrate noodle-making by hand, his dough fell apart. I was the only one in London who knew to add bicarbonate."

Mr. Poon declares, "I wouldn't have bothered with England if not for my high school sweetheart from Hong Kong." From the way she blushes through the years of kitchen exhaustion, we realize that he's talking about Mrs. Poon. For once, we've found a chef whose romance with food pales before his romance with his wife.

"She's the one who wanted to come here for the culture, the theater, ballet, and opera," explains Mr. Poon, while she nods away. There could be worse reasons for opening a restaurant than his claim that, "I've spent my life cooking so my wife can have her Shakespeare."

Between meals, I'm introducing Mei to this Sceptered Isle's civilized pleasures: the old map stores along Charring Cross, the dream bookshops lined with every Penguin edition every printed, a Pinter revival in the West End, *Volpone* at the National Theater. How is it that the British emote so much more genuinely on stage than in person? Mei is hardly impressed by the gray roast beef at Ye Olde Cheshire Cheese but can't stop humming the Kurt Weill turn "Surabaya Johnny" after seeing a production of *Happy End* staged in an Elizabethan bathhouse. Joining Leicester Square's after-theater crowds, this Johnny pauses to watch the medieval whirligigs mounted above the modern Swiss Center hammer their bells to toll another ding-dong London day.

"Thinking about your daddy?" Mei asks, always able to read my heart, if not my worrying mind. I'm thinking, in particular, about trips when he made sure I was outfitted in the sharpest oxford tweeds—advising me to "think Yiddish and dress British!" Now I realize how lucky I'd been to have parents who took me to the premiere plays of England's Angry Young Men. Though at age twelve, how could I know all the things in the world to get angry about? Continuing our journey in the midst of mourning only sharpens the preciousness of these moments with Mei—and of our once-in-a-lifetime excursion.

There's no time to get maudlin because we've got a Bank of China intro to China City, an unadorned two stories protected from Chinatown's bustle by a landscaped courtyard. To each side are wings "shaped like a bucket to catch customers." At least, that's the concept according to K. C. Tang, co-proprietor with the unrelated Ivan Tang. But this Ivan "hain't no Russian." He's our first Chinese with cockney accent, a curled-up do like Elvis Presley, plus a cocky attitude like Michael Caine's Alfie.

"After work, most 'usbands 'ead for the pub, and when the pub closes, it's Chinese or Indian takeaway. Lately, we've overtaken the Pakis as the number one food in the U.K. Of course, there hain't much choice, considering what the English put out." He may not realize it, but he's seconding the opinion of philosopher Lin Yutang, who once wrote, "The only time an Englishman thinks about his stomach is when it aches."

Despite his indelible, incongruous Britishness, Ivan concedes, "I been thinking about pushing off to America. If I could come eight thousand miles to make a quid, what's a few thousand more?"

He's an earthy character straight out of one of those classic proletarian plays I'd seen, *Chips with Everything*. Only now it's fried rice with everything. While the China City packs them in with Hong Kong cooking that's one rung above the norm, the co-owner admits, "We can't go to extremes like they do back 'ome, what with killing off a thousand birds to make a dish o' their tongues."

But Ivan Tang very much wants us to know, "For gettin' a license 'ere, you got to study the sanitary procedures an' all." He fairly summarizes all our research by adding, "This hain't just a matter of 'anging out yer red lantern."

The Sultan's Takeaway

The West's Chinese food may have begun in the East End. On the way there, I pause to give Mei a turn around the London Tower.

"This could fit in one courtyard of the Forbidden City," she observes, unimpressed to say the least.

"But don't you want to see the royal family jewels?"

"I've seen those already!"

At the moment, she's more interested in tracing the lineage of Old Friends, oft-mentioned as England's most venerable Chinese restaurant. An elevated rail extension takes us out of touristland to the fabled Limehouse district. Instead of finding some dank Dickensian scene, Mei and I enter a hot house of full-blown urban blight. Squat blocks of council houses are set between burned-out lots, boarded-up groceries, and red-brick bedsitters covered with graffiti instead of ivy. Things are looking less than friendly until a Pakistani grocer points us toward a rare intact block of storefronts. One of two neighboring Chinese places is indeed called Old Friends.

Though covered with balloons in anticipation of a birthday party, the dining hall is unoccupied. Co-owner William Leung has plenty of time to explain. "The partners who began this establishment were from the same village back in the old country. That's probably why it was called the Old Friends. Later, one of 'em broke off to start the Good Friends. Others try to copy the formula with the Young Friends."

We never get a sense of his culinary skills, but Mister Leung is clearly an avid historian. "From 'ere, we're close to what used to be the East India Dock. That was the busiest in the world once. Naturally, the Chinese sailors who came ashore 'ere didn't want to roam far. They made smaller settlements in Liverpool, even Glasgow. Some of 'em still 'ad their pigtails. The place was loaded with cheap rooming 'ouses."

So is it London or San Francisco that can claim to have given birth to the prototypical Chinese lunch counter? "Oh, all the first places advertised 'San Francisco Chop Suey.' The sailors had picked up the taste in America."

I'm just about to accept the distinction for my hometown when he adds, "There's only been Chinese restaurants here for about 170 years." A neat trick, since that would easily predate the founding of San Francisco.

The only evidence in the area to verify any timetable are signs for Canton and Mandarin streets, a Chinese retirement home. Explains William Leung, "This area was 'eavily bombed in the war. With the Docklands development, the largest new 'ousing site in Europe, most Chinese moved away. By the sixties, they'd put Chinatown over in Soho to accommodate the influx of poor farmers from 'ong Kong. If they'd kept their land over in Asia, those poor buggers would be rich men today! Now, thanks to Mrs. Thatcher and 'er quotas, you've got to 'ave a 'alf million pounds to get into Britain."

With evident bitterness, Leung tells us, "Because I was too old when I come over, I can never get over the barrier. The caliber's not there. My English hain't good enough." Still, he considers his menu second to none. "Chinese people don't want swans made of carrots or radish pagodas taking up 'alf the plate. That may be 'igh fashion. The food, if you'll excuse me, is rubbish. But you go back to Kensington and try all the Misters you like."

Under "Restaurants, Chinese" in the London phone directory, there are at least six such honorifics listed. From Mister Chin's to Mister Chow's of Knightsbridge, I'm surprised that one of them hasn't become a "Sir"! But I can't find the fabled Mister Kai of Mayfair, a character stocked away in my childhood unconscious along with such Anglophile bric-a-brac as who fought the battle of Agincourt or how many parts Alec Guinness played in *Kind Hearts and*

Coronets. In a windy dusk, my fair lady and I seek out Mayfair's best—wandering London's most exclusive area in search of what had once been the most exclusive Chinese fare in town, perhaps in the world. But the helpful bobby standing before the statue of Franklin Roosevelt in Grosvenor Square can't place the name. And I can't help wondering why I'm strolling past so many Rolls Royce limos on the same day that I've visited the grave of Karl Marx. After an afternoon peek at Sigmund Freud's couch in his house at Swiss Cottage, I'm willing to admit that this entire journey may be one retrogression into oral fixation.

An elegant foyer hums with customers at the restaurant that's now smartly shortened as "Kai." In double-breasted beige suit, two-tone shoes with tassels, greased hair parted straight down the center, and a rimless pince-nez, the Mister in charge fairly bulges with prosperity. His card reads "Don Tan" and he readily admits, "I'm not sure whether the original Mister Kai is with us anymore."

Someone named Lung Kai is quoted on the frontispiece of the grandiloquent, barely grippable menu we're handed. "Mister Kai's was the show biz stop in London, but it faded badly over the last five years," Tan admits, once he's had time to pull up a chair at our back table. "A restaurant of mine had gone under because of the Gulf War, so I got the call to come over and revive the place." The result is decor long on black marble and wrought-iron suns; as Mr. Tan bluntly puts it, "A Chinese restaurant that doesn't look like a Chinese restaurant." Away with all ghosts and dragons—especially in interior design. His motto: "The only things that should be Chinese are the chopsticks, the staff, and the food."

Even the latter has been made to sound like some rich relation. What's happened to such masterpieces of truth-in-labeling as "sautéed beef globules" and "fried cattle valves"? Here, we choose between "The Whims and Fancies of Empires" and "The Encirclement of the Sleeping Phoenix." Could "The Union of Land and Sea" be the old turf-and-surf platter? Is "Hokkien Opium" suddenly legal? Can there be enlightenment in the "Yin and Yang Sole"? Will we benefit from the egg rolls called "Parcels of Prosperity"? Or profit from "The Enrichment of the Surprised Piglet"?

Despite the euphemistic verbiage, we're pleasantly pleased by the down-to-earth soft-shelled crabs and Kai's showpiece, lobster on a bed of noodles swimming in a tangy, Singapore-style hot sauce. "We don't compromise to please the Western palate," Don Tan insists over the lulling tones of a live harp, adding, "Everything at the new Kai has a Malaysian flavor." Not only is the manager a native of Penang, but the head chef is Malaysian and so is the owner, a barrister who spends "lots of time on the golf links" but "signed the remodeling checks" to the tune of 700,000 pounds.

"In the restaurant business," huffs and puffs Mr. Tan, hopping up and down from his seat like a well-tailored frog, "you don't sweat to bring people in but to keep them coming back." To that end, the new Mister has brought along his younger, no-nonsense Missus to keep an eye on the register and books. Beneath all the high-cost pretense, this is just another family operation.

"So when is there time for a marriage?" I ask.

The answer comes only indirectly, through our usual discussion about food's importance in Chinese culture. "For us Chinese, I'll admit, food isn't just the number one need. It's the only unconflicted pleasure."

His words remind me of a statement I'd heard back in China: "Give a Chinese man a choice between a beautiful girl and a great meal and he'll always take the meal." By now, I know that's no macho boast. Don Tan covers his mouth and glances up to make sure his wife is out of hearing range. "I'll be honest with you. In our way of thinking, sex is considered somewhat of an obstacle. It's not supposed to be good for the man's health. So we substitute food for the sex"—Don Tan gives us a wink—"which leaves plenty of energy to create new dishes!"

The term, I believe, is *sublimation*. Don Tan doesn't know that he's making Doctor Freud proud.

"I do it all for the benefit of a nineteen-year-old son who has Bruce Lee for an idol!" this pudgy dynamo jokes, rolling his narrow eyes. Since he channels his urges into an eighty-hour work week that includes real-estate management, Mr. Tan knows it's Asian money that is keeping the London economy growing. "When the *London Times* wrote that Malaysia's prime minster took bribes, and my country threatened an embargo, the *Times* begged for forgiveness and recalled their reporter. They know who's running the show. Malaysia used to be a colony of Great Britain. Now Great Britain is a colony of Malaysia."

Kai looks to be annexed to the United Arab Emirates. Most of the other diners on the main floor wear khaftans and veils. One table for twelve appears to be occupied largely by one fellow's wives, kept happy with all the Peking duck they can eat. Give or take a few dietary restrictions, Chinese food really is global grub.

It takes another Mayfair encounter before I realize just how far one man's love of Chinese takeout can go. Don Tan introduces us to a fellow at the next table who looks like the suave heir of some Hong Kong investment group. Jimmy Man, handsome with sympathetically bushy eyebrows, manages Kai's nearest competition, "just down the road" at the Dorchester Hotel. Back in 1988, the Sultan of Brunei, whose oil reserves reputedly make him the richest man on the planet, decided that it was more convenient to own his favorite London inn than to be a mere paying guest. And one of the sultan's first requests was the addition of a world-class Chinese restaurant. So much less bother than ordering out!

The result is the Oriental, the only Asian restaurant in England to rate a Michelin star. Tucked away at the back of the Dorchester, this exclusive indoor balcony is done up in Kama Sutra carvings, Chinese scrolls, and Thai Buddhas that purposely blur the lines between Eastern influences. The menu, thanks to Simon Yung, a wizard chef plucked from the ranks of the Shanghai Sheraton, is aggressively contemporary Cantonese. In charge of it all is our newfound friend Jimmy, the very model of a modern Mandarin in tux. I doubt whether the lords and ladies with whom this gentlemanly lad seems to be on such friendly terms would guess that his family immigrated to England when Jimmy was eleven. Mr. Man's old man ran a restaurant, of course, but hard work and affirmative action programs have given the son a far swanker joint. No rented wardrobe, no amount of training in food management can account for Jimmy's being such a jolly good fellow.

His only worry, one that almost any other maitre d' would envy, is to keep a few tables free each night for the Dorchester's guests. "You can't very well turn away people who are paying fifteen hundred pounds a night," he whispers to us during a pre-dinner chat held on the foyer's raw silk divan. Of course, all bookings are thrown off-kilter each time the Sultan himself breezes into town with his entire floor's entourage of maids, drivers, bodyguards, and wives. "I believe he's only got two at the moment," Jimmy says. "Naturally, it slows the whole kitchen down when we get a hundred room service orders."

We're joined at the last minute by a guest who could not be less suited to these surroundings. We had met Joe Grahame, an ebullient, Generation X entrepreneur, standing beside a pro-Cuba literature table in the midst of Notting Hill's Caribbean carnival. Now he has taken us up on our invitation and brought along a six-pack of his pet project: Che beer, as in Comandante Che Guevara.

"Banned in the U.S.A.—It has to be good!" boasts the label, branded with a heroic image of the bearded guerrilla in black beret. As Joe tells it in a confident, upper-crust drawl, "The whole thing started as a lark, when I went on a beach holiday to Cuba. I fell in love with the place and wanted to help them improve their balance of payments." Now he's thrown over a career as an investment banker to crusade for a product barely tolerated in Cuba. If his beer catches on, there could be a whole line of spirits dedicated to the spirit of revolutions past. "There's always room for Lenin lager," I suggest. Or how about Mao Red Label?

I don't think our Joe has ever had a Chinese meal like this. Perhaps we haven't either. Doled out by waves of deft waiters are dishes like supple and moist duck slices alternated with fresh mango; marinated beef slices slightly charred to match stems of leek and lemon grass; e-fu noodles as fresh as any pasta, bathed in a hint of crab; a bass fillet subtly complimented, not drenched, in black bean sauce; chunky scallops on a bed of conpoy (dried scallop relish) to add tartness. Only bird's nest is missing from the carefully balanced bill of fare, due to the efforts of Britain's animal rights militants. For once, I even admire the Chinese-style desserts—a perfect tapioca cream and mango pudding.

Ever the salesman, Joe Grahame slips Jimmy Man a sample bottle of Che beer. This fruity brew is the perfect compliment to a superb cold dish of shredded duck, chicken, and jellyfish tossed with a mustardy blend.

That's the best thing about taste buds. They know no ideology.

But after eating at the Oriental, I don't see how the Yorkshire pie set can have any doubts about just who is colonizing whom. I trust the Sultan is satisfied.

Sole Fillets with Chili Bean Sauce and Asparagus Tips "Dorchester Style"

From the Oriental Restaurant

Ingredients:

8 skinned sole fillets
1 sole bone

Marinade:
Salt, 1 tsp.
White pepper, dash
Rice wine, 2 tbs.
Sesame oil, 1 tbs.

2 large dried black mushrooms, rehydrated in cold water
    and cut into 8 strips
Carrots, 3 oz. cut into 8 thin strips
Scallions, 3 oz. cut into 8 thin strips
Bamboo shoots, 3 oz. cut into 8 thin strips
Flour, 1 tbs. mixed with water
Cornstarch, 2 oz.
Vegetable oil

Minced onion, 1 tbs.
Minced garlic, 1 tsp.
Minced green pepper, 2 tbs.
Red Chinese vinegar, $1/3$ cup
Malt syrup
Salt, to taste

Sugar, 2 tbs.
Chili bean sauce, 1 $\frac{1}{2}$ cups
Cornstarch, 1 tsp.

Garnish:
Iceberg lettuce, julienned
Carrots, julienned
8 medium-sized asparagus spears, cut in half lengthwise

Marinate the sole fillets for several hours in the salt, white pepper, rice wine, and sesame oil. Boil a pan of salted water. Add the black mushrooms, carrot strips, and bamboo shoots and cook for 45 seconds. Drain and cool. Fill each fillet with this vegetable mixture, roll up, and bind together with flour paste. Coat the fillets with cornstarch. Deep-fry the fish bone and set aside, then deep-fry the sole rolls for 2 to 3 minutes.

Heat the remaining oil and stir-fry the onion, garlic, and peppers together with the remaining sesame oil. Add the Chinese vinegar, malt syrup, salt, and chili bean sauce, bringing to a boil. Thicken with cornstarch mixture.

Place the garnish on a platter, with the fish bone on top. Place the fillets atop the fish bone, spoon the sauce over the fillets, and arrange the asparagus tips at an angle so they look like oars on a rowing boat. Serve hot.

The Yin and Yang of Yan and Jan

Our first meal in Holland is served inside a windmill. Nothing could be more quaintly native, except that the owner is Chinese. Catherine Yan doesn't just run this continental *eethuis* ("eat house," I presume), but also the highly rated Dynasty and Manchurian restaurants.

"If the government of the United States can carry on without the president around, then so can my kitchens," says this Singapore-bred dynamo. After nineteen years, she hasn't forgotten her English or her indomitable Chinese pride. "When I first came here, the Dutch knew nothing about Chinese food beyond egg foo yung. Can

you imagine, all our restaurants had to call themselves Chinese-
Indonesian! And serve satays! But didn't Marco Polo take our onion
cakes and turn them to pizza? Didn't the Indians turn them to *naan*
bread? And the Chinese are so clever to have invented the fortune
cookie! Such a brilliant stroke of publicity! So that should change
all question marks to a full stop!"

As for Holland's small Chinese contingent, Mrs. Yan says "most
were rice farmers who came in the sixties when they couldn't scratch
up a meal back home. Why, I remember how my mother sent packets of pork lard back to her native Hainan Island during the famine!
So of course the Chinese prefer to start restaurants because we can
employ more of our family. Four in front and four in back, that's better than a laundry. And the staff always has enough to eat!"

At the moment, we're indulging in heaps of freshly smoked
gravlax salmon and wine-marinated duck breast *al sangue*. "If you
want to succeed, just walk a step faster!" that's Catherine Yan's
motto. "Right now, I'm trying to create a fund for more Chinese to
study here. The Dutch are so good at agriculture, tulip bulbs and all.
And they're very tolerant people—especially when we Chinese are
so law-abiding. We eat a few cakes when the moon is up and we light
some firecrackers! If they tell us to go right, we go right! If they say
left is better, we go left. But in my old age, I want to go back to
China. That's home, with a capital *H!*"

After lunch, Catherine Yan guns her B.M.W. across the myriad
bridges and locks of Amsterdam. Befitting this alternative city, we're
dropped in what has to be the world's most curious Chinatown. Groceries reeking of dried fish and tropical fruits, all-Asian video parlors
and beauty salons—even a Chinese "marriage bureau" that's not for
matchmaking but for sewing satin gowns—are stretched along the
Zeedjik. This narrow, cobbled bend with bone-white storefronts is
pressed between canal tissues like a Chinese paper cutting.

Straying ten meters to one side, we find clumps of desperate
Africans openly trading in heroin. A door or two down an alley from
simple noodle specialists like the Eethuis Nam Kee, Mei and I enter
the territory of what Confucius called the number two human drive.
Bestride the world's oldest culture is its oldest profession. Instead of
withered ducks, the windows display the slightly less costly per-

278

pound flesh of Amsterdam's vaunted prostitutes. The glassed-in cubicles feature plenty of Asian fare, a surplus of Thai peasant girls dolled up in fancy lingerie. Chinatowns aren't fussy about their neighbors.

"Amsterdam—Capital de Mal Gusto!" reads one graffito in the train station toilet. Up the main drag to the square called the Dam, bad taste central is lined with Burger Kings and T-shirt shops. Postcards feature the Pope entering peep shows, a brushstroked Van Gogh with spiked hair, tattoos, and nose ring. I had planned to introduce Mei to the wonders of marijuana—a key feature in my cultural revolution, not hers—but neither of us can get past the unappealing portals of "coffee shops" that serve up joints along with Dutch pancakes. With youth revolts, West or East, there's not much to look at once the smoke clears.

"I'd rather be in Venice," is Mei's slogan as she strolls the embankments of this too-chilly version. Instead of gay pastels, the waters here reflect utilitarian browns. "Or maybe it's just that Italian men are better looking."

These ultra-tidy towns of northern Europe remind me of cats that spend the whole day licking their own fur. Few societies know better how to remain prosperous and healthy. But the mechanisms of habit are so fierce that everything else is lost, including the reason for carrying on. So there's nothing much to do but head for the museum to ponder the copiously catalogued evidence of Saint Vincent's picturesque agony. What did these lowlands ever do for Van Gogh except bring him lower?

Amsterdam's Chinese dives are no more simpatico. Even a Chinese guide whom Mei boldly stops on the street can't honestly recommend any restaurant—not even the one to which he's leading a hapless Taiwanese tour group. Ever since the flavors of colonized Indonesia were brought back to enliven Dutch palates, the Asian restaurant has been presented as an upscale treat. We aren't fooled by the garish red carpeting and pagoda stories of the Sea Palace, one of the few floating Chinese restaurants west of Hong Kong's typhoon shelters. A few places serve respectable dim sum. But is it really possible to do them all that badly? At this point in the journey, we have merely to stare through the window at the relative crunchiness of heaped servings to rate Cantonese quality. There's even less temptation to do an indiscriminate sampling when the prices are among the most outlandish on earth. Twenty U.S. dollars for a plate of chow mein! Now I know what it feels like to emigrate with a satchel full of worthless Chinese *yuan*.

Shivering from wintry winds off the North Sea, Mei and I take refuge after spotting a sidewalk signboard for the "Greek Eethuis" Kriti. Surely, we can afford a grape leaf or two. Though minute in numbers, the Greeks nearly match the Chinese in world ubiquity—and ceaseless labor. But these heroes of the perpetually spinning *gyro* sure seem to have a better time. Entering a storefront painted azure blue to evoke a Mediterranean village, we find that the staff has already begun the nightly ritual of passing 'round the ouzo and revving up the *bazouki* tapes. Quicker than we can say moussaka, we're invited to share a table with a Dutchman named Jan who is helping a younger couple celebrate what seems like a rather hasty engagement. The underage bride-to-be, outfitted in her best sweatshirt, blushes down to her eyelashes with suppressed skepticism toward her dashing beau. This latter-day cad sports long curled locks and a black goatee that, except for the lack of white collar, make him look exactly like one of Rembrandt's swaggering, cigar-sucking burghers. But the first words out of his mouth are, "America! Ronald Reagan and Arnold Schwarzenegger are my heroes. Which are your two American heroes?"

He appears terribly disappointed when I can't think of one. Perhaps I've been away too long, perhaps not long enough. The older Jan terms the younger "a movie actor, just like Reagan." Apparently, he's appeared in a few swashbuckling action flicks. On the side, both work for the city government as "green inspectors," New Age Amsterdam's name for garbage collection. But none of these three talk like they're living in an eco-paradise. Like us, they're warming themselves with distant flickers of the hot-blooded south. Still, the Dutch are among the world's most genial people, once they've had a few. Fortunately, few of them haven't.

The Greeks at the bar, too, have sung themselves into full glow. One pony-tailed fellow with hooked nose and dreadful acne scars leads an urn-necked waitress into the center of the tables. They begin a slow circling, punctuated by the man's knee-bending dips and perfectly timed slaps at the point of one upraised black boot. Soon enough, the Greek beckons Mei to form a threesome. He is amazed at how quickly she falls into the lingering back-and-forths of their stutter steps. But then, he hasn't seen her impersonate flamenco, *Swan Lake,* or acrobatic woman warriors. When a small boy comes in from the cold to peddle roses, the lead dancer buys them all for Mei.

This restaurant owner introduces himself as Yannis, the Greek Jan. So where's the cool yin of our Ms. Yan to balance his alcohol-flushed yang? When we beg off on endless free rounds of *retsina,* he sends us back into Amsterdam's dark night with heartfelt embraces.

"Not even my own mother ever hugged me like that," says Mei. "Imagine how Chinese restaurants would take over the world if we could dance!"

In Holland, the world of Asia begins and ends with Indonesia. At an Indonesian restaurant meant to look like a rustic farmhouse, a red-haired Dutchman initiates us to the *rijstafel,* a banquet in miniature that is the most enduring legacy of old Batavia, tiny Holland's audaciously cruel occupation of the vast Sumatran archipelago.

"The rice table evolved as a Sunday afternoon ritual on colonial plantations," explains restaurant manager Michael. "In one meal, we bring together delicacies that a traveler would have to sample one atoll at a time." But this rice maven's enthusiasm began aboard ship in the Royal Dutch Navy. "Five days out of seven, we ate the *rijstafel.* Only two days were left to go Dutch." This bit of humor seems an admission that European meat-and-potatoes wasn't a fair match for the myriad flavors found at the business end of the spice trade. "Cinnamon, anise, bay leaf, clove, and nutmeg—these have all found the way into our native kitchen."

Thanks to another former Dutch holding, we wash everything down with some surprisingly decent South African wine. The curried stews and peanut-dipped skewers make a refreshing change—even if Mei brands them "glorified street food." We wait until we're quite stuffed to confess that tonight's feast is but a detour on our quest.

Our obliging Dutchman quickly gives us directions to Dynasty and Sichuan Food, Amsterdam's two most illustrious Chinese restaurants situated along a strip of high-tech gay bars and hashish houses. The Sichuan's owner, an effusive Hong Konger, offers Mei a rose and a chocolate. His notion of red carpet treatment extends to bearing each table's orders on a single silver platter, the stir-frys dolloped out like scoops of potato salad.

But Michael's top pick is located in an obscure, outlying Dutch village. At his insistence, we hop a morning commuter line out along flat canal banks, then switch in nearby Utrecht to a train where conductors are designated solely by nonthreatening badges worn on the hip of their blue jeans. On the phone, the Mandarin-speaking owner of Lai Sin's promises to fetch us from the station himself. The man who honks at us from the wheel of a plum-colored Citroen is at least six-foot-two in formal dark jacket. His mop of auburn hair is cut in jagged bangs, his smile is equally crooked. We figure this is some kitchen helper until the fellow addresses Mei in confident Beijing dialect. We try to suppress our amazed double-takes. Mister Lai Sin—or "Blue Star"—has seen a lifetime of them.

"My mother was Dutch but my father came from Wenzhou," he explains for what must be the millionth time. "I know, I don't look like I grew up in the kitchen of a chop suey joint!"

While his Occidental genes have proved dominant, the Orient clearly dominates this restaurateur's heart. "I prefer to be in the country," he explains, "so we know that our customers really tried hard to find our food!" He drives through the deadly quiet suburb of Dreibergen, then leads us down the canopied entrance of a white cottage with all the understated elegance of a European country inn. Our reserved window table is laden with carnations. Only a few lunching executives have joined us in making the pilgrimage to this culinary Lourdes. "You eat first and we talk later!" Lai Sin commands. "That's the Chinese way!"

Eat we do, beginning with two porcelain soup spoons laden with smoked squids plopped into a misolike sauce of cold bean curd with herbs. I've never tasted anything like it. The Sichuan dumplings, triangles of dough floating in chili oil, take me straight back to Chengdu. The shrimp may not be live, but come in three sauces. There's "wooly lamb," seared strips laid atop crispy white noodles, soft-shell crabs à la Shanghai, and ground pigeon saturated with garlic then wrapped in lettuce leaves. Alas, we don't get to the sautéed duck and pistachio, the frog legs and macadamia. No Chinese restaurant in Europe boasts so authentic, yet innovative, an assortment of dishes.

"We only change our menu when the old ones get dirty," Lai Sin jokes at the end of the meal. "Had you ordered ahead, you could have tasted the only true beggar's chicken in Europe, done in the proper clay pot!" Unlike the many owners who have conspired with a smile to keep us out of their chaos-ruled kitchens, this one is eager to demonstrate his faith in the Chinese belief that simpler and smaller is also better. Two woks, one oven, and steamers made from tin cans with holes punched in them—this is the spic-and-span laboratory of a lost son of China, aided by Hong Kong's Wong Kwong On.

"My Dutch mother still thinks that my chef does everything!" Lai Sin jokes, surrounded by plaques and awards from gourmet societies. After the VIPs have been sent on their way, we join this contented owner over his belated lunch that's mainly a bland bowl of *juk*, or rice porridge. "Peasant food is all I need," says this innovator who seems so unaffectedly Chinese in his easy hospitality. "I suppose you could call me a kind of missionary. My father had worked in the rice fields and taught himself to read at night. His restaurant was just a simple noodle place with a smelly toilet. But the Dutchmen, they didn't know any better. Slowly, over time, I began introducing our customers to more exotic flavors."

In his early twenties, Lai Sin qualified for an "Overseas Chinese" scholarship to spend a year studying in Beijing—right at the start of the anti-foreign Cultural Revolution. Still, he tells us with a sheepish grin, "I was popular because I had enough money to take my roommates out to eat once a week." Life was austere in the capital, with little meat available. "I remember, there wasn't a soul at the Great Wall, not a souvenir stand. You had to bring your own food with you."

Where most other boys from the West might have been disappointed by so spartan a homeland, Lai Sin grew even more determinedly Chinese. "I really had no choice," he confesses, "after I discovered Fang Shan"—the showcase of imperial recipes in Beihai

Park. "Chinese cuisine grows out of the decadence of the top ten percent, where new dishes always had to be created. But it also reflects the values of the common people, for whom every grain of rice is earned with a drop of sweat."

Obviously, Blue Star's place is more than a business. "The Chinese kitchen is so rich in history, we can't afford to lose that. And learning a cuisine is like learning a language. One's study never ends."

From the quick tosses of a great chef to the brushstrokes of a master calligrapher, everything about Chinese culture appears maddeningly simple, literal, obvious. Yet a lifetime's worth of curiosity can't exhaust all the lore, sample all the flavors. Having eaten at Lai Sin's, Mei and I are content to leave Holland without bothering to investigate a last lead about one mentor to Chinese students who supposedly owns as many restaurants as he keeps "foreign ghost" mistresses. How can we tell all the tales, chart all the fates, read every menu? The wisdom of the East ends up humbling all who pursue it—because the sum of what's found never comes close to the sum of what one is missing.

Far from Amsterdam or the emperor, a teenager shows up at Lai Sin's cottage asking if he can order some pork fried rice to take out. "Nay! We don't do that," Blue Star tells him wearily. "Please try Chin's on the next block."

Au Petit Panda

Ah, Paris in the fall! Against a frowning sky, the bohemian garrets turn virginal white. The pompous regularity of royal arbors is softened with the brownish tinge of changing leaves. The chill air is made cozy with the characteristic scent of baking baguettes, roasted chestnuts, forty-franc *poulets* on the spit, and Mei's new-found favorite, those mostly marmalade *crepes au grand Marnier*.

But where's the biggest edible canard of all, *canard laqué au Pekin*? How dare we enter the bastion of haute cuisine in service of its main culinary challenger? And how can we keep our eyes off the brioches and concentrate on an older cuisine's entrées? In a city where high standards and high-grade meats have produced better Arab restaurants than in the Levant, more sumptuous Vietnamese spreads than you'll find anywhere near Dien Bien Phu, we've got to believe that there must be some quality Chinese food among three thousand restaurants Asiatiques et étrangeres. At the very least, we should be able to establish some common ground between the two nationalities most serious about what goes in their mouths.

Any place with art and eats of this quality is Mei's kind of town. I know this from the frequency of snapshot poses she enforces: one on every bridge, one for every gargoyle and every steely cloud change.

"Very old, very beautiful!" goes the mantra Mei picks up from some ogling Iowan tourists outside Notre Dame. "Very old, very beautiful!"

We newlyweds can hardly resist the charms of the City of Light, especially when family friends are providing us a place to stay within striking distance of the Rue Mouffetard's open-air food orgy. Long ago, I'd accompanied my father on shopping rounds for pâté and Roquefort down these same cobblestone alleys made slick with goose fat. Is it possible to gorge in memoriam? Now it's my turn to pass down a love of Paris inculcated as a childhood assistant in lithograph collecting along the Rue de Seine. But everyone must find their own Paris.

On a tip from our hip host Julien, a burgeoning young artist whose own tour begins and ends at the grave of rock icon Jim Morrison, we dutifully search out a shaded street facing the back of the ruined Cluny baths. It's hard to miss the fire-engine red facade of Chou Chen, which advertises itself as le plus ancien Chinese restaurant of Paris—and looks it. Founded in 1929 as an offshoot of a nightclub called Le Lotus, Chou Chen—Mei says the name means "sound of the trees"—fuses the faded elegance of Hemingway's Paris and the delicate exoticism of the East. Its decor goes straight to the core of a historical relationship to the East defined mostly as a fashion statement. Would student radicals from the nearby Sorbonne have gone Maoist if red weren't the best color to paint the town? At Chou Chen, we find a Bertolucci film set patrolled by ochre-vested waiters doing their last tango. Spiral stairs lead to a white balcony, held up by white columns and trimmed with Oriental scenes painted on lacquered wood panels. A back wall that's all mirrors is plastered with sparkly red letters, "Bon Anniversaire, 65 ans."

Owner Antoine Bertucci, a.k.a. Monsieur Tang, has a distinguished Gallic nose. While his mother was Cantonese, his father was an adventurer named Dominique Bertucci who first ran a French restaurant in Shanghai called "Domino's," then a factory for making an imitation Martini & Rossi vermouth, which he jokingly labeled Bertini. Known for "loaning money to every fellow Corsican," Mr. Tang's father stuck it out in China until 1950. "He must have liked the place," says his son, "because he married two Chinese women."

Over the house specialty of Shanghainese dumplings, Chou Chen's owner admits, "I stopped speaking Chinese for almost sixteen years." He needed other vocabulary to help develop fuel injection for sports cars. The proof is a framed photo of Monsieur Tang in the pits of the twenty-four-hour rally at Le Mans. Another souvenir of decades gone by is a bullet hole in one of the painted Chinese panels, left by a celebrant of France's liberation from the Nazis.

"Before I took over the restaurant, the rice used to come served in a soup bowl. You could take as much as you liked. Some poor students helped themselves too liberally and were asked to leave." Now hungry denizens of the Left Bank stoke up at McDonald's. Monsieur Tang keeps busy as the Vice President of the Parisian Shanghai Association. "Mostly, all we do is sing karaoke and go on outings to Eurodisney." Only in Paris would the proprietor of a Chinese restaurant admit, "Without fail, on my weekly night off, I treat myself to a fine French meal."

The Sino-Franco community, some three hundred thousand strong, boasts a decidedly higher class of refugee. Sure, French soldiers joined in the looting of Beijing's Summer Palace. But icon André Malraux would later give revolutionary Shanghai the honor of exemplifying his novel title, *La Condition Humaine (Man's Fate)*. Despite recent restrictions meant to limit the expanding Chinatowns of Porte d'Ivry and Belleville, socialist President François Mitterand made his country a haven for escapees from the Tiananmen Square debacle. One young painter, just growing his first wisp of a goatee, readily admits that he was once on China's most-wanted list. His harrowing escape was completed only when he was smuggled into the hold of a ship, then posed as part of a Taiwanese tour group.

At a modest lunch counter near L'Opera delightfully called *Le Petit Panda*, Mei looks up a former "rightist" who made three escapes from a campus jail run by Red Guards now a petite and doll-like *Madame*. But few Chinese emigrés to France suffered the romantic tortures of artist Li Shuang. Through the usual, efficient grapevine, Mei knows to find this modern-day Juliet at the swank showcase for Chinese artists that she and her bubbly French husband run in the trendy Marais district. Once a prisoner of love, she's now privileged enough to have a studio in the basement of her own gallery. But the self-assured Li Shuang is someone who would have style no matter where she lived. Finishing up a surreal collage, she models denim apron, pink rubber gloves, and a flowered bow in her pageboy hairdo that perfectly matches her designer tunic. Still, she confesses that she's just at the point of growing comfortable with her public persona.

"Though I've lived in the midst of turmoil, I never was very political," Li Shuang prefaces her tale. "I prefer to live in my dream, but sometimes I just couldn't follow the rules of the game." Her professor father, an environmental scientist still "working for China, not the Party," was jailed for years in a basement cell on his school campus. On the verge of suicide, he was saved by a glimpse of his own daughters at play. Because of such counterrevolutionary lineage, Li Shuang was sent to a labor camp where she began making charcoals of bucolic scenes. Hidden in a photo album, these sketches eventually won her a chance to learn set design back in Beijing. By 1979, she helped organize the Star Painters Association, who sold their works on the street as China's first self-proclaimed "avant-garde" artists. Despite police harassment, they even staged a human rights protest on National Day. "After that, we all waited at home to be arrested."

But the government was straining to show tolerance at the start of Deng's reforms. Li Shuang would get into real trouble when she was told about a cultural attaché at the French Embassy who liked her paintings. Before their first meeting, he did not know that Li Shuang was a woman. She did not know that Emmanuel Bellefroid spoke such good Chinese. Soon, the two were living together inside one of the capital's heavily guarded diplomatic compounds. One day, while Emmanuel was in Hong Kong, she was lured off the grounds and whisked away by Security Police.

"We were so naive!" Li Shuang admits with a laugh. "But it's clear that they wanted to have an excuse to expel my husband, who had extensive contacts with Wei Jingsheng and others in the early democracy movement." Back in France, Emmanuel began a publicity campaign to free his fiancée. He went over the heads of wary diplomats by playing on the French fascination with tales of *l'amour*. Meanwhile, Li Shuang was offered release in exchange for a confession of spying.

"I didn't even think of Emmanuel as a foreigner! The guards would try to convince me by saying, 'Can't you tell? Just look at his face!'" Sentenced to two years of solitary, she had plenty of time to test her faith in a man she had known for so short a time. "Of course, I had doubts. But I didn't want to do anything that I would regret later."

When French President Mitterand visited China, he mentioned the case to Communist Party head Hu Yaobang—who immediately asked aides about "that girl." The next day, Li Shuang was released. She still had to wait six months for a passport and reunion with Emmanuel. "It was a hard adjustment, because I wasn't psychologically healthy and all the publicity made me feel like a puppet. Besides, my image of the West was all rock and roll and neon lights. Some people got upset when I said that Paris had too much dog shit on the streets!"

Leading us past the nearby Musée Picasso, she admits, "Back in China, Matisse and Picasso were my idols. It was a shock to come here and see that their works weren't always perfect. Every artist has to find their own door and open it. Strangely enough, it was when I was in jail, and asked for Chinese history books to pass the time, that I first started to admire my own culture."

Now Li Shuang leads Mei and me through an increasing drizzle to a little-known pocket of Chinese life just north of the Pompidou Center. "Chinese in France are mostly invisible," she says. "It's the Arabs that the French don't like. With us, everyone is most polite—though I've heard that a Chinese engineer will never get paid the same as a French one. And they still make a lot of false assumptions about us, as though we're creatures out of a fairy tale."

Before we find the restaurants, there are several blocks of earnest commerce—wholesalers in purses, belts, and other cheap leather goods. "This has always been the trade of Wenzhou people in France," explains Li Shuang. As in Italy, Spain, and Holland, the enterprising, seafaring inhabitants of that isolated port were the first to start a pipeline to France. As though making a statement that Asians are here to stay, the oldest standing building in Paris, plainly medieval in its crisscrossing beams, is occupied by a Chinese hairdresser and a Vietnamese noodle parlor.

Around the corner on the Rue du Maire, the many family-run storefronts are pure Wenzhou operations. Befitting China's coastal provinces, the menu at the popular Dragon d'Or des Arts et Metiers is heavy on seafood and soups. Both are combined in the unique house specialty: a soup filled with noodles made of rice flour and fish meal. The result is a most subtle, and most typically Chinese, combination of fishiness in two forms and at least three textures.

There's nothing artsy about Li Shuang's choice of dishes. She makes us try the mix of duck intestines and gelatinous chunks of duck blood. Having asked for three dumplings, we're given three full orders! Mei gives the seal of authenticity to the dried bean curd with celery and the braised noodles topped with spicy chunks of stewed beef. At the next table, a Chinese family has even come all the way from London to have the place cook up soft-shelled crabs brought from the market. Thanks to Li Shuang—and Paris—we've finally found some Wenzhou people making earthy Wenzhou food.

Still, I'm just not sure that Mei and I are prepared to die in the line of gastronomic duty. Everywhere we look, groups of soldiers are on patrol. Inside the metro, garbage cans have been sealed for reasons of *sécurité*—as Algerian fundamentalists besiege the sagging ramparts of the French Republic. Our first stroll to Notre Dame is interrupted by police cordons and a bomb scare. Parisian sirens wailing their characteristic *wha-wha* make us feel like we've entered some grainy, Gallic detective flick.

Each time we pass through the Rue Mouffetard market, Mei and I feel like we're infiltrators—crossing culinary enemy lines. Call us food terrorists, swooping down fast and furious to snatch perfect raspberries and green beans. On the way to eat moon cakes, we pop into a bakery to snatch two coffee-flavored eclairs. Stuffed to the gills with stir-fry, we indulge any leftover appetite with baby quiche. Back when the markets of Hangzhou so dazzled Marco Polo, China must have seemed as supremely bounteous a land as France now appears to us. The French have always made more of more while the genius of Chinese cooking is to make more of less. So how to compare the supreme expression of surfeit with the supreme expression of scarcity? And how to get these chefs back on the collective farm after they've seen Paree?

Champs of the Élysées

"The more times get chaotic, the more Chinese want to eat."

If Wu Gang is right, then the times we've been traveling through must be the height of confusion. But Mei's classic-minded cousin, a neatly groomed, soft-spoken forty-year-old who laughs by crinkling his nose, has cited this proverb out of nostalgia. Reunited after twenty years, the two instantly recall group suppers and ice-skating outings when both they and China savored one last burst of socialist innocence. "When the news spread that the Gang of Four had been arrested," Wu Gang recalls, "the shelves emptied because everyone wanted to celebrate with a meal."

This wandering son of a Beijing Opera leading lady manages to carry on the family tradition by photographing Chinese troupes in France. Understanding the importance of food to the culture, he is eager to arrange an introduction to the two Parisian restaurants that he considers to be "genuinely Chinese." This does not include the dozens along nearby Avenue d'Ivry, all of which have undergone, to use the Nixonian term, "Vietnamization." Despite the treeless avenues lined with Oriental signs, the giant Asian markets with names like *Tang Freres*, this thirteenth arrondissement Chinatown possesses neither exoticism nor the requisite squalor. After some hard years in an attic, Wu Gang managed to send for his family and settle them in one of the neighborhood's low-income housing towers. Everyone entering the building is Asian except me. Most wear rubber sandals more appropriate to the Mekong Delta than this wintry evening. While Wu Gang's beloved daughter, Mimi, is getting a French education and a pet whippet, Wu Gang's wife doesn't appear especially thrilled by the West. In proportions and amenities, there isn't much to distinguish their upper-floor apartment from similar units in Beijing.

The next day, we've gone from the projects to the penthouse—

and straight into the belly of the Michelin-rated monster. Over the phone, the proprietor of the renowned Chez Vong had asked fearfully, "What do I have to pay to be in your book?" He presumes us to be part of some shakedown operation, or worse, yearbook salesmen. In person, William Vong, or Vai Lam Vong, is far more hospitable. For thirty-five years, this wiry ex-interior decorator has been welcoming the French elite to his dark rosewood repository of Chinese antiques. Mei and I have hardly sat down at a front table when we are presented with photo albums featuring guests like Brigitte Bardot, Mick Jagger, and that French idol, Jerry Lewis. As the longtime mayor of Paris and practiced hobnobber, President Jacques Chirac has his own book's worth of snapshots.

With his nervous rush of words and odd Franco-English— every second noun requiring an added *ment*, as in *change-ment* and *complaint-ment*—William Vong does not strike me as a born maitre d'. His forebears were successful Hong Kong jewelers who dispatched their son to learn watch repair in Switzerland. Little did they know they were creating France's best-known Chinese restaurateur! He fell in love with Paris and switched to art school without telling the folks. Eventually, the family yielded to his aesthetic bent, backing him in a restaurant as the safest bet. So Mr. Vong channeled his design skills into making Chez Vong a showplace He leads us to an upstairs banquet room to show off his pride and joy, a Qing Dynasty opium bed, inlaid with mother of pearl and occupied by a bronze reclining Buddha.

"Most of our customers pride themselves on their sophistication," explains William Vong. "If I offer them a knife and fork, they get very insulted." Still, he concedes, "For a Chinese place to be popular, you have to include Vietnamese dishes." Accompanying superb dim sum stuffed with shark fin and chives, Chez Vong's lip-smacker is *ban coun*, a half-melted rice noodle cannelloni. One bite of the deep-fried taro root croquette makes Mei muse, "Crisp on the outside, soft in the middle. It's perfecto!"

Mr. Vong credits "having the same chefs for eighteen years." But he quickly adds, "These days, some of my French help try to get fired so they can go on unemployment. They put salt in the sugar bowls or on top of the fried bananas."

There are few Chinese in Chez Vong. A clientele of embassy delegations, plus Mei's cousin *et famille*, are awaiting us at the nearby Au Mandarin. "The next booth," claims Wu Gang, looking formal in a blue blazer, "is reserved for I. M. Pei when he comes to Paris." This carving-filled, second-story box just off the Champs Elysses is billed as the "more traditional" adjunct to the ultra-*luxe* Tse Yang, flag ship of the largest chain of fancy Chinese restaurants in the West.

"At this restaurant, I've got more items with bones because the Chinese like that," explains the owner as he joins us. "Also foreigners tend to have false teeth!" By coincidence, Mei's cousin has led us to Andre Yang, father-in-law of the well-bespoke lawyer Larry at New York's Tse Yang.

"Whatever I want to do, I say," declares this godfather of eateries with a throaty, Brando-style rasp. "And whatever I say, I do!"

Soon, he'll be enlarging his empire with a Tse Yang in Beirut—largely at the urging of the family of the Lebanese president. In fact, this gruff warrior with squinty smile and graying hair seems to prefer opening restaurants to running them. Mr. Yang's secret of success is to maintain a high quality of ingredients traditional to his ancestral home of Yangzhou, near Shanghai. The point is proved by excellent versions of a smoked fish appetizer, cold, wine-soaked drunken chicken, lobster claws in black bean sauce, and caramelized spare ribs.

"Just call what we do Chinese cuisine," Andre Yang insists, a trifle defensive that his other restaurant is so frequented by the tourist trade. As Wu Gang later explains in a whisper, the local community "cares only about price, not ambiance" and doesn't patronize the Tse Yang close by the Hotel George V, where a banner hung above the stone lions advertises *gastronomie chinoise*. "How," Andre Yang asks, "can they deny that I run a Chinese restaurant when I've got Chinese vases and shark's fin soup?"

Mr. Yang has become French enough to share a dislike for the British "because of the way they ruled Hong Kong." Having fled there from China at fourteen, he found studying wasn't his "cup of tea" and joined an uncle in his restaurant kitchen. On a whim, he took—and passed—a test to become head chef for an American official about to start a Chinese restaurant in Paris. Since 1954, he's founded a string of restaurants to which loyal patrons have followed. Recently, he's had to divest some of his German operations because "Chinese partners always think they know everything." Instead of "two Jews, three opinions," this ethnicity's motto could be "two Chinese, three menus."

More problematic was Mr. Yang's partnership with the late Tang Na, first husband of Jiang Qing, better known as Madame Mao.

"Madame Mao told everyone that Tang Na, a scriptwriter, was her true love," Mei informs me with a whisper, though I'm not sure how she's privy to such information. "To her, Mao Zedong was just a country bumpkin . . . After she left, Tang Na jumped off a building. But he survived and moved to Paris."

Only a Chinese would turn to running a restaurant! "Oh no! That always happens in a revolution," Mei wisely observes. "Back in Shanghai, plenty of White Russian nobles worked as waiters."

About Madame Mao's first mister, Andre Yang tells us, "He was a very educated man, but he liked to drink. When his past became known in the press, we had lines outside the restaurant."

"Didn't you have trouble during the Cultural Revolution?" I ask.

"Not much," says Mr. Yang, redefining trouble. "My partner just had to disappear for a year or so."

But Chinese food transcends all matrimonial and ideological disputes. "Later, Chiang Kai-shek's son was among our best customers," adds Mr. Yang. "And now I've been asked to consult for the catering on the first Shanghai-Beijing bullet train. I will always love my country. I approve of what the government did at Tiananmen Square, too. Suppose the people in my kitchen wanted to take over my restaurant, what would you expect me to do?" Asks the town's head Mandarin, "If Deng Xiaoping doesn't retire at ninety-one, why should I?"

Of course, the hard line is easier to dish out when you're sitting in Paris. "You have to shoot Chinese people to get their attention. While Americans talk but don't act and Russians act but don't talk, my countrymen are foolhardy enough to do both. They weren't afraid of American bombs in Korea! They ride their bicycles through everything!"

As Andre Yang sees it, "Any country that is backward and has a long history, the people will care first about how they dress and how they eat." But here, within walking distance of so many four-star restaurants, he has to admit, "Since the sixties, Chinese cooking stopped developing. Like the French, we should have been busy starting our own nouvelle cuisine. But their restaurants are backed by an entire nation supporting cooking schools and encouraging the highest standards."

In Paris, I finally comprehend the full degree of complaint that I've been hearing all along from those who truly care about Chinese cooking. What would the world make of French claims to gourmet superiority if there were millions of Froggy takeaways slopping out the cheapest versions of *pot au feu* and *rein à la moutarde?* A French chef goes to Escoffier's, then gets his own country inn and a cookbook contract. A Chinese chef pays his dues stuffing dim sum at four in the morning and, after fifty years or so, retires with a clean undershirt.

The table talk turns to one prize-winning Chinese cook that Mr. Yang was planning to hire. This head chef had been working in a Vienna restaurant owned by the spoiled son of a Beijing hotel manager. When he'd failed to be paid for months, the chef threatened to take his case to a lawyer. Then he mysteriously disappeared. Several weeks later, the newspapers printed the gruesome picture of a severed arm found in the snow of the Austrian Alps. One of the kitchen helpers recognized a characteristic cooking burn on the hand in the front-page photo. Police were led to the restaurateur's chain saw and found traces of human bone.

Mr. Yang adds the proper Taoist tone by concluding, "There's no completely good or completely bad person in the world. Even the bad one has plenty of friends." This has to be a case for Hercule Poirot. Call it Murder at the Golden Dragon.

Duck and Mango Salad

From Chez Vong

Ingredients:

Roast duck meat, 12 oz.
Fresh mango, 5 oz.
Fresh red pepper, 1 oz.
Cilantro, chopped, 1 tsp.

Celery, julienned, 6 oz.
Salt, dash
Sugar, dash
Prepared mustard, 2 tsp.
Chinese vinegar, 2 tbs.
Sesame oil, 1 tsp.
Sesame seeds, 2 tsp.

Cut the duck meat into thin shreds, then mix in a bowl with celery, red pepper, and mango, all julienned to the same size as the duck. Stir together with salt, sugar, mustard, vinegar, and sesame oil. Sprinkle with pan-roasted sesame seeds. Garnish with cilantro.

Cheating God

"The first thing Chinese look for when they arrive in a new land," Mei reads from a Paris magazine printed for emigrés, "is not a bank, a dentist, a playground, or a school, but where to buy soy sauce."

No people are more steadfastly loyal to their customary forms of feeding, even if that means missing the whole point of a place like France. As we'll be told at our next stop, "An average Chinese tour group with a week in Paris might try a single French meal."

Why should they bother when Cantonese investors have constructed a place like Chinagora? This facsimile Forbidden City features three stacked restaurants, a ten-story hotel with pagoda roof, a shopping mall and exhibition hall encased in a facsimile Great Wall. Nine years in the planning—and run by the son of Shenzhen's ousted pro-democracy mayor—it is the first all-Chinese development in Europe. In a sense, Chinagora may be the forerunner of many imperial outposts—only this time, it's the East conquering the West. But this showplace highlights vacuousness and vulgarity, the unthinking imitation of empty forms.

"Not very old, not very beautiful," mutters Mei. The persistently foreboding Parisian sky makes quite a good match for the concrete vastness of this fake Mongol castle, set at the far eastern end of the metro at the promontory where the Seine River meets the Marne.

"This site was chosen among ten because of the *feng shui* belief that water brings prosperity," says the manager of the Chinagora's first-floor restaurant. Water certainly improves the view to all sides of his boxy, low-ceilinged dining room, fronted by a bandstand. Mei's cousin Wu Gang has photographed many a wedding function here—though he and the manager scoff at the illiterate Chinese-Cambodians who marry with the red ribbon for the groom mistakenly pinned to the bride.

Our utterly Cantonese lunch certainly doesn't need any labeling, though the cold chicken has been roasted in tangerine juice and red crab eggs have been added to the hefty scallops. *Excusez-moi*, co-quilles St. Jacques! Even with this MSG-laced fare, I wonder if a Michelin-star counterpart could come up with so many tastes at one sitting—including straw mushrooms, carrots, duck, mango, shrimps, squid, Chinese broccoli, pan-fried noodles, and barbecued pork. One stomach is hardly enough to deal with it all. Instead of four stars, give me twelve courses—a soft bean curd before crème brûlée. Does this mean I'm turning Chinese as well?

Besides, the Parisian restaurateurs whom Mei has stubbornly en-treated have turned up their noses at having us conduct a Franco-Sino taste comparison. Instead, we save room for a dinner party thrown in our honor by a gathering of Chinese exiles. The ringleader is Mei's family friend Mr. Ma—or should I say, Monsieur Ma? This merry fig-ure of a man, with sharp Manchu features, suavely brushed mop of hair, and expanding Parisian gut fairly defines the term *Francophile*.

"I am Voltaire from another life!" he swears with a Beijinger's belly laugh. Having left an ex-wife and two sons back in Beijing to pursue his bohemian calling, Mr. Ma pursues bit film roles while scratching away at an apocalyptic novel. Later, we'll see his atelier—one shared hot plate and a single, padlocked room equipped with bunk bed. "The upper berth," quips Mei, "must be the guest room."

Not only does he sport a wrinkled trench coat and black beret, but Mr. Ma brings along a French actress half his age—plus a more attentive woman from Sichuan who reads everyone's palms as the party progresses. Affluence is in my future, the palm-reader claims, but Mr. Ma is the same ne'er-do-well that he was on the frozen lakes of Beijing. Dispatched to a re-education camp, he gave his precious ice skates to young Mei. "Do you remember?" she now asks him. "When you came back to claim them, I had to admit that we traded the skates for a chicken!"

In an oblong, red-papered living room that doubles as the office of something called Euro-Chine Exchange, a group of post-college kids mix copious amounts of beer with *vin ordinaire*. We're invited to sample the host's long-stewed pig's feet along with Mr. Ma's version of the noodle dish Ants Climbing a Tree, which this playboy has renamed "Ants Climbing into Bed." By the time the cigars are passed out, this midnight soirée has merely passed through the first of three obligatory phases.

After the food, comes singing. Each member of the party is teased, cajoled, and outright pressured into coming up with some remembered childhood ditty, soppy love song, or high-peasant folk tune. The most resistant is Mei's cousin, Wu Gang. But our host, so halting in speech, turns out to be the most proficient at flowing declamations. He even belongs to a club that meets weekly to sing classic Beijing-style arias. Not many things make Mei homesick, or even admit that China may still be her home. But Wu Gang's singing prompts a nudging elbow and her appreciative nods. Though many in the room have risked everything to rebel against Maoist conformity, the performance devolves into one continuous, high-pitched declamation from one of Madame Mao's "model operas." Even if the lyrics are about virtuous communes, and evil landlords, these verses are lovingly retrieved from aborted childhoods.

Old loyalties carry over into the inevitable political free-for-all. A pimply, aspiring conductor starts the debate with a staunch defense of the government's use of force in Tiananmen Square.

"China needs a strong hand to prosper, so things won't fall into chaos like Russia," he argues. Six years and several hundred glasses of French wine later, he is willing to concede that the youthful protesters were after free love as much as free speech. "In Tiananmen Square," he brags, "the blood of the martyrs mingled with the blood of the deflowered virgins!"

A bearded comrade seconds, "Back in my hometown in Inner Mongolia, people think I'm somebody because of 1989. But I did nothing that I am ashamed of and nothing that I am proud of!"

To a man, these Chinese also figure that the C.I.A. must be funding exiled activist Harry Wu in his crusade to expose slave labor in Chinese jails.

"Why exaggerate and lie about prison conditions when the people outside live worse?" one argues perversely. Now I see why an organized opposition has never developed abroad. Once they're far from home, and dependent on import-export hustles, even exiled protesters echo the party line.

"But what about a free press? What about freedom from fear?" Mei translates my astonished questions.

"Ah, Klee-chee, you do not understand!" Apparently, I've been given a new Chinese name.

"If China is so wonderful," I continue, already knowing the answer, "what are you all doing in Paris?"

"I am here for my country," the staunch conductor insists.

"So now you can see that the West is not such a perfect place," Mei castigates. More than ever, I appreciate her ability to remain loyal to the best of Chinese culture without resorting to false superiority or defensive inferiority. "You are right to stand up for China, but a China that doesn't just offer foreign corporations all its goods and cheap labor. We need to keep the valuable things from the past, the feeling of people pulling together. But we don't achieve anything by jailing writers or the Tibetans."

"Oh no, we must never give up Tibet!" is the vehement reaction of one former pro-democracy student. Apparently, he can't give up the concept of an imperial China. Another student admits that he never defined the "democracy" that he once demanded. These modern-day children of the Yellow Emperor still crave an all-powerful authority. And they blame every obstacle to China's rise to power on the United States. At one point, the beret-toting Mr. Ma has to rise to defend me by bellowing, "Klee-chee is not the American secretary of state!"

Until two in the morning, the room swirls with the crises that preoccupy global China in every spot where the Chinese can manage a quorum. Should stability take precedence over personal freedoms? How to modernize without losing all moral footing? Will there be war over Taiwan? "One Chinese can beat one Japanese," observes a student at the end of the night's disagreement. "But ten Japanese will always beat ten Chinese."

Everyone in the room gets his point about the Japanese aptitude for unity. Thank God, the Chinese—divided by loyalties to family, clan, region, philosophies—can never manage to march in lockstep. Still Mr. Ma, the veteran bohemian, exits shaking his head at how easily the younger generation can have their logic obscured by "the cloud of nationalism." Only afterward, in the privacy of our apartment, does one scruffy artist in ponytail and leather jacket voice a less confident view. Pointing to the plate of French cheeses we offer, the artist says, "This is just like China's past—rich and fragrant, but rotting."

For him, the few remaining grapes on a half-eaten cluster represent the present. "There is nothing left to it. Since the British dismembered our country, it's been all downhill. Young people have no inspiration to draw on."

He offers only one nod to Chinese civilization. "In art, at least, ancient Chinese were very advanced, in the sense that they painted for pleasure, not in the service of some religion." But he sees no future in the forms he has inherited, calling them "spiritually dead"—like the Chinagora project we've just visited. Even Chinese cooking largely involves the dutiful replication of time-tried dishes. The tradition can only grow by becoming increasingly internationalized. After so many millennia, Chinese food—like Chinese culture—can't really get any more Chinese.

Now this lost soul tests out his latest escape plan by inquiring, "Is it true that painters in America sell their works on the street?"

Mei and I try to disabuse him of any notion about striking it rich. When I ask how he survives in Paris, he declares of himself and his ilk, "By cheating." He sounds like a character straight out of some Victor Hugo novel that the young Mei had read in secret. "We cheat others, we cheat ourselves, we even cheat God."

Is that what Malraux meant by "the human condition"? On our final afternoon in Paris, the artist accompanies us to yet another terminus of the metro line. In a small auditorium near the Chinese embassy, a concert is being staged to commemorate the fiftieth anniversary of the end of what Chinese call "the anti-Japanese war."

Several of the exiles with whom we argued are performing as members of a people's chorus. Again, there seems to be no conflict between their outcast status and patriotic fervor—though one poor fellow admits to divided emotions as he scans the hall for his Japanese girlfriend!

"Friend," an impassioned narrator begins a stirring cantata before a full auditorium barely settled in plush velvet seats. "Do you remember your beloved Yellow River and the day when the Japanese ghosts came to plunder our land?" This is followed by a hostess in slinky white dress stiffly announcing a cavalcade of acts. The Chaozhou Family Association has sent its drummer corps—a half-dozen old gents who listlessly bang gongs without cracking a smile. Caught in the midst of what others term "fun," the Chinese look most like they're engaged in dreary duty. A violinist pops a string while performing Paganini variations on Peking opera. On his second try, half his bow flakes away.

"Must be made in China!" whispers Mei. It seems that every Chinese diva being schooled in Europe has gotten on the bill. Hefty exemplars of the operatic race join in duets that always end with show-off high notes. Even I get the message of unsubtle lyrics like "Wo ai ni, Zhongguo"—I love you, China!—or "Wo di Zhongguo xin"—I have a Chinese heart!

Mine are not the only tears in the house. On this day and forever, the people around me aren't Chinese—that's a made-up approximation, the barbarians' empty fiction. They are Zhongguoren, middle country people. Even the very term Overseas Chinese implies the impossibility of total escape. Chinese people are only able to leave home because they are so good at taking home with them.

After the show, everyone streams down the block and through the gates of the embassy's commercial section. "Tea and cakes" will be served, but after a year as an honored guest, I know better than that. As soon as some VIP makes the toasts, the crowd wades in to loot a table full of shrimps, red-stewed beef, chow mein, and dumplings.

"If Paris doesn't have the best Chinese food," Mei concludes, "it definitely has the best embassy food."

Kung Pao Kafka

The Inter-City Antonin Dvorak looks more like the Toonerville Trolley. This early-morning shuttle between Vienna and Prague consists of four cars, a fragile tether between the former West and East. The thrill of my first peek behind the old Iron Curtain is soon diminished by a Soviet-style iron maiden in conductor's drag.

"This terrible bad." She shakes her dirty blonde locks to frighten Mei and me into buying two more two-hundred-dollar second-class seats. "Different routing. Terrible bad."

Our passage purchased back in Italy delineates a slight variation in intermediate stops. But shouldn't all equidistant tickets be created equal?

"No dice! Ticket good," Mei insists, awakened by a cup of hot chocolate and the prospect of a noble stand. "We won't pay any more!" Since kindergarten, she's learned her lesson: with unwavering bureaucrats, never blink first. So we remain steadfast as three supervisors threaten to throw us off their closely watched train.

"After thirty years away, I can't stand them and they can't stand me!" says a longfaced Czech from Chicago who ambles into our car just in time to negotiate a compromise. In the boarded-up bowels of the Prague station's abandoned Austro-Hungarian shell, a conductress tails us to an exchange booth and takes a twenty dollar payoff.

On our way to the city of Franz Kafka's birth, we've already had out first brush with the Kafkaesque. Has any writer done so much to promote a destination without ever having written a single naturalistic description? I certainly wouldn't have added Prague to our itinerary if not for my attachment to this poet laureate of travel as the act by which one never arrives. Can there be any greater homage to the great ironist than to buy his face on a T-shirt at the gates to "The Castle"? Or to chart Prague's metamorphosis into a province of Chinese restaurants? What would Mr. K. make of our ceaseless gourmet trials? In a city that challenges all reason, Mei and I come looking for explanations.

"Just look at the map!" is the one we get from Miroslav, a Slavic hustler whose winning grin and hypnotically watery eyes have coaxed us into his Russian jalopy for a free ride to his rented room. "On one side, we have the Germans, who look down on us. On the other side, there's the Russians, who are just plain bad. And with Slovakia breaking away, we've just become twice as tiny! So what do the Czechs get to say about anything? They tell us we had a revolution, but the same people came away with all the money. I figure the KGB did it."

But what about Vaclav Havel, their champion of democracy? "He's a lot better writer than a president."

And what about Kafka, surely an even better writer? "Well, you know, he was a Jew—you see how much those people charge to get into their old cemetery!—and he wrote in German. So what's that for us to get proud about?" A true Czech indeed, Miroslav proves it with his nonstop disdain for everything that the world thinks of as Czech.

"Any problem with room, call me on my mobile!" When he's not trying to nab stray travelers at the train station, Miroslav works as a trainer at a local gym. "We got sauna, Jacuzzi, everything! You want try anytime, just call on the mobile!"

He hardly misses a beat when we tell him we're here to sample Chinese restaurants. "Good, my favorite is just around the corner from your room! It's called the Peking. But too expensive! Especially when our sausages and potatoes are so cheap and filling. Want to try world's best beer? That's one thing we got. Call me anytime on the mobile! Czech food? Well, we Czechs know that's not so good for us. Full of fat, but oh, quite tasty!"

Gallows humor has not gone out of style with Communism. If anything, capitalism has given the locals more rope from which to dangle. At least there are no twists regarding Miroslav's room. For thirty dollars, we get the partitioned back wing of a ground-floor apartment, complete with sitting room, lace curtains, a bookshelf of travelers' remainders, and a fiercely rigid bed. It's all a bit tatty by Western standards, but what isn't in a town where *babushkas* queue up for salami and the latest style of Levi's is treated as a priceless find? It's hard to believe that any society could have fallen so far behind the rest of Europe without having a plan. Perhaps it was a five-year plan.

We are just a short stroll from the shrine of Wenceslas Square, setting of the Prague Spring and untold humanist uprisings. But the place looks like Times Square without action; a slippery, sloped promenade of crushed hopes ringed with bratwurst stands and chubby prostitutes wearing vinyl go-go boots.

"This is a place without varnish," Mei chortles. Having grown up in such a society, she knows just how to make the best of Prague. Here, she senses a holdover of relative classlessness that makes for a refreshing change from the rest of the continent's fastidious shop-keepers and supercilious parlor intellects. The Czechs are all in this thing together, which is why their country is such an agreeable ruin to rummage about.

"A cage went in search of a bird" goes one of Kafka's elliptical aphorisms. That's just the way I feel wandering Prague's Old Town along with some of its twenty-five-million annual gawkers. Nothing cages the high-flying tourist quite as much as the sights we're all chained to seeing. No other activity requires so much time spent ex-ploring what others have already discovered. It's hard to remain un-moved by the view of spires from the Charles Bridge, the spell cast by the old churches, the various plaques aimed at convincing us Franz Kafka really was made of flesh and blood. Scorned by Nazis and Communists alike, the scribbler now faces the more formidable enemy of commercialized adulation. Nor can his haunted alleys re-tain much meaning once they're spruced up with puppet shops and fern bars.

The real symbol of Prague's absurdist underdog status, and the souvenir that Mei can't resist, is a marionette of the good sol-dier Schweik, the antiwar everyman created by novelist Hasek. "Shuai-ke!" she cries with glee at the sight of the dumb figure mod-eling his frayed private's uniform. Now Mei realizes that her favorite character in Chinese kiddie comics was really a Czech.

Prague's other oddball attractions include Dixieland jazz amidst Dracula settings, prewar Cubist architecture, and post-everything scrounging. String quartets squeak out discount Mozart in every church while on-the-cheap pockets of grunge culture blast out heavy metal. The heavily hyped "black light theater" shows off an avant-garde form instantly frozen into absurdist kitsch. A community almost devoid of living Jews runs a Jewish cemetery so crammed with generational layers that the tombstones litter the black earth like strewn teeth. The corroded hippie sentiments on the John Lennon Wall stand beside street stalls crowded with surplus Red Army fur caps. And our "mobile" man had been right: the world's finest beer comes with nearly the world's plainest grub. Creamed beef à la Stroganoff and pork shoulder à la caveman are served up with stale rye bread in cellars with about as much atmosphere as bomb shelters. Now this is one cuisine that will never leave you hungry again in an hour! Can Chinese food be added to the mix without turning the whole thing into some sort of Dadaist gravy?

Could it be that we've finally found a place far enough from China to be far enough? We've heard that Vienna is crammed with Chinese places—no doubt, to the quiet horror of the Aryan populace—and that Budapest is rife with Asiatic gangs. Perhaps there's little lure for the Chinese in ex-Czechoslovakia, neither a fraternal ally under socialism nor a "free market" jackpot. Yet close by the statue of good King Wenceslas, we pick up the first clues in our Sinological scavenger hunt. First, a newly opened casino features Chinese writing on its canopy. Next, a crowded restaurant that's Oriental in name serves the soggy creations of an all-Czech kitchen crew. And walking along those indeterminate, unsung boulevards that provide space in every town for cut-rate clothing outlets and surplus electronic parts, we immediately stumble upon a couple of musty, uninviting *Cinske Restaurace*—Chinese restaurants, my dear Watson!

At a rag store called Hong Kong Fashions, Mei coaxes the Chinese proprietress to name the best. She obligingly sends us around the corner to Zlaty Drak—Golden Dragon—a slick variant of the local model, with polished ebony bar and a back wall comprised of smoked mirrors. Lunch hour has passed, so the only ones in the place are a couple of bow-tied bartenders and a handsomely graying gent wistfully nursing a cigarette. Peter Chow is the "Monsieur Rick" of this Chinese remake of *Casablanca*. He exudes a been-everywhere, done-everything confidence—maybe because he has. For his last gambit, he ran a logging operation in Liberia. "That damned war destroyed ten years' effort. We got out with our lives."

Now he's betting on the stability of a regime barely five years old.

"Though the taxes are high, they really want to encourage new business," he tells us hopefully. "When younger people take over the government, there will be a change for the better. Just like in China. I'm waiting for the day."

We don't have to wait long for some modestly accurate home-style bean curd and pork with pickled vegetables. "We can't get much in the way of fresh seafood," he admits, though even this is an improvement on Stalinist bloc days. "There was only one Chinese restaurant in Prague. It's the Vietnamese who came here on technical exchanges, but now the Chinese government runs its own place, the Confucius." What we've already seen confirms Peter Chow's view that, "Once the Czechs get some cash, they worry first about a car. They are crazy for new wheels. But eating! What's dinner to them but a hot dog barely warmed and dipped in mustard?"

His tone suggests the unspoken "barbarian." But, the owner argues, "the people accept us because they know that foreigners are going to give them a beautiful city," which he defines as "a place where you can eat everything you want." Come to think of it, what's the point of putting up with a city if you can't? But something doesn't jibe about a man of such broad ambition who is content with so modest a domain—ruled over by a painted vixen in black dress leading the rest of the crew in an afternoon game of mah-jongg. A display of photos, including one showing President Havel struggling with chopsticks, confirms that this is no lady, this is Peter Chow's wife. When we ask him about the presence of Chinese gangs in town, he grows oddly vehement. "Russian criminals pour in without anyone noticing! But when a reporter spread rumors in his column about some Chinese Mafia, I told him that I didn't want him to come back."

Still, Peter Chow starts filling us in on the details of Chinese smuggling operations. "A few years ago, we had thirty thousand Chinese coming through, but now, it's down to a trickle. At the airport, you used to see the snake heads waiting for their ducks." The former term stands for Fujianese gangsters, the latter for unsuspecting immigrants. "Sometimes, the ducks get kidnapped and held for ransom. Other times, the ducks' relatives are alerted and capture the snake heads instead. There used to be a lot of action because this is an easy port of entry to Western Europe. From here, you can pack into a van with some Vietnamese and hide until you cross into Austria. Others used to go to Germany the hard way—until a few lost their fingers climbing over the mountains."

Peter Chow professes no desire to travel. "America, that's much too dangerous. How could I take my family to a country where I'm afraid to go outside?" A moment later, he pulls back his gray linen jacket to reveal a holster shoved into his pants on one hip. Out comes a pistol. The handle is made of fine wood, the kind you instantly want to stroke. I wish he'd put the thing away, even if this is the first time we've encountered firearms in a Chinese restaurant.

"I have five of these, all registered and legal! I'm going to protect my family." Against what, Peter Chow won't really say. Perhaps this tenacious proprietor is like Kafka's fictional "Stoker"—a man whose unbounded faith in his powers of survival only leads him further into his own trap.

Speaking of traps, it's easy enough to see why Chinese food, properly prepared, would appeal to taste buds the world over. What's irrational is the way diners of all nations seem to lap up the stuff even when it's atrocious. At one popular outpost near the Charles Bridge, every dish comes dripping in a reddish-brown Elmer's cornstarch. Two waitresses straight out of the People's Republic lounge by the cash register, fondling one another's long locks and short apron strings. They've held their indentured station seven days a week, ten hours a day for the four years they've been in Europe. Quizzed by Mei about real Chinese food, the girls grudgingly mutter, "Great Wall." But how do they know?

Some detective work leads us to the satellite neighborhood of Pankrac. After a pleasant subway ride—is it some holdover from coal-mine culture that the cleanest places in Prague are under the earth?—we alight in a setting that could be Bulgaria or West Pittsburgh. Beneath a sky the color of concrete, more concrete: housing blocks alternating with empty-lot rubble, a local market featuring plenty of potatoes and state-of-the-art plastic shovels from Albania. It takes five or six inquiries before gypsy peddler recalls anything "Cinske" out here. The rain is coming and of course, we've forgotten our umbrella. We take sanctuary in a smart new business hotel, reminiscent of ones in outlying Beijing for its grandiose senselessness. Luckily, the concierge points out that we're just across a patch of barbed wire from what we're seeking. There's Chinese writing atop the poured-concrete, lantern-festooned jewel box set ludicrously atop a supermarket that looks more like a barracks.

Inside the Great Wall, we've really arrived in Beijing: the same screens and scrolls, same doilies and antimacassars covered in plastic, same vast number of unoccupied tables. The boss is away this afternoon, but a young waiter who has lived in Vienna provides us with a sampling of Northern-style food. He even insists, at great risk, to knock down our bill. For this true son of Beijing, it's a matter of pride, not p. r. And the chef here has something to be proud of. The shredded pork in "Northern sauce"—actually *jing jiang*, Beijing's characteristic bean paste—features the garlic-vinegar in perfect balance, barely kissing the diced meat. The *ma po* bean curd and pan-fried *guo teh* are as robust as it gets. So the reluctant waitresses coughed up the correct skinny after all. With its view of vacant lots and crumbling concrete, this is one of the secret finds of Europe.

In his classic parable "The Great Wall of China," Kafka ponders why humans toil on endeavors whose results they'll never see, why they find relative freedom in obeisance to far-off authorities. In the Great Wall restaurant, I ruminate on how they manage to singe the eggplant skins with the taste of fire. I try to figure out why Prague, of all places, should offer some of the continent's most authentic Chinese food. The relative lack of demand among the Czechs has thus far saved the cuisine from bastardization. Chinese cooking's history here has been short and sweet, not sour.

Two more subway stops, then a bus ride out onto a plain of twenty-story housing encampments, takes us as far as we can get from Kafka's inward-turned center. We've come to find a long-lost American who once roomed with my mother when they worked together in New York's Russian-American Institute. Joy—whose sister is named Hope—was so much a Communist zealot that she gave up her U.S. citizenship to build the new order. Though our arrival is a complete surprise, Joy welcomes us into her homey two-bedroom unit while she continues a widow's weekly ritual of putting away enough coleslaw for the entire winter. Still vivacious in curly, streaked hair at nearly eighty, sporting a Brooklyn chattiness that borders on the compulsive, Joy brings out photos of her "simply gorgeous" and "too Aryan" husband. He had been a professor who took over an administrative position, as Joy explains, "to warm the seat of a friend who was finishing his thesis." A victim of bad timing, Joy's husband ended his life washing windows as a result of the purges that followed the crushing of the reformist Prague Spring. Insists Joy, fairly gritting her teeth, "Neither of us ever turned stool-pigeon." This personal vindication seems more important than any final judgment on the system to which she's devoted her life.

"The struggle's never over," she says with a sigh, an unnatural cook struggling with her cabbage grater. "You think we got it better now?"

Like most elder Czechs, she's worried about the rising cost of health care and the looming privatization of an apartment that she figured would be hers forever at subsidized rates. Her son, a Czech architect, proves as shy and sputtering as Joy is forthright and uncensored. He is also more cynical. "Now we are China without the investment," he muses, seconding our observations. "We are ready to build something new, but there's no money to do it. And Havel is more interested in showing the world that his hands are clean."

Joy's budget is obviously tighter than ours, so we treat her to lunch at the last restaurant on our list—a top pick of Prague's English-language ex-pat's weekly. Whether or not the food is good, the Chinese Still Life has to win some kind of award for the strangest restaurant name we've come across. Once we spot this tiny establishment on the bottom floor of yet another grim housing block, Mei tells me that the Chinese lettering simply reads "Chengdu." Joy, a lifelong translator, points out that the Czech *Cinske Zatisi* actually means a "restful place," perhaps a tranquil garden. This ultra-tidy establishment, its dowdy wallpaper festooned with fan-shaped mirrors, does provide some measure of tranquility. And the food is perfectly Sichuanese, starting with a superbly subtle cold hacked chicken, boiled to tenderness, then smothered in rice wine and sesame oil, chopped garlic, and green onion. I'm hardly disappointed with the *dan dan mien*—fresh noodles with a Italian-style dollop of hot bean paste—when it's a small miracle to find them at all.

Even the hostess has the small frame, square jaw, and rounded eyes that cause many Chinese to praise the good women of Sichuan. The jaunty young owner with flimsy mustache was actually an instructor in the famed culinary academy that we'd been unable to find back in the real Chengdu. He has published articles, been on television, and did a cooking stint in Canada at the Sichuan government's behest. "But I saw there are not many Chinese restaurants here," he tells us. "And it doesn't take much to invest."

His only complaint is that he's had to hire two Czechs. "They work four days a week, but I have to pay them much more than the Chinese." That's alright, now that he's turning away dinner traffic. He's even thrilled to have signed a seventeen-year-lease.

I cannot imagine a less promising place to do business. But what do writers know? To me, it's not God but money that works in mysterious ways. I wouldn't want to lock myself into a satellite city that makes the main wing of Sing Sing prison look like the Ling Ling Teahouse. My idea of liberation isn't getting in on the ground floor of nowhere. But the immigrant may be the ultimate Kafkaesque creation—a "hunger artist" willingly trading on his self-abnegation, the man who not only plots his own alienation, but takes comfort in it.

If Franz Kafka were roaming the streets of Prague today, I don't think he'd hang out in the marionette shops, youth bistros, punk dungeons, or Tex-Mex chili parlors. But you just might find him sipping tea under red tassels, in a quiet corner of a Chinese still life.

Sichuan Cold Chicken

From Cinske Zatisi

Ingredients:

1 medium-sized fresh chicken
3 scallions
Fresh ginger, 4 slices
Salt, 2 tsp.

Shaoxing cooking wine, 5 tsp.
Peanut oil, 3 tsp.
Garlic, 4 cloves
Sesame oil, 1 tsp.
Cilantro, 5 sprigs

Heat a large pot of water, enough to cover the entire chicken. When the water comes to a full boil, add the whole, cleaned chicken along with the ginger slices and 3 tsp. cooking wine. Boil fifteen minutes or until the chicken appears eighty percent cooked. Turn off the fire and let the chicken stand until the water cools naturally, up to eight hours. Remove the chicken and cut as desired—lengthwise or in strips, deboned or with bones. Put on a plate on a bed of lettuce. Mince the scallions and garlic very fine and mix together in a small bowl along with salt. Heat the oil in a wok and add the scallion-garlic mix, along with 2 tsp. of broth used to cook chicken and the remaining 2 tsp. of wine and sesame oil. Finish mixing and smear evenly atop the cold chicken. Garnish with cilantro and serve.

Dessert
. . . .
FROM HUNAN TO
WHO KNOWS

Featured Restaurants:

China Inn, Bedford, Pennsylvania
Mark Pi's China Gate, Columbus
Panda Garden, Terre Haute
The Imperial Wok, Santa Fe
Avalon, Gallup, New Mexico
Kim Chuy, Los Angeles
Empress Palace, Los Angeles
888 Seafood, San Gabriel
Charming Garden, Monterey Park
Chinois on Main, Santa Monica
Mandarette, Hollywood
Yujean Kang's, Pasadena
Good Chances, Rosemead
Sam Lok, San Francisco
Yank Sing, San Francisco
Hong Kong Flower Lounge, San Francisco
Tommy Toy's Haute Cuisine Chinoise, San Francisco
House of Nanking, San Francisco
China Moon Cafe, San Francisco
Brandy Ho's Hunan, San Francisco
Sichuan Taste, San Francisco
Chef Chu's, Los Altos
Happy Cafe, San Mateo

Terre Haute Cuisine

What comes East Coast must go West. Wiping a heap of fall leaves off our trusty Honda left in a Boston driveway, Mei and I are past the point of delighting in the inauthentic. On our return trip cross-country, we can hardly keep our tongues hinged to the tongue-in-cheek.

Our first night falls in Bedford, Pennsylvania, once an old Amish outpost but now little more than a pit stop where the boxy, yellow China Inn stands as the only hint of a world as yet unfranchised. The only other diners are a van full of giggling church kids, each red-haired and with braces, who wrinkle their noses at the five qualities and seven fragrances while heading straight for the duck sauce. The waitress is Caucasian—never a good sign—but the proprietress is clearly moved by Mei's use of Mandarin and her plea for "real Chinese food." In a jiffy, we get some cold and properly chewy thin-sliced cured beef, dumplings that barely hint at meat fillings, and a bony white fish sprinkled with scallions.

"Too light for you?" the owner asks, echoing Mei's frequent concern. Chinese food is much the same as Chinese art: perfection is often no more than a wisp of fog. Chinese fear that Westerners, while adapting quickly to tangy sauces, will never appreciate the comforts of simplicity, the joys of blandness. How has this wife of a Taiwanese Ph.D. in physics ended up slaving away a hundred miles away from her family down the Pennsylvania Turnpike? How can this plainly intelligent owner keep from feeling that she's living a lie, and helping others ingest it?

Sometimes, our own worst enemy is the ability to rationalize nearly anything—like Mei and I eating here, on our way to driving nearly eight thousand miles across won ton wastelands. Whatever it is that keeps these scattered chefs going must be what keeps us going. Call it obtuseness, obsessive thoroughness, or an excuse for lengthening the distance between ourselves and settling down. The two of us suffer from an excessive amount of "ants in the pants," what my ancestors denigrate as *spielkas*, what Mei's elevate as *c'hi*. But the anxiety of plotting and planning our next move is gradually being replaced by the anxiety of wondering how Mei and I will maintain public and private passions once the search is exhausted.

313

As a time-consuming car game, I suggest that we try to count up every meal we've endured or relished in a year.

"And what about every soy sauce stain that I've had to wash out of your pants?" Spoken like a married woman.

Somewhere near nowhere, I announce, "We're over three hundred restaurants so far. Why am I ready for more?"

"Chinese food tastes better than one-a-day vitamins," answers Mei. Is this joke on us? Just as we'd set out on April Fool's Day, we're heading back on Halloween. We don't realize this until we pull into a small town McDonald's, only to find the entire staff transformed with peaked hats into a brood of witches. They rustle about with macabre grace, filling orders for deathly fries. An afternoon kaffeklatsch of seniors chomp on Big Macs and hot apple pies through the impermeable openings of five-and-dime Dracula masks. All fake smiles are masked, rubber wrinkles hide real ones.

I have planned lunch in Wheeling, West Virginia. Twenty years back, on a youthful cruise in a Chevy Impala affectionately named "Jerry," my cousin Mike and I had a memorable encounter here with some Chinese waiters who took the orders in perfect southern drawl. "Y'all want some chow mein?" They had set down the fortune cookies with, "Y'all come back now, you hear?"

Traversing streets made for country-western sorrows, we find the one gaudy red representative of pagoda baroque has recently failed along with much of the local economy. The main way I know that I'm in hillbilly country is by a donut shop sign that warns patrons of a leaky roof: "Please do not set here!"

Before long, we're in steel-sprouted, cold-hearted Columbus. We follow secretaries out of the Ohio chill into a mall almost as brassy as in pace-setting Singapore. Near the down escalator is Mark Pi's China Express, a lunch counter where open woks give off the proper sear and hiss. This looks like a reasonable effort at turning the world's oldest cuisine into the latest convenience food. If Chinese food hasn't spawned its equivalent of Mexican food's Taco Bell, the problem may be that Chinese food may be as quick to cook as it is messy for immediate scarfing. Who wants to risk the fast lane with a lap full of *moo goo gai pan?*

We try the China Gate, a swankier sit-down version in the basement, hoping to find Mr. Pi squared. Instead, we meet a waitress from Shanghai, married to an Ohio State grad student, who answers our inquiries about real Chinese eats near the campus with "*Mei you.*" Sorry, Charley. So we settle for the dread combination platters: black bean chicken cut in gooey chunks *à la Americaine*, Singapore noodles missing the scent of curry.

Somewhere along this stretch of road, the size of belt buckles makes a noticeable increase. So does the outlandish jollity of gas station cashiers who hand over pink credit card receipts with the admonition, "This'll keep you in the pink!" But November is kissing the corn fields, turning sky and earth into mirrors of barrenness, making this no time to dawdle in the Midwest. Call me a blonda-phobic, but southern Indiana seems a place where terrible things may break loose at any moment, tornadoes or murder sprees. Terre Haute blazons in the highway night, no high ground as far as I can see, but a major conglomeration of clashing neon. The notion of haute cuisine doesn't appear to be any more elevated than "The Boston Connection," a beanery fronted by local hoops hero Larry Bird.

In the far corner of a Formica-white strip mall, we find our Hoosier heaven at the Panda Garden. The menu posted outside the door is actually authentic enough to call their squid-and-shrimp sauce *ma la*—for numbing hot, just like in Sichuan. At last, we can pooh-pooh the assorted deep-fry called a *pu pu* platter! Too bad the oblong storefront is divided by a jungle of plants, drenched with recorded music, and lit by the sort of pink bulbs butchers use to freshen the look of their meat. The surplus of cheerleading wait-resses, charming in their off-the-boat mix of eagerness and awkward-ness, are enrolled at nearby Indiana State. The college's foreign students make this town something of a culinary oasis. But Panda Garden is the carefully crafted creation of one Mr. Cheng, the out-front son of tireless parents in the back.

"Sometimes, I work so many hour, face get stuck!" He means from smiling, which I can see is not something that comes naturally to this determined young man. But he soon warms to the task of host-ing us. "In America country, everybody, even Terre Haute mayor, pay attention to reviews!"

This is one of the working maxims that the owner has acquired through eleven years in Chinese dives from Waco, Texas, to Northampton, Massachusetts. "What I like is the mountains and sea coast," he admits. But the Chinese view their personal likes and dislikes as faint breezes before the stronger gusts of commerce and fate. So the Midwest beckoned because "we could introduce something better." Back in his native Taiwan, "the dimensions of the slicing must be exact. Here, all that counts are big portions." As Mr. Cheng quaintly puts it, "In China, chow mein is for old men with no teeth! But in America, that's all the young men eat!"

After our long day's journey toward dinner, I'm thrilled to eat reasonable, if somewhat overdrenched, approximations of Beijing-style bean paste pork, jellyfish and General Li Hong Zhang chicken. Judging from the numbers of generals thus memorialized, it seems that poultry is all Chinese armies ever ate. I'm willing to enlist. Better yet, this young/old man presses on with a banquet of factual tidbits and twice-cooked statistics.

"The average American, he consume Chinese food one time every two week," he starts in. "Market share for Chinese restaurants is twenty percent, compared to forty percent pizza, five percent for Japanese and Mexican. Four factors for restaurant success are food, smell, service, and cleanliness." Judging from his place, elevator music runs a close fifth.

Our host's most compelling bit of unconfirmed trivia is his assertion that "the average diner's stomach absorbs pound-and-a-half of product per sitting." I wonder if this holds equally true for Sumo wrestlers and bulimics, whether the "product" consists of canned corn, Rocky Road, or *mu shu*.

"Used to be, one month's salary in the States paid for a year in Taiwan," he calculates, reducing all manner of diaspora into another easily digestible form. "Now about equal." Mr. Cheng has to stay on top off his data, since he's the only one of five brothers without a graduate degree. "Average life expectancy for Chinese restaurant, it's five years. That's when you do first remodel." This must be lesson one. "If you can't afford, you're stuck in cycle going down." But he still thinks it pays to be humane. "I had bosses so stingy that they wouldn't even give waiters boiled water. I want my people to enjoy work here. Every New Year's, all my regulars invite for free."

This free course we're getting could last all night. "Do you know we had a customer who tried to get out of paying by saying he was from F.B.I.? What kind of trick he play! I know enough to ask to see badge. All kind of things happen in restaurant! Disgruntled waiter, he phone in a bomb scare. Guy find a half tooth in the sesame chicken salad, turns out it's *his* tooth!"

For Mr. Cheng, gleefully describing calamity after calamity, there's no business like the pound-and-a-half product business.

"Ever had any trouble with Indiana people?" I interject.

"You never know you have a problem until something happens," answers the owner, trying to do his diplomatic best. But one waitress seems to think that West Terre Haute is where it could happen.

"When we go fishing, we always come home before dark," this co-ed pipes up with a giggle. "One time, we heard some shooting over there. That's the place where they got a lot of *san* K." Now I know *the three K's* is Mandarin for the Klan.

Chinese with Reservation

How do we make it from Indiana to Oklahoma in a single day? No Chinese place tempts us to stop. We pass through St. Louis too early and by afternoon are bouncing across the mitigated bleakness of the lower Ozarks. In Cuba, Missouri, neither Castro nor Mao are in evidence. One of the eternally grinning girls at McDonald's steers us to a place in the next town that she pronounces, "Reeeely good." But Wong's Chinese-American kitchen is run by Vietnamese and deep-fries egg rolls at a pace to rival any drive-in. From a stack of glossy brochures at Big Mac's, I find that Asia is represented in the glut of Vegas-style "show theaters" that attract tourists to Branson, self-proclaimed "middle of mid-America," navel of nowhere. Shoji Tabuchi, a schmaltzy violinist in sparkling white Liberace suit, has not only made himself into a star, but enlisted his American wife as emcee and their daughter as warbling co-attraction "when she isn't busy with homework."

By dinner, we're zipping past Tulsa, its office sentinels and sandstone malls pulsing with the power of oil money. We figure that we'd best wait for Oklahoma City, where we can get hot tips from our Chinese hosts. Yes, Mei has close relations in the land of Will

Rogers. In fact, few are closer to her than a cousin who gave up a career as a promising coloratura soprano to help her husband start—guess what?—a Chinese restaurant. But the restaurant has been sold to help fund a U.S.-style theatrical farce back in China. With the couple having just returned to introduce situation comedy to Beijing, we can only commune with their spirits. Except for the strewn piles of Chinese newspapers, their vast, ranch home is about as American as anything can get. The master bedroom's monster bed even comes equipped with giant ceiling mirror—one furnishing that would never have passed muster back on the commune.

House-sitting Chinese students more accustomed to packaged noodles can't think of a single restaurant to recommend. Mei and I take our chances by cruising a downtown that seems seedily stuck in the Dust Bowl era. The only Okies we find are Vietnamese.

"Maybe we should have quit while we were ahead in Tulsa. . . ."

"You're here now," is Mei's standard answer, "so enjoy it." That's not easy at a drafty Chinese-Vietnamese night club where the chicken comes with fish sauce and the plate comes with cockroaches.

Before heading out in the morning, Mei and I make a detour past the bombed-out Federal Building, now a bulldozed hole surrounded by churches where workmen still replace blown-out glass. Six months after the country's most destructive act of right-wing sabotage, impromptu memorials hang onto stretches of cyclone fencing. Between wind-ravaged corsages are baby photos of the victims—many of whom *were* babies. The fence is hung mostly with T-shirts, fluttering like scarecrows, bearing the names of high school football teams and magic-markered, "Miss ya!" and "Luv ya!" When it comes to having a history, Americans are still awkward adolescents.

We've already seen at least three signs claiming the spot "Where the West Begins." It really begins out in the high plains near the border with Texas. Here, the first flat-topped mesas appear, the sky overwhelms, and the long freight trains can be seen chugging away twenty miles off the road. It's where I first have to expand Mei's vocabulary with the word *tumbleweed.* For some reason, I feel giddily content in this huge void, where even such hardy cultural weeds as Chinese food can't make it. Surely, there must be more to the freedom out here than a mere license to speed.

Traveling down Route 66 back in the late sixties, my VW van broke down near McLean. In what amounted to the quintessential hippie nightmare, my long-haired companions and I were nearly strung up at the Amarillo county fair. This time, I'm looking forward to lunch in that bastion of ten-gallon xenophobes. Too bad we barely find an open grocery, let alone a restaurant, in downtown Amarillo. The tiny Chinatown Cafe turns out to be a Thai restaurant—"they all look alike, y'all!" The better eats are out in suburbia, we're told by two thoroughly assimilated Asian teens who use their restaurant mainly to rehearse their rock band and sell laminated sets of Dallas Cowboy cards.

By the time we get back to mall-land, everything is closed for the afternoon but the China Express. This is a semi-fast joint where a variety of stir-frys are ordered from a single cashier and emerge on paper plates. The place is the branch-child of a Shanghainese who also owns a chain of Mexican joints. Since I'm in Texas, I go for the beef *kung pao*—nicely seared, though dosed with semi-rancid peanuts. A do-it-yourself Mongolian barbecue is also on offer, but the portions don't look properly ranch-sized.

By evening, we've retreated into New Mexico's bastion of good taste. How is it that this adobe oasis of interior design should survive the general homogenization? Mei has never seen Santa Fe, so we jog north to browse for Indian jewelry on the sidewalks of the plaza. In fresh mountain air, we hike up exclusive Canyon Road. But we don't have much time to browse through the cavalcade of art galleries catering to the rage in southwestern pastels. We're pointed upward and upward to the Imperial Wok, a swank night spot with roofed-over atrium, where yet another wayward mechanical engineer from Shanghai turns out passable specials of sweetened purple eggplant wedges and too tangy fish-flavored pork. In how many lands have my hopes for this dish been shredded?

It's easier to find Chinese amidst the pueblos than to picture my sedentary, intellectual father having lived his student days among these Zuni stomping grounds, chasing the ghost of D. H. Lawrence while rousing *bracero* miners to militant action. During Depression days, he came here to follow a best pal poet taking a tuberculosis cure and the two curly-headed dreamers nearly wound up as the state's entire Communist Party central committee. Now I exchange yellowed letters and faded handbills with the friend's daughter, Bayita, who lives on Bayita Lane, surrounded by Yemenite rugs strewn over adobe additions, sheep and pigs kept under the shade of golden aspens. Her puff-bread *sopapillas* with red beans give us a real taste of the local cuisine, while Mei contributes the best drunken chicken to be found in the Land of Enchantment.

In Albuquerque, we get a recommendation from June, a steely-eyed woman with the kind of solid voice that belies a lifetime of heartache. Born into an all-American family that observed strange rituals she would later come to recognize as Indian, June married a Navajo man and works trying to build self-esteem among the tribal reservation's many alcoholics. She insists that we stop at the Avalon in Gallup, a place described as a "meeting ground between the Navajo and the Chinese." Sounds like our kind of place. From the description, I imagine a dim bar with teepee-like shafts of light where wizened elders pass around holy chopsticks like they're peace pipes. Instead, our cruise along the honky tonks and western wear shops of old Route 66 lead us to an archetypal coffee shop.

The only hints that the Avalon is Chinese-American are the pagoda symbols stenciled to the windows, barely visible behind newspaper vending machines. It's the sort of place that should have gum-cracking soda jerks on roller skates and flip-through juke box selectors at each table. Sunlight floods the cracked linoleum. Families out for a Sunday treat are stuffed into every booth. Yet this all-American scene has nothing to do with the white bread culture of fifties' nostalgia. The Americans here are dark-haired and brown-eyed people of the earth, with sun-parched skin, rock-moving shoulders, and cactus-torn hands. There's such a bawling, familial mix in here that it would be futile to break them down into census labels like Native American, native Mexican, Chicano, Tejano, or other.

When we inquire after the owner, a barely of-age waitress who is a dead ringer for the Virgin of Guadalupe, answers, "Me no speak inglis." In this ethnic melange, it's tough to pick out any Chinese—until a few start emerging from the kitchen. The young Chinese looks scholarly in glasses but is all too busy at the grill turning out man-handler meals for oversized people. Monstrous specials of half chickens and mounds of mashed potatoes whisk past us. By the time we've perused the Avalon's limited footnote of a Chinese menu, we're introduced to the owner.

"George Hoo Soo. How can I do you?" With a red Nike swoosh cap and glasses case stuffed into the chest pocket of his apron, he is Chinese down to his baggy eyes but thoroughly Western in accent, friendly manner, and ambling gait. He'd come to America from a town near Canton way back in 1934.

"I got my social security card the very first year that they passed the social security," he says proudly. He had run another restaurant down in Winslow, Arizona, until '46, "when the railroads moved out." Long before that, his grandfather had worked for Union Pacific "at fifteen bucks a month" and was a housekeeper for a San Francisco banker, doing "so much handwashing on a laundry board that the tips of his fingers plain wore off."

With easy, uncomplaining tones, this fount of Chinese oral history recalls the time "when it took a hundred days to come over on a Chinese junk and the boat fare that every Chinese tried to scrape together was ninety-four dollars." He hasn't forgotten all the years of exclusion either, when "the Chinese were scarce, until President Lyndon Johnson changed the quotas and ended the discrimination."

Now the Avalon has three or four competitors right along Gallup's desert strip, serving "strictly Chinese stuff." As George tells us, "We've even got one Chinese around these parts who married a Navajo woman to try and get in on some reservation business. But you can't just get a license to sell pottery or run your own casino. The Indian nation, they've got pretty strict rules about that. Now the fella is drunk most of the day."

As for the local tribes, George has always felt "right at home" in their midst. He asks matter-of-factly, "Don't you know that the first Indians came from Asia anyway?"

Many experts believe so. One grizzled Chinese professor, with whom we'd shared a hot pot back in Sichuan Province, has spent years attempting to prove that the Mayas and Incas, even the Japanese, descend from China's mountain-dwelling Miao tribe. In this diner, there's more evidence to solve the anthropological mystery. George tells us, "Why, there are even plenty of words in the Navajo language that sound pretty much like Cantonese. The words for sweeping and washing, for instance." Could this have helped the Germans crack all those American war secrets transmitted in Navajo?

Soon enough, we'll hear that clicking tongue on FM stations as we cross the reservation, but no reservations are necessary at the Avalon. Here, I find myself eating, and enjoying, my first chop suey. If there was a place to try that ultimate Chinese-American concoction, it is among these descendants of Chinese railroaders. Even Mei approves of the dish as homemade by Mrs. Hoo Soo. Heaped to the rim of a thick crockery bowl, this greenish, brackish soup is thick with tender strips of pork swimming on reefs of fresh-cut celery, adrift bean sprouts, and cabbage. When it comes to abject acculturation made tasty, little can top this. There's no point in traveling any further into America.

By dark, we're poised at the edge of the Mojave on the cusp of greater Los Angeles. The roads to Las Vegas and the Grand Canyon meet in Kingman's nest of discount motels. Amazingly, the off-duty psycho at our front office points us toward Chin's, one of three or four Chinese restaurants on this strip alone. More amazingly, the only pedestrians we spot along the way have Oriental features. Like us, they're scanning for that next neon pagoda, ready to take a chance.

"Gamblers," Mei calculates much quicker than me. "Chinese even go to the desert to tempt their fate."

Cruisin' for Stinky Tofu

Sooner or later, the whole world ends up in L.A. So does our search.

The city that once defined beach boy blandness has become the ultimate immigrant grab bag: one unadorned, unaesthetic supply center subdivided into ethnic aisles. I just hope all those seekers after the good life don't land where Mei and I do, in the smoggy apotheosis known as Echo Park. Trying to work out my crosscountry kinks with a jog, I can barely breathe, let alone follow an urban par course that zigzags to avoid the hazards of trained pit bulls and gangs of unemployed teens slinking about in baggy pants that make them look like menacing clowns. Along the street where we're staying, half the houses are boarded up and the other half blare Mexican polkas across claptrap porches claimed by permanent garage sales. On our first morning in the City of Angels, we wake to find every lock on our car jimmied by a robber who couldn't get in. Now we can't either.

Fortunately, our host lives up a set of Mediterranean terraces leading away from the mean streets. Within a compound of white stucco that's evolved into an informal commune is the one-room studio of quite another type of immigrant. Unlike the Chinese we've been charting, the Taiwanese painter who signs his name *Tu-2* (too-too) is after the inspirations of an ennobling poverty. A photojournalist back home, he came to L.A. for film school but ended up staying to keep away from Taipei's hectic social pace and competitive cliques. We'd met at the Venice Art Biennale, where he was an informal interpreter for the Taiwanese delegation. Now Tu-2 folds his futon to make room for totemic sheets of canvas that form a remarkable series entitled "Mickey Mao." The Great Helmsman is redrawn with Disney ears and rodent overlap, metamorphosed by rubber nose or shifty Nixon eyes. The possibilities are infinite: Mao as tattooed gang member, an O.J. Mao. More touching is Tu-2's self-portrait as a hopeful child, posed with engineer parents amidst the ghoulish progress of a Taiwanese power plant.

Tu-2, as the name tooted on his answering machine implies, is his own most resplendent creation. He's neither archbishop nor ballerina but an ultra-internationalist hippie whose shoulder-length locks, gaunt frame, brown skin, and sculpted cheekbones make most people mistake him for Cochise.

"How can the ladies resist me?" Tu-2 asks, a most un-Latin lover with highpitched cackle. His combination of boundless energy, artistic insecurity, and unabashed self-admiration has won over a string of pantheist girlfriends. His latest is the sensitive offspring of Holocaust survivors who makes a good living as a psychic to the stars. "We're taking a break right now to resolve some class issues," he tells us in proper L.A. speak. I guess he's referring to the anxiety that comes up when she looks through her crystal ball at a future with a starving artist.

"Never mind all that negativity. I just go out each day and kick my balls," says Tu-2. This unfortunate malapropism refers to the artist's attempt to hone his soccer skills to the level of an all-Mexican neighborhood league he's just joined. Though past forty, this self-described "skinny monkey" displays the lithe, slipper-footed form that once made him a judo champion. While letting down his formidable hair over continually brewed thimbles of tea, Tu-2 admits his martial arts skills once enabled him to serve as part of the elite bodyguard unit for Generalissimo Chiang Kai-shek.

"When you've seen a man up close, then you know he's really a fascist," he says of the experience, which included the absurd discipline of learning to "undress and shower in no more than fifteen seconds. If you couldn't make it, you had to keep showering again! I tell you, I got really clean!"

Now our bad boy barely has a bathroom at all and repays his old boss with the ultimate insult of finding him unpaintable. Between shows in Europe and Taipei, this hip offspring of anticommunism lives off the generosity of an archetypal, wholegrain American lefty. Tu-2's landlady Isa reminds me of my own radical relations, with her graying pigtails, her house crammed with back issues of *Monthly Review* and Guatemalan oven mitts, plus her strident attempts to get the idle class in her building to join early-morning neighborhood tree-plantings and protests against a new L.A. football stadium.

She calls the lucky members of her low-rent *rancho* "a family," but I'm not sure how Tu-2 relates with a taciturn British screenwriter and a bearded anarchist dermatologist who is the spitting image of George Bernard Shaw sitting amidst the succulent garden. Then there's the overtly gay and equally joyous white director for black theater companies who immediately invites us to watch the smog set and sip wine during each evening's purposely unmotivated "porch time." Passing his porch in the morning, we involuntarily witness the dramaturg's gnomic form greeting the day with yoga in the nude. Tu-2's prim Chinese mom had received a more rude initiation to the "land of fruits and nuts" by taking a trip to this neighbor's toilet, wallpapered with pinups of male porn beefcake. "Now that," jokes Tu-2, "is where too much Chinese food gets you!"

While we wait for higher-priced establishments to fax their invitations to "tea for two" with Tu-2, the artist packs us into his high-raked, four-wheeled Mitsubishi jeep. Intimidating as O. J.'s Bronco, it's perfect for an urban safari down the wilds of Sunset Boulevard. Just before the refurbished Union Station, we come to the core of L.A.'s old Chinatown. Too bad it's nothing like the atmospheric finale in Polanski's film of the same name—or even as Chinese as Hollywood's campy Grauman's movie palace. Like Australia's gold fields, this area was first inhabited by migrants from Canton's Sze Yap district. The population grew significantly after Chinese fled San Francisco's 1906 earthquake. But while the writing on the wall is still in pictographs—no gang graffiti here—Chinatown's streets have lost their necessary clamor. Parking garages far outnumber pagodas. In Angeleno style, the neighborhood has devolved into two parallel strips become glorified freeway ramps.

As for eats, the Sam Woo chain has piped-in Tex-Mex music and is popular mainly for offering steamed crabs at under six dollars a pop. Tu-2's first choice, and that of many others, is a noodle joint called Kim Chuy—where all the character is in the food, a rarity in L.A. "I used to come here with a film-school girlfriend," Tu confesses. "When we broke up, she admitted that she missed the won ton more than me."

We've barely sat down before we're served broth-soaked coils of especially luscious noodles. "These are Chaozhou-style, which are less tough because we use more eggs than water," explains the owner, an older gent who ought to know, since he bills himself "the king of Chaozhou noodles." His place is also pretty royal when it comes to mashed taro and white lotus, grilled rice-flour onion cakes, and more noodles served in *sha cha jiang,* a Chaozhou trademark sauce and the Chinese homage to satay made from peanuts, dried shrimps, and sesame.

Fleeing the Japanese, the king had left the coastal Chaozhou homeland in northern Guangdong to set up shop in Cambodia—or so I gather, since his story gets passed from Chaozhou dialect to Cantonese to Mandarin to Californian as it moves around the table. Aside from the Khmer Rouge, Kissinger's carpet bombing, and the killing fields, conditions weren't bad for noodle-making. By comparison, L.A. had proved a bit more hospitable. Living off the patriarch are more members of his clan than there are diners—though there are enough of those to form a continual wait. As the head of the Chaozhou Association, Kim Chuy's proprietor also helps provide old age benefits and proper funerals for a community that has swelled with Southeast Asian Chinese to the tune of seventy thousand Chaozhou. Not even the U.S. census can verify such claims in a town where illegal migrant populations are tossed about as lightly as five-figure movie options.

Like most Chinese, the Chaozhou have moved away from this dirty, expensive Chinatown to sunnier, suburban climes. Before heading that way ourselves, Mei and I are invited to the Empress Palace, astonishingly opulent inside a half-abandoned mall. The restaurant is like Hong Kong in every detail, down to some of the best dim sum I've had in ages, including mushrooms wrapped in sticky rice-flour rolls and transparent dumplings stuffed with a biting pesto of Chinese chives. Our host is a physics professor at Cal State Northridge with a no-nonsense manner, a straight-up Ozzie Nelson hairdo, and so many ballpoints in his shirt pocket that I'm reminded of Mei's favorite taunt at me: "If you carry one pen, you're a writer; if you carry two pens, you're a scholar; if you carry three pens, you're a pen repairman."

According to our host, "Being a writer is best of all, because no foreigner can ever take your job away." Somehow, I never thought I possessed so much job security. Having sponsored many other Chinese, including the film star Joan Chen, the prof's years in L.A. have left him thoroughly Americanized. He's also Chinese enough to have lived about four other lives. Before physics ever entered the picture, he'd fled China and become a Taiwanese tuna fisherman, a "long liner" as they were called. According to him, all the waters of the South China Sea had been pretty much fished out generations ago. Now he hopes to publish a novel based on his seafaring days. Who knows, there could be a movie in this! And we're just one of a thousand cozy groups in the cavernous dining hall, dreaming of deals done over chicken feet. The Chinese didn't just invent paper and gunpowder. They perfected networking, too.

Supposedly, it was in L.A.'s Chinatown that baker David Jung first created the fortune cookie. Inspired by ancient Chinese rebels placing secret messages inside buns, he conceived of them as a way of handing out cheery slogans to down-and-out World War I vets. In the beginning, they were just sweet egg rolls stuffed with biblical one-liners. In those days, a bowl of rice here cost five cents and it was fifteen for chop suey—and people actually ate chop suey. But not even the sharpest cookie could have predicted what one old-time restaurateur terms "L.A.'s great change." Before immigration restrictions were loosened in the sixties, there had been thirty-five thousand Chinese in the city. Now, some estimates put the number at seven hundred thousand, or nearly a third of all Chinese in America.

"There was one Chinese bank," this old-time chef recalls, "and now we've got more than two billion in assets." Without the white backlash to the Rodney King riots, liberal councilman Mike Woo would have been elected the country's first Chinese big-city mayor.

More dramatic still has been the creation of fully incorporated, all-Chinese towns known collectively as Little Taipei. Alhambra to Monterey Park to Rosemead. West of downtown, a notch below Pasadena, the San Gabriel Valley is the Middle Kingdom's main place in the sun. Sooner or later, Mei and I are bound to end up in this Chinatown in Cinerama. As it turns out, the call comes that very evening. We're invited to try our luck at the lucky, lucky, lucky 888 Seafood Restaurant. (Since *eight* sounds like "wealthy" in Cantonese, the numerologically mad Chinese find nothing quite so propitious as being "behind the eight ball.")

We invite along Isa, who makes us detour through her beloved Elysian Park, its palm fronds barely glimpsed through the dusk and pollution, avoiding the much-loathed freeway in favor of what feels like an unending demilitarized zone. At last, we emerge onto a strip where the signs are all in Chinese. But the concrete flatness takes away any sense that this is any place other than another Azusa (everything from *a* to *z* in the U.S.A.) It isn't easy to spot the 888 among the estimated two thousand Chinese restaurants in the area, most of which are inside covered arcades or set beside Lucky's Drugs and Ralph's Supermarkets. Arriving early on a weeknight, we find more fish in the display tank—eight, of course—than people dining in the vast, overlit dining room. This allows us to be supervised with fearsome desperation by a wise-cracking Chinese-Vietnamese.

"This my brother!" he keeps saying with a cackle about a newspaper photo of himself in younger days. Quickly, we become this manager's brother, too. Even Isa, a militant vegetarian, gets the full treatment—including a salad featuring mayonnaise and mock crab with fruit, in a style termed "Chaozhou plus Cantonese plus nouvelle." Somehow, it all works, as does the yin-yang shrimp, peppered or mild and serving with the ubiquitous tart "X.O." sauce. The crabs are as good as they could be outside of Vancouver; the braised *e-fu* noodles don't make me say, "Phooey!" I even learn that the name is derived from a boil-then-bake method perfected by the renowned E family. The owner, another self-made Chinese from Saigon, calls himself Harry and has eleven siblings, six employed here. "So," jokes his manager, "we have to expand soon!"

But Isa wants to raise consciousness among these money-driven newcomers, asking sternly, "Are you aware of all the heavy metals in large forms of marine life?" These Chinese want their marine life as heavy as possible. They prefer to test their sauce on live animals. "I can't stand to be cruel to a crustacean," says Isa.

By dessert, the manager gathers his courage to tell a joke about a Chinese greenhorn who is thrilled to discover that his favorite brand of meat is available all over America. Thinking that a "hot dog" is something canine, he reacts to the sight of the tubular sausage by declaring, "I didn't say I wanted that part of the dog!"

Isa barely musters a titter at the sexist humor. But the manager cracks up at his own cleverness, covering his embarrassed smile with cupped hands the way Korean ladies do when picking their teeth. When Isa demands a doggy bag lest her Chinese greens go to waste, invoking the starving children of East L.A. instead of China, Mister 888 replies, "Not correct to call it doggy bag! Here, we call it the human box!"

Our host is far slicker at Charming Garden, the first and best Hunan-style restaurant in Little Taipei. Hang Feng is a sober boss who also runs a seafood distribution company while managing the U.S. branch of a business begun by his illustrious father.

"He was once a student leader for the Kuomintang in Shanghai. Number three on the list to be killed by the Communists," claims Hang Feng. In exile, Chiang Kai-shek "pushed my father into becoming a city councilman," but the elder Hang got fed up with politics and turned to show business promoting. Says Hang Feng, "My dad was the biggest. He brought the Osmond Brothers to Taiwan."

In some cultures, it might have been a comedown for a one-time politician to turn restaurateur. But Hang Feng's father even made his son work two years as a waiter to learn his rigorous trade from the bottom up. "Just when I was making good money, my father called to tell me to go work in the kitchen!" There's no saying no to Pops in the Confucian order. "I did all the worst jobs for a year and a half. Now the cooks know they can't fool me."

They fill us with an afternoon feast of raw flounder poached in soup at our table, Hunan-cured ham stuffed between flat bread leaves, minced pigeon in lettuce leaves, a superb, crusty General Tso's chicken, finished off with a sweet, hot puree of walnuts. The Charming Garden is Chinese cooking at a level that should be so easy to replicate, yet one that hardly exists in the United States. Consistency, care, and pride—and no greasy residue, no indefinable brown sauce.

Never mind gangs, smog, or drive-by shootings. After this first taste, we've got to brave the freeways and head back to Little Taipei that very evening. Besides, this time, we're riding high in Tu-2's jeep. When the address we've got for a Shanghainese pick turns out to be outdated, we begin cruising willy-nilly. Isn't this, after all, the truest expression of our quest's original concept? I don't mind doing it in this neighborhood anyway, where pot holes are outnumbers by pot stickers and each takeout kitchen offers a different regional flavor. Maybe we can get our driver a bumpersticker that reads, "I Brake for Dumplings."

Our first stop is the Taste of Sichuan takeaway, where perfect folds of fresh won ton dough are soaked in slippery chili oil. Everything in these parts comes in styrofoam, but I feel nonetheless like I've been transported straight back to Chengdu. Standing by the kitchen pass-through is a chunky woman with blue eyes and short, dirty blonde hair, packed into a gray flannel uniform with handcuffs jangling from her belt loops. The cooks are astonished when this off-duty security guard blusters out her order in perfect Shandong dialect—laced with a vernacular of insults. Mei is shocked as well and can't help mur-

muring, "Your Chinese is so good!" The women continues on in Mandarin, insisting with nasty impatience, "I was born in China. I speak Chinese. I am Chinese!"

Mei doesn't dare attempt to solve the mystery, but she's convinced when this swaggering tomboy tells the restaurant staff, "When you want to kill someone, don't aim for the head. Shoot them in the stomach and let them bleed." In Monterey Park, everything is just like home—even this cruel empress of Pinkerton's.

Meanwhile, Tu-2 has slipped off to the next bare-bones mall stall with six tables and several generations of women working miracles in a galley kitchen. He goes into paroxysms of nostalgia over the stinky tofu—a deep-fried cake of fermented beans that doesn't taste nearly as bad as it smells, or smell half as bad in the States as it did in Taiwan. I'm proud to swallow several chunks, though I can't quite grasp the appeal.

"This is very Hakka and I'm Hakka to my bones," Tu-2 reveals as he coos over smoked bean curd with pork intestines and pickled greens. "That's why I can relate so well to Jews!" This still doesn't quite clarify for me how the Hakka "guest people" became the wandering Jews among Chinese.

"Growing up, I was always ridiculed and ostracized by the mainlanders. But that's not as bad as what the mainlanders did to the native Taiwanese!" Tu-2 cries, reaching a note high enough to shatter his glass of tea. "When the Kuomintang took over the island, they murdered at least fifty thousand!" I don't know if the numbers are true, but I'm not surprised that my education in Taiwanese history can only be completed in Southern California. Or that Tu-2 wants to get some respect for his native food from Mei.

"She's my long-lost sister," he tells me. "You are lucky to have found a true Chinese woman. With true Chinese values!" Stung by her jibes at his unintentional, L.A.-style self-promotion, he promises, "Little sister, I will study my Confucius and become more humble every day."

For the next two hours, Tu-2 happily leads our motorized conquest of Valley Boulevard, which passes through Alhambra, San Gabriel, and Rosemead on its monotonous way back to the Forbidden City. Shall we sample that old diner turned into a Shanghai dumpling parlor? Go for some Beijing wheat cakes or another seafood splurge? There are no Denny's or Wendy's out here. Just a million Wong's and Woo's, a speeding Sinophile's dream.

At one strategic intersection in San Gabriel, we turn into a vast, cheery, two-story shopping center that's more parking than building. Somewhere among these dairy-white facades is the only American branch of Dong Lai Shun, Beijing's most fabled hot pot emporium. And that's just for starters. Could this be a culinary theme park, something like the mini-China in Canton where tourists can get from Tibet to the Great Wall in a hundred easy steps? Too bad the atmosphere is deadly and previous snacking has killed our appetites. I should have known that L.A.'s greatest hits would end up in a mall. Connected by escalators between outdoor rungs, this one developers' fancy just might constitute the best Chinese restaurant of all.

Beef with Ginger and Scallions in Clay Pot

From Charming Garden

Ingredients:

Beef, $^1/_2$ lb.
Scallions (Green Onions), 6 pieces
Ginger, 3 slices
Chinese marinated black bean, 1 tbs.
Cornstarch, $^1/_4$ tsp.
Peanut oil, 1 cup

Marinade:
1 egg white
Soy sauce, $^1/_2$ tsp.
Rice wine, $^1/_4$ tsp.
Cornstarch, $^1/_2$ tsp.

Sauce:
Wine, $^1/_8$ tsp.
Chicken broth, $^1/_2$ tsp.

Slice the beef thinly and against the grain. Pour the marinade onto the sliced beef. Gently fold the sauce into the meat slices. Slice the scallions into 2-inch long pieces. Put the garlic cloves through a press. Place the black beans in a bowl, cover with water, let stand for ten minutes, then drain the water and mash the beans. Blend the cornstarch and water until smooth.

Heat the oil in a medium hot pan; sauté the beef briefly, then remove it for later use, leaving the oil in the pan. Add the garlic and beans to the pan; sauté them and then return the beef to the pan, stir-frying until fully cooked. Add the sauce, then the cornstarch mixture, and stir for another thirty seconds.

Pour a little oil into a clay pot and heat on the stove. Add scallions and ginger until they become fragrant, then add the mixture from the pan and serve.

Raisinets and Mandarettes

L eave it to L.A. to be on the cutting edge of "New Age Chinese." Naturally, this is the place where five thousand years' tradition must be fused with yesterday's fad. Sprightly Viennese chef Wolfgang Puck, not content to feed the stars at Spago's and the masses with frozen California pizza, has begotten Chinois on Main. Can we find a contender for our top ten in sea-blown Santa Monica, amidst bagel shops, movie memorabilia, and fern-loaded cafes that offer organic smoothies along with surfing the World Wide Web?

The decor of Chinois is mostly Southwestern turquoise and pink, the one Eastern touch an incongruous Buddha statuette reclining, untempted, above the wine rack. Our waiter has a French accent so thick that I suspect he's a kid from Des Moines doing his best Charles Boyer. The busboys are burly Fernando Valenzuelas trucking about languorously in black mandarin frocks. Not even in L.A. have they yet dared to offer the all-eunuch wait staff.

Puck's open kitchen is bicameral, symbol of an uneasy coexistence. Fronted by a sushi bar and prep table, two sets of ranges are set back-to-back. On one, there are several grimy woks; on the other, only long-handled sauce pans. But nearly all the staff is working concentratedly over the latter, making sure that the *coulis* has a perfect consistency and the crème (with ginger) is correctly *brûlée*. Our Chinese chicken with cashews has a sauce so soupy that it can't stick to the quiveringly Caucasian chunks of bird. Baby eggplants, smothered in red pepper strips, are even soggier. As Puck explains in a cookbook for sale at the bar, he disdains cornstarch and so prefers to do his stir-frying in butter!

"Not half bad," pronounces Mei. But which half is that?

At Chinois, East and West may be hooked up to the same gas pipe, but their twain has not met. Perhaps the marriage can only take place when Chinese themselves are exposed to new flavors and clientele. The result is certainly more satisfying at Mandarette, a spare corner eatery along a campy strip that has given the world such landmark boutiques as "Cowboys and Poodles." Despite Tu-2's glowing endorsement, I'm skeptical that any decent food can be served in a laundromat now outfitted with track lighting, painted a weathered gold, and decorated solely with unfurled Chinese robes. But the bill of fare is as tastefully pared down as the surroundings. Homemade onion cakes, a fish fillet in fresh chili sauce, everything comes from the kitchen as a less oily, more playful version of a Chinese standard. Like most of L.A.'s leading Chinese owners, this one hails from Taiwan and turns out to be an inveterate gourmet. He's just been hired as a consultant to Lettuce Entertain You, an upscale chain in Chicago, and soon begins raving about a new Mexican place there that serves its fruity desserts inside a sweet, soft-shelled taco.

"But have you ever had Wenchang chicken? Lotus root in mustard?" Always thinking to aid the cause, Mei starts filling in the owner on the best dishes of every place we've been in the world. I nudge her under the table to stop, or at least ask for a consulting fee.

"The key in L.A.," this knowing gent assures us, "isn't the food, but constant remodeling." Is it image or eats that wins knowing nods from Mandarette's all-Caucasian, all-satisfied clientele? "Warren Beatty and Bruce Springsteen eat here," says our host, as though reading from a plaque. "Madonna, she orders vegetables only."

Back in his four-wheel ricemobile, Tu-2 imitates, dreaming of glory, "The artist Tu-2, he orders only oysters . . ."

"Especially," adds Mei, "after kicking his balls."

On a final, sunny afternoon, Mei and I head out to stately, mon-eyed Pasadena to check out the highly rated Yujean Kang's. Some years back, there had been a place with that same unusual name on the outskirts of Berkeley. There, it was but one of dozens aimed at luring student traffic, but this present branch has become L.A.'s number one Chinese according to local magazine rankings. Lunch-time is packed with businessmen and blue rinse matrons. There are few tanned movie people here, but even fewer Chinese. Hardly hob-nobbing with the almost-famous, the man whose name is on the marquee can barely be coaxed out of his basement office. Yujean Kang is an unaffected, hands-in-the-pocket sort. His broad face is topped with a squared-off military haircut, his burliness accentuated by a thick tan sweater stretched several sizes too big.

"Customers spend less in America. They treat Chinese food like pizza," huge Yujean shrugs at his success, taking off on a series of apologies for why Chinese food in the States can never match restaurants like the one his mother ran back in Taiwan. "Over there, all the cooks are trying to outdo one another. Here, we do our best within the limitations." For instance, "Italian prosciutto works better with our green beans than the original Yunnan ham."

With an unseen snap of Yujean's fingers, his staff bears perfectly understeamed sea bass with fermented black beans as a kind of bitter icing, crowned by a wreath of baby bok choy. All the items on Yu-jean's menu are ingeniously combined and thoroughly Chinese with-out being too terribly exotic.

"Whenever a Chinese knows how to cook good," grouses Yujean, "they call it nouvelle."

Maybe so, but what else can I call his kumquat polenta? Fusion food? Or is this just ordinary fare in a looney-tunes town where everybody can eat their favorite fantasies even if they can't live them out?

During rush hour, Mei takes me along to beautiful Burbank where an old college friend known for her spiked blond hair, now covered with a beret, is moving up the ranks of Walt Disney animators. We get the studio tour through cubicles of drafting tables where, amidst exposed pastel ducts and ping pong tables, a corporate army of Santa's helpers inch along to complete storyboard quotas whose fairy tale progress is charted on every bulletin board in sight. Then we meet Tu-2 at a nearby projection room for the world premiere of a ten-minute short that a film school pal has taken six years to complete. So agitated is this director about his premiere that Tu-2 had to ferry him to the hospital this morning to have his stomach pumped. Who wouldn't, when showing the first reel in a proposed feature about seven past girlfriends? Number one is a guitar-strumming earth child, quite pregnant by another man, who bares all in a confessional, weekend encounter.

"Poignantly Woody Allen. Cassavetes real . . ." Everyone in the screening room raves about the effort, no doubt hoping to land a spot on the crew in case more funds are raised.

"Since I didn't get discovered," quips Mei, "I'll just have to discover myself."

To touch base with any reality in this town, we have to return to the sections that speak a foreign tongue. By the time we've coaxed Tu-2 into a last cruise back down the San Gabriel Valley, the main strip is half-dimmed, the few restaurants open are dumpling houses or those that advertise themselves as "Hong Kong–style Western." Featuring the black bean club sandwich. A lurid purple sign lures us into taking a chance at the Good Chances Restaurant. How can we go wrong with a name like that? "In Chinese," gropes Mei, as we ascend one last time from our Darth Vader jeep, "the characters mean something about the tender feelings that keep falling like the rain."

There's no rain in L.A. and we're a long way from the proprietors' native Taipei. Moved by his tender feelings, or an attempt to test the outer limits of my sensibilities, Tu-2 orders such Taiwanese favorites as snail meats stir-fried with basil and garlic, strips of smoked bean curd and pork with yellow leeks, and crab roe atop sautéed loofah—a vaguely bitter, mint-green squash baring little resemblance to the popular scrubbing sponge. Our midnight treat ends with a stomach-smothering blanket of rice porridge laced with sweet yams.

Good Chances will never have the good fortune to gain a Gault-

Millaut rating. But someday, I'd like to return to try the Mint and Duck Tongue, the Three Cup Rabbit, the Clam and Winter Melon Soup. To my taste buds, these combinations are playful and resourceful enough. Take a pass on menus that spin computerized variants of "chicken with cashews, chicken with snow peas, chicken with chicken . . ." Real Chinese cuisine has been nouvelle since old Lao Tzu was still a tot.

Besides, no pan-Asian bistro can offer us the garnish of fresh-grated history. At Good Chances, the lone waitress tells us to stick around to meet the head chef. "You know, he once cook for Mao!"

I suppose Chinese scullions of all loyalties could do with this pedigree. At this point on the journey, we've heard the claim more than a few times, beginning in Yue Bin, our first and favorite Beijing hole-in-the-wall. But this obscure dinette on a dark block in Little Taipei seems the least likely place to find a revolution's kitchen help. Emerging from his labors, this one appears the quintessential Chinese cook: pallid, drained of passion, but seemingly tireless, ageless, and possessing those agile yet perpetually water-logged hands. However, Meng Qing Chuan can list some unique work experience on his resume.

Back in '64, just when the Cultural Revolution was about to break loose, this Beijinger was plucked from the kitchen of the opulent Anglers' Roost State Guest House to serve as part of a three-man galley crew on Chairman Mao Zedong's personal train. Aside from a brief investigation to make sure that his working class lineage was "red to the roots," Meng never had to show any special talent nor receive special training. Along with his beloved Hunan stewed pork, the Great Helmsman had simple wants.

"Just three dishes and a soup," says Meng. "The leaders ate like the people ate." Though he remained on the train for sixteen years, he seems to have had little chance to converse with the man himself. At least, this is as much as I can get from Mei, who can barely keep up with every tenth sentence once this seemingly laconic fellow gets up to speed. No word either on whether Mao was a good tipper. The chef does recall the day he was sent through the train to find a certain young miss only to realize by process of elimination that she had to be in Mao's bunk. He also has strong memories of an infamous assassination attempt by Mao's scheming second-in-command, Lin Biao.

"We sat for days in the Shanghai station behind a special wall. Four leaders came to warn Mao and the train took off. We usually went sixty kilometers an hour, but this time we went one hundred forty. Since we couldn't make our usual stops, we soon ran out of water for cooking. I had to empty the sinks and toilets of the passenger compartments." That must have been some hot and sour soup.

With the revolution off the rails, the chef was reassigned by Mao's successor, Hua Guofeng, then offered a chance to try his skills in a New Jersey restaurant. When this enterprise went under, the chef stopped off in L.A. to see a friend. "My ticket back to China was already in hand," he swears. But the dinner he cooked convinced the guests that he should stay and work for them. Now what would the Red Sun of Tiananmen say about his former charge deserting to Tinseltown's wrong side of the ideological tracks? And cooking up Taiwanese specialties yet?

"I thought of Mao as a great person. But I never worshipped him," says this primal proletarian. And now? "Now, I think nothing."

Not even of Mickey Mao? The answer, like the conversation, seems all too matter-of-fact. For Mei and Tu-2, this is just another chance encounter with one of millions of woeful brethren. It's only me, the outsider, who is thrilled to see our journey coming full circle back to lofty Peking's inner circles of power. Once more, I'm reminded that the divide between cooks and leaders is never that great. One is always privy to the gossip, no matter how distant from the source. One is always Chinese, even close by the San Bernardino Freeway. I feel humbled to be part of this fraternity, so global in reach and yet so discreet, this life behind kitchen doors that has nothing to do with the cars whizzing past, the valley girls, and the bible salesmen; the motorized procession going nowhere because it can never get home; America's endless boulevards that aren't nearly so long or illuminated as the story of China.

San Fan City

An hour from home after nine days on the road, fourteen months of Chinese food, and nearly three years without a permanent address, Mei insists that we brake for—dare I admit?—sushi. In Cupertino, across eight vapid lanes from the world headquarters of Apple Computer, is her longtime favorite high-class Japanese, serving the finest raw fish to the Silicon Valley's top programmers. Given the Chinese belief in foods both warm and cooked, it's remarkable how much Mei adores sea urchin eggs and unboiled sweet shrimp. While she ingests plankton to her heart's content, I eavesdrop on the dinner conversation of some well-heeled, Nike-shod technocrats. While I've been off learning ancient cooking terms, my homeland has created new ones like *home page, workfare,* and *Gingrichite.* When America changes, does it always change for the worse? The only hopeful sign is that liberals and conservatives still share slices of yellowtail.

Mei and I know that we're really home when we have to drag our Chinese trunk and other valuables out of the car and up sixty steps into one of those San Francisco Victorians as haughtily upright as a spinster reacting to a sexy postcard. The same journalist responsible for my having met Mei outside the Berkeley cinematheque welcomes us back with a note telling us that she's out at yet another flick. Where every new sensation is available, none are ever enough. And the talk of this town is always about the latest restaurant and the latest hair salon. The search for both items is about as enduring as anything here—when nothing should be easier to find than a good haircut or a good meal.

The trouble is that San Franciscans remain tourists in their own town. True natives are about as rare as Republicans or rubber galoshes—and the rest of us, refugees from America's grimy East Coast or the world's teeming East, still have trouble convincing ourselves that we actually deserve a permanent perch on the wind-scrubbed hillocks of this multicultural sand castle. *San Fan City,* as the Chinese half-Anglicize, may be the best term for a town whose biggest civic celebrations are Gay Freedom Day and Chinese New Year. With its Zen fogs and brown shingles, beat cafes and end-of-the-line wistfulness, America comes West only to find that the Orient has got there ahead of them. After all, San Francisco's Macao and Woosung, run by a Mr. Asing with pigtails under his stovepipe, was supposedly America's first Chinese restaurant! The Chinese presence that's been central to the city's identity right from the start has served as a license for all new arrivals to get off-center, if not mystical.

When friends invite us to their latest find, the Yellow River Hakkanese, we find a waiter who has immigrated to major in English Lit., quoting Melville and Hemingway while bearing the salt-baked prawns. At this point, Mei and I are more impressed by the two-pound, bean-filled bomb canister of a Mission district *carne asada* burrito. But ours is a concept that just won't quit. Even after we stop looking, the restaurants come to us. When Mei is offered a part-time job leading orientation seminars for oil company execs being transferred to Beijing, I come along to lecture on culture shock. Here's one subject where I've earned my advanced degree. As Chinese eating etiquette will figure heavily in future business dealings, Mei and I soon find ourselves getting paid one more time to eat Chinese food.

We initiate our students at the Cantonese-sounding Sam Lok, decorated like many Chinatown dives with a huge blowup of Hong Kong harbor, but recommended to us as the one true Sichuanese restaurant in town. Indeed, they actually heap their stir-fried kidney with the numbing, clove-sweet peppercorns that I didn't think had yet reached our shores. Owned by mainlanders, Sam Lok is susceptible to the un- even efforts of mainland chefs. Our trainees get an accurate preview of all the spongelike, oil-soaked bean curd they'll have to choke down! Wu Kong, a sedate place in the shopping center carved from downtown's former Rincon postal center, bills itself as a "breakthrough" restaurant. While I had already come away with a flaccid lunch special complete with cold hot-and-sour soup, Mei knows how to find the Shanghainese standards that this place does best. The only upscale Chinese that's worth the ensuing loss in atmo-sphere is Yank Sing, a financial district dim sum house with impeccable standards and a giant spinach dumpling that in one bite outdoes all the tortellini in nearby North Beach.

Before the seminar ends with an educational video—the very

same *Wild East* film in which Mei had appeared to discuss bound feet and post-Maoist foreplay—the schedule calls for a stroll through Chinatown. The only disclaimer that Mei and I can offer about the world's most picturesque slum is that any resemblance to China, real or imaginary, living or dead, is purely coincidental. Even the pagoda-like turrets along Chinatown's Grant Street were part of a calculated plan to create a tourist fantasyland. When San Francisco's powers-that-be threatened to move all Chinese out of the city center after the 1906 earthquake, a clever land developer saved the day by commissioning American architects to create an environment they considered "exotic."

Fortunately, the Chinese have a way of subverting all attempts at glamorization. T-shirt shops and electronics marts—run by Israelis who greet Mei like an old pal from her days as a Chinese opera promoter—are still outnumbered by outdoor vegetable stands combed over by the world's wariest shoppers, squares full of decrepit chess players, smelly back alleys, and housing projects that could pass for Chinese torture chambers. Aside from the abundance of fresh crabs and braised noodles at the lime-green Yuet Lee and various Hong Kong–style joints, much of the food isn't so much unreal as unkempt. How to comment on a highly praised vegetarian lunch counter where a boiled head of lettuce comes drenched in bottled oyster sauce? The food is even worse at a series of banquets where we discover Chinese "champagne"—a fizzy cider that's all food coloring—and observe the number of times that suave new Mayor Willie Brown pays obeisance to rich Chinese contributors. Mei and I develop a customary route: a favorite bakery for barbecued pork buns; the best market to pick up fresh snapper and crabs, and even fresher pea flowers; and a stop to see the world's best-named bank officer, Wells Fargo's Tiger Wong. Chinatown is a great place to shop, but we don't necessarily want to eat there.

Our "orientation" course concludes with a trip toward the ocean to the Richmond District, San Francisco's newer and truer Chinatown—and the neighborhood where Mei and I were living when we met. Having once dismissed this corridor along the north flank of Golden Gate Park as less than truly San Franciscan—no hills out here, no "painted lady" Victorian homes—I've come to feel that no other section so accurately reflects the city where the United Nations was founded. In this intermediate stop between immigration and assimilation, you scarcely realize how much of the world has moved in next door until you go looking for a restaurant. On Clement Street—say "Cle-*ment*" and never say "'Frisco"—there's a veritable United Nations of eating, with respectable Chinese entries like the Shanghainese breakfast snacks at the Fountain Court, the seafood at the Ocean, *jiao zi* at the Taiwan, clay pots and gritty salt-baked chicken at the Hakkanese chain, Ton Kiang. Only Geary's legendary Hong Kong Flower Lounge, part of an international group whose outlet near the San Francisco airport has been packed ever since its opening, lives up to its reputation for consistency with a few stellar specialties like their stuffed tofu in the shape of the pi-pa instrument and tender fillet of lightly smoked black cod.

Now is our big chance to meet a San Francisco legend. Like Herb Caen, Dashiel Hammett, and Emperor Norton, Tommy Toy is one of those names that have become wedded to the city's image of itself. I think of him as a man born in tuxedo, noodlemaker to the stars. His latest incarnation, Tommy Toy's Haute Cuisine Chinoise, is a somber, over-sumptuous lair that's decidedly for the executive set. The place no longer has the show-biz pizzazz or the menu of the 1950s. With the emphasis on "signature dishes" like beef fillets and steamed lobsters that are barely dressed in a hint of ginger, this is Chinese food that is definitely "chopsticks optional."

Still, I'm not surprised to find that Tommy himself is minding the store. "I got the idea for our new menu in Hong Kong, because I knew that we could do it here for one-third the price," he rightly explains, though the point of this restaurant isn't a bargain. He upholds the elegance with dark blue shirt and expensive suit, but Mr. Toy's choppy bangs looked permed and dyed. "Yes, I catered for Nixon at San Clemente. Frank Sinatra was one of my regulars," he states offhandedly. "But I don't think of myself as that successful. I started out as a dishwasher and I've always put in a good day's work. It's even tougher when your name is on the canopy. This is where my father was born and I've never lived anywhere else."

Somehow, there's always room to leave a mark in this oddball city. Perhaps San Francisco ranks high solely at creating uncanned, eccentric originals. When Peter Fang came from Shanghai fifteen years back, he hardly expected to become a doorkeeper trying to regulate the flow of the city's longest line. At lunch or dinner, the sidewalk on the last block of Kearny before curving into Columbus is packed with the hip and the restless patiently waiting as though at the food stamps office to enter the narrow portals of Fang's funky House of Nanking. With two woks facing the front glass and furiously fired to feed them all, "House" is probably the ultimate hole-in-the-wall. Though his tiled walls are cluttered with four-star reviews and culinary distinction, Peter Fang can barely bring himself to expand into the next storefront. Maybe he likes crowds. In a slick aviator jacket worn with the flaps up, hawk eyes, and hair done in a burr hairdo flared out at the side in square edges, Fang prowls the crowded galley beside his precious few tables looking like a Chinese James Dean. But just like Tommy Toy, he's still the nervous immigrant who worked seven days a week to establish his American foothold and stays close to the store to keep failure at bay.

What packs in his loyal clientele are immense portions, served on sizzling skillets, of dishes unusual enough to be sought after and ordinary enough to be readily savored. Creativity meets home cooking in the baby eggplants over noodles and the staple Nanking chicken—deep-fried strips of breast meat coated with sesame seeds and a seared, almost hot, sauce. For Chinese, however, Fang prefers to put out his flash-fried catch of the day, smothered in wilted, vinegar-pickled greens. The saltiness, and lack of sauce, bespeak his native Shanghai, yet there's no way to categorize the small-is-beautiful menu as anything but pure Fang. "You can taste love in every one of Peter Fang's dishes," one review on display exclaims. Amazing, how often love tastes like garlic!

Mei and I are finding that our hometown is just a bit too casual—and Cantonese—to produce a truly world class entry. Our last hope is the very Californian China Moon Cafe, a modified luncheonette done up in bold black-and-white checkerboard softened by a single symbolic hanging orb. Caucasian chefs with their long locks in nets put on a window display of prepping and tossing.

I'm a bit skeptical of a Chinese restaurant without a Chinese hand in sight, but creator and self-described "China nut" Barbara

Tropp proves to be a one-woman Gang of Four. A wiry, intense woman with enormous eyes highlighted by chic short hair, Tropp admits, "I was just another Jewish kid from a small town in Jersey who made it to Princeton." Then she made it to Taiwan to study Chinese and found herself feeling incredibly at home in a culture where "people actually sit around and talk about what they're going to eat tomorrow." So she decided to devote her life to honoring the Confucian phrase about the importance of eating that we've heard so often. Only Tropp's translation gives *min yi shi wei tian* an American twist: "For the salt of the earth, food is where it's at."

In voluminous cookbooks, Tropp has shown off her devotion to much Chinese lore. This has even extended to her faith in Chinese medicine to combat a lengthy illness. Now she admits that she plans to close her beloved China Moon rather than let its name be sullied by others.

"Restaurants are part fantasy, a little like theater," she tells us as we jam together into a tiny back booth. "In this one, I try to project my love for all things Chinese." While the portions are minute and dolloped out onto Japanese ceramic trays, the prices more in the range of the charge-account set, Tropp's creations are, as she claims, "Chinese at the roots and Western in the branches."

Mei, the toughest judge, nods her head in agreement after we've sampled flat breads stuffed with pork and smeared with sweet hoisin, a mahi-mahi fillet topped with a carrot-and-cashew relish, duck slices combined with cold lotus root. "This isn't Pan-Asian food," Tropp insists. "Like the Chinese, I try to cut chicken with the bones, to honor the Chinese love for things slimy and chewy. We remember that oxygenated water makes the best tea."

She's also Chinese enough to admit that "the best cooking is really at home. But often I discovered that the dishes I tested at home didn't work in a restaurant. When you cook in a commercial setting, you've got to turn up the volume—and make the food at once more obvious and more complex. It's something like putting on heavy makeup for the stage lights." Observes the unadorned Tropp about her competition, "Most of the Chinese restaurants here are afraid to use all the wonderful native California produce. They'd rather use something from a jar to stay traditional."

But this isn't a town for the traditional. As Tropp explains her presence here, "I just never felt comfortable in New Jersey." Spoken like an honorary Chinese—and a true San Franciscan.

Smoked Black Cod

From the Hong Kong Flower Lounge

Ingredients:

Fresh black cod, 2 lb. cut into $1^1/_2$ inch-thick fillets
10 celery leaves
Carrot, 1 thinly sliced
Cilantro, 3 sprigs
Powdered ginger, pinch
2 scallions
Sugar, 3 tsp.
Chinese rice wine, 1 tsp.
Chinese cooking wine, 1 tsp.

Marinate the fish fillets in all the ingredients for 2–3 days. Score the top of the fish with the grain, then bake the fillets at 450 degrees. Pour a small amount of butter or vegetable oil atop the fish and serve.

So Can Chu

While I've left my heart in San Francisco, I've stored my junk in Oakland. On the final day before a year's rental runs out on our self-stuffed bin, Mei and I borrow a flatbed truck from a Chinese building contractor and begin reassembling a home.

Unfortunately, a winter storm blows up right on cue. Mei has to help me rope down my belongings so they won't blow away on the Bay Bridge. I never thought that I'd see my bride wearing a flattened cardboard box on her head to keep from getting drenched. Transporting a messy writer's twenty years of first drafts beats living through the Cultural Revolution, but not by much.

A month of trying to get a step ahead of the classifieds crowd lands us a one-bedroom roost with a view of Mediterranean hills. The place is just big enough to be bearably cozy and the bushy-topped Monterey pine looming over the garage suggests to Mei the promise of future prosperity. The owner is an ex-hippie lawyer who immediately invites us to a Chinese restaurant in upstate Santa Rosa. Who says you've got to kill all landlords?

After bedding down in so many anonymous hotels, now comes the hard part. We have to agree on the firmness of a mattress and the design of our futon cover; integrate Chinese scrolls with Russian constructivist prints, Persian carpets and Che Guevara posters, collections of baseball cards and classical sheet music. And what will we do without room service or that next restaurant? We've managed to get married without receiving a single crock pot, blender, or set of flatware. Mei's bottom-line request is a dishwasher, which she calls "the marriage saver."

To further guarantee a good outcome to our domesticity, we pay a visit on Lin Yun, a renowned master of the "Black Hat" Buddhist sect who has been a shadowy presence in my life ever since he successfully predicted the imminent death by asphyxiation of a friend in Hong Kong. A Chinese mover and shaker by moving in the otherworldly, this jet-setting seer must have more frequent flyer miles than any other holy man—advising businesses, lecturing at colleges, and soothsaying on television throughout the Pacific Rim. "BEST CHI" (as in "life force") reads the license plate on the master's Mercedes, for Lin Yun is among the top authorities on *feng shui*, pronounced "fung-shway" and literally translated as "wind water." As we've already seen by the mirrors and red tassels in a hundred restaurants, this set of ancient Chinese beliefs—which Chinese beliefs *aren't* ancient?—govern the placement and design of homes, offices, and even tombstones to achieve luck in life and harmony in the afterlife. Beside a life-sized bust of himself in the plush lair of a colonnaded mansion, Lin Yun explains that he's set his world headquarters in Berkeley because of "the abundant *ch'i*, the deer which still come out of the hills, the intellectual activity in this place." And what about the resale values?

At his side for our marriage consultation—and, we hope, a Chinese lunch—are the usual bevy of devoted female followers, led by his dedicated Taiwanese girl Friday and mantra-chanter, Crystal Chu. There's a mysterious attraction to this heavy-set, giggling Lama who is half Sumo wrestler and half Howdy Doody—with Marine crew-cut, Buddha eyes too close together behind oval spectacles, and garlic-bulb nose. "The journalists in Taiwan always ask me about the movie starlets who dine with me," he will offer a perfect in-your-face karmic retort. "But they never write a word about my talks at M.I.T. So I tend to think that they must be revealing their own interests."

With thousands of restaurants having turned to him for "transcendental insurance," he also has plenty of choices when his interest turns to food. So I'm a bit disappointed when the entourage heads out for downtown Berkeley's sloppy, student-oriented Long Life Vegi-House. The food is hardly special, but Lin Yun shows us how the place has been made to seem larger and grander with a back wall of mirrors, how red tassels break the bad spell of a low ceiling, and how air circulation—and the circulation of tips—is improved by the addition of a wind chime or hung bamboo flute.

"The ch'i over China is very turbulent now," observes the master over his meal. Lin Yun believes that any push to unify with Taiwan is against the natural cycles of Chinese history—that now point toward a period of division and fragmentation. "From the point of view of ch'i," he observes with a chuckle, "either the current leaders do not possess sufficient wisdom, or they are so brilliant that no mere mortals can grasp their logic." That's about as partisan as his political remarks get—except to note that Bill Clinton wasn't born with "the unique, noble ch'i of President Bush."

Mei and I are honored when Lin Yun shuns more luxurious vehicles for a ride back in my creaky Honda Civic. "This car looks like a writer's car," he observes. But he's hardly disapproving of the mess and even gets a hearty laugh out of the gold-tasseled portrait of Chairman Mao hanging from my rearview mirror. I'm not sure if the device improves the *feng shui* in my car—or even if a car can have *feng shui*. At least, Lin Yun sees "longevity" in our forthcoming marriage—though he warns Mei and me of "unresolved problems." Instead of reading our minds, this Chinese must be divining the balance of our bank account.

"All can be overcome by throwing yourself into life," says Lin Yun. "Do not take the posture of waiting for death." Neither of us dare ask for more from a man who is as close to a psychic as I ever want to meet.

Berkeley must indeed be a good place for gurus because it's here that we find the reigning wizard of Chinese cookbooks, Ken Hom. Considering that we've already tried his Imperial City in London, and that he codifies and champions the international dominance of Hong Kong–style cooking, it's a bit surprising to see this young, hyperenergetic American-born Chinese working out of a ramshackle, two-story Victorian in the mostly African-American flatlands of Berkeley. A back conservatory overlooking a profuse California garden has been turned into a study lined with every cookbook known to man. A drafty old kitchen has been outfitted with several state-of-the-art restaurant stoves and a giant copper-covered vent. It's here that Hom and his longtime partner prepare a lunch in which every ingredient is measured to the half-ounce and poured from dixie cups. The results are tested by Mei and me, along with several workmen in paint-splotched coveralls taking a break from some house renovations.

The encounter encourages us to make one last stab at meeting the Bay Area's other culinary dynamo and the man who has come to virtually monopolize the business of popularizing Chinese cuisine in America. Martin Yan, whose virtuoso slicing and rapid-fire punning has made *Yan Can Cook* the most entertaining cooking show ever on television, appears to live his life at the speed with which he manipulates his cleaver. A number of messages finally bring the reply of a quick call from the San Francisco airport. Yan's about to board a plane for another of the culinary tours he leads to Asia, but promises to share a meal upon his return. "Just don't say that I am endorsing any one restaurant as the best," he insists. "The Bay Area has so many good chefs and I have so many friends that I wouldn't want to choose between them."

Since many of them have followed affluent Chinese to the south of San Francisco, we meet Yan at a private table on the second floor of Chef Chu's, a squat, bustling dinner house claiming a busy corner of the flat suburban strip of El Camino Real. At first glance, the place doesn't seem all that elegant or especially authentic. Yan himself leaves quite a different impression in person.

"Something happens to me when I'm in front of a camera," he half-apologizes. "Otherwise, I'm really quite boring." Actually, Yan looks even more handsome now that he has dropped his grinning persona. And his English doesn't slip into the humorous singsong cadence that he uses while performing. Shaking his hand, what amazes me is how disproportionately tiny it is, considering the miracles it performs on a cutting board.

"I learned everything from my mother in Canton, then left at thirteen and worked in Hong Kong restaurants," he recites. "The show, the success, it's all been unexpected. I endorse a lot of products now, I'm in demand at trade shows, but I want to be associated with quality products. I lost fifty thousand dollars on one of my tours to China, but I wanted the American chefs to see the real thing." Like a good Taoist, this most enthusiastic of wok-men insists, "If you are good at what you do, the people will find you. I really don't like to resort to hype."

I realize why we've been invited here as soon as our host for the evening appears. With Larry Chu around, Martin Yan can have a night out of the spotlight. In this tall, well-coifed, and authoritative man sporting his very own "Chef Chu" polo shirt, the TV personality has met his match in articulateness, self-promotion and zealous devotion to food. "If Yan can cook," he declares, "so can Chu!"

For the next three hours, he proves his point—with glazed pecans ringed with half-sour cucumber chunks, piles of tender facsimiles of Yunnan ham, a soup of "eight treasures" including abalone and shark's fin that slide down easily, braised ox-tail, and a wood-ear-laced *mu shu* pork accompanied by the thinnest of crepes that Chu describes as "the industry standard." The food is hardly groundbreaking but consistently complex and heartily northern without getting gritty.

"Our family practically patented Mandarin cooking in America with the Mandarin Kitchen," says Chu, hardly the bashful sort. As usual, this author and instructor who has built a cooking classroom under the stairs to the second floor, began his career by coming to Berkeley to study architecture. "But I had a relative who worked at the original Trader Vic's and before I knew it, I was in the restaurant trade. Instead of designing houses, I was designing dishes."

His original takeout started with twelve items and grew to more than a hundred. Is it the confidence born of a long culture, or is something about the way children are reared that makes so many of China's unbound sons so boundless in energy and ambition?

"In China, it's not what you know but who you know," confides Larry Chu, repeating the familiar immigrant comparison. "In America, it's not who you are but what you do."

What Larry does best is coordinate "texture, flavor, and visual harmony" to make sure "the last bite is best" by "using the large wok to cook small and the small wok to cook big." I'm glad Martin Yan knows what he means. "The secret to Chinese cooking is the pretreatment, the marinades, the attention to small detail. Every Chinese dish involves three or four independent processes. That way, you can get good results from mediocre ingredients. It's a testament to the patience of the culture."

So is the Chinese obsession with proper shopping, which soon has Chu, Yan, and Mei comparing notes on how to select the best uncooked chicken. "Always feel the knuckle at the top of the feet. That will tell you if the chicken is fully grown or not. . . . Check the stomach because the birds are sometimes fed small rocks to increase their weight. . . . Observe the limpness of the head when slaughtered. That can indicate how vital the animal may have been when alive."

Chu's tips for longstanding prosperity include profit-sharing and lots of community involvement, including catering for charities and Rotary clubs. Over a superb dessert of fresh, warm pears poached in a mix of herbs traditionally used to quell coughs, Chef Chu proclaims, "There's only one Elvis Presley! Am I right?"

He must be talking wok 'n roll. Yet success hasn't really gone to his head. At the end of our meal, he wants us to know, "I hope my children will always know the feeling of a Chinese family's Sunday night dinners—the storytelling and love that makes life a celebration."

In the presence of Martin Yan and Chef Chu, I suddenly have the feeling that this whole restaurant racket is but an attempt to honor lost allegiances, a vast network of remembrance in which cash and fame are but stepping stones home.

Dinner at the Happy End Cafe

A journey like this has no real finish, just a pause between courses of a lifetime banquet. Yet Mei and I must have reached satiation when we can no longer rouse ourselves from our roost upon hearing a new recommendation. Who can bother with Redwood City when you've been to Fiji? Is it possible that we've overeaten the planet?

If that's so, then, in the spirit of Chinese food, we'll probably regain our wanderlust after an hour or so. Anyway, a travel writer always gets to take his trips twice. So creating this book will give me a dose of double digestion, a kind of Chinese chewing of the cud. Soliciting recipes from all corners of the planet, Mei and I are awakened in the middle of the night with faxed lists of ingredients, most often without accompanying instruction. I should have known—not only does the Chinese world ignore time zones, but it doesn't necessarily share our definition of a recipe. Several restaurants in China send brochures instead. Another problem is matching flavors with all the chefs and owners. Business cards I have known and loved!

Soon enough, all our favorite Chinese on the planet pass through town to provide a handy recapitulation. Famed composer Tan Dun, once known at Beijing's music conservatory as "Little Hunan," drops into town for a world premiere performance of a work for string quartet and bowls of goldfish, and, despite my fear of being found not just behind the times but tasteless, pronounces the whole garlic cloves with ham at Brandy Ho's Hunan to be "Fahn-tah-steek!" His fortune cookie reads, "Talent does what it can but genius does what it must."

The conceptual artist Ai Wei-Wei, father figure to China's avant-garde in his Mingus goatee and baggy pants, has emerged from rummaging Beijing flea markets for Sung Dynasty treasures to invite us for dim sum during the hectic shooting of a Chinese TV series, *Moon over a Foreign Land*. About the quality of the script, he concedes, "You can't make a noodle soup that both Chinese and Americans will like." As the art director for this soap opera about two musicians forced to become maids in America, he offers a cameo role to Mei—who, as usual, handles the part of a sympathetic landlady with aplomb, and no rehearsals. During the shooting, I lead Mei's old pal on an expedition to Haight-Ashbury thrift shops in search of bric-a-brac from America's brief imperial reign. Acting the part of a burly Charlie Chan detective, Wei-Wei purchases a postcard portrait of the forlorn Franz Kafka to whip out of his overcoat. He asks each passerby, "Have you seen this missing person?" Not a single passerby on hip Haight Street can provide a positive I.D.

Every Tibetan in town recognizes Phunkhang Goranangpa, who spends a month on our couch, snoring to shake down the walls and devouring all the lamb roasts and prime fillets that we buy in bulk from the Price Club. He's come to the States seeking investors for everything from a new credit card network for China to a cast-of-billions movie based on an ancient Tibet epic whose plot has been passed down by children speaking in tongues. At a picnic in honor of the Dalai Lama's birthday in a Berkeley park, Tibetan exiles defer to this renowned giant wearing a multi-pocketed photographer's vest. They don't seem to know quite what to make of a countrymen who still manages to live within the occupying country that so strains the limits of their Buddhist forgiveness.

But no arrival is more surprising than that of Li Ying, a.k.a. Sincere Li. After being turned down for a U.S. visa numerous times due to her young age and unmarried status, Mei's half-desperate half-sister has finally made it here, thanks to an assignment to purchase airline parts in Milwaukee. Suddenly, Mei and I are a step closer to becoming a true family through having to show the ropes to this new, twenty-seven-year-old dependent. Her first blue skies, gay bars, and redwoods hardly seem to bowl her over. She has no promised-land plan beyond dating Ph.D.'s and improving her "English level." When we find her a room in the beachside stucco cottage of a Taiwanese city clerk, we figure that we've shielded little Sis from some of the worst of the immigrant experience—until her stingy landlords keeps the water at so low a trickle that it's almost impossible to shower.

"Water seeks lower ground, people seek higher," goes the proverb

Mei uses to explain the relentless migrations of the Chinese. One day in the not too distant future, the greatest achievement of China's revolutions—both socialist and capitalist—will come when people like Li Ying (and all the nation's best and brightest) no longer have any motive to leave home. In the meantime, we introduce her to Vietnamese noodles, Thai beef salad, and Boston Creme Pie. When it comes to Chinese eats, we've reached the point where no place seems worth the effort. Once in a while, we take Chris home through the fog-bound Sunset district via a blazing red storefront emblazoned Sichuan Taste. Actually, this is a Hakkanese joint run by a Cantonese who just hasn't bothered to repaint his sign—and doesn't have time considering the constant crush of Chinese families who, like us, are after the basic value of six dishes, including scrupulously fresh sand dabs and shrimp, for under twenty dollars. The chef/owner is nearly as fast a worker in romance as he is in the kitchen. His American-born wife confesses that she met her husband when he asked her for directions upon arrival at the San Francisco airport!

After all our searching, my appreciation for Chinese cuisine reaches new heights right in our own ill-equipped kitchen. Though I'm glad to whip out a pasta anytime—even a repertoire of stir-fry that rarely meets Mei's approval—I'm amazed at the way she can always create something bracing out of a few dried mushrooms, a packet of rice-thread noodles, a scrap of celery, and less ginger than is visible to the naked eye. I soon see that there's no better way of reestablishing friendships after a year out of town than the lure of live and carefully selected Dungeness crabs along with bowls full of Mei's homemade chive dumplings.

Our final investigation is a visit to the world headquarters of Martin Yan, that televised cooking master. We get a peek at the rock garden and kumquat trees that his culinary magic have earned, the shelves full of products that he endorses, the quick instincts by which Yan instructs a phalanx of test-kitchen helpers to add a second coat of cornstarch to taro root pastries. But Martin Yan has brought us here to view hundreds of videotaped scenes from his travels in China. By sneaking these quick spots into his show, the chef feels that he's using cuisine to educate the world about the best aspects of his homeland. I find that I'm wiping away the tears as I watch the noodle makers of Canton, the fishermen along the Yangtze, the dead ducks of Peking. Am I missing all those people and eats, all that history? Is this a backhanded way of grieving for my dad? Has a connection to China become symbolic of my attachment to all humanity? If so, I've got more than a billion real specimens to care about.

Whether or not Mei and I ever come around to producing an off-spring, despite losing the closest blood tie that I'll ever know, the past year has made me an honorary member of humankind's largest and most supportive clan. Where I once viewed this one-fourth of the world as walled off and marginalized, I now see them as an engine churning with workaholic frenzy at the center of every aspect of the planet's shared future. And that's not just because all the hair dryers in Walgreen's are marked "Made in China." Instead of wondering how the Western world may be affected by developments among the Chinese, I look first at how the much wider and more unified Chinese world will be affected by the rest of us.

It doesn't matter that I haven't quite come up with a unified theory to explain why food means so much to the Chinese. The only questions worth asking are the ones that are too deep in the blood to be answered. But I do know that if I ever want to assess some local economy or political struggle, I'll seek my advance intelligence among sharp-eyed Chinese restaurant owners. Never again will I discount the presence of some small, bony, mop-haired man huddled over his hot stove labors. Take another look and he just may be a licensed healer on two continents, fluent in five languages; a former physicist, a moonlighting temple-tender, clan chieftain, or one-man charity. An exiled poet. An expert calligrapher. Or simply a master at taming fire.

At this point, I'm no longer surprised when Martin Yan takes the opportunity to load us up with a box full of soy sauce, bean paste, chili oils, marinades, and even an ultra-sharp Martin Yan cleaver. Having entered a universe enjoined to give all its goodies away on the way from "Hunan to who knows," I cannot help wondering just what I've done in some previous life to deserve all these feedings. Perhaps some earlier incarnation of the spirit currently occupying my forty-five-year-old coil once scored highly on the examination for Confucian scholars or led the victorious conquest of Shang states over the Qin.

Waving good-bye from his front steps, Yan surveys million-dollar homes bordering coastal hills choked with deer and black oak. He sends us off with the joke, "Welcome to Chinatown!" I'm glad that the Chinese have persisted in planting their community of the heart on yet another alien soil.

Appetites whetted by video visions of stacked bamboo steamers, Mei and I stop in suburban San Mateo's irrelevant downtown to make one more search. On this sleepy, still evening—one of those few windless winter nights the Pacific grants—there is hardly any traffic beyond a few pickups jacked up toward heaven. Remarkably, we quickly come upon Mei's Restaurant. Knowing by now how to tell the genuine from the plastic at a glance, we resist the temptation with one peek through recessed plate glass.

A check in the phone directory reveals that the Happy Cafe, touted by a local distributor of kung fu flicks, is just around the corner, fronting the old Southern Pacific station. Our final find consists of bare walls, a few strips of track lighting mounted on a sparkly ceiling, and six hastily arranged white Formica tables. But those tables are crowded and, better still, the patronage is entirely Chinese. A single waitress, full of bounce in white Reeboks, stands behind a cash register that blocks the entry to a tiny kitchen. With no door in between, we glimpse the reflection of woks flaming up, making the back end of the restaurant blush with fire.

The hastily typed menu, stuffed into a clear plastic sleeve, features a dozen specialties typical of Shanghai. Mei can hardly choose between all the dishes that her mother used to make for her. By this point, I almost feel like my mother made them for me, too. There's small chunks of red-cooked pork, barely visible in a bowl filled with sponges of deep-fried bean curd and knotted ties of tougher bean curd skin. There's so-called crab shell buns, a hard, white roll covered with crackling sesame seeds and stuffed with more pork and leeks. There's excellent steamed *bao zi* and more uniquely egg-yellow dumplings in a soup chockful of white cabbage and cellophane noodles. Everything we order is rough, bland, and brown. Everything is delicious.

"Munch on!" instructs Mei. Neither she nor I can quite believe that the trip of a lifetime is over—especially when we can find another course of China's eternal banquet being dished out for us right around the next corner. "After all those meals together," she adds, "we're still pretty close, aren't we?"

"That's predictable. We never even got a cold!"

"Must be all the garlic . . ."

"And one-finger zen every morning."

"After this," she brightens, "we can start in on the world's best Japanese! Mmm, sashimi! Or do you prefer Italian?"

"You're always one step ahead of me . . . and three times as beautiful."

"Only three times?" Mei teases.

"If we try this again, we'll wind up three times fatter." Deep down, we both know that no other goal but this one could ever give us this much latitude to scour longitudes. But dare we, after all this time, name a single best Chinese restaurant?

"How can we rate imperial banquets against a peasant stall?" I still want to know. "Or compare Sichaunese to Hakkanese?"

"An apprentice on a good day versus his master on a bad one?" adds Mei.

"VIP treatment versus the average Eat at Zhou's?"

"You could lose your marbles!" Mei declares.

"Correct." Three stars and four forks can't do justice to a journey of ten thousand meals. While we're lingering over our version of a last supper, Mei and I wander through a remembrance of banquets past to construct a single dream dinner—as if we could pick and choose from all the world's menus for home delivery.

"I know you'll want to have the Fragrant Garden's bird's nest soup . . ."

"Too subtle for you!" Mei counters. "I bet you'd choose mock shredded duck in pancakes from Please the Guest."

"How did you know?" I ask.

"Because you're predictable! And you still don't know much about real Chinese food!" At least, by now, I know enough to admit that my wife is right.

The purpose of all journeying is to change one's mental map of the world. In this case, I've changed the menu. Not only have I learned to eat like a Chinese—and shop like one, combing the smelly Chinese markets like another sharp-eyed Cantonese house-wife in search of the freshest pea pod shoots—but I've started to think like one, too. This trip has not only been about getting from one restaurant to the next, but about moving on to another phase of my life. With Mei's concern and world view to help me over the last hump of a midlife crisis, I've learned a lot about knowing my limits, lightening my worries, leaving behind my regrets. My perspective, while not entirely Eastern, does seem longer and clearer. She's even taught me the value of a little toe-tickling "play" to go with our morning exercise.

I'm proud that I've freed her to use a lifetime's diary writing to be-gin a first novel. Her story deals with the rights of children no less, but safely in Chinese and beyond my criticism. All I know is that she hits her computer keyboard more readily and devotedly than this old pro. In turn, she has freed me from the writer's habit of taking the dim and dramatic view. Now I try to emulate Mei's dogged optimism to lighten the dual burden of two literary lives. I don't mind that she's willing to make awkward phone calls to editors who always have paychecks "in the mail." When it comes to other people, I ac-cept more and try to ask for less. Instead of calculating what's in it for me, I've begun looking forward to picking out gifts for others. Oc-casionally, I actually catch myself feeling like one pretty fortunate cookie. If my story with Mei has hardly reached some tidy finale, we two can always enter our own Happy End Cafe—where the joys come in modest, digestible doses. I know that I've never been hap-pier than I am now, sharing dishes and discoveries.

After all, we dream of another world but we eat in this one. More than ever, I'm certain that a restaurant really is "the place where the spiritual meets the material," as the good man of Sichuan told us. No other money-making enterprise does such a necessary job of "serving the people"—in this case, billions and billions served. With every fine Chinese meal, necessity fuses with whimsy, sheer survival be-comes pure inspiration.

"O soul, come to feed on the food it loves!" goes the ancient ad-monition of that Chinese poet named Anonymous. Now I know on which side of the great yin-yang sea my soul, and soul food, lies. Not just stuffed but sustained, not merely fortified but revitalized, I must go where steamers mist, fogging windows and world-views; where dancing broths froth, insistent cleavers hack, and the lazy Susans glide like perfect karmic wheels of eternal ingestion.

Then another bow-tied foot soldier steps forward to shatter the reverie.

"Look, he can use chopsticks very good! Say mister, where in the world you learn that?"

Appendix 1:
John and Mei's Dream Menu

A Fantasy Banquet from around the World

Cold Dish
Squid, Abalone, and Celery Rolls—Fu Yuan
Squid in Cold Bean Curd Sauce—Lai Sin's
Duck with Mango—The Oriental
Cabbage Hearts in Mustard Sauce—Li Li's

Rice and Noodles
Ban Coun (Vietnamese Ravioli)—Chez Vong
Yangzhou Fried Rice with Fresh Water Chestnuts—Kong Yi Ji
Five Flavor Noodles—Shahe Restaurant

Poultry
Kung Pao Frog Legs—Shun Lee Palace
Wenchang Chicken—Guangzhou Jiujia
Crispy Chicken—Hai Tian Lo

Vegetables
Fresh Bamboo Shoots and Ji Vegetable—Lao Fandian
Imitation Crab Meat—Prima Tower
Temple Goose—Jing An Temple

Meat
Dong Po Pork—Tien Hsiang Lo
Shredded Chicken and Pork in Omelette, Peking-style—Yue Bin
Hunan Ham in Pancakes—Peng Yuan
Charred Beef with Scallions—The Oriental

Fish
Sea Cucumber—Chongqing Seafood
Hunan Squid—Shun Lee Palace
Smoked Black Cod—Hong Kong Flower Lounge
Steamed Crab—Carrianna

Soup
Bird's Nest Soup—Fu Yuan
Buddha Jumps over the Wall—Hai Tien Lo
Minced Pigeon Soup in Winter Melon—Peng Yuan

Sweets
Deep-fried Candied Yams—Black Earth
Bean Flour Mock-Fruit Pastries—Chongqing Seafood
Three No-Sticks—Prima Tower

Specialty Items
Medicinal Hot Pot—Landmark
Beijing Duck—Beijing Kao Ya
Roast Goose—Yung Kee

Appendix 2:
How to Find the World's Best Chinese Restaurant

To search for the best Chinese restaurants, several basic tips apply. If you can't judge a book by its cover, you can judge a Chinese restaurant through the window. When every dish looks the same color, or is drowned in too much sauce that's brown or congealed, try the next place down the block. Establishments that advertise as cooking in several regional schools, like "Cantonese-Sichuan-Hunan," probably aren't good at any. When in a French restaurant, you wouldn't order Italian; when in a Shanghainese, try to stay away from the specialties of other regions listed in the menu out of obligation to general tastes.

Ordering rarely turns a mediocre restaurant into a great one, but can often make a very good one mediocre. Try to get someone to read Chinese listings, point at what Chinese customers have ordered, or, barring that, follow the advice of the waiter or choose from the listed chef's specialties—unless you suspect them as merely being the most expensive. Don't be afraid to ask which fish are freshest, which vegetables are in season. For large groups, have some cold dishes, one noodle or dumpling dish, one soup, and one whole fish, plus a variety of vegetables and stir-fryed meats in varied sauces. Rice should be as minor a part of the meal as a dinner roll. Fried rice is rarely worth ordering, soy sauce rarely worth adding. And always try something new—you'll never run out of tastes. Indecisive? When in doubt, do as the Chinese do. Order more.

What follows is a list of recommended restaurants grouped alphabetically in two categories—those worth a trip and those worth trying. Addresses, chefs, and ownership are subject to change without warning.

John and Mei's Top Forty

Au Mandarin
100 Champs Elysées
Paris
Tel.: (33) 43594848
Diplomats' Haven

Chongqing Seafood Restaurant
205-1668 W. Broadway
Vancouver, B.C.
Tel: (604) 73401668
Sichuan

Beijing Roast Duck
Bldg. 3, Tuanjiehu Beikou
Beijing
Tel.: (1) 5072892
Ultimate Duck

Ding Tai Feng
194 Xinyi Road, Sec. 2
Taipei, Taiwan
Tel.: (02) 321-9827
Dumplings Galore

Bei Yuan
202 Xiao Bei Road
Guangzhou
Tel.: (20) 3330087
Cantonese

Fang Shan
Beihai Park
Beijing
Tel.: (1) 4011879
Imperial

Charming Garden
111 N. Atlantic Boulevard, #351
Monterey Park, CA
Tel.: (818) 458-4508
Hunan

Fu Yuan Restaurant
No. 17, Lin Yi Street
Taipei, Taiwan
Tel.: (02) 321-0279
Haute Chinoise

Chef Chu's
1067 N. San Antonio Road
Los Altos, CA
Tel.: (415) 948-2696
Northern

Guangzhou Jiujia
2 Wenchang Road South
Guangzhou
Tel: (20) 8862286
Essence of Cantonese

Chez Vong
27, rue du Colisée
Paris
Tel.: (33) 43597712
Cantonese-Vietnamese

Hai Tian Lo
Pan Pacific Hotel
Marina Square
7 Raffles Boulevard
Singapore
Tel.: (65) 3368111
Cantonese with a View

Hong Kong Flower Lounge
5322 Geary Boulevard
San Francisco, CA
Tel.: (415) 668-8998
Cantonese

Hong Yuen Xuan
Baitasi
Beijing
Mongolian Hot Pot

Imperial City
Royal Exchange, Cornhill
London
Tel.: (171) 626-3437
Eclectic

Joe's Shanghai
136-21 37th Avenue
Flushing, NY
Tel.: (718) 539-3838
Shanghainese

Jing An Temple
Nanjing Xi Lu
Shanghai
Vegetarian

Kai
65 South Audley Street
London
Tel.: (171) 493-8988
Elegant Malaysian-Chinese

Kenneth Lo's Memories of China
Harbour Yard, Chelsea Harbour
London
Tel.: (171) 352-4953
General

Kong Yi Ji
Dongsibeidajie, Alley 6
Beijing
Zhejiang Style

Landmark
3344 Cambie Street
Vancouver
Tel.: (604) 872-2868
Hong Kong Hot Pot

Lai Ching Heen
Regent Hotel
18 Salisbury Road
Kowloon
Tel.: (852) 2313-2336
Nouvelle Cantonese

Lai Sin's
Arnhemse Bovenweg 46
Driebergen,
The Netherlands
Tel.: (31-0) 3438-16858
Better Than Going Dutch

Lao Fandian
242 Fuyou Lu
Shanghai
Tel.: (21) 63282782
Solid Shanghai

Li Li's
71-73 Stanley Street
West Melbourne, Australia
Tel.: (03) 9326-5790
Aussie Imperial

Longchaoshou
No. 8 Chunxi Road
Chengdu
Tel.: 676548
Sichuan in Sichuan

Mandarette
8386 Beverly Boulevard
Los Angeles, CA
Tel.: (213) 655-6115
Modern Northern

Meilongzhen
91 Jiangning Lu
Shanghai
Tel.: (21) 62173326
Shanghai Knees

Moi Kong
22 Murray Street
Singapore
Tel.: (65) 221-7758
Hakkanese

The Oriental Restaurant
The Dorchester
Park Lane
London
Tel.: (171) 629-8888
State-of-the-Art Cantonese

Peng Yuan
305 Building 12
Zhonghsiao East Road, Sec. 3
Taipei, Taiwan
Tel.: (02) 752-9766
High-class Hunan

**Prima Tower Revolving
Restaurant**
201 Keppel Road
Singapore
Tel.: (65) 272-8822
Northern in the Tropics

Shahe
318 Sanlet Road East
Shahe, Guangzhou
Tel.: (20) 7714323
Temple of Noodles

Shun Lee Palace
155 East 55th Street
New York, NY
Tel.: (212) 371-8888
Solid, All Schools

Tien Hsiang Lo
The Ritz Hotel
41, Minchuan East Road, Sec. 2
Taipei, Taiwan
Tel.: (02) 5971234
Hangzhou

Tse Yang
34 East 51st Street
New York, NY
Tel.: (212) 688-5477
Power

Victoria Restaurant
Royal Centre
1055 West Georgia Street
Vancouver, B.C.
Tel.: 669-8383
Ostrich

Yue Bin
43 Tsui Hua Hutong
Beijing
Tel.: 5245322
Holy Hole

Yung Kee
32-40 Wellington Street
Central, Hong Kong
Tel: (852) 552-1624
Getting Goosed

Yujean Kang's
67 North Raymond Avenue
Pasadena, CA
Tel.: (818) 585-0855
Sino Fusion

And Many More Along The Way . . .

Avalon
1104 E. Old Route 66
Gallup, NM
Tel.: (505) 863-5072
Chop Suey Diner

Brandy Ho's Hunan
217 Columbus Avenue
San Francisco, CA
Tel.: (415) 788-7527
Hunan

Beijing
40 University Square
Madison, WI
Tel.: (608) 257-8388
Manchurian

The Bull
238 Flinders Lane
Melbourne, Australia
Tel.: (13) 9650-5964
Shanghai

Black Earth
9 East Hepingli Street
Beijing
Tel.: (1) 421-2792
Manchurian

Camy Dumpling House
23-25 Tattersalls Lane
Melbourne, Australia
Tel.: (3) 663-8555
Shanghai

The Box
1366 Yan'an Zhonglu
Shanghai
Tel.: (21) 62176452
Home-style Shanghai

Carrianna
8511 Alexandra Road
Richmond, B.C.
Tel.: (604) 270-8233
Chaozhou, seafood

Chen Ma Po Dofu
33 Jiefang Bei Lu Er
Chengdu
Tel.: 331636
Tofu for You

China City
White Bear Yard
25A Lisle Street
London
Tel.: (171) 734-3388
Cantonese

Chinagora Restaurant
1, place du Confluent France-
Chine
Alfortville, France
Tel.: (44) 45 18 33 09
Cantonese

Chinese Garden
310 N. Fourth Street
Coeur d'Alene, ID
Tel.: (208) 667-6014
Rocky Mountain High

Chou Chen
3, rue de Cluny
Paris
Tel.: (44) 43.54.99.85
Franco-Shanghai

Cinske Zatisi (Chinese Still Life)
Batelovska 120/5
Prague
Tel.: 612 18088
Sichuan

Dai Village Big Shack
Guangdongdian Nanjie
Beijing
Tel.: (1) 508-9186
Yunnan

East Lake
3711 No. 3 Road
Richmond, B.C.
Tel.: (604) 270-1122
Seafood

888 Seafood
8450 Valley Boulevard, #121
Rosemead, CA
Tel.: (818) 573-1888
Eat, Eat, Eat

Fatty Lee's
Malacca, Malaysia
Fat Shrimps

Flower Drum
17 Market Lane
Melbourne, Australia
Tel.: (3) 9662-3655
Tuxedo Cantonese

Gandi Restaurant
Taman Lila
Singaraja, Bali
Indonesia
Tel: 0362 21163-22980
Suppressed Cuisine

Golden Dragon (Zlaty Drak)
Anglicka 6
Vinohrady, Prague
Tel.: 266250
Czech Mate

Golden Pheasant
318 N. Higgins Avenue
Missoula, MT
Tel.: (406) 728-9818
American-Chinese

Good Chances
408 W. Valley Boulevard
San Gabriel, CA
Tel.: (818) 282-0388
Taiwanese

**Grand China Princess Hotel
Restaurant**
215 Yaowaraj Road
Samphatawong, Bangkok
Tel.: (662) 224-9977
Cantonese

Great China
2015 Kittredge Street
Berkeley, CA
Tel.: (510) 843-7996
Shandong

Great Wall (Dlouha Zed)
Pujmanove 10/12/18
Prague
Tel.: (422) 692-2374
Beijing-style

Great Wall
1309 Grand Avenue
Billings, MT
Tel.: (406) 245-8601
Cantonese

The Great Wok
Bau and Laucala Streets
Flagstaff, Suva
Fiji
Tel.: 301285
Almost Sichuan

Happy Cafe
250 S. B Street
San Mateo, CA
Tel.: (415) 340-7138
Home-style Shanghai

Hong Kong City Hall
City Hall, Low Block
Central, Hong Kong
Tel.: (852) 2521-1303
Dim sum

Hong Kong Palace
Main Street
Sidari
Corfu, Greece
Fed up with Feta?

House of Nanking
919 Kearny Street
 San Francisco, CA
Tel.: (415) 421-1429
Hearty

Ja-Ja
1210 Dillingham Boulevard, #14
Honolulu, HI
Tel.: (808) 842-5695
Northern

Kazakhstan Gourmet
Dixon Street Arcade
Sydney, Australia
Dumplings

Kim Chuy
727 Broadway, #103
Los Angeles, CA
Tel.: (213) 687-7215
Chaozhou

Li Family Restaurant
11 Yang Fang Hutong
Beijing
Tel.: 601-1915
Imperial

Long Yuan
Sandweg 113
Frankfurt, Germany
Tel.: 4970770
Wunderbar

Mao Family
No. 4 Hepingli Middle Road
Beijing
Tel.: 4271404
Campy Hunan

Maple Garden
909 Isenberg Street
Honolulu, HI
Tel.: (808) 941-6641
Northern

Maple Garden
99 Penang Road
Penang, Malaysia
Tel.: (04) 634185
Cantonese Seafood

Mask of China
117 Little Bourke Street
Melbourne, Australia
Tel.: (3) 9662-2166
Chaozhou

Mui Chun
B1-03 Funan Centre
109 N. Bridge Road
Singapore
Tel.: (65) 3397766
Hainan-colonial

New Flushing Seafood
36-57 Main Street
Flushing, NY
Tel.: (718) 460-8989
Shanghai

Panda Garden
3540 Riverside Plaza
Terre Haute, IN
Tel.: (812) 235-0515
Northern

Poons in the City
Minster Pavement, Minster Court
Mincing Lane, London
Tel.: (171) 626-0126
Artistic Cantonese

Quanjude
No. 32 Qianmen Street
Beijing
Tel.: (1) 511-2418
Beijing Duck

Sam Lok
655 Jackson Street
San Francisco, CA
Tel.: (415) 981-8988
Authentically Greasy Sichuan

Seven Stars
205 N.W. 4th Avenue
Portland, OR
Tel.: (503) 228-2888
Cantonese

Shanghai Garden
524 - 6th Avenue South
Seattle, WA
Tel.: (206) 625-1689
Shanghai

Shark Fin House
131-135 Little Bourke Street
Melbourne, 3000
Australia
Tel.: 663-1555
Dim sum

Shen Shen (Sunshine)
No. 8 Fuxing West Rd.
Shanghai
Tel.: (21) 473-3182
Chinese coffee shop

Shu Rong Dofu
Jinsong West Entrance
Beijing
Tel.: (1) 772-1385
Sichuan

Sichuan
51 Xi Rongxian Hutong
Beijing
Tel.: (1) 603-3291
State-run spice

Snake Restaurant
43 Jianglan Road
Canton
Tel.: 8884498
Snake

Sui Yuan
24 Meishuguan East Street
Beijing
Tel.: (1) 407-5051
Hunan Hole-in-the-Wall

Szechwan House
625 N. Michigan Avenue
Chicago
Tel.: (312) 642-3900
All-purpose

Tempio del Paradiso
San Marco 5495 (Rialto)
Tel.: (041) 522-4673
When in Rome . . .

Tommy Toy's Haute Cuisine Chinoise
655 Montgomery Street
San Francisco, CA
Tel.: (415) 397-4888
Status Cantonese

Tse Yang
25, avenue Pierre 1er de Serbie
Paris
Tel.: (44) 47 20 70 22
Haute Chinoise

Wall Sea Street Restaurant
135-05 40 Road
Flushing, NY
Tel.: (718) 762-8585
Taiwanese

Xin Yeh
375 Xinyi Road, Sec. 4
Taipei, Taiwan
Tel.: (02) 725-1025
Taiwanese

Yank Sing
427 Battery Street
San Francisco, CA
Tel.: (415) 781-1111
Dim Sum